THE REAGANS

ALSO BY ANNE EDWARDS

BIOGRAPHY

Sonya: The Life of Countess Tolstoy

Vivien Leigh: A Biography

Judy Garland: A Biography

*Road to Tara: The Life of
Margaret Mitchell*

*Matriarch: Queen Mary and the
House of Windsor*

*A Remarkable Woman:
A Biography of Katharine
Hepburn* (UK title: *Katharine
Hepburn: A Biography*)

Early Reagan: The Rise to Power

Shirley Temple: American Princess

The DeMilles: An American Family

*Royal Sisters: Elizabeth and
Margaret*

*The Grimaldis of Monaco:
Centuries of Scandal/Years of
Grace*

*Throne of Gold: The Lives of the
Aga Khans*

Streisand

*Ever After: Diana and the Life
She Led* (UK title: *Diana and
the Rise of the House of Spencer*)

*Maria Callas: An Intimate
Biography* (UK title: *Callas:
Her Life, Her Loves, Her Music*)

NOVELS

The Survivors

Shadow of a Lion

Haunted Summer

Miklos Alexandrovitch Is Missing

The Hesitant Heart

Child of Night
  (UK title: *Raven Wings*)

La Divina

Wallis: The Novel

AUTOBIOGRAPHY

The Inn and Us
  (with Stephen Citron)

CHILDREN'S BOOKS

P. T. Barnum

The Great Houdini

A Child's Bible

THE
REAGANS

PORTRAIT OF A MARRIAGE

ANNE EDWARDS

Guilford, Connecticut

An imprint of The Rowman & Littlefield Publishing Group, Inc.
4501 Forbes Blvd., Ste. 200
Lanham, MD 20706
www.rowman.com
Distributed by NATIONAL BOOK NETWORK

British Library Cataloguing in Publication Information available

Library of Congress Cataloging-in-Publication Data available

ISBN 978-1-4930-3646-2 (paperback)
ISBN 978-1-4930-3647-9 (e-book)

♾️™ The paper used in this publication meets the minimum requirements of American
National Standard for Information Sciences—Permanence of Paper for Printed Library
Materials, ANSI/NISO Z39.48-1992.

Printed in the United States of America

FOR

Maxwell Edwards Sadler
Casey Edwards Sadler
Hillary Anne Edwards
Liza Elaine Citron
Aaron Lieb Citron

The Future

CONTENTS

FOREWORD

The Hollywood of my youth—the 1930's to the early 1950's—was marked by a broad political divide between leftist Democrats and far-right Republicans. There seemed to be no middle ground. The devastating McCarthy hearings tore it farther asunder. For Ronald Reagan, during his years as president of the Screen Actors Guild, this presented a personal and professional time of self decision. He had happened into acting by circumstance. His early success during a time when great numbers of the population were still mired in the muddy roots of the Great Depression appeared to have sealed his fate. But early on he was well aware of his passion for politics. He kept on acting as it was "as good as any way to make a living," and he now had a wife and two children to support. His wife, the actress Jane Wyman, felt he was "devoured by something" she "could not define." His position in the Screen Actors Guild and his career left little time for her and when they did have time together his dark moods and Wyman's inability to deal with them derailed their marriage, ending after eight years of what the Hollywood press had written in bold type was a "Fairy Tale Marriage." She has said that the "Guild could have been named the other woman in our marriage." Reagan concentrated on both arms of his career, but the Guild took precedent.

President Roosevelt, a Democrat and a man who had seemed a God to him, and had steered the nation through the Second World War, had died not seeing the end of the war. The years that followed brought Reagan closer to the right and a powerful man in the industry. His life was consumed yet somehow there seemed a vacuum to be filled. Enter Nancy. The rest is history.

I had never met Nancy when I started work on this book—truly a Part Two to my *Early Reagan*. However, we did have numerous mutual friends and I had earlier, during the writing of *Early Reagan*, struck up a friendship with his daughter, Maureen. I had done a great many interviews. My foundation was solid. I requested an interview with Nancy. I received a kind note in return, but at base it was a refusal. Shortly thereafter, my husband took seriously ill. We were living in Connecticut at the time and the doctors informed me that he had, if possible, to be moved to a sunnier clime. I chose Beverly Hills, California as that was my childhood home. The Reagan Library was only a thirty minute drive and I planned to do work there, with one condition, I would have to bring my wheelchair husband with me. One day I received a call from an assistant to Nancy who told me that she had learned who I was (a niece of the restauranteur, Dave Chasen, who had been a special friend of the former first lady and President Reagan). Nancy had been informed of my husband's situation and had arranged for his comfort while I was working. I was informed where to park (it would say "Reserved for President Reagan"). When we pulled in we were greeted by staff who took us upstairs and to the President's private study (Reagan was in the final stages of Alzheimer and no longer used it.) It was furnished with the same furniture as he had had in the White House. Predominantly red flowered chintz on chairs and chaise. Very warm and well kept, as though Reagan might walk through the door at any moment. We were told that a tray would be brought up with his lunch if he would call on the telephone when ready. There was a television and current books and magazines on the cocktail table that fronted the sofa.

Nancy did not give me an interview per se, but she dictated a letter to me with some of her remembrances and comments on *Early Reagan.* I worked with my husband close by for several months. On my final day I was given a note that Nancy would see me before I left and that she wished to show me something and her assistant would come to get me in a short time. This was so mysterious I could not imagine what it might be. When her aide came to collect me I followed her to the elevator and then down to the basement of the giant building. Giant was not the proper word for it. It seemed as large as a stadium. There were many, many rows of glass fronted cases, shelves, displays—this is where the gifts to President Reagan were kept and displayed—about the size of a department store level. From jeweled saddles to the smallest offering were displayed. My guide turned me aside and we walked to the other end of the room where Nancy stood waiting before what was once a red booth from Chasens. We exchanged greetings. Nancy was quite welcoming.

"This is the very booth from your uncle's restaurant where Ronnie proposed to me," she explained, "I bought at the auction when the restaurant closed." She handed me a framed photograph of herself, Reagan, two close friends and my uncle—all smiling widely—seated in the booth. "I loved Dave," she said. "He always welcomed us so warmly." She saw me back to Reagan's office. Dallied for about five minutes and then departed. I sent her the book when it was published. I got a simple thank you card which was followed by a lovely holiday greeting at Christmas. A mutual friend said she liked it although she thought I could have been a little kinder to her. President Ford, who had lost the Republican nomination to Reagan in 1976, (who had become a good friend of mine after his help on both this book and "Shirley Temple") wrote me:

"Dear Anne:

"I deeply appreciate an inscribed copy of your book. . . . Very interesting and enlightening. I approve of your comments where I am involved. President Reagan & Nancy, despite some differences, became friends. It is tragic that Ron is so ill. Betty & I have great sympathy for Nancy.

With appreciation, admiration, & very best wishes.

Gerald R. Ford."

President Reagan died on June 5, 2004 at the age of 93; President Ford on December 26, 2006 at the same age. Reagan was buried on the grounds of the Reagan Library and I was asked by a national television station to cover the Simi Valley rites. The Reagan family (Maureen now gone) stood side-by-side in front of his grave, united. Dutch, as he was known as a young man, was finally at peace after enduring many years of a devastating disease. For several years and to the end, he did not recognize Nancy. But she somehow carried on his spirit and I much admired her for that.

CHAPTER ONE

ENTER NANCY

One evening in mid-February 1952 Edith Luckett Davis and Dr. Loyal Davis, parents of thirty-year-old Hollywood contract player Nancy Davis, were sitting down to eat dinner at their Scottsdale, Arizona, home when the telephone rang. Edith answered it. Ronald Reagan, a forty-one-year-old divorced movie star of waning celebrity, and father of two, was on the line.

"He asked me for Dr. Loyal Davis and I said who wants to speak to him and he said Ronald Reagan," Edith, a onetime touring road actress known for her out-front responses, recalled. "I thought what the hell's he doing calling Loyal? I didn't know what it was for. I said, 'Just a minute.' I went in and said to Loyal, 'Ronald Reagan wants to speak to you.' And he said, "Me?" And I said, 'Get to that phone 'cause I want to know what in hell he wants.' Anyway, Loyal went to the phone. He said, 'That's interesting [in answer to Reagan's admission that he wanted to marry Nancy]. Are you sure you can [support her]? Yes [when Reagan asked if he approved].' And they talked and after [they hung up] Loyal said to me, 'He wants to marry Nancy.' And I said, 'Oh, go on!' He said, 'No, I'm not kidding. He wants to marry Nancy.' And I said, 'That's very exciting, very exciting.'

"Then she called and I said, 'Why in hell is that man calling your father for this?' And she said. 'We want to get married but don't want to marry unless you and Daddy want me to.' And I said, 'Of course. If he's a nice guy and you like him, then I'm sure it's all right.' And she said, 'He is, you'll love him.' I said, 'Find out what you want for a wedding present. It can't be extravagant, but I want you to have what you want.' She called back [in a little while] and said, 'I'll tell you what we want. We want a camera that can take moving pictures and a screen that we can show them on, and that's all we want.' And I said, 'Sold.' "[1]

It seems probable, due to her emotional attachment to Reagan at this point, that Nancy would have married him despite any objections Dr. Davis might have raised. But for Reagan at his age to make a call to Nancy's elderly parents seeking permission for him to marry their mature daughter exhibits Nancy's early influence over him and the strength of his feelings for her. She had urged him to do so despite his initial reluctance. For her entire life Nancy had sought approval from her parents—the mother who left her with relatives as a small child to go on the road with a theater troupe, and the father who made her wait years before he adopted her so that she could legally bear his name.

Nancy Davis was born Anne Frances Robbins in New York City on July 6, 1921. Edith was fond of saying that Nancy was supposed to be born on the Fourth of July, but the Yankees were playing a doubleheader that day, and being a die-hard fan, she delayed the birth for two days. Edith was a plainspoken woman who peppered her Southern-inflected speaking voice (she came from Petersburg, Virginia) with gritty phrases, and very often four-letter words. She had been on the stage from the age of three, then quit school in the tenth grade and joined a stock company. Her chief assets were a pretty face and a well-turned ankle, but Edith quickly picked up the tools of her trade, an ability to learn her lines and speak them clearly and to move on stage with confidence. She developed into a creditable actress and for the next decade traveled up and down the East Coast with various companies, playing supporting roles in plays that starred better-known performers: Walter Huston, Louis Calhern, and Alla Nazimova, a highly stylized actress of the stage and silent screen who had been trained in Russia by the great theater producer (and originator of the Stanislavsky method of acting), Konstantin Stanislavsky, and became known by the use of only her last name. Edith and Nazimova were friends, and when Edith gave birth to her daughter, she asked the ofttimes bizarre older woman to be the child's godmother.[2]

Nancy's father, Kenneth Robbins, was a shoe salesman from Pittsfield, Massachusetts, with claims of attending Princeton and of being the scion of a rich family who had come upon hard times but were still well-off. It seems this was mostly untrue. The Robbins family had never had great wealth and were just scraping along; moreover, the Princeton archives do not list Kenneth Robbins as either a graduate or former student. Nonetheless, his parents, Anna and John Robbins, did not approve of their son consorting with an actress who was five years his senior, and who—at the advanced age of twenty-seven and still unmarried—had no doubt led a less than prim, virginal life. Robbins possessed a certain charm and a persuasive manner; he also boasted that he would be heir to a comfortable estate upon the death of his terminally ill father. Edith was determined to marry him, and marry him she did, and quit the stage. A year later John Robbins died, and the inheritance his son had promised Edith turned out to be a pittance.

It was a miserable marriage, filled with resentment, and a hard-scrabble life. Ken tried his hand as a theatrical booking agent but was unable to find any clients. While he later joked that he represented "a one-legged tap dancer and a cross-eyed knife thrower,"[3] that seems to have been an example of his style of humor. When America entered World War I in 1917, he enlisted in the army and left Edith to cope for herself in New York. Edith managed by returning to the stage, appearing in supporting roles in several Broadway shows. When Ken returned in January 1919, they set up housekeeping together again in New York City. Ken hated the city and the theater, and in the next two years had a succession of jobs that did not pay enough to cover their rent. He insisted that Edith return with him to Pittsfield where he thought he could find gainful employment working on cars, something he enjoyed doing. Edith refused to go. She was three months pregnant with Nancy, but he left her anyway.

Nazimova and other friends came to Edith's financial rescue, and as soon as she was able, she joined a touring company carrying the daughter she now called Nancy in a cradle fashioned from a wicker laundry basket. When Edith was giving a performance, Nancy was left in the care of other players, stage managers, and people at the rooming houses where they stayed. In two years Edith had performed in forty-two plays in almost as many cities, playing everything from the mother in *Little Lord Fauntleroy* to Michaela in a nonmusical version of *Carmen.*

Ken Robbins did not have much interest in his daughter. Things had not gone well for him in Pittsfield, and in 1922 he and his mother, Anna, moved to Glen Ridge, New Jersey, where Ken went into the real estate business. With the small insurance money his father had left Anna, he purchased an old, many-bedroomed house on Fairway Avenue in nearby Verona, which he then rented to a Mrs. Mae Palmer for use as a sanitarium. This appears to have been Ken Robbins's main income for a great many years to follow. He and Edith were divorced, but he contributed nothing either to her support or Nancy's.

Shortly after her daughter's second birthday, Edith decided that there were too many difficulties in keeping the child with her on the road. One contributing factor was her need to establish a life of her own. Edith was still a young, attractive woman with natural desires and the hope of marrying again—next time with more security for herself and her daughter. Also, Nancy was an active child and could no longer be confined to a makeshift cradle or a room in a boardinghouse of strangers. Edith took her to live with her sister, Virginia Galbraith, in Bethesda, Maryland. Virginia's husband, Audley, worked as a shipping clerk for the railroad. They had a daughter, Charlotte, who was three years older than Nancy. The Galbraiths owned a modest, but comfortable three-bedroom house in Battery Park, an area near the Bethesda railroad station. Nancy was later to say that the Galbraiths "treated [her] with great love." But it was not the life or the love she was longing for. Her relatives were "darling people," she would admit, "but I wanted my mother."[4]

For the next six years Edith would pop in and out for visits that lasted from a few hours to a day or two, a situation that went on for six years. The two sisters had very little in common. Virginia—"Virgie" as she was known in her family—was a homebody, modest, puritanical, and without much individuality. "Mother was not only outgoing and gregarious; she was also capable of uttering words that would shock a sailor, and was one of the few women I've ever known who could tell an off-color joke and have it come out funny," Nancy would recall.[5] Edith also had an aura of glamour. She wore artfully applied makeup that emphasized the largeness and blueness of her eyes. Her lips were painted in "bee-stung" fashion, and her blond hair was lightened with peroxide. She smelled of sweet lavender and always carried items in her pocketbook to intrigue a little girl who wanted to be more like her mother than like her painfully plain aunt.

Nancy's favorite times were when her mother was appearing in a play in New York City and Aunt Virgie took her by train to visit. She would watch Edith perform from the wings and "quickly came to love the special feel and musty smell of backstage." On those visits she would "dress up in her stage clothes, put on makeup, and pretend she was playing her parts." Her most treasured possessions were a "curly blond Mary Pickford wig" given to her by Edith, and a small dollhouse built for her by the stagehands in one of Edith's plays.[6]

Going back to Bethesda was the worst part. Sixty-five years later Nancy would write, "I always dreaded the end of my visits, when I had to leave Mother again. When she wasn't staying in a residential hotel, she would live in the brownstone apartment of a friend who was traveling with some other show. To this day, I still get a sinking feeling in my stomach whenever I'm in New York and pass one of those buildings."[7]

In later life Nancy would rationalize her mother's having left her with relatives while she continued on the road. After all, Edith had to make a living to support the two of them, and touring seemed the only thing she knew how to do. During Nancy's childhood, however, there was resentment and deep pain accompanied by a need to defend her mother's actions. When she was five, she was struck down with a virulent case of double pneumonia, often fatal in those days. Aunt Virgie nursed her through, but Nancy could not contain her anger that she was sick and her mother "was thousands of miles away in a touring company. I remember crying and saying, 'If I had a little girl, I'd certainly be there if *she* was ever sick.' My aunt repeated this to my mother," a form of betrayal that turned Nancy against her aunt and did not bring Edith hurrying to her side.[8]

Nancy's life took a new turn in the spring of 1929. President Herbert Hoover was promising a chicken in every pot, and the country was enjoying what appeared to be a secure prosperity. Edith arrived in Bethesda on a warm April day, beaming with evident happiness. She led Nancy by the hand out to the front porch, and they sat down together on the lumpy couch where, although there was not much of a view, you could watch the cars go past.

Edith told Nancy she had "fallen in love with a wonderful man." He was Dr. Loyal Davis, a neurosurgeon who lived in Chicago. Edith had met him on shipboard when he was going to England to attend a medical convention and she was a guest of friends who had invited her for a holiday abroad. Davis wanted to marry her, but there would be a short wait as his divorce was not yet final. When it was, mother and daughter could be reunited in a fine home in Chicago. Nancy claims that Edith then asked for her permission to say "yes," for if she did, Edith would then retire from the stage and they could "live together as one happy family. It's up to you."[9]

Surely Edith's question was as rhetorical as Nancy's was later to be. Here was a forty-year-old mother asking her eight-year-old child, who had been separated from her for nearly six years and who desperately wanted to be loved by her, whether she would agree to be part of one happy family. For a moment Nancy was too overcome with happiness to speak. Then she looked up at her mother with the large brown eyes she had inherited from her hated father and immediately agreed.

The wedding, to take place in Chicago, was scheduled in June to enable Nancy to finish out her school year in Bethesda. As Edith's sole bridesmaid, she stood gawky but radiant beside her mother wearing a pale blue taffeta dress and carrying a mixed bouquet of summer flowers. "I was happy for Mother, but I can remember, even then, feeling twinges of jealousy—a feeling I was to experience years later, from the other side after I married a man with children. Dr. Davis was taking part of her away from me, and after being separated from Mother for so long, I wanted her all to myself."[10]

Whereas many young people had their lives torn apart during the Depression, Nancy's was made whole. Many of the occupants of the elegant apartments like the Davises' on Chicago's Lake Shore Drive had their share of bankruptcies and suicides. Nancy was able to block these things out. As a young woman she made only two visits to New Jersey to see her real father and grandmother, who were living in extremely reduced circumstances. She later claimed that her father had been abusive to her, locking her in the bathroom when she defended her mother against his allegations of her "impure past." Whether or not this incident occurred as she related, Ken Robbins denied it, and she never returned to see him.

The doctor had a son, Richard Davis (also to become a doctor), two years younger than Nancy, who lived with his mother, Dr. Davis's first wife, in California. He would visit his father during the summer. Richard's first memory of Nancy was when she was "in the third or fourth grades [eight or nine years old]. In those days she wore a school uniform: tunic, knee socks, and beret. At the beginning of the school year, my father and I would walk her to the corner of the drive [Lake Shore Drive]. With each step the tunic, which was too short, would sort of pop up in the air and we'd see her bloomers. Father would say, 'Richard, Nancy has on those dreadful navy-blue bloomers, doesn't she?' and I would dutifully agree. And then he'd say, with a big, broad smile, 'Isn't she just the most wonderful child,'" which could not have been good news for a little boy of six or seven whose father now had a second family, and a child who lived with him year round when he only spent a few months a year.[11]

During summers the Davis family, Richard included, were often guests for several weeks at the home of actor Walter Huston and his wife in the San Bernardino Mountains in southern California. There was swimming and tennis, and Nancy entered into some homespun theatrical performances in which everyone, including the infinitely untalented Dr. Davis (to much good-humored ridicule), played a part.

Dr. Davis was the key figure in Nancy's life. Richard claims, ". . . no question about that." Dinnertime, once they returned to Chicago, meant open family discussions, and Davis was always interested in what Nancy had to say in their lively conversations. "She really adored my father," Richard averred. "There was a great relationship between the two of them."[12]

"They were too close in my opinion," a family friend insisted. " 'Nancy's not going to want to leave Loyal if this keeps up,' I told Edith. 'And if she does she'll measure every man against him.' "

" 'That ain't all that bad!' Edith replied."[13]

Nancy's life in Chicago was the fruition of a dream—except for one thing. She still did not have the right to her stepfather's name and was registered at the elite Girl's Latin School as Anne Frances Robbins. She was called Nancy by her friends, but she wanted to obliterate her birth name forever. Although fond of Richard, she envied him his right to bear the Davis name. Perhaps the doctor feared that his son's inheritance might then be in jeopardy, but the legal aspects were also daunting, because Robbins was still alive and might very well have wanted a considerable figure to sign a document that negated his parentage.

"She called [Loyal] 'Daddy' and he certainly encouraged her awed devotion," Edith's friend, Margaret McLean, recalled. "They were very affectionate together. It seemed to please Edith, and Lord knows, Loyal—never in my presence, anyway, and I lived in the same building and saw quite a lot of the Davises—showed any irritation when she fawned around him."[14]

The doctor found it difficult to display overt affection to his son. A young girl was different, especially one who tried as hard as Nancy did to win his approval, and who seldom, if ever, misbehaved. His laws were rigidly followed. Cleanliness was next to godliness in his household. Order was important. Silence was expected when he needed quiet to work on a medical article or report. But he also wanted "his girls," as he called Edith and Nancy, to entertain him when he wished to relax. For Nancy there had been all those years without a father, never quite feeling a daughter to her Uncle Audley when she lived in his home. Ken Robbins had not been a father to her. Longing for a paternal relationship, Nancy clung to Dr. Davis and guilelessly charmed him in the way of young girls.

"She was a flirt, no doubt about that," Edith said. "Aren't all little girls? She always tried to get Loyal's attention and he responded. Why wouldn't he?" Eventually, Nancy became almost as important in the doctor's life as he was in hers.[15]

Finally, on April 19, 1938, after relentless pleas on the part of Edith (pressed by Nancy), and of pressure on Robbins (who claimed Nancy wrote him a vindictive letter that he would never forgive), a petition was filed in Cook County Circuit Court, Illinois, stating that "the father [Kenneth Robbins] of said child [Anne Francis Robbins] consents in writing to the adoption of said child by the petitioners [Edith and Dr. Davis] and waives the issuance of process, that said minor child [Nancy was sixteen] being more than 14 years of age likewise consents in writing to her adoption."[16] There is an irony to the timing of this. Davis's first wife had recently died and fourteen-year-old Richard had moved to Chicago to live with the family. It seems that Davis might have felt that having his son in residence would be uncomfortable for Nancy unless she also bore the Davis name.

"You can call me Nancy Davis," she proudly told her school chums the following day.[17] When she graduated in June 1939, her class picture caption read: "Nancy's social perfection is a constant source of amazement. She is invariably and suitably dressed. She can talk, and even better listen intelligently, to anyone from her little kindergarten partner at the Halloween party, to the grandmother of one of her friends."[18]

From Girl's Latin, Nancy went to Smith College in Northampton, Massachusetts, taking with her a significant wardrobe. This women's college, which was housed in handsome brick buiidings set in a thickly wooded campus, attracted the daughters of some of the most socially prominent and well-to-do families. They were generally sophisticated, well traveled, and well read, and, as Nancy had been forewarned, wore tremendously chic clothes. Except for one classmate, Jean Westcott, no one knew Dr. Davis was not her birth father. Early in every new relationship Nancy managed to mention that her father was a famous brain surgeon, her mother a well-known, retired stage actress, her godmother the legendary Nazimova, and Walter Huston, star of stage and screen, such a close friend of the family that she called him Uncle Walter. "Some of the girls thought she was pretentious," one of her Smith chums said. "Others that she was insecure. I concurred with the latter. She was quite short and somewhat chubby, but she dressed well. Clothes were important to her. So was finding a rich, suitable husband. She had boyfriends, but I wouldn't call her popular. She was keen on being an actress, but I never felt this was paramount in the choice of her future. Nancy wanted to marry someone as rich and famous as her father. That was her ultimate goal."[19]

Nancy had said it so many times that it has become legend, "My life didn't really begin until I met Ronnie." No doubt she came to sincerely believe it. But, in doing so, she was negating the very essence of herself.

She was twenty-nine years old when she met Ronald Reagan—a meeting she neatly engineered. The big 3–0 was stalking her, and gaining ground, while marriage had so far eluded her. Everything she had ever truly wanted had been late in coming and only achieved after much struggle, steely determination, and clever and unrelenting manipulation. Meeting the newly divorced and eminently eligible Ronald Reagan was not the beginning for Nancy, but the culmination of a life's ambition to find the man who would bestow upon her the same status, respect, and security that her mother had gained by marrying the prestigious Dr. Davis. Until her arranged first date with Reagan, no suitable marriage prospect had appeared, although she had access to some of the most powerful and famous men at Metro-Goldwyn-Mayer, the studio to which she was under contract.

By her own realistic judgment (and that of her peers and the public), Nancy was neither a gifted actress nor a great beauty. Nor did she possess the physical dimensions that invited instant masculine desire. Hers was a trim, petite figure. Her arrival in Hollywood at twenty-eight (the studio press corps took two years off her age for publicity purposes), placed her at a disadvantage in a town obsessed with youth and early success. Yet her greatest handicap in finding a husband was that she had been signed by the studio under the protective auspices of Benjamin Thau, former booking agent for Loew's Incorporated, who after two decades at MGM, had worked his way up from casting director to administrative assistant to the all-powerful studio boss, Louis B. Mayer.

Thau was not a personality in the Hollywood sense of the term. He lacked the flamboyance, the aura of power of studio moguls like Louis B. Mayer, Samuel Goldwyn, Darryl Zanuck, and Harry Cohn. Nor was he considered a creative genius like Irving Thalberg, who guided some of MGM's greatest early films. But Thau's behind-the-scenes power at the studio was never questioned. He had Mayer's ear, and that was akin to being the king's general. He was fifty, believed to be a confirmed bachelor, and famous for his casting-couch dalliances. When Thau gave the go-ahead for Nancy Davis to get "the star treatment" in the screen test he had arranged for her, all the producers on the lot received notices, signed by him, requesting their attendance at the showing. Since this was tantamount to a royal command, the reasoning on the lot was that Nancy Davis was Thau's candidate to succeed Greer Garson, a top Metro star known to have been his mistress and whose screen test he had given equal attention a decade earlier.

"Screen tests [in 1949] were very pro-forma," Armand Deutsch, a producer on the lot during Nancy's tenure, recalled. "The person being tested faced the screen—for fifty percent of the test full face and for twenty-five percent left and right profile. If a lady was being tested, you only saw the back of the head of the man [who was feeding her lines]. All these tests were done by test directors [a special unit which did not include directors of feature films]. So I see Nancy [Davis] for the first time in my life and I was astounded because the slate said 'Directed by George Cukor' and 'Photographed by George Folsey,' and the back of the head belonged to Metro star Spencer Tracy." (Deutsch was mistaken. Howard Keel, newly signed to a studio contract, not Tracy, fed Nancy her lines in the screen test).[20]

"I had never seen anything like this. I watched the test and went back to my office. The producers didn't check with each other but we are kind of a cruel lot I guess. I wrote in my report, 'Forget about the girl and sign the director.' But they did sign Nancy."[21]

For three weeks before the screen test, Nancy had been coached by

Lucille Ryman Carroll, then head of MGM's talent department. Benny Thau, she recalled, asked her to do what she could with Nancy, who had acquitted herself well. No one (especially Carroll) felt she had star potential, but all concurred that she could play sincere, unglamorized types—faithful wives and mothers of good breeding. Although the camera was kind to her, she simply did not project that special quality that made a star. Thau's extraordinary contribution to her screen test, and her subsequent signing to a six-year contract with options, sent up red flags that weren't lowered when single men working for the studio, like Deutsch, were requested to escort her to dinner parties and previews where Thau was often present, acting therefore as "beard." Everyone knew everyone else at Metro and exchanged backroom gossip. Thau, it was said, did not want his relationship with Nancy to become public knowledge (that is, outside studio circles) and avoided having his name linked with hers in Hollywood columns.

Nancy possessed impeccable manners. She dressed in good taste. She made no secret of the fact that her father was a pioneering neurosurgeon and chief of surgery at Northwestern University Memorial Hospital in Chicago, that her parents lived on that city's fashionable Lake Shore Drive, and that she had graduated from Smith College, representing herself as a young woman with a background of some social prestige. This was fairly truthful, but not the sort of personal information usually bandied about on a movie lot where the chief executive, Louis B. Mayer, and many of his staff, had neither university degree nor socially prominent family connections.

"I think Nancy's relationship to Dr. Davis was her defense," a former contract player at MGM recalled. "She didn't really know *who* she was and it was, therefore, terribly important for her to *be* a famous surgeon's daughter. She was reserved. Never one of the gang. It gave some of us the feeling that she looked down on us. Now, I feel she might have suffered from feeling inadequate with so many far more beautiful girls also signed to contracts. But at the time, her stand-offish attitude fed the rumors that she was Benny Thau's girlfriend. Although there was nothing remarkable about Nancy's looks or ability, she had been given star treatment in her test. There seemed no other explanation why a director of

George Cukor's stature on the lot would direct her test." (Cukor had obtained remarkable performances from Greta Garbo in *Camille*, Katharine Hepburn in *The Philadelphia Story*, and Ingrid Bergman in *Gaslight*, to name a few.[22]

Nancy signed her contract with the studio at a starting salary of $300 a week on March 2, 1949, with six-month options that, if the studio did pick them up, would in the final year, 1955, raise her salary to $1,250 a week. Two days after her contract went into effect, she began work in *Shadow on the Wall*, a B film starring Ann Sothern. Nancy had a supporting role as a psychiatrist treating a child who had witnessed her mother's murder.

Nancy wrote in her studio biographical questionnaire: "My greatest ambition is to have a happy marriage"; what she hated most was "superficiality, vulgarity esp. [*sic*] in women, untidiness of mind and person—and *cigars* [the emphasis is hers]." While most young players stressed their desire to become a star by learning everything they could about making movies. Nancy saw her new career as a bridge to a successful marriage.[23]

No one knew quite what to make of her. She did not form friendships with the other young contract players and lived alone in a garden-style apartment at 941½ Hilgard in Westwood Village, across the road from the UCLA campus. There were rumors that she had had casual affairs with both Spencer Tracy and Clark Gable in New York, where she appeared in the small role of Si-Tchun, a lady-in-waiting in the musical *Lute Song*, which starred Mary Martin and Yul Brynner, before coming out to the Coast as Thau's protégé. For the first year that Nancy was on the lot, there was no other man in her life. At her request, Thau had accompanied her to see her parents in Scottsdale, Arizona, where the Davises had recently moved from Chicago. This had not been a successful encounter. Loyal Davis was not thrilled at Nancy's close association with a Jewish man twenty years or more her senior. On their return to California, the romance cooled off.[24]

After her breakup with Thau, Nancy briefly dated the troubled actor Robert Walker, who was struggling with alcoholism and manic depression after his wife, Jennifer Jones, left him to marry film mogul David O.

Selznick, the producer of *Gone with the Wind* and *Rebecca*. Nancy developed a strong crush on Frank Sinatra, also under contract to MGM and appearing in musicals, mainly in buddy roles with Gene Kelly—*Anchors Aweigh, Take Me Out to the Ball Game,* and *On the Town.* At the time Sinatra was married to his first wife and carrying on a furtive affair with the beautiful Ava Gardner. Nancy would stop by a soundstage where he was scheduled to shoot a scene and, if allowed in, would stand well back during shooting, then edge her way closer to exchange a word or to with Sinatra between takes. At lunchtime in the studio commissary, she would pause at his table on her way in or out. "Sinatra knew Nancy had the hots for him, but he was otherwise engaged," the late Peter Lawford said.[25]

"Nancy was desperate," an MGM player recalled, "although her career seemed more secure than many of us. If you were signed because you were beautiful and sexy, if you hadn't become a Lana Turner or Ava Gardner or Elizabeth Taylor [the three most glamorous stars at MGM when Nancy was signed] by the time you were twenty-three or twenty-four—forget it. It wasn't going to happen. But Nancy could go on playing plain-Jane supporting roles in B films for years. She claimed she wanted to be a fine and recognized actress like her godmother, Alla Nazimova. I always felt that was a scrim. Nancy was in hot pursuit of a husband."[26]

Yearning for social status of her own, Nancy was convinced she needed to marry a man who had already attained it. Her childhood had been filled with traumatic partings, of accepting what had been dealt to her grimly, but with grit and determination. As a teenager, she had set about reinventing herself and her early hard-knocks life.

Most youngsters fantasize about their futures to some extent. Nancy laid out a plan, and with remarkable steely reserve made things happen as she wished they would—one slow, self-rising step at a time. Though not beautiful or glamorous, she was always well groomed in conservative but stylish outfits, with much attention paid to matching accessories. She entered a room with an interested smile, cultivated to give her a look of assurance, the look of someone who grew up in comfort as the daughter of a distinguished neurosurgeon. The early life that Nancy would later try so firmly to negate had honed a dauntless spirit of resolution that would in the end serve her, or at least her needs and ambitions, well.

Shortly before her thirtieth birthday, she sat down one day and made a list of the men she considered to be Hollywood's most appealing and eligible bachelors. In a culture where youth was valued above character and, often, intelligence, time was growing short if she wanted to achieve her aim of being Mrs. Somebody. Her ideal marriage partner had to be a man Dr. Loyal Davis would welcome as a son-in-law.

Ronald Reagan topped her list. Not simply a movie star, Reagan was president of the Screen Actors Guild and exuded a certain charismatic power during his tenure. Moreover, his stand on the possible infiltration of Communist propaganda in films would certainly find approval with the archconservative politics of Loyal Davis. Then there was the man himself. Nancy had viewed several of Reagan's movies, and she had liked what she had seen.

Reagan was a handsome oak of a man, tall and muscular, his arms attached like strong branches to his athletic trunk. His weathered complexion reflected his love of the outdoors. He wore an easy smile on his face, not forced or turned on just for the camera. His voice had a reassuring masculine timbre. When Nancy attended a large SAG meeting over which he presided, the late actor Roddy MacDowall noted, "Her eyes were glued on him the entire time."[27] Reagan and Jane Wyman had recently divorced, and Nancy had heard that Ronnie was in shock, vulnerable, and looking for companionship. Nancy made up her mind that she would somehow manage a personal introduction.

Among the first friends Nancy had made at the studio were Dore Schary and his wife, Miriam. It was a smart move. Harsh times hit Hollywood in the late forties, when Nancy was signed at Metro, and her home studio was no exception. Furthermore, the films the studio had recently produced had not won their usual lion's share of the Academy Awards. Studio chief Louis B. Mayer was pressed by the New York office to hire Schary, who had risen from writer to successful production chief of RKO-Radio (a position he now held at MGM) and was thought to be a young man with ideas who could bring the studio out of its doldrums. Nancy had quickly found herself two protectors—Thau and Schary. It was Schary who cast her in a small role in *East Side, West Side*, to follow her appearance in *Shadow on the Wall*.

The movie, based on a novel by Marcia Davenport, was directed and produced by Mervyn LeRoy and starred Barbara Stanwyck, James Mason, Ava Gardner, and Van Heflin. Nancy was cast as Mason's obsequious secretary, who informs his wife (Stanwyck) of his affair with the sensuous Gardner. This would be the one film in which Nancy appeared with a star-studded cast. At the time it seemed the credit might elevate her status. She also had faith that Schary, who was primed to take over the studio from Mayer, could make that happen. Now that her relationship with the powerful Benny Thau was over, Nancy was seeking higher ground.

Nancy and the Scharys were a curious match. Although Nancy was not all that politically minded, she had spent many years listening to Loyal Davis's conservative Republican opinions and outright prejudices. Nancy did not share the latter with Davis, choosing to confront him not verbally but through her choice of friends. Benny Thau was Jewish and Dore Schary was both Jewish and a dedicated liberal Democrat. Miriam Schary was not one of Hollywood's social leaders for several reasons. First, with the snobbism of many New York intellectuals, Miriam considered Hollywood a vulgar place and pursued her own interest—art. In addition, a facial disfigurement caused by an accident that had paralyzed some nerves discomfited certain people, especially in a town where feminine beauty was so overvalued. Nancy was immediately sympathetic to Miriam.

One day, during a telephone conversation, Nancy mentioned to Miriam that she would like to meet Ronald Reagan. Miriam was not enthusiastic. Even though Reagan was a Democrat, his actions as president of the Screen Actors Guild were worrisome to liberal members. There was talk that he might be a secret agent for the FBI, transmitting private information garnered from SAG files on fellow actors whom he suspected of belonging to Communist front organizations. This made him a possible informant, an idea that the Scharys found intolerable.[28] Nancy countered that it was equally intolerable to accuse him without knowing the facts.

Reagan's easy smile was deceptive. He could be a bulldog when he chose. Jack Dales, director of SAG, recalled that he was often "two men . . . aggressive fighter across the [negotiating] table, then in conference among ourselves [SAG] in our caucuses," losing his temper.[29] This worked well for the Guild in studio negotiations, but it did not make him popular on a personal level with the members.

Reagan's dedication to a cause reminded Nancy of Loyal Davis, who passionately fought hospital boards and medical unions to win concessions for his profession, and she was intrigued even more. She persuaded Miriam to give a small dinner party—to which both she and Reagan would be invited. Miriam agreed, thinking it would provide the opportunity for her to confront him about his current agenda for SAG and his dogmatic anticommunist stand. As with most dinners at the Scharys, their children were present; Miriam believed they should learn about life firsthand. Their daughter, author Jill Schary Robinson, a teenager at the time, vividly recalled that evening in late August, 1949.

"There was a lot of political talk and some arguments. [My parents] were liberals and they looked at the current situation in Washington as a witch hunt. The rights of American citizens were being frighteningly abused. Reagan made his [anticommunist] views very clear. [Miriam also made hers clear, while Schary played the role of mediator.] He was very articulate. Nancy listened to him attentively. She was sitting opposite him at the dinner table and she kept smiling at him in agreement. Reagan truly believed Russia was plotting to conquer the United States and was using movies as a means of propaganda. He also felt it was his duty to fight this in order to preserve his country's freedom."[30]

The Scharys' suspicions of Reagan's work as an FBI, informer, were not relaxed in his company. Jill described the evening as rather contentious. Reagan had recently shattered his right thighbone during a charity softball game, and his leg was still in a cast, so he departed soon after dinner, having taken little notice of Nancy. It was obvious that his relationship with the Scharys was not close. He had accepted Miriam's invitation because, as president of an actors' union, he needed to maintain channels of communication with studio heads.

The Reagans both claimed to have met at a date later than the Schary dinner party. However, in an interview in 1983 with this author, Miriam Schary corroborated Jill's recollection. "Reagan met Nancy that night at my house," she said. "But he was obviously preoccupied and there were ten for dinner that night. I don't recall his saying much to Nancy. I asked him beforehand if he would pick up a guest [Nancy]. He replied that he wasn't sure he had the time to do so as he would be coming directly from a meeting at the Guild. I believe that Mervyn LeRoy collected her and took her home."[31] This means Reagan knew, when he later arranged a meeting with Nancy, that she was an attractive young woman, which might well have caused him to agree to meet with her personally over a problem she then claimed to have.

Two months passed, and Nancy was ready to shoot her final scenes in *East Side, West Side* with Mervyn LeRoy, who had many top hits to his credit—among them as producer of *The Wizard of Oz* and as director of *Waterloo Bridge, Random Harvest, Madam Curie*, and *Thirty Seconds over Tokyo*. Reagan and LeRoy were friends, and Nancy used that connection to her advantage. On October 29 an article in the *Hollywood Reporter* appeared listing the name *Nancy Davis*, the wife of producer Jerome Davis, along with over two hundred other signatories to an amicus brief calling upon the United States Supreme Court to reverse the conviction of screenwriters Dalton Trumbo and John Howard Lawson for refusing to disclose their political affiliation to the House Un-American Activities Committee.

The chief objective of the committee was to declare the Communist Party—a legal party at this time, but viewed by HUAC as a criminal conspiracy—illegal. The men who led the anticommunist purge—which became exercises in harassment that left behind broken families, shattered careers, and suicides, as well as compromised, disillusioned men and women, some never again able to function properly in society—were often out to settle old scores or to gain quick notoriety and power.

Some, like Reagan, honestly believed that the Communists had already infiltrated Hollywood and had to be rooted out.

In his 1990 autobiography, *An American Life*, he would write, "In the end, we stopped the Communists cold in Hollywood, but there was a dark side to the battle; unfortunately, it was a story with victims as well as villains. . . . Many fine people were accused wrongly of being Communists simply because they were liberals."[32] Dalton Trumbo, one of the convicted Hollywood Ten, was to say, "None of us—right, left or center—emerged from that long nightmare without sin."[33]

But at the time Nancy went to LeRoy, paper in hand, and with a tone of desperation asked him to help clear her name so that no one would confuse her with this *other* Nancy Davis. LeRoy wanted to know what he could do. "Call Mr. Reagan and ask him to please see me so that I can clear this up," she requested. LeRoy might well have decided this was none of his affair and sent her to the front office for assistance. But he had his own agenda. His film was near completion, and he did not want HUAC creating problems for a member of his cast (such allegations, if true, could lead to Nancy's being removed from the production and so leaving scenes to be reshot). He called Reagan and explained to him that the Nancy Davis in his film had no interest in left-wing causes and was not the Nancy Davis listed in the *Hollywood Reporter*.

Reagan checked SAG files and confirmed the Nancy Davis appearing in LeRoy's movies could not to have been the same woman and called LeRoy back to assure him of this.[34]

Nancy pressed LeRoy to call Reagan again and tell him of her continued anxiety regarding "the name confusion," saying that she would feel better if she could meet with him again to be sure there would be no more such accusations. LeRoy did so, adding that Nancy was attractive and suggesting that Reagan "take her out to dinner and tell her the whole story yourself."

"Taking out a young actress under contract to MGM," Reagan recalled, "didn't seem like a bad idea to me—and I could call it part of my duties as president of the Guild." Reagan made a date with her for that evening, arriving to collect her at her Westwood apartment on two canes, his leg injury not yet fully healed. They dined at La Rue's, a popular Hollywood restaurant.

Nancy brought up the problem of the other Nancy Davis. He suggested that she change her name, an idea she refused to consider.

Soon enough the subject was dropped. "He didn't talk about himself, his last picture, his next picture," Nancy recalled. "There was none of that. He talked about horses and the Civil War." He said later that "her eyes mesmerized" him. Never had anyone seemed so intent on listening to what he had to say. Not wanting the evening to end, he suggested, "Have you ever seen Sophie Tucker? She's singing at Ciro's just down the street. Why don't we go for the first show?"[35]

They stayed through two performances, and Nancy did not return to her apartment until three A.M., after agreeing to see him again that night. He picked her up around eight P.M., and they drove down to the ocean and had dinner at the Malibu Inn, seated at a window table with "a starlit sky turning the night sea into glittering sparks of light as waves rose and crashed against the rocky beach shore,"[36] as Reagan later supposedly described in full purple Hollywood style to a staff writer on *Movieland* magazine. With his immediate and flattering interest, Nancy expected the relationship to accelerate into something more serious. To her extreme disappointment, however, he also continued to date several other attractive young women who appeared with him in photographs taken at various restaurants and nightclubs.

On Reagan's thirty-ninth birthday, Nancy felt she was making inroads when she was his beaming date at a banquet held at the Beverly Hills Hotel, where he was honored by six hundred Friars (representing the film industry's most prestigious members). Film giants Cecil B. DeMille, Harry Cohn, and others gave speeches in tribute to his work for the industry to avoid the recent crippling danger of a major actors' strike.

By that spring Ronnie and Nancy were seeing each other on a weekly basis but still not exclusively. Nancy accepted dates arranged by the studio for publicity purposes. Although Ronnie remained somewhat aloof, she chose to overlook it, aware that he was under mounting pressures. The machinations of union clashes and HUAC, his own battle with his conscience over this issue, and the conflicts between major film agencies and the studios all whirled around him. He was busy giving speeches, writing articles as guest columnist for *Themis* magazine, presiding at SAG meetings, and hotly conspiring to win points for the Guild, or at least for his position on the various controversies then raging (excerpts from one of his columns appear in appendix 1). At the same time, he was having problems with Warner Brothers, where he had been under contract for thirteen years.

Because his contract called for yearly increases, Reagan was earning more than he ever had. But his movies were not doing well at the box office, and his studio felt he was now too mature for the youthful roles he had been playing. They also did not believe that he had the charisma of enduring stars like Cary Grant, James Stewart, Spencer Tracy, Henry Fonda, and John Wayne, who were his age and older but whose movies retained tremendous box office magic. His political activities had further eroded his image.

Convinced that Ronnie was *the* one, Nancy tried a new approach: She took a vigorous interest in his work at SAG. When actress Joan Caulfield left the board, Nancy told Ronnie that she would really like to become involved in Guild activities and that perhaps he could propose her name as a replacement. He considered that plausible enough to follow through on the idea, although the board rejected it on the grounds that "the Guild is in need at this time of name strength on the Board [meaning a member of star stature]."[37]

Nancy refused to let this daunt her, and realizing that she had found a connection that would bond her closer to Reagan, she intensified her knowledge of what was happening at the Guild. Reagan found this comforting. Jane Wyman, who had always hated his intense political activity, chose never to discuss it with him. The women he had recently been dating understood very little of such matters. But with Nancy he could expound for hours as she listened enraptured, asking just the right questions to spur him on. In November 1950 her name was once again placed on the SAG ballot. She was voted down a second time.

Reagan still remained uncommitted to the relationship, but Jack Dales and the Scharys considered Nancy and Ronnie a couple. That summer, Reagan claimed, he awoke "one morning and couldn't remember the name of the lady sharing my bed. That was it." This was the time to admit that he was in love with Nancy. With his solid Christian background, that meant marriage. At this point he feared he might have waited too long; as he later wrote, he "had done everything wrong, dating her off and on, continuing to volunteer for every Guild trip to New York—in short, doing everything which could have lost her."[38]

This was in February 1952, and Reagan had been dating Nancy for two years. Shortly after this epiphany they were seated in their favorite red-leather booth in the front room of Chasen's, having a quiet dinner together. Ronnie leaned across the table and said, "Let's get married." Nancy, her hand on his, looked into his eyes and said, "Let's."[39]

Then she requested that he call her parents and ask for their permission.

CHAPTER TWO

ALL SHE EVER WANTED

Nancy had no intention of being lost. The pride in the loving looks she gave Reagan were not mere feminine wiles. Nancy was wholeheartedly in love. Everything she had ever said about wanting a marriage above a career, about knowing when the important man came into her life, was now valid. For two years she had not complained when Reagan chose Guild business over a date. She made no attempt to make him jealous or to pressure him into a proposal. Although they maintained two separate apartments, they were mostly cohabiting, and whether or not Nancy knew it at the time, she was, in fact, one month pregnant. This was not a situation that Reagan would have taken lightly, had he been informed. Reagan was a man who greatly respected Christian values, which had been drilled into him by his mother, Nelle, the woman by whom he judged all other women. One of the first things he had done when he began seriously dating Nancy was to take her to meet Nelle. His brother Neil was present.

Nelle was small, no more than five feet tall, and looked frail and pinched, no loose flesh on her sharp bones. This had always been misleading. She was in her midsixties now and still could lift a weight greater than herself. God gave her the strength, she was fond of saying, to work and to endure. And she had endured much. Times had been easy for Nelle only after her two sons grew up and the younger, Ronald, began acting in movies. But even then she refused to have anyone do work for her that she could do for herself or ask for anything more than was necessary to live a clean, Christian life.

Since Reagan was not in the habit of bringing his lady friends to meet her, Nelle paid special attention to Nancy Davis. She provided coffee and homemade cookies and studied Nancy as she talked to Ronnie and Neil. When she was clearing the dishes, Nelle took Nancy aside and looked hard into her eyes. "You're in love with him, aren't you?" she asked. "Yes," Nancy replied. "I thought so," Nelle said, her words couched in hidden meaning.[1] Although she had never stood in the way of her son's choices, Nelle had not liked Jane Wyman, whom she had believed to be neither a good wife nor a good mother. "Jane was too involved with her own career to suit Nelle," a family friend commented.[2] Knowing how deeply hurt her son had been by the divorce, Nelle did not want him to suffer through another failed relationship. She watched closely as Nancy's glance followed Ronald's every move with wide-eyed adoration. This was a woman who would be a dedicated and caring wife, and for that reason Nelle liked Nancy from the very start.

Neil, on the other hand, reserved judgment. "Well, it looks as if this one has her hooks in him!" he said after meeting her this first time. Nelle, he recalled, was thoughtful for a few moments. "I suspect your father's family said that about me after our first meeting," she finally replied.[3]

Nelle was the youngest child of Thomas A. and Mary Anne Elsey Wilson. She was born and lived most of her life before she married John (Jack) Howard Reagan on a farm in an area known as North Clyde, about eleven miles from Fulton, Illinois. The Wilson family found their chief pleasure in their religion. They strictly observed the Sabbath, regularly attended worship, and conducted Bible studies at home. Nelle's mother died when she was seventeen and was courted by Jack, whose father worked at a grain elevator in Fulton. The Reagans (Jack had a brother and a sister), all practicing Catholics, had a love of music and dance. Family gatherings meant sprightly reels and jigs executed with great enthusiasm. Corn whiskey was consumed in great quantities. To be a hard drinker without becoming a drunk was a test of character, a means of demonstrating a man's self-control. It often proved too great a test for Jack.

He had Irish charm aplenty, dark good looks and no desire to end up at a grain elevator like his father. He took a job in a local dry goods store where shoes became his speciality and where Nelle, small, perky, blue-eyed, and auburn-haired, also worked. "Nothing better than to spend the day admiring the turn of a pretty girl's ankle," he was known to say.[4] Nelle and Jack fell in love, and despite her father's objections due to Jack's religion, the two were married. Nelle was certain that she could bring some stability to Jack's life, that he would stop drinking once she was able to give him a sense of worth.

The young Reagans moved to nearby Tampico, where their two sons, John Neil Reagan (September 16, 1908) and Ronald Wilson Reagan (February 5, 1911), were born. While Jack was a good salesman, his drinking took a large slice of his salary. Whenever he lost his job, the small family moved from one city in Illinois to another: Tampico to Galesburg to Chicago and then back to Tampico. Finally, in 1920, they settled in Dixon, Illinois, population 8,191. Despite the advent of the telephone, radio, and the train, Dixon had remained a backwater, an isolated and overgrown prairie village squat in the middle of undeveloped farmland, a town whose workers were in the lowest income bracket in the nation.

Still, a young boy fed stories by a father with a glib manner and a penchant for exaggeration might view the town "not in the drab hues of reality, but with a certain enchantment."[5] Jack had a job in a shoe store and Nelle watched over her two sons—Moon (Neil's nickname) and Dutch (as Ronald had been called from birth because Jack thought his second son looked like a little Dutchman)—to see that they did not stray. They were by all accounts typical American boys. They got into fights and defended each other. They stole grapes and apples from a neighbor's farm, and Nelle made them go back and confess and offer to rake leaves or otherwise make up for their thievery. The boys did as she told them to do. After they had raked leaves for several hours, the neighbor presented them with a bag of fruit. On their return home, Nelle sent them both out to hand it over to the church as a further penance, although she well could have used the food to supplement her meals, and the boys had had hopes of a fruit pie, a rare treat, for dinner.

The country was enjoying postwar prosperity, but the Reagans still suffered hard times. A strong personality with a distinctive voice, Nelle was the center of her household. Such luxuries as chicken on Sunday or fruit pies were too expensive for her meager budget. Liver (mostly pork or beef) was considered pet food and often given free with another purchase. Nelle would buy soup bones and the butcher would throw in a pound of liver, no doubt knowing full well that she was using it to feed her family, not a dog or a cat. She grew onions and potatoes in a small plot at the back of the modest house they rented on Everett Street. There was soup, potato and onion pie, macaroni and cheese on Sundays, when she could scrape up the few extra pennies for the cheese, and always a big bowl of popcorn set out on the kitchen table to quell any hunger pangs the boys might experience. Nelle refused to borrow from any member of her own or Jack's family. When bills came due, they had to be paid immediately. Material debt was the Devil's lure, Nelle believed; the only debt man should have was to God, and so the Reagans made do.

For extra money Nelle took in a roomer and moved the boys down to the enclosed porch, "which was fine in summer but nippy in winter,"[6] Reagan remembered. She turned the larder, which was usually empty anyway, into a sewing room where she hemmed a dress for fifty cents and a coat for a dollar. She did all she could to build up their father in the eyes of his sons. Jack was good-natured and well-liked. Although Dixon was right in the center of solid Republican country, the Reagans, like many American-Irish Catholics, had always been fervent Democrats, and Jack became actively involved in the local ward. Fellow workers overlooked his drinking, and Nelle taught her sons tolerance of their father's "bouts with the dark demon in the bottle."[7] In one of the most dramatic episodes of his youth, Dutch, age eleven, half-dragged, half-carried his stocky, inert father into the house from the front porch where he had collapsed in a drunken stupor, fragrant with the stench of too much alcohol. There were repeated incidents and times when both

Moon and Dutch had to collect Jack, in less-than-coherent shape, from local bars.

Dutch always treated his father, drunk or sober, with respect, as did Moon. Jack Reagan was loving, given often to sentimentality. He was also something of a dreamer, glib—an honest man whose ambitions were too large for his talents. He was never shy of a day's hard work but, at the end of it, his failure to accomplish what he wanted to do was too heavy a load and he drank to blur the edges of self-disappointment. He never became an unruly or angry drunk. "He just would drink until he collapsed," a fellow Dixonite recalled.[8]

Nelle was dedicated to her work for the Christian Church of Dixon, whose members saw themselves as liberal Fundamentalists. It was a poor congregation, with no church in which to worship. Meetings were held in the basement of the local YMCA, and members were expected to tithe one-tenth of their income to support it. Despite having to struggle ten percent harder to take care of her family, Nelle never missed a week of tithing, and to make sure that she never shorted her obligation, she kept a record of every fifty cents she earned. (Reagan continued his mother's practice of tithing ten percent of his income until at least 1986, when the pastor of Hollywood Christian Church, Benjamin H. Moore, stated, "The President still contributes weekly to the church.")[9] Nelle's church was part of a religious revival that had as much of an impact on the twenties as Prohibition. Members followed five fundamentals of belief: "The infallibility of the Bible; the virgin birth of Christ; the Resurrection; that Christ died to atone for the sins of the world; and the Second Coming."

Dutch was baptized in 1922 at the age of eleven. He was to say that he had felt "called" at the time of his baptism, that he had experienced a personal epiphany "when he invited Christ into" his life.[10] At fifteen, along with Nelle, he taught a Sunday School class for boys his own age and was a leader at prayer meetings. The congregation was much taken with his voice and delivery, which they believed owed a great deal to the private elocution lessons his mother (who had harbored early hopes of going on the stage) gave him. Church parishioners recount how Dutch could "make the Bible seem personal, like a phrase might just have been written."[11]

Nelle Reagan's personal ministry grew to extend beyond members of her family and church. "If Nelle had had the education, I think she would have mounted the pulpit," a contemporary commented. Bone-skinny, "a real tiny, little thing," with a commanding voice, given to dramatic readings, she regularly visited patients at the state mental hospitals and scheduled weekly visits to prisoners in the local jail, where she quoted from the Bible and dispensed "Christian comfort" to the "poor souls who were all God's children" in these institutions.[12] On her Saturday visits, Dutch would accompany her. "She had a way of givin' out her religion that wasn't offensive," Dixonite Louis Sindlinger explained. "She was very good at reading the Bible. The men [prisoners] looked forward to her coming. Some of them were released in her custody and slept on a cot in Nelle's sewing room until they found another situation."[13]

Not until he was eleven had Nelle realized that Dutch was severely nearsighted. Glasses were prescribed, but he still had to sit on the bench for most of his school years when he was yearning to get out on the football field and prove that he could run the field as well as the best of them. He took drama classes at high school, often playing the lead in school performances, and became the only lifeguard on the Rock River at Dixon's Lowell Park for seven summers. He claimed to have saved seventy-seven swimmers from drowning in the river, and he had cut a notch in a log on the bank of the river for each rescue. He saw himself as a hero and so did many Dixonites. While Moon was an extrovert, a great promoter and salesman for whatever he wanted, Dutch was introspective. He read late into the night, tried his hand at writing, was earnest about his religion, and was more reserved at home than in public. He lived in what he called "a pretend world." He basked in the acceptance of outsiders and always gave that "extra something"—a special boyish smile, blue-gray eyes "looking straight at you."[14]

Dixon historian Charles Lamb boasted that "Dixon was always a small town. It always has been and it always will be. Folks had dreams [to move away and be successful] . . . but most never realized them."[15]

Dutch had dreams *and* he realized them. He was graduated from Eureka College, which was affiliated with the Christian Church, whereas only eight percent of Dixon's high school graduates continued their education. At Eureka, football was his first love, but he was once again relegated to the bench for most of the games by the coach, Oklahoman Ralph "Mac" McKinzie, whom he admired with a true fan's devotion, for Mac had been a star player on his own and had brought Eureka the limited glory it had attained. "Dutch," he recalled six decades later, "I put him at the end on the fifth string. . . . [Nobody who wanted to play football at Eureka was excluded from the team.] The first year I never let him play a game. Guess he hated me for it. But I had a team to consider. He was nearsighted, you know. Couldn't see worth a damn. Ended up at the bottom of the heap every time and missed the play because he couldn't see the man or the ball movin' on him. Gotta say he was regular at practice. And took his knocks."[16]

He never gave up hope of one day carrying the ball over the goal line, but he won swimming medals, became a student leader, and headed a student rebellion. He gave a stirring speech in the school chapel in favor of removing Eureka's president, Bert Wilson, who had placed severe restrictions on the social activities of the students, including smoking and dancing. When Reagan urged them to unseat Wilson by nonviolent means—a strike that involved not attending classes—the entire student body rose to its feet cheering. The strike was successful, and Wilson tendered his resignation. Dutch had experienced a new, exhilarating feeling that filled him with a developing sense of power. He had so connected with an audience that he had been able to sway their emotions into a mass reaction. Elected senior class president, he gave the student address at graduation. Then he was out on his own. Moon had left home, and his parents were now reduced to living in a one-room apartment; Jack, having been fired from his job at a local shoe store, was unemployed for most of a year.[17]

Dutch's childhood and youth was one of unrelieved pinching and saving, doing without, being grateful for little in the way of luxury. His immediate ambition was not riches, just better conditions—bills paid, money in the bank for an emergency, and enough put aside to take care of his parents. He feared his own conservative nature would force him to compromise, to abandon a crazy dream of standing alone on a stage as he had at the chapel on the campus of Eureka College with everyone looking up to him, being influenced by what he said. He believed in working for the essential needs in life, but he knew he could never be happy until he was *somebody*. He did not have the urge to drink, did not smoke, and did not subscribe to the idea of accepting handouts. Nelle had instilled in him the belief that you had to work hard for everything you got in life. There would be no free rides, and in the end it was the Good Lord who placed you where you belonged, so there was no use griping about it.

At the time he left college the man was fully formed, and that included the charismatic personality that gave him a kind of power over others. Yet he did not use it to his advantage, although after the night of his speech in the school chapel, he knew he could if he wished. In November 1932 he voted for Franklin D. Roosevelt in the presidential election. Although the Depression was at its lowest ebb, Reagan talked himself into a job as a sports announcer on radio station WOC in Davenport, Iowa. Within a year he moved to Radio WHO, an NBC affiliate in Des Moines, Iowa. He continued to tithe and to send his parents an equal amount from his small paycheck and, although three years younger than his brother, to assist Neil in completing his self-imposed interrupted education at Eureka College. (Neil had hoped to get a job to assist his parents, but was unable to do so with the Depression causing vast unemployment.) This left Dutch with very little for extras. All this changed suddenly in March 1937. Reagan was in Hollywood, ostensibly to accompany the Chicago Cubs on a training trip to Catalina Island, a short boat ride from Los Angeles, for a sports-related story. While he was in town, he looked up a former girlfriend from his WOC radio days, Joy Hodges, a singer who was now playing small roles in the movies. She introduced him to an agent, and the next thing he knew, he had been offered a contract at Warner Brothers Studio. After some nervous deliberation, he signed for seven years with options every six months at the starting salary of $200 a week, four times what he was making with Radio WHO.

Upon signing, the first thing he did was to telegraph his parents that he was sending them railroad fare and had rented a house for them in West Hollywood. If he could help it, Nelle would never want for the necessities of life again. His hope was that his father would stop drinking, especially since Jack now had a chronic heart condition that prohibited large alcohol consumption. But four years later, having never kicked his habit, Jack Reagan died of heart failure. Nelle was alone but free of the worry caused by Jack's addiction to alcohol. Moon had graduated from Eureka College, was married, and had a good job as manager of radio station WOC in Davenport, Iowa, where Dutch had once been employed. Nelle's attention turned to her younger son, now Ronald Reagan, rising movie star (she hoped), and to work at the West Hollywood branch of the Christian Church.

From early childhood, Reagan had been handicapped with exceptionally poor vision. To balance this defect, nature had endowed him with a photographic memory and a fascination with ferreting out little-known historical facts. Lawrence Williams, an actor who appeared in five films with Reagan during their mutual tenure at Warner Brothers from 1937 through the early forties, recalled that between long takes on ten-hour shooting days, "Ronnie would express animated views on an infinite variety of subjects to us, his fellow actors—captives on the set. Statistical information of all sorts was a commodity Ronnie always had in extraordinary supply, carried in his head. Not only was this information abundant, it was stunning in its catholicity. There seemed to be absolutely no subject, however recondite, without its immediately accessible [mental] file. He had the dope on just about everything, all history's baseball pitchers, the optimistic outlook for California sugar-beet production in the year 2000 [this was in 1940], the recent diminution of the rainfall level causing everything to go to hell in summer in Kansas and so on. One could not help but be impressed."[18]

He was also a diligent worker, agreeable to all he was asked to do. As he was photogenic and moved well before a camera, his career progressed. His coworkers recall that in his early days in Hollywood he was a loner, not a playboy or a social animal, seldom without a book in hand, and often seen off to himself, wearing his familiar thick, horned-rimmed glasses, nose close to the page as he read, glancing upward from time to time as though "committing what he had just read to memory." In 1938 he appeared in *Brother Rat* with Jane Wyman, who worked at the same studio, and they fell in love. It was an attraction of opposites and seemed doomed from the start, but with his Christian upbringing Reagan believed marriage was a commitment before God, and divorce something that would never happen to him.[19]

When she was dating Reagan, Nancy did not give much thought to the fact that he had two children, Maureen, eleven, and Michael, six. Both children had been placed in Chadwick, a boarding school situated about a half-hour's drive from their mother's home where they joined her on weekends and holidays. Sometimes Reagan would drive up to their school to visit with them, and other times he would take them for a weekend to his new ranch, Yearling Row, in Malibu, which was larger and more elegant than the horse farm in Northridge.

"It was obvious to us kids that Dad and Nancy were very much in love. They held hands, and when they didn't think we were looking, they sneaked kisses," Michael remembered.[20] From the beginning, Michael confessed, he felt like he was in the middle of a battle between his mother, Jane Wyman, and Nancy, and an outsider to his father and Nancy's great love for each other. Because he had been adopted and Maureen was not, his sense of estrangement was even more painful. Wyman was a strict disciplinarian who used a riding crop—ten whacks on the calf of each of Michael's legs when he misbehaved. Both of the children had suffered some form of either emotional or physical abuse by Wyman, but never carried tales from one parent to the other for fear that she would refuse to let them see their father, which she often threatened. Neither Wyman nor Reagan was a demonstrative parent, but Reagan took the greater interest in his offspring. He never raised a hand, or his voice, to either child. He always fell back on reasoning, explaining in detail what the child had done wrong and what they should do to right it. Michael idolized him and desperately wanted to feel his closeness, but as Michael much later put it, "Dad could give his heart to the country but he just found it difficult to hug his own children."[21]

The young boy bonded with Nancy on the weekends that they spent together and on the trips they took in the car, when he would sit next to her in the front seat and she would rub his back. It was the nearest thing the boy had known to physical affection. He and his sister "talked about Dad and Nancy, and we both agreed it would be wonderful if they got married because then we would have another mother. Most of all, I hoped that if they got married they would have me move in with them. I would have a Mom and Dad and a normal house like many of my friends and I wouldn't have to board at school."[22]

"Nancy and I got along right away," Maureen stressed in her auto-biography *First Father, First Daughter*. She also had warm memories of the car rides when they would sing duets. "Although she gave the impression of being strong-willed and determined—Nancy seemed to me to be a warm, compassionate person, certainly sympathetic to the problems of a young girl dealing with the kinds of things I was having to deal with at the time [her own antagonism toward her mother, her burgeoning sexuality, and her conflict with Wyman over her imposed Catholic education]."[23]

When Nancy and Ronnie were married at the Little Brown Church in the Valley on March 4, 1952, she gained a ready-made family. The ceremony was simple, with only Reagan's good friend William Holden and his wife, Ardis (known on screen as Brenda Marshall), present. Nancy wore a gray suit with a white collar and a small flowered hat, and carried a hand bouquet. It was not the wedding that she had always dreamed of having. "Ronnie still wanted to keep things low-key . . . no press."[24] Michael and Maureen were at Chadwick and waited in the small house next to Maureen's dorm for a promised phone call to confirm that the marriage vows had been exchanged. When the telephone rang, their father simply told them, "O.K. It's official."[25]

"I would have preferred a bigger wedding with all our friends," Nancy admitted. "I understood how [Ronnie] felt and if he thought a private ceremony was more appropriate, that was okay with me. By then we felt we were already married [indicating that they had been living together for a considerable time]."[26]

After the ceremony, they went back to the Holdens' home where Ardis had a three-tier wedding cake with the traditional bride and groom on top. Ardis had also hired a photographer so that there would at least be wedding pictures. Champagne toasts were raised and a catered dinner for four served. Nancy claimed she was in such a daze throughout the day that during the ceremony she had to be prompted by Holden to say "I do," and never realized until much later that Bill and Ardis had not exchanged a word, remaining aloof from each other the entire day. The Holdens' marriage was on rocky ground at this point, mainly because of his drinking and extramarital affairs, and they had had a terrible row directly before leaving for the ceremony.

Mrs. Ronald Reagan at last, Nancy glowed all afternoon, her arm through Ronnie's whenever possible. They spent the first night at the Old Mission Inn en route to Phoenix, where they stayed at the luxurious Biltmore Hotel and spent most of their time visiting with Edith and Loyal Davis. The two men hit it off fairly well, but it was Edith to whom Reagan gravitated more naturally. (From that time, every July 6, Nancy's birthday, Ronnie would send Edith a telegram thanking her for giving Nancy "the gift of life so that she could share it with" him.)[27] Neither Nancy nor Ronnie thought it odd in any way that they should be spending their honeymoon with the bride's parents, meeting Loyal Davis's friends, one of whom—Arizonian Barry Morris Goldwater—was running on the Republican ticket for senator from that state and would have a great influence upon Reagan's future.

Goldwater was "a damned hard man to dislike," Loyal Davis once said.[28] His friend was a big man, bristling with energy, dogmatic, a Republican with eyes set beyond the Senate. The Arizona sun and his love of the outdoors gave him a salubrious glow, and he was open and frank in his opinions. Reagan could not help but admire and identify with him. Goldwater (his father was Jewish but he had been brought up an Episcopalian, his mother's faith) was an expert pilot, a confident speaker, and a power in his own state set to break the Democratic grip on the Senate.

Of their honeymoon Nancy wrote: "After just a few days in Phoenix, we started back for Los Angeles, where Ronnie had a picture commitment [Hong Kong]. On the way home, there were high winds and they split the top of Ronnie's convertible. So the honeymoon ended with me on my knees in the front seat ... holding down the top. We had to stop every once in a while so I could warm my hands."[29]

Shortly before the Reagans married, there had been indications that MGM might not pick up Nancy's next option. In the four years she had been under contract to the studio she had appeared in eight films, acting the female lead in three of them: *The Next Voice You Hear,* opposite James Whitmore, in which she played his very pregnant wife (a singularly unglamorous role, but her best); *Night into Morning* (taking third billing to Ray Milland and John Hodiak); and *Shadow in the Sky,* which again costarred her with Whitmore and with Ralph Meeker. All three movies were low-budget affairs made under Dore Schary's auspices, containing worthy themes that defeated them at the box office. Nancy's career was heading downhill fast, and MGM was taking a dive as well.

In 1951 Louis B. Mayer, who had gone from immigrant junk dealer to powerful head of Hollywood's most famous studio, had engaged in a power struggle with Schary, his former aide, and lost. Public taste had changed, television was an active threat, and age had encroached on MGM's long list of famous stars who had brought the studio the epithet "the glamour factory." Mayer was voted out by the stockholders and replaced by the literate Schary, twenty years his junior. In his eight years as chief of production Schary was responsible for the studio's transition from movies that entertained to those that carried a message, and that led, ultimately, to his and the studio's downfall.

Nancy was one of the first of Metro's contract players to go. She gave interviews saying that she was retiring from the screen to become a full-time wife, which was what she had always wanted. The truth was that she was being offered no parts. Unfortunately for the newly married Reagans, Ronnie was at a professional crossroads in his life as well.

CHAPTER THREE

A HOME OF THEIR OWN

With his most recent movies box office losers, Warner Brothers failed to renew Reagan's contract. For the first time in his film career, he was independent of studio control. There had been great changes in the movie industry, and Lew Wasserman, president of the Music Corporation of America and Reagan's agent, was responsible for many of them. MCA had as its clients some of the greatest box office stars in Hollywood, many of whom had been locked into contracts at salaries that were not commensurate with the income their appearance in a movie generated. Wasserman was convinced that once a star was a free agent he or she would be empowered to strike their own deal with a film company, bringing in a story of their choice, and maintaining control over many other creative elements. He tested the waters in 1950, making a multimillion-dollar package deal for James Stewart, *Winchester '73* (an exceptional Western script by Borden Chase and Robert L. Richards), and Anthony Mann as director, MCA retaining a percentage of the film, as well as demanding a high-six-figure salary for the star. The deal made Stewart a very rich man and an actor now in charge of his own career. Feeling he should be able to achieve the same goal, Reagan went to Wasserman, whom he considered to be a close friend, to discuss this possibility.

An elegant man, beam-tall, spike-lean, Wasserman set the executive style personifying Hollywood power that Reagan later adapted in his role as politician—the smoothed-back hair, the Italian silk tie, impeccably tailored dark suits, and French-cuffed white shirts. The son of poor immigrant parents, Wasserman had worked his way up from movie usher in Cleveland, Ohio, to band booker to agent to president of the largest theatrical agency in the world. Reagan admired him and often sought his advice, which Wasserman had always been happy to dispense. But lately he had passed him off to other, less powerful MCA agents. Now Reagan sat opposite Wasserman in his large, wood-paneled corner office, the faint, spicy scent of the occupant's cologne in the air.

"Lew," Reagan ventured, "what you did for Jimmy [Stewart] was great. Don't you sort of think it's my turn now?"

Wasserman adjusted his signature, oversized black spectacles and leaned forward in his leather chair. "Ron," he replied, in a quiet but forceful voice, "Jimmy has been a major star for many years. His films have been big money makers. You haven't got the same numbers going in as he had."[1]

Reagan was enough of a realist to accept the harsh truth when confronted with it. He wasn't in Stewart's league, and he knew it. The fact that he believed he was a damn sight better than the material the studio had given him, did not alter the fact that his films had not made money or received critical acclaim. Wasserman suggested Reagan go out and look for a strong property (script, play, book) in which he could envision himself as the star and then the agency would see what it could do. The offer did not come with much enthusiasm or a guarantee.

Reagan now had two families to support. Wyman (who had not only reached star status but maintained it after winning a Best Actress Oscar for her "superb portrayal of a deaf-mute rape victim in *Johnny Belinda*" and a recent nomination in the same category for the 1951 film *The Blue Veil*) had just signed a multimillion-dollar contract, so he might not have had to concern himself about Maureen's and Michael's present welfare. Nonetheless, his background decreed that a man took care of his children. With a new wife, a third child on the way, and a ranch—the 350-acre Yearling Row—it was imperative that he find lucrative work soon. He would not consider selling the ranch. Yearling Row was a place in which he could revel in the outdoors, work with his hands, and breed, raise, and ride his horses. The ranch gave him a sense of freedom and empowerment.

His high expenses forced him to accept roles in two turgid dramas, *Hong Kong* and *Tropic Zone*, both opposite Rhonda Fleming, for which he would be paid $45,000 each, less MCA's ten percent agency fees. The producers, Pine-Thomas, made low-budget action films that were released through Paramount. Neither script met with Reagan's approval. In each his character was two-dimensional, and both would be shot on limited time schedules on mostly back-lot mock-ups of exotic locales. Although the films could possibly diminish his star image, Reagan felt he had no choice.

For some years, there had been remarkable juxtapositions in Reagan's career. At the same time that he was appearing in movies that might be inane and sometimes worse, having to rattle off dialogue to a chimpanzee (*Bedtime for Bonzo*), an Indian chief who spoke no English (*The Last Outpost*), and a Chinese boy with a minuscule vocabulary (*Hong Kong*), he was—and had been for six years—the president of the Screen Actors Guild, debating technical and controversial issues on which the lives of thousands of people were balanced. He was also much in demand for lectures and commencement addresses. His impassioned speech "America the Beautiful," delivered to the graduating class at William Woods College in Fulton, Missouri, clearly displayed his brilliance as a communicator. Portions of the speech are immensely stirring, with word pictures that spring immediately to life. (See excerpt in appendix 2.) William Woods is a small, private Christian school, which at the time was for women only. Speaking to about five hundred young students, Reagan made it crystal clear that, along with his fundamental American philosophy and his view of Russia as the Evil Empire, he believed the feminine role was to provide emotional support for the men in her life— father, husband, brother. He also subscribed to something he called momism—that women were responsible for most of the great and noble deeds that men achieved and that when they failed in their given role, their men failed in theirs.

We see the direct result of this philosophy in his relationships with

Nelle and Nancy, both of whom he placed on pedestals. Nancy had no intention of ever being less than his idea of the perfect wife. Her first consideration was always Ronnie, who was then at a difficult point in his career. Acting had been a choice that had been thrust upon him, not one that had its roots in a love of the theater and performing. Although he had taken easily to it and it had given him the wherewithal to support his family during the darkest days of the Depression, it had never completely satisfied him. Given his ability as an orator, which owed a great deal to the church and to Nelle's evangelistic talents and teachings, he possibly could have had a rewarding life as a preacher. But, despite his strong Christian beliefs, from youth he had striven to find for himself a more popular pulpit.

Both he and Nancy strongly felt that his potential had never been realized, that the power and charisma that he exuded in his SAG dealings and in his speeches should have been transferred to the screen. After Reagan's discouraging meeting with Wasserman, he was aware that he was unlikely to reach that level of stardom, that he simply had to press forward along another route to achieve the financial security he desired. Certainly, husband and wife discussed the idea of a future in politics. But at this time Reagan's loyalties were torn. His ideology had strayed from that of the Democratic Party, which he claimed had left him. Yet his deep regard for Nelle's feelings (she had faithfully supported Jack in his Democratic political beliefs and still maintained them) kept him from aligning himself publicly with the Republican Party.

Members of the Democratic Party in Los Angeles County approached him to consider running for the U.S. Congress. There were long discussions with their representatives and with Nancy. He confessed to Jack Dales at SAG and to others that he was having serious problems with the direction he believed the Democratic Party was going. Although he had idolized Franklin D. Roosevelt and had always voted Democratic, he cast his ballot in 1952 on the Republican side, for Gen. Dwight D. Eisenhower. Some of his leaning to the right can be fairly attributed to Nancy, who had been reared in an arch-Republican household and longed for her husband to please her father so that she could bask in that approval.

Nancy would always contend that she had no influence over Ronnie's political decisions. This was untrue. He always listened to Nancy's views, especially concerning which people to trust, for he felt she was more perceptive than was he in that area. It was through her opinions about Reagan's allies and advisers that Nancy most effectively exerted her power.

With Ronnie under extreme pressure, traveling constantly to cover all his commitments, Nancy devoted herself to being the supportive wife. She shielded him from household problems, diligently adhered to the budget he set for them, and somehow managed to look "cool and well turned-out" in both public and private. He once confided to his mother-in-law that "even at breakfast" Nancy was "a tidy sight, everything neat and a lovely picture."[2] When he was away—which was a good part of the time—he spoke to her daily and sent her letters and telegrams, often mushy enough to be associated with adolescent behavior. He called her Nancy Poo or Nancy Poo Pants and signed some of them Daddie Poo. There were also imaginative letters, funny, caring, frequently accompanied by small, humorous line drawings he made, or two inked hearts emblazoned with their initials, an arrow through them. Nancy's letters were far more prosaic, but she did use many of the same schmaltzy terms of endearment. "Dear Daddie Poo," she would begin.

As she waited for the birth of their child, she readied the house they had bought at 1258 North Amalfi Drive in Pacific Palisades, about a half-hour drive from Malibu and Yearling Row. In late 1950, after their relationship had deepened, Nancy moved from Westwood to an apartment in Brentwood that afforded more room and privacy. On their return from their Arizona honeymoon, they took up residence in Ronnie's handsome bachelor quarters on Londonderry Place above the Sunset Strip. It had a spectacular view and a king-size bed but not much storage space. Nancy held on to her apartment and shuttled between the two apartments and Amalfi Drive. Her aim was to complete the nursery and make the rest of the house at least livable before her due date, and to do so on a limited budget that did not include funds to furnish the living room. They had paid $42,000 for the property—half of it with a mortgage (Reagan also had a mortgage on Yearling Row).

Reagan felt an emotional tie to Pacific Palisades, a community founded as a new Chautauqua in 1922 by the Southern Conference of the Methodist Episcopalian Church. The Chautauqua, a national organization named for the town in New York where it originated, was part of the Inter-Church World Movement. Before World War II, the organization held church seminars and presented visiting lecturers for a short time in small towns across the country. People who came from a distance lived in tents, and the campsites took on a fairgrounds atmosphere. Some of Reagan's happiest childhood memories had been when the Chautauqua set up on the banks of the Rock River, just a mile up the road from where he was a lifeguard at Lowell Park and at the end of Dixon's trolley line. Every day during the two weeks that the Chautauqua was in Dixon, he and Nelle (his brother, Neil, who adhered to his father's Catholicism, did not attend) would ride the trolley to the site, where they listened to the lectures and Bible readings intermingled with theatrical entertainments. Mother and son would lunch on apples and crackers—all Nelle could afford—in the picnic area. Nelle would often give Bible readings and was diligent about their attendance at lectures, but she enjoyed equally with Dutch the entertainments, which varied from musicians playing on washboards to demonstrations of wireless telegraphy.

Although the Chautauqua influence had faded, many streets in the Palisades were still named for the bishops of the Methodist Church. Because the area's western border of oceanfront bluffs afforded spectacular views to those who chose to build homes on these higher elevations, the Palisades had become an upwardly mobile neighborhood with a quaint business district that gave the place the aura of a country village. The Reagans' seven-room, two-story frame house on Amalfi Drive was in the so-called flats that lay at the base of the bluffs. Its most distinguished feature was its very ordinariness, hemmed in by hedges with houses on either side of the narrow, well-manicured frontage. Inside, the rooms were generous and light. Bow windows faced the street, and sliding glass doors led to a rear, bricked terrace. There were three bedrooms and a bath upstairs. A bath also adjoined the downstairs den, which for the time being would substitute for the yet-to-be-furnished living room. The house was modest, but the Palisades boasted wide residential streets, and on good days on Amalfi Drive—when there was a breeze and no smog—there was the scent and spray of the nearby but not visible Pacific Ocean.

The house was postwar, with a modern kitchen, but Nancy did not cook. The most she could do was breakfast. Even cooking a steak on the grill threw her into a panic. "Dave Chasen [owner of Chasen's], . . . sort of took me under his wing," she recalled. " 'Nancy,' he said to me not long after our wedding, 'Why don't you come with me [to the meat-packer's] and I'll show you how to pick out good meat and how to have it cut.' Of course, I said, 'Yes,' and down we went. He was such a dear man."[3]

She never did learn how to cook. From the start of their marriage a housekeeper with proficiency in the culinary arts was essential. When that person (and cook-housekeepers came and went with some frequency) was off, or they were between staff, Ronnie would manage a meal or they would dine out, most often at Chasen's, which became their home away from home, chosen for the privacy it afforded and its clublike ambiance. (Its membership was composed of some of Hollywood's most famous citizens.) Dave Chasen's warm friendship offered a true oasis in a town of tinsel and con men. He allowed no photographers, booths were large and conducive to intimate conversation, food—if requested—could be prepared specially. Dave had been a successful vaudevillian and star of the Broadway stage, and the restaurant had been a Hollywood fixture since the mid-1930s. He was considered an insider, someone to be trusted during a time of fear and trembling of the McCarthy and HUAC hearings. Chasen's was a rare safe zone where differences were checked at the front door and people could table-hop among old friends if they chose, whatever their political beliefs.

On October 22, 1952, Patricia Ann Reagan was born ("go ahead and count, a bit precipitously . . . ," Nancy would confess years later),[4] at Cedars of Lebanon Hospital (now Cedars-Sinai) after many hours in labor followed by a cesarean section. She was almost immediately called Patti, and weighed seven pounds three ounces at birth, which would make it difficult for anyone to believe that the child was two months premature. Nancy had been under tremendous stress in the last trimester, knowing that this situation had eventually to be faced, and she was insecure as to how to handle it. Today, the fact that a couple who had been going together for two years had conceived a child two months before their wedding would raise no eyebrows. But this was Hollywood 1952, where it would have been a scandal. The press was informed that Patti was two months premature—no birth weight given. Nancy, they were told, had suffered complications and was healing slowly.

No professional photographs of mother and child were taken, as was often done with new celebrity parents. Ronnie, between movies at the time, remained home for six weeks to help care for Nancy, a point that was made sympathetically in media coverage. The true facts of Patti's birth, and the suspect story that she was later told about it, would eventually cause a bitter rift between mother and daughter.

"[What I was told was that after] eighteen hours of what my parents have described as excruciating labor, the doctor decided to do a Cesarian section . . . What they lifted out of [my mother] . . . was a baby who had performed the superhuman task of hooking its fingers onto her ribs. This extraordinary baby came out with scabs on its tiny fingers and was then put into an incubator for two months . . . because this little girl was supposed to be born eight weeks later." Patti's birth certificate makes it clear that a newborn baby weighing over seven pounds would not have needed to be placed in an incubator unless the child had serious physical problems—which Patti did not. "My parents have never gone for simple, state-of-the-art lies. They weave bizarre, incredulous [sic] tales and stick by them with fierce determination," she once bitterly alleged.

Nancy remained in the hospital for two weeks. Ronnie brought her home alone. The baby joined them later in the arms of a nurse. "Despite the fact that I was innocent of the crime of punching my way through my mother's uterus, shoving a few organs out of the way, and grasping her ribs," Patti wrote in her controversial autobiography, *The Way I See It*, "I was guilty of something else. I was a girl and my mother, by her own admission, had wanted a boy."[5]

This was true. Nancy had hoped all through her pregnancy for a boy, which she believed would have pleased Ronnie. Reagan was an outdoorsman, and with a son he could share his love for horses, shooting, and the land. Of course, there was Michael, whom Reagan always considered a true son. But Jane Wyman controlled the boy's life, and her influence created a barrier. It contradicted many of the things Reagan presumed right in the raising of a child, including the time spent with his father, the age when boarding at school was acceptable, and the ability to choose his own religion as Ronald and his brother, Neil, had done. There was also a strong sense of competition between Jane and Nancy, who had yet to meet. Quite naturally, Reagan stood behind his current wife in any dispute. Whatever Nancy thought was right for Michael, Reagan backed with full knowledge that Wyman might not agree and so further isolate the boy from his father.

"I didn't know much about being a parent," Nancy has admitted, "and I was an insecure mother."[6] However difficult this made-up scenario of her birth was to become for Patti, the guilt-hinged secret bound her parents even closer. Reagan's background was so riddled with Christian righteousness that he would not have wanted anyone—especially his mother, Nelle—to know that he had "violated" Nancy before they had exchanged their vows.

Until Patti's birth, Michael and Mermie, as they called Maureen, and Nancy and Ronnie functioned as a family unit. Jane Wyman had remarried (to Fred Karger, a bandleader and musical arranger) soon after Nancy and Ronnie were wed. Both children were now in parochial boarding schools, placed there by Wyman, who seemed unable to cope with a new marriage (which also included a stepdaughter close to Mermie's age), a new house, her booming career, and two children; moreover, as a fairly recent convert to Catholicism she was determined that her children be reared in that faith. Reagan appeared never to have been asked whether he wanted his children to be raised as Catholics or to attend out-of-state schools. He voiced objections, but that was as far as it went. Wyman refused to compromise, and he left it at that, either with or without Nancy's approval. His time with Michael and Mermie was now limited to holidays and weekends during the summer.

Before motherhood, Nancy had spent almost every weekend at Yearling Row, which was where Michael and Maureen would come when they visited their father. After Patti's birth, Nancy accompanied Ronnie to the ranch, but seldom when the other children were there. Nor did she encourage Ronnie to bring them to the house in the Pacific Palisades. There was a distinct feeling of "yours and *ours*" and a distancing from *yours*. Both children missed Nancy, perhaps Michael the most, for he felt unwanted and insecure at home with his mother and her new husband and had always fantasized living with Nancy and his father as part of one family. Nonetheless, the limited time he had with his father was the one stabilizing influence on his life.

"The few times I felt good about myself," he wrote, "were when Dad took me with him to the Malibu ranch . . . but my favorite time was when we'd hunt ground squirrels together, Dad with his semi-automatic rifle with scope and me with my single-shot rifle. Dad had bought Nancy a black .22 caliber Ruger six-gun so that she would have protection at home when he was out of town. He tried to teach her how to shoot, but Nancy hated guns [so] Dad let me use the gun [which had] a black holster, and I taught myself how to quick-draw just like Paladin [a TV character]." Michael was boarding at St. John's, a Catholic school he likened to a "miniature Alcatraz. I had no one to talk to as Maureen had been sent to [a Catholic school] in Tarrytown, New York [St. John's was in California, but he would later be sent to Arizona] . . . Mom was convinced that all our problems were caused by Dad [and Nancy, who] had poisoned my mind against her."[7]

Nelle, whom Mermie and Michael called Gramsie, was their one female softening influence during this difficult time. Nancy had betrayed them. For the two years before she married their father, she had led them to believe that she honestly cared for them, offering them warmth and seeming to welcome them fully into her own relationship with their dad. Suddenly, with a child of her own, she had made them feel, as Michael would title his autobiography, *On the Outside Looking In*.

The early years of the Reagans' marriage were certainly not easy for either of them. In 1953, Reagan resigned from his position at SAG to spend more time on his career. But the good scripts were not coming his way. He was unemployed for six months in 1953, and when he finally got a film in December, *Prisoner of War* at MGM, he received only eighteen thousand dollars, a dramatic cut from his previous salary. Angry at

Wasserman and the agency for not finding him better roles, he was in a black mood, and often a wall arose between them that Nancy could not penetrate. He remained at the ranch for longer periods leaving her alone with a baby who cried for hours on end. The baby had colic, a common complaint for infants. An English nanny, Penny, was hired. This only added to the expenses that were creating such problems for the Reagans. Nancy's solution was to go back to work if she could find a means to do so.

She was offered the female lead in *Donovan's Brain* opposite Lew Ayres, who played a scientist who keeps alive the brain of a vengeance-seeking industrialist in his laboratory. A modest production, it was an intriguing story, but not much of an improvement over its forerunner, *The Lady and the Monster*, made by a small independent only eight years earlier. "The shooting took six weeks [for which Nancy was paid $3,000 a week]. It wasn't a classy picture but it did pay some bills," she commented. Although appreciated by Ronnie, Nancy's working to pay their debts hurt his pride. He was all for her having a career if she so chose, but not to pay for the things that he believed were his responsibility.

After *Prisoner of War* nothing came Reagan's way. He suspected that Wasserman, a strong liberal Democrat, had turned cold to him because of stories circulating that he had fed names of SAG members to McCarthy and to HUAC, causing many actors to be blacklisted. In his mind he had done his patriotic duty, but in later years he would question his choice. Nancy was convinced that he wasn't being offered jobs because of his work for SAG, which had often brought him in conflict with the studios. To tide them over Reagan took guest star spots on various television shows. Although he was unaware of it at the time, Reagan's movie career was nearly over. Later, Nancy recalled that one evening he came home from a SAG meeting, after his term as president, humiliated because he overheard someone say, "Well, at last Ronald Reagan is having his picture taken."[8]

The humiliation was not to stop there. Reagan was now being represented by MCA agent, Taft Schreiber, who found him a gig in Las

Vegas where name performers were being paid high salaries. The first offer was for him to appear as Master of Ceremonies in a show at the El Rancho Hotel that would star, not Reagan, but a well-known stripper. Reagan was furious. Schreiber called back later to tell him that the Last Frontier Hotel would sign him for two weeks at fifteen thousand per to work with the Continentals, a male quartet that had appeared as the star act at many nightclubs and on Milton Berle's and Ed Sullivan's popular television shows. Reagan discussed it with Nancy, who had grave doubts about the wisdom of doing a nightclub turn at this stage in his career. Still, the money was seductive and much needed. So she agreed with his decision to take the offer.

Leaving Patti in the care of the nanny, the Reagans boarded a train for Las Vegas. There Nancy sat through all the rehearsals, "some up to four hours long . . . sipping nothing more than a glass of ice water."[9]

The Vegas show opened on February 15, 1954, with Reagan, the Continentals, the Blackburn Twins, and a line of long-legged blond showgirls wearing two-foot-high plumed headdresses and brief South American–inspired costumes. Reagan cracked jokes in an Irish brogue, a straw hat perched on his head. He was the Continentals' added fifth member, sunk to a humiliating low in an old-time baggy-pants vaudeville routine. For a finale he stood "alone, spotlighted center stage in his black tuxedo, and recited a sentimental poem about the glories, sacrifices, and contributions made by actors."[10]

"Is Las Vegas going to have to suffer a retreating army of fading Hollywood stars?" one critic questioned in print.[11]

Nancy was beside herself with concern. On the ride home Ronnie was a desolated man. She tried to cheer him as best she could, noting that there had not been an empty seat in the theater for any performance and that he was applauded grandly. Still, she knew in her heart that a portion of the audience had come to see how bad he would be. "Never again will you accept anything just for the money," she insisted. He agreed, and when they reached Los Angeles, he called Schreiber to repeat their edict.[12]

The bond between Ronnie and Nancy was tightening. While Reagan might have feared that motherhood would draw her away from him, it had achieved quite the opposite. Nancy's life centered obsessively on Ronnie. She believed in him so sincerely that she infused him with the same confidence.

CHAPTER FOUR

CORPORATE WIFE

A s Patti had been born on a Tuesday, Ronnie gave Nancy an enameled brooch with the words *Tuesday's Child* engraved on it. An accompanying card read: "So you won't have to be too far from our 'Tuesday's child,' ever. And because I intend to be as close to both of you as Eggs are to Easter."[1] The summer of 1954 brought them frequent separations due to a thankless and underpaid costarring role he had opposite Barbara Stanwyck in *Cattle Queen of Montana*, which was filmed on location in Glacier National Park, Montana. At the time he was also negotiating a deal engineered by Wasserman to host a television series for General Electric. He had to make several trips to GE's corporate headquarters for discussions. Reagan believed, as did other movie players at the time, that appearing in television would spell the end of his career. Wasserman thought otherwise and steered MCA into becoming the progenitor of television's most successful early series, cleverly dividing his client list into the haves (those who were big stars) and the have-nots (those who fell into a middle category). He made movie deals for the haves and television deals for the have-nots.

Reagan had been helpful to MCA in 1952 when he was president of SAG. He had pushed through a waiver that allowed the agency to produce films for television while representing actors on their list. (This would later be the basis for a grand jury probe into possible antitrust violations by MCA.) Although still angry at Wasserman for palming him off to Shreiber at the nadir of his career, the Reagans were in need of funds and eager for the GE project to be settled.

At the time they were just managing to meet their bills. The GE series would guarantee them a solid six-figure annual income for at least three years, with enough money left over to establish a fund for the future. MCA had developed a half-hour anthology format with Reagan as host and a guest star from their list, whom the agency would guarantee for each episode. "How MCA baited the stars in was, one, you could choose the kind of vehicle you would be in. For example, Bob Hope could be a Sam Spade–type detective if he wanted to [actually, Jack Benny wanted to do that and did]," GE executive Earl B. Dunckel explained. "The other bait was that we kept the program for three or five showings, and after that [it became the property of the guest stars]."[2] (General Electric made individual deals with the guest stars. The bigger the name, the sooner the star obtained rights to the program in which he or she had appeared. There was no way for them to individually market one episode. However, the guest performer received a generous amount each time the segment was shown after GE's rights had expired.)

GE broadened the duties of the host. He would have to be a good spokesperson able to go on the road to talk at the various GE plants across the country as part of the company's extensive Employee and Community Relations Program.

"We had been very definite," Dunckel continued, "as to the kind of person we wanted. Good moral character, intelligent. Not the kind with the reputation for the social ramble. We looked at several people [Edward Arnold and Walter Pidgeon were also being considered]. You don't construct a top ten program overnight. . . . In a large corporation, if you try something new, your biggest obstacle is your own people. I then came up with a plan to have Ron meet and charm these G.E. vice-presidents all over the country so that they would stay off our back long enough for us to get the program moving."[3]

"The wife of our man was also an important component," another GE chief executive added. "Corporate wives have to be a special breed. If Ron was going to be out there representing General Electric, Nancy had to display the [high] moral standards. We liked the idea that she was a new mother, that she had, more or less, given up her career to be a homemaker. The plan included her home being on display."[4]

At first Nancy was reluctant to have her family's privacy invaded. GE raised the ante. They would build her a new home, completely modern, using all GE equipment. "Where?" she wanted to know. "Well, wherever you like" was the reply, with a generous offer for the purchase of the land and the construction of a house on it. The Reagans chose the higher reaches of the Palisades, which would afford them a view and an air of upward mobility.[5]

Reagan signed a three-year contract contingent upon the show's longevity. He would emcee all the shows and appear in four episodes each season in scripts of his choice. As host, he would receive $125,000 a year (plus expenses), $15,000 more payable for each show in which he appeared, and, as an added incentive, a hefty percentage of income from episodes after their fifth replay. MCA then brought Nancy into the mix. She flew to New York in August to join Ronnie and to meet the heads of various departments at GE. "There was nothing of the posturing, nothing of the 'I am a star' [with Reagan]," Dunckel recalled. "He was a regular guy. I liked him right away. . . . And I could see the two of them together, as an example of a good, G.E. representative couple."[6] Nancy was guaranteed a minimum of three shows in three years as a supporting performer in scripts of her choice at $10,000 per episode. The security that they had hoped for was finally theirs. They had no idea that the series would make Reagan a very rich man and end up preparing him for a brilliant career in politics.

The first *General Electric Theater* with Reagan as host was aired from the CBS studios in Hollywood on Sunday, September 26, 1954. Finding it difficult to read the cue cards, he memorized his lines, talking directly into the camera in a very relaxed manner. The program and Reagan were an immediate success. Nancy appeared opposite him on October 10, playing the wife of a man on the brink of a nervous breakdown. Shortly thereafter she learned that she was pregnant, and hoping for a brother for Patti and a son for Ronnie, she remained at home, helping in the plans of the house that General Electric was to build for them. In February 1955 she had a miscarriage. She would have a second one the following December.

With Nancy unable to travel with him, Reagan was forced to do extensive trips on his own. "With all the 'missing you,'" he wrote her from Atlanta in April 1955, "there is still such a wonderful warmth in the lonliness [sic] like looking forward to a bright warm room. No matter how dark & cold it is at the moment—you know the room is there and waiting.... I'm such a coward when you are out of sight—so afraid something will go wrong if I'm not there to take care of you so be very careful."[7]

For Christmas he had given her several nightgowns. The accompanying card, with a child snuggled up to a sleeping Santa, was written in his uneven, somewhat childish hand. (Reagan was naturally left-handed. As a child he was forced to write with his right hand, and still did so, but his handwriting was uneven and would always be so.) "For My Mommie Poo—Even though it curbs my pleasure they will adorn the one I adore—Love Poppa." On Valentine's Day 1955 he wrote, "You are my cuddely [sic], wuddely [sic] little pink Honey Pot. XXXXX Guess Who?"[8] Cards and letters began with "Dear Nancy Poo Pants Mommie" and were mostly signed "Poppa." They expressed his longing to be home with her, his love for her, an occasional reference to "Patti Poo Pants." He does not discuss in much detail the work he is doing but does convey the joy he feels in doing it, except for the traveling.

General Electric manufactured everything from refrigerators and other household appliances to medical and industrial equipment. Reagan's first GE tour began at the giant turbine plant at Schenectedy, New York. Nothing had prepared him for the vastness of thirty-one acres of factory under one roof. He stood stunned on the balcony above at his first sight of it. The noise of the machines was deafening. He refused to wear his new contact lenses anywhere that people were smoking or there were fumes as his eyes became too irritated. Dunckel and another executive led him carefully down the three flights of open iron stairs to the factory floor. "He couldn't see a hand in front of his face," Dunckel recalled.[9]

Word spread quickly that Reagan was there, and the machines ground to a halt until the workers were told to return to their jobs. Reagan walked the thirty-one cement acres back and forth for four hours, stopping at each machine, talking to almost every one of the plant's factory employees, signing autographs and "generally having a hell of a good time getting acquainted." He followed this routine at each one of his stops.

"The women would come running up—mash notes, autographs and all that kind of thing. . . . One woman bared her breast and asked him to sign it [he turned red and substituted an autograph on a slip of paper instead while she buttoned her blouse]. The men would all stand looking at him, obviously saying something very derogatory—'I bet he's a fag,' or something like that. He would carry on a conversation with the girls just so long . . . then he would leave them and walk over to these fellows and start talking to them. When he left them ten minutes later, they were all slappin' him on the back saying, 'That's the way, Ron.' "

By the spring of 1955 he was speaking with increasing frequency in open factory areas and auditoriums and before the country's most powerful clubs: the Kiwanis, the Lions, the Elks, and the American Legion. He talked about America the beautiful and the need to retain wholesome values, the family, the country's economic problems, taxes, juvenile delinquency—all subjects with which everyday people could associate. He'd intersperse his talks with humorous Hollywood or personal anecdotes. No hifalutin language. Down-home, homespun. Very soon he was perceived as a spokesman for management, although he was careful to skirt such subjects as employee's benefits, wages, health insurance, or work-related conditions that might produce health problems. These questions he replied to with cagey ambiguity.

For example, Dunckel explained, "They might ask, 'What do you think of this business of General Electric telling our union to take it or leave it?'

"[Reagan] would say, 'When I was heading up a union, I recognized that there always came a time when you were at the make or break point and where it had to be one way or the other. All the argumenting, all the discussion had taken place. We had passed that stage. Now it was,

'Am I going to accept your plan? Are you going to accept my plan? Are you going to go on from here, or is this going to remain a deadlock?' That's essentially what take it or leave it amounts to.' "[10]

Reagan toured about twenty weeks a year, visiting every one of GE's 139 plants and talking to over 250,000 of GE's employees. He had a fear of flying and had it written into his contract that he would only travel by rail. "I got to see a lot of the country through the windows of a moving train," he later wrote.[11] The success of his tours gave him a new image of himself, more politician than actor. Nancy could see this happening but was not prescient, nor was he, of where it would take him—and her as well. New friends like Earle and Marion Jorgensen, Betsy and Alfred Bloomingdale, and Charles and Mary Wick entered their lives. They did not desert their old friends—Jimmy and Gloria Stewart, Ursula and Robert Taylor, Harriet and Armand Deutsch, and silent-screen star (known for her roles as a jazz-age flapper) Colleen Moore, who was a buddy of Edith's and also was Patti's godmother. Most of their new friends were Republican and, as time went on, increasingly active in Reagan's growing political presence.

With her husband's newfound popularity and high profile, Nancy's life was changing. No longer did the couple have to struggle financially. Neither was given to great extravagance, but Nancy upgraded her wardrobe considerably, defining her personal style, possibly with the good advice of fashion-conscious Betsy Bloomingdale. At Christmas and on her birthdays Ronnie's presents to her often came from a Beverly Hills jeweler.

All of this prosperity did not come without some sadness. In the mid-1950s Nelle developed what the doctor called early senility. She could not continue to live alone without the danger that she could harm herself unintentionally—perhaps by starting a fire or leaving the gas on without lighting it. Nancy was unable to cope with a youngster and her responsibilities to Ronnie while having a failing mother-in-law live with them. Nelle's condition was in fast decline, and the Reagans were advised that eventually she would become totally dependent. A decision was made to place her in a comfortable nursing home close to them so that the family, including Neil and his wife Bess, could visit often.

Once Reagan signed with *General Electric Theater* (the name chosen for the anthology program), the Reagans saw more of Nancy's parents. The doctor and his son-in-law had a growing rapport. During his travels Reagan found it easy to stop off in Arizona, where he would spend time with his in-laws and Senator Barry Goldwater. The Davises also traveled to the Coast several times a year to see the Reagans. Edith recalled that on one trip she and Loyal went to the church wedding of a friend's daughter in Beverly Hills where Jane Wyman was also a guest.

"I went over to her and I said, 'Oh, I'm so glad to see you, I'm Nancy's mother.' and she said, 'Oh, I'm so glad to meet you. Thank you for being so nice and coming over.' And I said, 'Oh, no, honey. Anybody who wouldn't be nice to you is a fool.' "[12] Exactly what the forthright Edith meant by that remark is anyone's guess, but she was well aware of Wyman's ability to institute revenge if she felt wronged—or slighted.

Nancy had not inherited her mother's down-to-earth brashness and often coarse language. In her youth and early adult years these aspects of Edith's personality had embarrassed Nancy and propelled her into a closer relationship with her stepfather. Her parents' marriage had been both a miracle and an enigma to her. She had never been able to fathom the nature of their mutual attraction, but it had allowed her to redefine who she was—or, at least, who she wanted to be. Her ties to her mother were strong, but she did not use her for a role model, perhaps wrongly. Curiously, Edith had won the doctor's heart by the very things that Nancy found offensive. "Edith taught me to change my asocial tendencies and habits," Davis later explained, "to develop a sense of humor, to retain my desire and energy to succeed but to relax and enjoy the association of friends."[13]

Edith was an open, honest, earthy woman, worldly, comfortable in men's company, who never pretended to be other than who she was and who put on no airs even when she married the already eminent doctor and was thrust into Chicago society. She was what her friends would refer to as "a man's woman." She loved sports, a good, dirty joke and in her eighties would say that the one thing she missed in old age was sex.

Dr. Davis was a hard-line Republican who thought bleeding-heart Democrats would lead to the ruination of the country. He feared the

Russians and believed that Communism was America's most virulent threat. Roosevelt, he claimed, was in bed with the Jews and the Commies. Davis also subscribed to the pursuit of excellence and to the doctrine that men were to be the leaders and women followers. The doctor's life had been pedagogic before he had met Edith, and despite his claims, he still had not learned how to relax completely. When Nancy was a girl, he resorted to writing notes of appreciation or warmth and placing them under Edith's door or on her breakfast tray. And he would hide behind an implacable smile when Edith in her own childlike way would suddenly get up and do a little soft-shoe dance to some old-time music on the radio. He was a man not of great contradictions but of much repression. He could not be vulgar or tell a dirty story. Yet he would prod Edith to do so and at the end turn his head away so that his reaction was concealed.

Reagan shared many similarities with Dr. Davis. They both were from small towns in Illinois, Davis having been born in Galesburg. Both had attended a small college, Knox University in Davis's case before he went off to Chicago to study medicine at Northwestern University. In many ways, except in matters of tolerance toward blacks and Jews, Reagan held to his father-in-law's political ideologies. But Nelle's early training had left an indelible mark on her son. Nelle considered it a mortal sin to look down on anyone's color or religion.

Nancy saw a different set of likenesses between her father and her husband. Both were strong men with whom a woman could feel thoroughly feminine and yet who would invite their wife's participation in decisions of a personal and a business nature. If one tightly squinted one's eyes, they even bore some resemblance to each other. They were about the same height and build, although the doctor was thickening some with age, and both had strong-boned faces and the inimitable sound of the Midwest in their speech.

Nancy desperately wanted her father and Ronnie to become good friends, for Dr. Davis to recognize what a wise choice she had made and for Ronnie to see, firsthand, why she so admired her father. Reagan did, in fact, enjoy a close friendship with his father-in-law, and Dr. Davis had a great influence on Reagan's thinking and on his switch not long afterward to the Republican Party (despite his claims that he was already headed in that direction because the Democrats had moved away from his views).

Both of the Reagans voted for the incumbent president, Dwight D. Eisenhower (with Richard M. Nixon as vice president), in the 1956 election, Reagan's second vote on the Republican side of the ballot. Nancy was registered as a Republican, but Ronnie was still listed as a Democrat. Reagan's schedule was too crowded for him to do any campaigning had he wanted to do so. But many of the things he spoke about and stressed in his talks at the GE plants fitted well into the Republican platform. As his GE contract allowed him to appear in films but not in another television program, he and Nancy accepted a script sent to them by Columbia Pictures, titled *Hellcats of the Navy*. It would be Nancy's last film. The Hellcats of the title were the troubleshooters of the submarine service. Reagan played a naval commander sent to Japan during World War II on a daring mission—what other kind was there in the movies?— to scout enemy waters for Japanese mines. Nancy was the navy nurse Reagan loved. Reagan had concluded that his film career, due to his exposure on television, was over. *Hellcats* renewed the possibility that if the movie was a hit, he could have it both ways—television and the big screen. The script read better than it filmed, however. Reagan had hoped for a fast-action, patriotic film like John Wayne's *The Wings of Eagles* and *Jet Pilot*, made that same year, but *Hellcats* had a limited budget, and the movie turned into a jingoistic potboiler. Reagan gave a credible performance, though Nancy's role was sadly one-dimensional.

Reagan's lifelong fear of flying and a tendency to claustrophobia made the long hours spent in the reproduced conning tower of the submarine during shooting of *Hellcats* a nightmare for him. He later said that he "could not wait to get out of there at the end of every take." Movie audiences suffered the same experience. Although the movie only broke even, the Reagans received good fees for their participation.

Whatever extra time Reagan did have was spent with Nancy poring over the architectural plans of William R. Stephenson for the building of their all-electric dream house, which would be known as "The House of the Future." The spectacular site in Pacific Palisades that the Reagans had chosen, 1669 San Onofre Drive, was a steep, densely wooded shelf carved into the southern slope of the Santa Monica Mountains, high above the street and affording an unimpeded view of Los Angeles and the ocean.

"It will have everything electric except a chair," he joked to reporters.[14] And it nearly did. There would be electrical items not yet on the market—electric gates and garage doors, a dishwasher with a built-in garbage disposal, retracting canopies for indoor or outdoor dining, and multicolored dining room dimmers to set the mood for any occasion. Additionally there would be a built-in rotating outdoor barbecue spit, a heated pool, a movie projection room, air-conditioning throughout the house, heating on the terrace, a built-in oversized refrigerator and freezer, and a near-professional laundry room with a pressing machine.

The interior walls were mainly of stone and glass. To offset the high-tech ambience, Nancy decorated the family rooms with large couches, giant tub chairs, roomy ebony-and-glass coffee tables, with her favorite color, red, splashed everywhere—the upholstery, the drapery fabric, the paintings on the wall—set against plush gray carpeting. "Nancy and Ronnie are just alike," Edith laughed, and then with unabashed political incorrectness added, "They don't care—just so it's red . . . it makes her furious when I say that . . . but [it's] like I tell you—like the niggers—any color so it's red."[15]

The move into the new house did nothing to help the relationship between Nancy and Patti, who claims she was frightened of her mother. Whenever her father was not present in the house, Patti recalls, Nancy would quarrel angrily with their small staff and find fault with her daughter. Penny, the British nanny whom Patti had loved, had not made the transfer from Amalfi to San Onofre, nor had Julia, the black cook, to whom the child had become attached. "I was never told why," Patti recalled.[16]

Maids came and left in alarmingly short time spans. "What happened between arrival and departure was yelling," Patti recalled. "I remember sitting in my bedroom with my hands over my ears because I could hear my mother's voice in the kitchen, yelling at the maid about dishes in the wrong cupboards or something not being prepared right. I would sing to myself to block out the sound."[17]

Patti admits having felt unwanted by Nancy but loved by her father, who unfortunately was gone a good part of the time. There is little doubt that her daughter was difficult, throwing tantrums at times, being uncooperative, trying in whatever way she could to get her mother's full attention, even if it meant testing Nancy's patience and incurring her anger. The child would thus be disciplined—confined to her room or spanked, at least when Ronnie was not at home. There were also times when Nancy tried to be affectionate and hug and kiss the little girl. But these times were too often when they were in public and usually came at a price: Patti had to look like and be "Little Miss Perfect." The child gave vent to her frustration when she was alone or with other children. But she also forced confrontations with her mother, well aware that she would be chastised or spanked. Any attention would seem better than none.

Nancy did not know how to deal with the situation. Perhaps, because her mother was absent during her early years, she found it difficult to relate to her own child. Reagan seemed totally unaware of the standoff between his wife and his daughter. The way Nancy told it was that Patti was difficult but that she was a forebearing mother. His empathy, therefore, settled on his wife.

In September 1957 Nancy learned that she was once again pregnant. This time she was determined not to miscarry. She had met privately with a mystic—the beginning of a lifelong relationship between Nancy and a string of astrologer-mystics—who told her that this child would be a boy. Ronnie would have a son of his flesh. He was seeing Michael infrequently at the time. Despite her dedication to the Catholic faith and its tenet against divorce, Wyman had divorced Fred Karger. Michael was nearly failing school and was deeply depressed. What neither Wyman nor the Reagans knew was that a camp counselor had molested the boy when he was eight years old and that a terrified Michael had been carrying this guilt around with him ever since, believing from his Catholic teachings that he would one day go to hell and that his illegitimate birth would seal this horrible fate.

"It seemed Mom and I couldn't have a conversation about anything without it becoming a quarrel," he recalled of the period between 1956 and 1957 when he was twelve. One row escalated until it ended with Wyman shouting, "We won't have any more problems because you're never going to see your father again. . . ." She then grabbed the riding crop and "whacked" him on his legs. "She finished with a swat in the middle of my back. That last blow shocked and hurt me so much that the anger in me boiled up and I could no longer control it. I turned around and shouted, 'I've had it with you, Miss Wyman!' To my shame I slapped her on the cheek."[18]

Michael's problems were not known to Nancy and Ronnie. Had they been, it seems impossible to believe that Reagan would not have attempted in some way to meliorate the situation. But nothing was done. The Reagans were too involved with their own lives. Nancy had to take extra caution during the first trimester of her pregnancy. Ronnie was still traveling often for GE, speaking out about issues. He had also returned to active work on the board of SAG. Nancy attended every board meeting with him even though her obstetrician, Doctor Benbow Thompson, had told her to restrict her activities. Nancy admitted fear that if she were not careful she might lose the child she so desperately wanted. But she was torn. She also wanted to spend every minute she could with Ronnie when he was in Los Angeles.

"So help me God, I think she was at a board meeting until the night before the baby was born," a fellow board member, actress Ann Doran, recalled. "She was so uncomfortable she could barely breathe and she had to sit there for hours without moving. . . . The tie between the two of them was so strong by then that she did not leave his side and he didn't leave hers. I've never known two people who were so much one when they married. It was strange, very strange . . . as if she just submitted her whole soul to him."[19]

Ronald Prescott Reagan was born at 8:04 A.M., May 21, 1958, by cesarian section, at Cedars of Lebanon Hospital, weighing in at 8 pounds, 8 ounces. (The child's middle name, Prescott, was the family name of Barry Goldwater's wife, Margaret Prescott Goldwater.) Reagan had been adamant that he did not want his son to be a "Jr." Actually, he was called Skipper almost immediately.

Nancy should have been the happiest of women. Certainly Ronnie was a contented man. He had a wife who thought about him above and before anyone else. He was financially secure, Yearling Row was a horse farm of which he was proud, and he and Nancy lived in a dream house with the perfect family—a daughter, and now a son. Nancy was the center of his life, his four children on the perimeter, and he considered that to be the way it should be. Yet for Nancy there seemed to be something wrong with this picture.

As happy as she was to have had a son, Nancy felt equally uncomfortable being a mother. That was particularly true in her relationship with Patti. She had discussed with Patti the fact that she would soon have a sibling. She let the little girl feel her stomach, more or less following the guidance of psychology books dealing with sibling relationships in children. But Patti had been acting up in the last weeks, causing Nancy to be upset when she should not have been. And then there was Michael and Maureen. Nancy had never told Patti that her father was also a dad to two other children. The fact that Maureen had been in school in Tarrytown, New York, and that Jane Wyman had kept Michael from seeing his father during much of the past year had only put off a situation that Nancy was loath to confront.

Nancy hated, not Maureen and Michael, but the very idea that there were others who had a claim on Ronnie. Shortly after Skipper's birth she was finally forced to reveal the existence of a half sister and half brother to Patti. Michael and Wyman's relationship had become so fractious that Wyman sent the youth—now thirteen—to a psychiatrist. After several sessions the doctor suggested that it would be better all around if Michael could be sent to live with his father.

"I thought that at last I would be living with a family unit just like a normal kid. I would have a new family and a new start. What I didn't realize was that Nancy was as strong or stronger than my mother."[20]

The house on San Onofre had been built to meet Nancy's specifications, and it had not included an extra room for either of her stepchildren. There was the large master bedroom suite, a room for Patti, a nursery for Skipper (with a cot for the live-in nurse), and a room off the kitchen for the housekeeper. Michael had to sleep on one of the two couches in the living room, waiting until any guests left to make it up as a bed before going to sleep. Patti was told that she now had a half brother.

"The 'half' part of the label tugged him away from me, told me he wasn't supposed to matter as much as the baby my mother held in her arms [and whom she was not allowed to hold in hers] . . . I was told that Michael had a different mother, but he was my father's son. He was going to start living with us on the weekends; during the week, he would be away at boarding school. His bed would be the living-room couch," Patti wrote.[21]

Michael had hoped that he would be going to day school. Instead he was once again boarding, this time at Loyola, another strict Catholic school, but at least in the Los Angeles area. When Michael suggested that maybe he could go as a day student and Nancy drive him back and forth (a thirty-minute trip each way), his father replied, "She's too busy with [Skipper] and Patti. Don't you think it is enough that she has opened up her home to you and invited you in?"

For a youngster who had come to his father and stepmother hoping to find a real home, this was a bitter pill. "Like everyone else in the house, including Dad, I was a little intimidated by Nancy," Michael admitted. "She, like Mom, seemed to go through maids and cooks every month, and I was always worried that with one wrong move I might be the next to go." The only time he had to be alone with his father was on the occasions when he accompanied him to Yearling Row on the odd Saturday when Nancy could not. During one of these excursions he made some complaint about Nancy to his father.

"There is a wall building between you and Nancy," Reagan told him, "and it's up to you to tear it down."

"Why is it up to me to make peace with Nancy?" the boy asked.

"Because I'm married to her" was the reply.[22]

They were also not a family that prayed together. Michael was not included in their Sunday morning family church visits. This again was attributed to Wyman's decree that Michael be reared as a Catholic. But for the young boy this meant yet another exclusion.

Maureen graduated from Tarrytown that summer. Michael had been living with his father and Nancy for only a few months, and Patti hardly knew Maureen at all. When Maureen came to visit one day, Patti confided to her that she had two brothers, not one. "Michael is my older brother," the seven-year-old said.[23]

"Yes, and do you know what that makes me?" Maureen asked. "I'm your older sister."

With that news, Patti burst into tears shouting, "No, it doesn't! No! it doesn't!" and ran to her room.

"Actually, it was more like an eruption," Maureen added.

"I remember feeling confused," Patti wrote. "How many more brothers and sisters were going to arrive at the house and be introduced to me?"

Terribly upset by the scene and Patti's volcanic reaction, Maureen went to her father to discuss it. "Well, we just haven't gotten that far yet," he hedged.

"And there was a reason they hadn't gotten that far yet," Maureen explained. "I wasn't there.... They'd just gotten to Michael, and only after it was decided he would move in with them."

The Reagans were telling Patti about her father's other family on a need-to-know basis, and "until that time there had been no need for her to know any such thing about me," Maureen reasoned.

"Dearest Mommie Poo," Reagan wrote to Nancy about this time from Yearling Row on a weekend when she had remained at San Onofre. "You are stuck for Mike's $4.00 each weekend [the allowance Reagan usually gave him]. I love you Mommie and I already miss you more & more & mucher than that. Let Mike *cab* [Reagan's underline] back to school—don't you drive down in that district. I love you Poppa."[24]

Their family was becoming more and more dysfunctional, but neither of the Reagans appear to have had any insight into what was evolving. It was all right for Michael at thirteen to go alone in a taxi "down in that district," Loyola's area, where there had been a rising crime rate, but not for Nancy. It was acceptable for both Maureen's and Michael's relationship to be kept hidden until it had to be revealed, despite the pain and possible repercussions this might cause all their children. Nancy had no cause to question her own actions in this regard because Ronnie supported her without question. Reagan's fear of possibly losing Nancy overrode any commonsense judgment regarding the well-being of his children. A small part of this could be attributed to his distraction over Nelle's fast-failing health. In 1957 she suffered a series of heart attacks, and she wrote her good friends Mary and Jay Sipe in Dixon: "I am a shut in. I can't drive a car any more so it was sold this last week. I will be 74 years young this month of July, and am very grateful to God, to have been spared this long life. Yet when each attact [sic] comes I whisper—'Please God, let it be now, take me home,' but He still isn't ready for me, or He would take me; there must be something I haven't done, and he don't [sic] want me until my tasks are done."[25] (The full text of her letter can be found in appendix 3.) Within a short time, Nelle lost her memory and no longer recognized either Neil or her beloved younger son, although he paid her a weekly visit whenever he was in Los Angeles (a terrible foreshadowing of what one day awaited both her sons).

"His mother's decline decimated Ronnie," an old friend said. "He was a reserved man, he would smile and charm you. But it was hard to know what he was really thinking and feeling. But after his visits to Nelle he often looked as if he had been crying. It was easy to see that he had been strongly affected."[26]

Nancy was the only sun in his life. She had always wanted unconditional love from a man, and Ronald Reagan gave this to her. What she did with it was up to her. So far she had handled it ill-advisedly in terms of the children, who could not help but be affected by her actions. Yet she had bound Ronnie ever tighter to her. Fearing that somehow these ties could unravel, she devoted herself even more to his care, and had a way of portraying herself as a victim in any situation where her attitude might be questioned.

She also devoted a lot of time and effort to remaining attractive to him. As a young girl Nancy had had a weight problem. After Skipper's

birth she was heavier than usual and concerned she might become ma-
tronly. Thus, she started a regime of diet pills that did what they were
meant to do. Unfortunately, they also put her on edge, and so the doctor
she sought for help prescribed another pill to calm her nerves, and still
another to help her sleep.

CHAPTER FIVE

I LOVE YOU, NANCY

How come you moved in on me like this?" Ronnie wrote Nancy from the road about the time of their eighth anniversary. "I'm all hollow without you and the 'hollow' hurts."[1] His tours for GE kept them apart for about sixteen weeks a year, but he had made it a condition of his newest contract that the tours were not to last more than two weeks each. They had a special ritual for his departures by train. He liked to pack his suitcases himself, but Nancy would always sneak in some love notes and small bags of variegated jelly beans, his favorite candy. She would then drive him downtown to the last grand railway terminal to be built (1939) in the United States—the Spanish mission–style Los Angeles Union Passenger Station with its Moderne and Moorish details, majestic arches, handmade tiles, and fifty-foot-high central ceiling. They would wait together in one of the outside patios, brilliant with the colors of tropical flowers and foliage, until his train was called. She would then help him settle into his first-class sleeping compartment and remain for the final "All Aboard!" From the window he watched her small, tight figure as she stood on the platform until he could see her no more.

Train travel still had a certain elegance then. Black porters wore crisp white jackets. Passengers dressed smartly for meals. There were smoking cars, observation platforms, and dining cars with menus and freshly prepared food. Card tables were made of fine-grained mahogany, and telegrams could be sent and received as all the largest stations en route had Western Union offices. Reagan's to Nancy, sent daily, were typically sentimental. Once at his destination, he called as often as possible. He was always impatient to get back home, where Nancy never tired of hearing his "tales from the road."

She took an interest in whatever he liked most—Yearling Row, horses, baseball, politics, even shooting, which she hated but endured, under his instruction and cautious eye. Although well-informed, and able to hold her own in any conversation, Nancy seldom put herself forward when they were in public. After she had lost the weight she had gained with Skipper's birth, she reoutfitted herself, changed her hairstyle, and looked, while perhaps not glamorous, a very handsome woman. From the time of her fortieth birthday on July 6, 1961, she managed to maintain her spare size-six figure. Her short red-brown hair with its gold highlights was lacquered to remain in place should hurricane-force winds sweep through the Palisades. Her large, brown, wide-apart eyes dominated her face, and there was a determined strength in her jawline. She never looked ruffled or caught off guard. They made a striking couple, Reagan with his "good-guy" weathered looks, the crinkly grin, and the jaunty stance, Nancy, perfectly dressed, every detail correct, never a wrinkle in her clothes, even at the ranch. They were straight out of central casting. The cowboy and his lady.

There were multiple Nancys. With the children and anyone who worked for her, she presented a hard surface, grim at times, demanding, unbending, acerbic rather than amusing. Ronnie lived with another Nancy, this one feminine, warm, funny, never too busy or preoccupied to concentrate on his needs. Reagan thought of Nancy as vulnerable, a woman to be protected. Her friends from that era describe her as strong, forbearing, devoted to her husband, but also fun. She liked music you could sing and dance to—Gershwin, Cole Porter—and the records of her old crush, Frank Sinatra. She read current novels—mostly those on the bestseller lists—love stories, comic tales. She kept up with magazines of topical interest—*Time*, *Life*, and *Look*—and had a keen eye on what was happening in the movie and television industries so she could discuss these things with Ronnie. They attended church every Sunday. Ronnie never wavered in his tithing and often picked up his Bible to read a passage or a psalm aloud to her.

In understanding Ronald Reagan, it is important to recognize how much his religion, which was interfaith, meant to him and how it contributed to his great respect for other religions. That was one strong reason why he did not interfere with Jane Wyman's decision to raise their children as Catholics. Nancy was not a deeply religious person, but she did support his beliefs. She seldom, however, attended church services in those years if Ronnie was away from home.

When he was traveling, the house on San Onofre took on a brooding mood. Small things irritated Nancy. She became cross with Patti for minor misdeeds. The problem was that Nancy had given up her career not just to be a wife and mother, but to be in total charge of her husband's well-being. When he was gone she was unemployed, and inactivity got on her nerves. She saw her friends, tried to take an interest in Patti's school, and worked out a schedule of "togetherness" for Ronnie's return. She was anything but the modern woman who fostered her independence. And she did not have a great deal of tolerance for those women who did. She wanted only to be an integrated, indispensable part of Ronnie's life, including his career.

A place on the board of SAG had finally been found for her, so she had an honest reason to accompany Ronnie to meetings when he was off the road. The Guild was fighting to secure for its members residuals from old movies that were being, and would be, released for television. "We knew there was going to be a battle," Jack Dales recalled. "There was no secret about it—so we wanted a strong leader and everybody turned back to Ronnie Reagan." This was despite the conflicted emotions caused by his betrayal of members during the worst years of HUAC and the McCarthy inquisitions that had ruined so many careers and destroyed so many lives. But this was October 1959. McCarthy had died in 1957, a discredited demagogue. Now SAG was set to wage war on the producers, if necessary, placing the membership yet again in jeopardy.

"After a meeting with our officers, I called Reagan and asked him to come back for another term as president," Dales added.[2]

Nancy did not want him to accept. She believed that his last association with SAG as president had hurt his career, and she did not care
for that to happen again just as he was riding high. Reagan wanted time
to think about it. As he and Nancy argued the pros and cons, there
seemed more of the latter than the former. What if GE disapproved of
his holding a position that might put him in complete opposition to their
views? Jack Dales called back and said that SAG had to have an answer
in the next forty-eight hours so that they could press forward with their
case. Reagan rang Lew Wasserman for advice. Wasserman told him to
accept the position. "Nancy thinks it might be dangerous," Reagan
hedged.

"Nancy is not being asked to be president of SAG," Wasserman
replied.[3] This advice may appear puzzling on the surface. However,
MCA was fighting what would be a protracted and devastating battle
with the Justice Department, which was seeking to prohibit agents who
were also producers from representing actors—that is, from being, in
effect, spokesman for both sides. Wasserman clearly thought that if Reagan was in power at SAG, it would benefit MCA's case. The presidency
became a serious problem later for Reagan, who was called to testify
before a Senate Committee. He was not found guilty of any conflict of
interest but his position with SAG was the cause of the Reagans' stressful
IRS audits; the government was apparently searching to see whether
Reagan had received money from his agency to advance its cause in an
illegal manner.

Reagan accepted the position at SAG and almost immediately was
thrust into a series of explosive negotiations with the producers to ward
off a strike. For the next six months the Reagans' lives were so pressured
that they had very little time to spend together. When Ronnie was not
on the road or filming for GE, he was negotiating for SAG. Old movies
had become a new commodity for television programming as the number
of channels grew. The producers of past films and the studios where
they had been made now saw an opportunity to cash in, but they needed
an agreement with SAG members in order to have the right to reshow
in a new venue films in which they had earlier appeared. A deal was
finally cut in April 1960. SAG, under Reagan's lead, sold all TV rights

in films SAG members had made from 1948 to 1959 to the producers for two million dollars. The end result proved to be costly for actors and a bonanza for the producers, who now would not have to pay television residuals to any performer who appeared in a film during those years, which happened to encompass the most prolific period in the movie industry. These films have been in constant replay since that date, with the actors receiving no compensation. Those whose careers were ended by 1959 because of age, the blacklist, or changing styles no longer had any future income from their film work to rely upon. (A deal was struck some years later that gave SAG members residual income from films made *after* 1959.) Members called it a sellout, although Reagan had also negotiated a pension fund and health insurance that they previously had not had. The Reagans found themselves in hostile territory, and both resigned from their positions, Ronnie as president, Nancy from the board.

This was an extremely troubling time for Nancy, who always seemed to be on edge. Ronnie's eight years of security with GE (he was now earning over $250,000 a year and was a part owner of his episodes, with a bonus arrangement, too), were coming to an unsatisfactory end. The company had asked him to stop being so political on his speaking tours and concentrate on pitching their products. After all, they were paying him to be a spokesman for GE, not to parade his political views. Being a TV salesman was not what either Ronnie or Nancy saw as his image. He had not done the commercials on the show. "Selling toasters is not for me," he had insisted successfully. He did not intend to start now. And so he refused to sign another contract with them. One of the last episodes in which Reagan appeared costarred Nancy. Airing on July 1, 1962, it was called "Money and the Minister," and dealt with the moral issue of selling out one's beliefs for money even if for a good purpose.

Three weeks later, on July 25, after a long struggle with what was now known to be Alzheimer's disease, Nelle Reagan, aged seventy-nine, died clutching a teddy bear as she lay on a single bed in a full-care nursing home in Santa Monica. She had not recognized either of her sons for several years. The cause of her death was given as a cerebral hemorrhage. Reagan asked Neil if he could have their mother's much worn Bible, which his brother readily agreed to. Nelle left little of any value, her household possessions having been given to the Church when she moved into the nursing home. Her death hit Reagan hard. It would always sadden him that she did not remain lucid and live long enough to see how his life evolved.

Money was a serious consideration in the Reagan household—how to make it, how to save it, when to spend it, who to spend it on. Nancy was fearful that if something did not come through for Ronnie soon, they would have to start digging into their capital. Reagan had received a great many political overtures, but Nancy could not envision that his involvement in government would ever be more than an avocation.

They were both careful about spending, fastidiously keeping within their budget, entertaining mostly at home (Ronnie liked to cook and was an aficionado of California wines, which were good and inexpensive), and not given to great extravagance of any kind. Yearling Row was run frugally; the main house was no more than a cabin with Spartan bunkhouses for the small staff. Reagan used pencils down to the nub and both sides of the pages of his writing pads. They were, in fact, financially secure. But Nancy recalled what it was like to live from hand to mouth as a child with her aunt and uncle, and Ronnie had watched his family's small income consumed by his father's drinking problem and the vicissitudes of the Depression.

The children were made aware of the money issue in their home. Toys had to be "earned" by obeying Nancy's rules and getting good grades at school. They were constantly told how lucky they were and how hard their father had to work to earn the money to pay for their good care. They were never without the essentials and a good measure more. They lived in a beautiful home, attended fine private schools, had plenty to wear and food to eat—although Nancy was rigid about clothes lasting a long time and food not being wasted. Gifts were limited, even in the best of times, and had much to do with the approval rating of the children's behavior.

Nancy kept a closet where she stored gifts that she either did not need or care to keep. Many of these were dispensed to staff, friends, and family at Christmas. This became a sensitive issue with the children,

Patti, who interpreted receipt of such items as a measure of s estimation of her worthiness. The number of gifts given as another indication. Ron usually received the most gifts, ratti was next, then Michael. Maureen, "if she came by on Christmas Day, got a single present."[4]

The Reagans agreed that their children had to be taught the value of money, and who could blame them for that? But it was a fetish with Nancy. She did not believe in tipping, and although the custom at Alida Gray, the Beverly Hills beauty salon she had long patronized, was to do so, she never did. It was difficult to understand where Nancy's priorities rested. Michael had been sleeping on the living-room couch for several years (which must have been uncomfortable for all concerned), without a place to put any personal items, when suddenly a room was being built at the rear of the house. No explanation was given to the children. Michael was positive the addition was meant for him and that he would finally have a room of his own. Every day, as it was under construction, he would wander through the open beams visualizing how he would arrange things. When it was complete, it turned out that it was to be for Skipper's live-in nanny, who had shared the former nursery, as the little boy was growing and needed a space of his own. Michael was crushed, unable to tell his father or Nancy how deeply he was wounded. Shortly after the nanny moved into the new room, he asked his father if he could be sent to a coed boarding school, not Catholic, not in California. Although he had always hated the thought of not being able to come home for the weekend, he now felt pointedly unwanted. Reagan, asking no questions as to why the boy wanted to do this, promised him that it would be arranged if he could bring his grades up and if his mother, who had remained constant in her desire for her children to have a Catholic education, approved.

Skipper was Nancy's obvious favorite. She pampered and protected him, spending what extra time she did allocate to the children attending to his needs. He was a happy child, outgoing, loving, and seemingly unaffected by Nancy's special attention, which did not inspire any apparent jealousy in either Patti or Michael. He was also more independent, somewhat of a free spirit, the only one of the three young Reagans living at home who was not afraid to ask Nancy why she was doing something he thought was wrong or to blurt out what was on his mind. "Why do you always say we can't afford things?" he asked at the age of eight. "We aren't poor."

"Because you have to earn what you get," she snapped back.

"How do *you* earn it?" he countered, for which it seems Nancy had no answer and changed the subject.[5]

Nancy had more patience with Skipper than she had with Patti or Michael. In 1961, when Michael was sixteen, she angrily confronted him with his most recent report card, which had not shown the progress she felt it should.

"You are not living up to the Reagan name or image, and unless you start shaping up, it would be best for you to change your name and leave the house," she shouted at him.

"Fine," he reciprocated with injured anger, "why don't you just tell me the name I was born with so at least when I walk out the door I'll know what name to use."

"Okay, Mr. Reagan," she snapped. "I'll do just that."[6]

This information was concealed in state files, as was always done in adoption cases of that era, and the teenager thought Nancy's was a futile boast. A week later, however, when he came home for the weekend, she informed him that his birth name was John L. Flaugher. His birth mother had had an affair with a sergeant on leave from the army who was sent overseas and never returned. "You are the offspring of that relationship," she ended in a cold voice, confirming for Michael his worst fear—that he was a bastard and would therefore go to hell.

Before he could speak to his father, Nancy had presented her case to Ronnie, turning the story around so that Michael became the villain. The boy asked to tell his side of the story. "I don't need to hear your side," Reagan replied. "You're wrong. Nancy is right."[7]

San Onofre Drive had become a house of lies and self-deception. Perhaps it had always been. Nancy told movie critic and magazine writer Susan Granger that although Reagan seemed easy "he is more complex than people think."[8] More accurately, Reagan was far brighter than commonly perceived because he had an easy way about him. Those who knew him mostly from his film persona believed he was the man they saw on the movie screen, at least until his long GE stint. But from childhood Reagan had learned how to filter out the painful realities that crossed his life—his father's alcoholism and the embarrassment it had so often caused him, his early poverty, his failure at football because of his poor vision, and the insecurity that all these youthful experiences had engendered.

Nancy has also said that "what you see of him is what you get."[9] This does not suppose that Nancy did not understand Ronnie. She knew both the private and the public man and how he placed an invisible shield between the two. She was also deeply aware that he never revealed his true self in public or even to his children. He had chosen Nancy to be his only confidante and yet, even with her, he withheld emotions that he thought were better kept veiled.

He loved Nancy. She was necessary to him emotionally and sexually. With her, he believed he had found the one woman who could be his soulmate. Keeping Nancy happy was a prime requisite for keeping Nancy. Having lost Jane Wyman because proper attention had not been paid (he had pursued interests greatly divergent from hers), he was loath for this to happen again. It appeared that the one best way to keep Nancy happy was to remain on her side whatever the cost, and it would be high: their children's emotional well-being. Reagan's image was that of a loyal friend, ready to jump to your side should there ever be a need. But Nancy was only too aware that he could cut people out of his life without ever noticing they were gone. This was true of old friends like William Holden, who had been his best man and Patti's godfather, but Ronnie had not seen or inquired after him for years once Holden's drinking had accelerated. That would also be true in the years to come with staff members and even his children. Nancy needed to be all-important to him to make sure that would never happen to her.

In the decade between 1952 and 1962, Reagan's ideology took a sharp right turn. He had finally registered as a Republican and was campaigning for John Rousselot, a far-right California Congressman running for reelection. Reagan quit the campaign when it was revealed that Rousselot was the national public-relations director for the extremist John

Birch Society, something he surely should have found out beforehand, and perhaps he did. Then came his election-eve endorsement of Richard Nixon for governor, even though ten years earlier he had written an old Eureka College friend: "Pray as I am praying for the health and long life of Eisenhower because the thought of Nixon in the White House is almost as bad as that of 'Uncle Joe [Stalin].' Let me as a Californian tell you that Nixon is a hand picked errand boy with a pleasing façade and naught but emptiness behind. He has been subsidized by a small clique of oil and real estate pirates, he is less than honest and he is an ambitious opportunist completely undeserving of the high honor paid him [the vice-presidency]."[10]

Now he was saying: "Can you believe that a man like Dwight David Eisenhower . . . whose love of country is beyond question, could have closely associated with Richard Nixon, as he did for eight years, and now recommend him for high office, as he is doing, if he did not believe him worthy to serve?"[11]

Reagan's turnaround had been coaxed by his relationship with Loyal Davis and Barry Goldwater and his new circle of rich Republican friends. Nancy fostered this, perhaps more on a social level than a political one. She very much enjoyed her father's growing closeness to Ronnie, and she found her self-esteem puffed up by association with the wealthy and powerful men and women who now peopled their life. Moreover, since Nelle's death Reagan had grown closer to his brother, who had aligned himself for years with the conservative wing of the Republican Party.

Neil was a top executive with the advertising firm of McCann, Erickson, representatives for United States Borax Company, sponsors of the television show *Death Valley Days*. The host on *Death Valley Days*, known as the Old Ranger, was up in years and failing, and the show had dropped considerably in the ratings. This was in the late fall of 1963 and Neil recalled "Dutch [they still referred to each other by their childhood nicknames] had just finished G.E. Theater [actually, it had been more than a year] and wasn't doing anything . . . so I suggested to the client, 'What about Reagan?' He said, 'Oh, if you can get him, you're damned right.'"[12]

When Neil approached him, Reagan was not enthusiastic. First, it disturbed him that by hiring him, Borax would have to fire the Old Ranger, a favorite on the show—and of his—for many years. He also had doubts as to whether doing another television series would be a wise move, especially if it was not of the quality of the *General Electric Theater*. Neil had a hard time convincing him, so he called Bill Meiklejohn, who was his brother's new agent. (In 1958 MCA had acquired Decca Records, the Universal Studio lot, and all of Paramount Studio's pre-1948 film library. This brought about a government threat in 1962 to press charges of antitrust violations against MCA. Wasserman was forced to liquidate its talent agency and turn to film production in a compromise agreement and to make no more acquisitions for seven years. Thus all of MCA's former clients, including Reagan, had to find new representatives.)

A few days later Neil was seated at a front booth at the Hollywood Brown Derby on Vine Street, where he usually ate his lunch, and in walked his brother, who paused to talk to him. "If it wasn't for you I wouldn't be here this noon, dressed up with a tie on," he told Neil. He was, he continued, having lunch with Meiklejohn, who had agreed to pitch the idea to Reagan. The agent was obviously persuasive, because after lunch Meiklejohn stopped by Neil's table, smiling. "Go ahead and write the contract up [at the same salary as he received from GE] and send it over to him. He'll sign it," he said.[13]

"Ron can't be pushed; he can be coaxed," Nancy has admitted, and who would have known better?[14] But the money being offered was not easy to dismiss. There were many other considerations, and it would be quite a while before the contract was finally signed and production begun on the series. In the meantime, Reagan had made the switch to the Republican Party and was actually campaigning for several of its candidates. When asked why her husband changed parties formally by registering as a Republican in 1962, Nancy bridled, "Remember when Churchill left the liberal party to join the Conservatives? He said, 'Some men change their party for the sake of their principles; others their principles for the sake of their party.' Ronnie feels that way [the former] about becoming a Republican."[15]

Reagan had been a Republican in theory and practice for many years. Actually, his switch in his views on Nixon had come as early as 1960, and he actively campaigned for him against John F. Kennedy in that presidential election. Despite his opposition to Kennedy's views, he was as distraught as most people were when the president was assassinated. "It was the Communists," he insisted. "They want to destroy our very freedom to elect a president. But they can't do it. We're too strong as a nation, as a people." Maureen recalled that when they watched the tragic events in Dallas on television together, her father had tears in his eyes, the first time she could ever recall him displaying his emotions so openly.[16]

When Jackie Kennedy appeared on screen Reagan commented, "Couldn't she have changed her suit? There's blood all over it."[17]

Reagan believed that it was simply not right for the president's widow to make a display of her husband's blood, that there was something undignified about it. Kennedy's assassination, in fact, had strongly affected him. Jackie Kennedy would later recall that he wrote a moving letter to her and to her brother-in-law, Robert Kennedy, and Nancy always admired Jackie, especially her sense of style and elegance.

By 1964, with Reagan's contract with the United States Borax Company still in heated negotiation and not yet signed, he made *The Killers* (which would be his last film) and then plunged into politics. His speeches to help California Republican candidates raise money drew large crowds, and he was seen by the Republican Party as a great asset. The country had gone through grief and upheaval in the past year, first with the senseless assassination of Kennedy and then with the high casualty list in Vietnam, a war many Americans had not wanted. Kennedy's vice president, Lyndon Baines Johnson, had inherited all of the slain president's unresolved problems. Johnson, president for only the last year of Kennedy's elected term, was running against Loyal Davis's good friend Barry Goldwater in the 1964 election. Johnson stood on a platform of nonescalation (a policy that was abandoned after his election); Goldwater proposed the use of nuclear weapons, if necessary, to win the war.

Kennedy's murder had badly shaken America's confidence in itself. Liberals weren't sure they could trust the new president, who had not convinced them of his ability to end the war. Johnson was regarded as a tough, vulgar, power-driven Texan, and a hard-to-beat opponent. The

Republicans, still reeling from Nixon's defeat four years earlier, wanted power, and the man they chose to stand up against Johnson was Senator Barry Goldwater.

Reagan spoke for Goldwater at California fund-raisers during the summer and early fall of 1964. Basically, the speech he gave was the one he had been giving for the last year of his work with GE citing the expansion of federal government, "the proliferation of government bureaucrats who were taking control of American business," and the danger of socialism. He slanted his comments toward Goldwater's platform and brought in relevant anecdotes and personal stories. His main thrust was that "America is at a crossroads: We have a choice of either continuing on this path or fighting to reclaim the liberties being taken from us."[18]

After he gave "the speech" with some variations one more time before eight hundred Republicans gathered for a fund-raiser at the Coconut Grove (then a famous nightclub attached to the now-shuttered, legendary Ambassador Hotel in Los Angeles, where Robert Kennedy was shot while celebrating his victory in the 1968 California presidential primary), a group of top Republicans asked him if he would be willing to film the speech for a nationwide political television broadcast in support of Goldwater. He agreed. Without realizing it, his own political future was now on the rise.

Filmed in San Francisco, Reagan's speech, "A Time for Choosing," was aired nationally on October 27, 1964. His manner was straightforward, he looked into the eye of the camera as though it was an old and trusted friend. His voice was both melodious and commanding. He talked person to person in his own words for thirty minutes, no written pages to glance down to and so break the connection between speaker and audience, no cue cards. Most of what he said was memorized and had been rehearsed through the many times he had spoken almost the same words: He never mentioned Vietnam. It was the Red Menace, the Evil Empire, Communism (which referred to the North Vietnamese as well) that he impaled. His penultimate paragraph closed with the memorable words: "You and I have a rendezvous with destiny. We will preserve for our children this, the last best hope of man on earth, or we will sentence them to take the last step into a thousand years of darkness."[19]

The speech, according to the *Washington Post*'s senior correspondant, was "the most successful national political debut since William Jennings Bryan electrified the 1896 Democratic Convention with the 'Cross of Gold' speech."[20]

Reagan and Nancy were able to watch the pretaped address at home, where they had gathered a few close friends. When it ended, the others in the room told him that he had done well, but there was not a clamorous reception. This is perhaps because some of the Reagan's oldest friends, like Harriet and Armand Deutsch, were Democrats and uncertain about their reaction to Reagan's growing conservatism. On their guests' departure, Reagan felt uneasy, wondering if he "had let Barry down," and had been wrong in agreeing to give the speech.

"At about midnight," he wrote, "Nancy and I were awakened by a phone call from Washington, where it was 3 A.M. The call was from a member of Barry's campaign team, who told me the Goldwater-for-President campaign switchboard had been lit up constantly since the broadcast. Thousands of people, he said, had called in pledging support to Barry and the party. After that, Nancy and I both had a good night's sleep."[21]

There was a quality of instant communication to Reagan's delivery that had not surfaced in politics or war since Roosevelt and Churchill. This did not seem to help Goldwater with voters, for Johnson won the election by a devastating margin. Still, the signs were there that the conservative movement was alive and could succeed with stronger candidates. Over a million people had donated funds to Goldwater's campaign, and there had been double the number of volunteers to those who had aided in Johnson's campaign. Nevertheless, the Democrats remained in power. Crisis by crisis, the country was becoming more divided. What was needed in the future was a candidate who could speak to the neglected sentiments of the American people, not just of one party.

Republicans suddenly saw Reagan as their white hope. "After the Goldwater debacle," Holmes Tuttle, a wealthy car dealer and Loyal Davis's good friend, said, "I called Henry Salvatori and some others, and we went to Ron and discussed the idea of his running for Governor [of California]." Reagan dismissed the idea without any hesitation. "[But then] Holmes came up to the house specifically to see me," Reagan remembered. "I gave him the usual thing about [not wanting to run] for office. ['I'm an actor, not a politician. I'm in show business.']" After more than an hour, with Reagan still adamant, Tuttle finally asked, "Would you agree not to give us a flat no? Just kick it around in your mind?" Reagan agreed.[22]

He did not envision that there was a master plan behind these overtures, that this small group of men led by Holmes and including Justin Dart and A. C. (Cy) Rubel, the former president of Union Oil Company, might be conspirators laying the groundwork for him to run for the presidency one day on behalf of the conservative wing of the Republican Party. If he had suspected such a plan, he might never have followed the path he eventually took.

"Nancy," Reagan claimed, "had no more interest in my running for governor than I did and she was just as flabbergasted by the idea as I was. We loved our life as it was and didn't want it to change." He called his father-in-law to discuss it. Davis, whom Armand Deutsch had once accused of being "to the right of Attila the Hun," said he would be crazy to run for office; "he said there was no way a man could go into politics without sacrificing his honesty and honor, because no matter how well intentioned he was, a politician was inevitably forced by the realities of political life to compromise." Reagan began to back down.[23]

Holmes Tuttle, and the fast-growing group of wealthy, high-powered, and high-placed men who had formed a clique of like-thinking California Republicans, refused to take no for an answer. The pressure on the Reagans was tremendous. "It soon got to the point," Reagan wrote, "where Nancy and I were beginning to have trouble sleeping at night; the constant emphasis that I was the only guy around who could beat Brown [Edmund G. (Pat) Brown, the liberal Democrat incumbent governor of California who was planning to run for a third term] and heal the split in the party put a lot of weight on our shoulders. After a while we'd lie in bed and ask ourselves: *If they're right and things get worse for*

*the party and we could have done something about it, will we ever be able to
sleep at night again?"*[24] Cast in the role of her dreams, wife of a prominent
man, Nancy did not yet suspect the details of the final screenplay. Reagan was beginning to consider the idea. Nancy was certainly an integral
part of his final decision. He would never have taken on anything as
serious as running for public office, which would completely disrupt their
lives, against her wishes. She was not enthusiastic about the prospect of
campaigning or, if he won, about moving to the state capital, Sacramento.
But she assured him that she would completely back him in whatever
choice he made. As time went on and the pressure increased, Nancy
thought better of it.

"In the beginning Nancy was more reluctant than Ronnie for him
to enter the political arena," a close friend says. "Then there came a
time when she seemed to fancy the idea of being first lady of California.
Also she had extraordinary faith in Ronnie. In the end, it was Nancy
who was the one who was the key voter in the matter. Her life was going
to be turned upside down, and Ronnie had to be convinced that she
would be all right with that."[25]

While all this was going on, Reagan signed and fulfilled his contract
(twenty-one episodes) for *Death Valley Days*, a move he came to regret,
because it kept him away from home again for long periods as a good
part of the show was filmed in Death Valley, where temperatures rose
to 110 to 120 degrees, and tempers with it.

Six months after Holmes Tuttle first approached him, the pressure
increased. There was now an active committee, called the Friends of
Ronald Reagan, seeking his agreement to be the Republican candidate
for governor. "How do you say no to all these people?" he asked Nancy.
"I don't think we can run away from it." Nancy agreed, and on a television broadcast on January 4, 1966, she stood by his side, looking up at
him adoringly, as he announced his intention of seeking the Republican
nomination for governor.[26]

Pictures were taken of the family, excluding Mermie, who was now
married and politically active herself, and Michael (at boarding school in
Arizona). No mention was made in the press release of Reagan's divorce
or of his "other family," although it was public knowledge. Skipper,

seven, smiled engagingly, but Patti looked uncomfortable in almost every photograph. She was now in boarding school and had come home for Christmas break. Her relationship with both her parents had deteriorated seriously as she approached her teens. The hostility between her mother and herself grew ever darker. Patti has claimed, quite convincingly, that their frequent arguments before she was sent off to boarding school had become violent. She recalls that Nancy would find something to fault her on, take her into her bathroom, close the door, accuse her, wait for the young girl to reply, than crack her hard across the face no matter what she said. It was a scene that repeated itself with frightening frequency.

Patti was a difficult child. She had a strong rebellious streak, and she felt unwanted by her mother. Nancy did not know how to deal with the situation. Her early hope had been that her daughter would grow out of her rebelliousness. But Patti had a strong will, a mind of her own, and enough smarts to outfox Nancy at times. Even at the age of thirteen she knew there was something seriously wrong in her relationship with her mother and asked her parents if she could see a therapist, which several other of her classmates were doing. The Reagans were adamant: no therapist. There is no doubt she baited her mother with full knowledge that a violent act on Nancy's part would follow. This hardly excuses Nancy's response or covers the appalling deafness of the parents to Patti's obvious cries for help. They felt Patti was acting up to gain attention. Reagan never believed anything negative Patti told him about Nancy, and could not conceive that Nancy would strike her. "Why do you lie like this?" he would say. "Why do you hurt your mother so? She doesn't eat because she is so worried about you."[27]

Patti asserts that her mother was obsessive about staying thin and was on diet pills. They speeded up her chemistry, and heavy doses of Valium slowed it down, during the day; by her bedside every night was a bottle of Seconal and a glass of water. Patti was only twelve years old when she began to sneak pills from Nancy's large supply in her medicine cabinet, setting off on her own path to addiction.

On the afternoon of January 4, 1966, Nancy, wearing a neat red-wool outfit, ushered members of the press into the living room on San Onofre, which one reporter described as being "so splurged with color that even Reagan's black pants and black loafers seemed exuberant."[28] Reagan announced his candidacy and then settled back on the large, comfortable sofa, Nancy by his side. He began talking about his youth in Dixon, Illinois, and how he had come home from Eureka College to no work, then had hitchhiked to Chicago and finally gotten a job in Davenport, Iowa, as a sports announcer for five bucks a game. He was at ease telling his stories, told them well, and almost verbatim as he had recited them perhaps a hundred times before. Nancy sat, hands clasped, eyes raised in devoted attention.

Patti returned to school the day after her father declared publicly that he would run in the primaries for governor. Only Skipper was at home. In many ways this eased Nancy's mind. At least she would not have to deal with her perverse daughter. Then Mermie decided she wanted to be active in her father's campaign. Nancy was not pleased; nor, for that matter, was Reagan.

CHAPTER SIX

ON THE CAMPAIGN TRAIL

Nancy has said, "What I wanted most in all the world was to be a good wife and mother. As things turned out, I guess I've been more successful at the first than the second."[1] Her problems in raising her own children were difficult enough, but those with her two stepchildren seemed insurmountable. One of the roadblocks to understanding Maureen and Michael's situation was the total lack of communication between Jane Wyman and the Reagans. Both children were loyal to their parents and did not carry tales from one household to the other. Therefore, the Reagans were not cognizant of Wyman's harsh means of punishment, and Wyman was ignorant of Michael's sense of being an outsider in his father's home. Nor did the Reagans exert any power to keep Wyman from sending both children away to strict Catholic schools against their wishes, Michael at the tender age of five and a half. Having boarded in Tarrytown, New York, for four years and then gone to live in Washington, D.C., upon her graduation, Maureen was kept at such a distance for so many years that she unwillingly drifted apart from both her parents. She had, in fact, seen her father only twice and her mother once during that period. Now she had returned to California.

Those missing years had caused Maureen to suffer a deep sense of self-doubt as to her worthiness. She had not gone on to college because Wyman had demanded she attend a nonsecular school. Her interest in politics led her to the nation's capital. Unlike her father, she registered Republican in the first election in which she could vote. Reagan refused to give her money for her support, claiming he would have helped her to achieve a bachelor's degree but as she had not continued her education, she was on her own. Without college credentials, Maureen could find only clerical work. At twenty, a statuesque blonde, five foot eight with a strong resemblance to her mother—snub nose, square jaw—Maureen met and married John Filippone, a thirty-two-year-old divorced police officer who turned out to be a wife-abuser. She survived several violent beatings and hospital stays before she had the courage, despite his threats to her life if she did so, to divorce him. Too ashamed to tell her parents of the pain and humiliation she had borne, she soldiered on alone. Finally, in the fall of 1963, she fell in love with David Sills, formerly of Peoria, Illinois, and now a marine lieutenant stationed in Washington. When he was relocated to the West Coast, Maureen headed home.

Nancy made an attempt to heal old wounds, shopping with Maureen for a new wardrobe, which, with a major weight loss, she needed. Ronnie took a shine to Sills, championing his shared "small-town Illinois roots and his sharp political mind."[2] The Reagans hosted a reception at Chasen's following Maureen's and Sills's wedding at the Church of the Good Shepherd in Beverly Hills on February 8, 1964. At the church service Wyman was seated far apart from the Reagans. Although invited, she did not attend the reception. Her remarriage to Fred Karger and her divorce from him for a second time a year later weakened her relationship with her children, who found the situation at home confusing, especially since their mother imposed her religion on them and yet did not abide by it herself; the Catholic Church did not countenance divorce.

By the 1960s Wyman's career had wound down, with few offers of major roles coming her way. "Something happened in the sixties," she would later say. "It seemed that the time didn't permit women to be part [of movies being made] except in a secondary way." The roles that came her way were "murderers, old ladies that were senile [she was fifty at the time]. I'd read one of those scripts, I'd look in the mirror and say 'How could they think of me for this [part]?'" She had been offered the role that Bette Davis later played in the 1962 Robert Aldridge film *Whatever Happened to Baby Jane?*[3]

During Goldwater's presidential campaign Maureen had been a full-time volunteer. With her father's decision to run for governor of California, she was actively preparing to work on his campaign as well. To her shock, she was told by Bill Roberts and Stu Spencer, who were managing Reagan's candidacy, that they did not want either Maureen or Michael to be involved with their father's campaign. Their explanation was that Nelson Rockefeller's divorce and remarriage had caused his defeat in the 1964 Republican presidential primary (a campaign they had managed and which Goldwater had won). Spencer, a blunt man with a sharp tongue, was clear in telling her that they wanted no mention of "Reagan's other family" and that it would be best if she and Michael kept the lowest possible profile. Maureen claimed that he suggested to her husband that she "dig a hole and pull the dirt in over [herself]." Desperately hurt, and angry as well, Maureen called her father and asked him to intervene on her behalf.[4]

"If you pay someone to manage a campaign, then you've got to give them the authority to do it as they see fit," Reagan replied unsympathetically.[5]

Maureen, rebelling in the only way she knew how, worked independently for the California Federation of Republican Women, much to Roberts's and Spencer's fury. When Reagan came to speak before the San Diego chapter of the powerful woman's organization, Maureen was asked by the CFRW to introduce him. Stu Spencer was on hand. They barely spoke, but just before she mounted the podium to give her introduction, Maureen was handed a printed page that Spencer asked her to read. She studied it with amazement. The first two lines were: "Ronald Reagan and his wife Nancy have two children, Patti and Ronnie." Nothing followed to add that Reagan also had a son and a daughter with Jane Wyman.

"For me to read aloud those words [with their omissions], as his daughter, would have been the ultimate humiliation," Maureen said. "I wanted to run away and hide, but I also wanted . . . to stand up for what I felt was right."[6] So she looked up from the prepared text and in a chatty tone, the Reagan smile much in evidence, told the women's group a family anecdote that included her and Michael and underscored her father's sense of integrity and good humor.

Nancy was suddenly a candidate's wife. This required skills she had never developed—giving speeches and meeting hundreds of women in one afternoon, ladies with whom she would formerly have had little in common and less cause to engage even in small talk. Most of her appearances were to be before women's groups. There were brunches, luncheons, teas, dinners, and many weeks when, resentfully, she and Ronnie had only a day or two together. Early on, Nancy asked if she couldn't just do question-and-answer sessions. This was agreed and reduced the problem of speech-giving to a minimum. Reagan soon turned to the same method but for different reasons. He wrote and delivered marvelous speeches. The problem was that the opposition kept playing on the fact that he was an actor, saying that his speeches were being written for him—which was not true—and that he was then coached in delivery (also not true). A question-and-answer format refuted those accusations as he would have no idea what questions would be put before him.

The Reagans' acting careers did have their advantages, as many people enjoyed the idea of meeting a movie star—perhaps even more than a political contender and his supportive wife. Nevertheless, the Hollywood connection had serious drawbacks. Movie song-and-dance man, George Murphy, who had played Reagan's father in *This Is the Army*, had recently been elected to the Senate from California, the first professional actor to attain a major government office. A past president of SAG, Murphy was also a former Democrat and a founding member of the Hollywood Republican Committee. But the list began and ended with Murphy. Reagan was attempting to make the leap from film and television stardom to statewide office with no record to back him up other than as president of SAG and a fund-raiser for his party.

"Taking someone with celebrity status in one field and trying to shoehorn them into another is a very, very tough job. It doesn't automatically equate," Don Sipple, who has worked on numerous gubernatorial campaigns, said. "There has to be a transformation and a transition as far as the celebrity's motives and preparation are concerned."[7] Reagan had achieved that with his famous televised speech during the Goldwater campaign, and with the years he had spent touring the country for General Electric espousing his political beliefs. The Reagans' movie background was a weapon for his opponents to use against Reagan, both in the primary that he had won against George Christopher, a popular former mayor of San Francisco, and the current race against the incumbent governor, Edmund G. (Pat) Brown.

"I'm running against an actor, and you know who killed Abe Lincoln, don't you?" Brown told a group of children in his first television commercial after Reagan won the primary on June 20 with a two-to-one majority.[8]

"Brown's campaign against me," Reagan snapped back, "simply put, asked the question: What is an actor doing seeking an important job like the governorship of California?" As the campaign got underway, Brown seemed confident he'd win his third term in a breeze. He had previously beaten not only Richard Nixon, a former vice president of the United States, but also U.S. Senator William F. Knowland, an Oakland publisher who was another California Republican powerhouse. "I suspect," Reagan said, "he thought it would be even easier to knock off this newcomer to politics from Hollywood."[9]

Reagan's candidacy created some difficult times for his old Hollywood friends who remained loyal to the Democratic Party. But Republicans like John Wayne, James Cagney, George Murphy, Jack Warner, and many others lent him their financial support. There were also those who were undecided as to what they should do. Some feared that their lack of support would cause a schism in their friendship with the Reagans. Armand and Harriet Deutsch were two of the latter, along with Mary and Jack Benny and George Burns and Gracie Allen.

"Ronnie always voiced his views and we said, 'Shut up! Ronnie!' Deutsch recalled. 'You don't know anything about this.' But, oddly enough, long before he ever thought of running for governor, Jack Benny always called him Governor. I don't know why. When it did happen it all came about very rapidly. This was a very difficult time in my life. I decided that I was not going to vote for him for governor and I said to

Harriet, 'I gotta tell him.' Not to be a hero, but Holmes and all those guys were coming around for money. Harriet was very unhappy about it. We called and asked them [the Reagans] for dinner and had it right in the alcove [a small, charming dining area off their living room] and I was hoping we'd get through dinner. But before we did [Ronnie] said, 'Hey! What do you want to talk to me about?' A very difficult thing. I said, 'Ronnie, this is very hard for me, but I have to tell you that I'm not going to vote for you. I'm not going to vote for Pat Brown, but you're too conservative for me, and I'm telling you because it will reach you through Holmes and Justin Dart.'

"He got up. It was a round table of four, and he walked halfway around the table and placed both his hands on my shoulders. 'I don't care who you vote for,' he said. 'We'll always be friends.' Nancy was a little different. She cried at dinner and Harriet cried. But we weathered it."[10] (By the time of Reagan's race for a second term as governor of California, the Deutsches had switched parties and become backers of Reagan's campaign. They would remain friends throughout Reagan's presidency and beyond.)

His relationship with Lew Wasserman, a staunch Democrat, further eroded during his campaign. Reagan suffered mixed feelings over this. During the antitrust probe, he had gone to bat for Wasserman, who was now one of the most powerful men in Hollywood. Wasserman also emerged as a fund-raising force behind the Democratic Party, a welcome figure in Lyndon Johnson's White House who had been offered and refused a cabinet position as secretary of commerce. Not only had he once treated Reagan dismissively, Wasserman was "now working for the other fellows."[11] Yet it had been Wasserman who had talked him into the deal with General Electric that had changed Reagan's life and made him financially independent.

Northern and southern California were split over Reagan's run for governor. Hollywood was divided, not into *ward* but into *war* zones, with the liberal left represented by such high-profile names as Dore Schary, Frank Sinatra, Paul Newman, Shirley MacLaine, and her kid brother, Warren Beatty, who were campaigning for Pat Brown. Jack Dales recalled near-violent arguments breaking out after SAG meetings. "It was an explosive situation. HUAC and McCarthy had been vanquished. But there were too many walking wounded actors who SAG members knew had been betrayed by Reagan. They saw him as the worst kind of informer, and even those who were Republicans felt hesitant about his fitness to be governor."[12]

After a timid start, Nancy got into the full swing of the campaign. "Nancy was indispensable," a staff member for Roberts-Spencer said. "She was responsible for getting out a large segment of the women's vote. I don't believe she really liked campaigning, but she was a trooper. Women came to see if she still looked good now that she was in her mid-forties, and she did not disappoint them. She was always well-dressed, her hair perfectly coiffed. And she answered question after question with amazing patience. [She] must have consumed thousands of cups of tea and more bland luncheon fare in a month than any one would care to in their entire lifetime."[13]

A member of Nancy's staff, Kathi Davis, accompanied her to all her engagements. Often their schedules required the Reagans to fly the same morning to opposite ends of the state. Later they would meet in another town for a black-tie dinner, then Reagan would have to leave early to fly to his next destination, where he had an early breakfast meeting. They might not meet again until the weekend. Nancy's first taste of being a candidate's wife was a demanding and exhausting experience. Copies of Nancy's brutal schedules in the Reagan Library archives give a vivid picture of how hard she worked during the campaign, frequently without much letup. Yet her memos to Stu Spencer and members of his staff reveal, not concern for her own well-being but for Reagan's, with constant requests for care to be given that "Ronnie have time to rest and to eat a proper meal."

Campaigning was tough for Nancy as well. Often she would have to fly to two cities in a day, sleep fitfully in hotels with sealed windows, rise in the pre-dawn hours, eat at odd times and whatever food was available. She shook hundreds of hands, smiled when her feet hurt from standing on high heels for hours at a time, and always had to look her best no matter how exhausted she was.

What disturbed her most were the brickbats, poisonous remarks, and accusations that were flung at Ronnie. Brown realized early in the race that it was not going to be as easy to beat Reagan as he first believed, and he got downright mean in his rhetoric. Reagan had to conquer his fear of flying in order to cover the territory that was necessary if he were to win. No matter how exhausted he was, he seemed always to look fresh. He had not worn makeup since his first few movie roles, and he refused to do so on any of his television appearances. This gave him a natural look; Brown, on the other hand, was unflatteringly made up and stiff before the camera. What they called "the hormone vote," meaning women voters, came out in force to hear and see Reagan. His message— taxes, spending, morality (this was the era of Haight-Ashbury, kids on pot, and rioting on college campuses), and the dangers of Pat Brown's third-term candidacy ("Taxes, taxes, taxes!")—hit the public just where it should. Reagan was gaining backing and gaining it fast.

He corresponded frequently with Richard Nixon, now in New York City at his legal offices at 20 Broad Street. On June 9, 1966, Nixon wrote, "As I am sure you know the assault on you will reach massive proportions in the press and on TV as Brown and his cohorts realize that they are going to be thrown off the gravy train after eight pretty lush years. There is an old Mid-Western expression (my roots also are in the Mid-West) which I would urge you to bear in mind as the going gets tougher. Just sit tight in the buggy!"[14] (Although Nixon was born and raised in Yorba Linda, California, his parents were from the Midwest.)

On August 10, with Brown's campaign increasing in vitriol, George Murphy wrote from his Senate office, "I just talked to Barry [Goldwater] and he says Cal[ifornia] looks so good he is worried. He also says the [Los Angeles] *Times* has started the 'Smear.' Don't let it bother you. Just keep going as you have been. Love to Nancy—Murph."[15]

By October, with the campaign in its last month, Brown knew he was fighting an uphill battle. At one campaign stop the electricity failed. Brown commented, "They can cut off the electricity, but they can't shut up the greatest governor California has ever had." He added later, "I'm entitled to be reelected. It is ludicrous that the Republican party would nominate a man without experience."[16]

But Reagan took to the campaign trail as if born to it. For him it was an extension of his grueling tours for General Electric, and, as in those days, he was always prepared. People who knew Reagan well during this period repeatedly comment on his seeming detachment. Yet with strangers whom he wanted to win over, he had a warm, ready smile and a firm, lingering handshake. He made eye contact with supporters on reception lines and had an instinct for saying just the right thing, patting a man on the shoulder in a friendly gesture, blushing at a flattering remark by a woman. Was he acting? Perhaps he was, but speak to any number of the recipients of his small attentions and they will tell you, "He was a real guy," "He respected who you were and what you did," or "When he moved on [in a reception line] you felt he would remember you."[17]

Nancy was a dedicated coworker, doing all that was required of her at the same time as she vigilantly watched over her husband's well-being. She slipped packages of peanut butter crackers along with bags of his favorite jelly beans in his overnight case, and they talked several times a day. "She was a patient listener," a staff member recalled, "and she seldom complained of anything to him—unless it [had] to do with his staff's overworking him. To those of us who were with her on a day to day basis, it was a different Nancy. Once she had learned the ropes, she was a tough taskmaster. Mr. Reagan could display temper on occasion if pushed too far. Mrs. Reagan could get downright mean, although if she thought later she had been unfair, she would apologize to the aggrieved party."[18]

Reagan's composure, as his opponent turned his campaign into one of innuendo and unfounded accusation, was amazing. For example, Brown claimed Reagan had once belonged to a Communist front organization. Indeed, Reagan had once inadvertently joined an organization thought (later, even by him) to be a Communist front organization when he was not yet president of SAG. The group was the Hollywood Independent Citizens Committee of Arts, Sciences and Professions (HICCASP), originally formed as an instrument to further Franklin Roosevelt's New Deal programs, which in 1945 Reagan firmly believed in. At the time, his brother Neil was working as an outside agent for the FBI and warned him to "get out of that [organization]. There are people in there who can cause you real trouble. . . . Finally one evening, hell, it was about midnight, he called [and told me he thought HICCASP was a Communist front organization]."[19] Reagan resigned from HICCASP the next day. He was ultimately recruited by the FBI to work undercover for them, which he did with Neil's input and persuasion.

Brown also accused Reagan of being a puppet of big business interests that were manipulating him. He broadcast television ads showing Reagan in clips from the film *Bedtime for Bonzo*, which had been the low point of Reagan's movie career, holding his costar chimpanzee in a maternal clasp. Reagan refused to lower himself to the "dirty campaign" that Brown was running, but he didn't ignore it, either. In one televised interview he cracked—a sideways smile on his well-tanned face—that Brown was "standing in mud up to his armpits saying 'This is the dirtiest campaign I have ever been in.' "[20]

Nancy displayed her anger at her husband's detractors more openly. One time she stood up in the aisle of the plane taking her from Los Angeles to a fund-raiser in San Diego, turned to the men behind her who had been loudly deriding Ronnie, and shouted at them to listen to the speech he was to give that night and see how wrong they were. Kathi Davis did not have an easy time coaxing her to sit back down.

Family problems continued to plague Nancy along with the pressures of the campaign. Patti, fourteen, was at boarding school in Arizona, where she had run off with—and threatened to marry—a twenty-one-year-old dishwasher employed by the school. She was gone only a day, but that was long enough for her parents to become wild with worry. Their concern was quickly replaced with the fear that if the story broke, the publicity would hurt Ronnie, giving Brown a chance to throw more dirt at him. But Patti was found (the couple had not gone far or crossed a state line), the young man in question was dispatched, and the story was kept out of the press.

No attention was paid to Patti, who was obviously crying out for help and understanding. Before her failed elopement, Patti had turned to someone she felt she could trust, Michael, begging him to drive to Arizona to help her to falsify her age on a marriage certificate. Instead, Michael called Nancy—thinking this was the right thing to do—and informed her of the situation. Nancy decided that Patti needed discipline, not counseling. Because the couple were stopped and returned to the school, Patti felt betrayed by Michael and did not speak to him for years. The man she had sought to marry was fired from his job at the school. He later claimed that he did not know that Patti was a minor and that he was working to earn money to further his education.

Michael, having recently celebrated his twenty-first birthday, was living in Los Angeles, but acquiesced quite willingly not to involve himself in his father's campaign. He had discovered a love of boats and racing them and was deeply in debt financing what the Reagans believed was a frivolous hobby. To cope with all these family situations, hold up her end of campaign duties, and still be a helpmate to Ronnie, Nancy increased her intake of pills to get through the day (uppers) and to sleep at night (downers). Staffers noted a change in her personality. She was increasingly on edge and could exhibit "on the slightest provocation a cold front that hit the bottom of the thermometer."[21]

A week before the election, a weary Brown got aboard the *Grizzly II*, his campaign plane, en route to his next speech engagement and announced to the accompanying political reporters, "I'm going to do a little Harry Truman work and I think the glamour of this man is going to fade." He was referring to President Truman's surprising victory over Republican candidate Thomas E. Dewey in 1948. With Reagan's percentages gaining over his, Brown's optimism failed him. "Tired old governor," he said across the aisle to his wife, Bernice, on *Grizzly II* as they were returning from a string of speaking engagements with disappointingly sparse audiences. "Tired old wife," she responded.[22]

Reagan's last campaign speech was given in San Francisco. On the flight back to Los Angeles, his staff and the reporters who were covering his campaign were so confident of his victory that they were already whooping it up. Reagan sat resolutely reading a book, "trying to appear that he wasn't part of the group firing gin-filled water guns in the cabin of a United Airline's plane."[23]

On Tuesday, November 8, after dining with a close circle of friends and supporters, Nancy and Ronnie were chauffeured to the Biltmore Hotel in downtown Los Angeles, where the Republicans were holding their election night party. Nancy was extremely nervous. Reagan wore a calm expression, as he usually did under trying circumstances. It was nine P.M. and the polls were closed. The election seemed to be going his way, but he was never one to count on anything until it was assured—"the contract signed, sealed, delivered, the check in the bank *and* cleared," he was known to say. Still, both of them were optimistic. Reagan appeared to be far ahead of Brown, who, with the Democratic campaign team and his supporters, was holding vigil a few miles west at the Ambassador Hotel. Over the car radio the Reagans heard it announced that Ronnie had won the election.

The final count would give him the election by 993,739 votes. There was a tremendous ovation in the grand Biltmore ballroom when they arrived. Reagan's campaign song had been written to Jerry Herman's popular show tune "Hello, Dolly," and as the Reagans made their way through the cheering crowds, the band was playing and the crowd singing: "Hello, Ronnie! Well, hello, Ronnie! It's so great to have you here where you belong!"

Nancy stood radiantly smiling on the podium beside Ronnie as they waited for the sound of the cheering to ebb. He was not wearing his glasses, and the crowd was a blur as he smiled and waved at them. Later, he would tell George Murphy, "This is the first time in my life [facing the cheering throng] that I ever really felt like a star."[24] Unlike most winning candidates, they were not surrounded by family. Michael and Maureen had been asked to stay away from the Biltmore, and they had done so with bitter resignation. Patti was told she must remain at school in Arizona, and Nancy had decided that Skipper, aged eight, should not be exposed to the media cameras and enthusiastic revelers. And so this was a high point the Reagans would share alone.

One of the first congratulatory telegrams Reagan received was from Nixon.

CONGRATULATIONS. THE MOST SIGNIFICANT NEWS OF NOVEMBER EIGHTH IS THAT REPUBLICAN GOVERNORS WILL BE IN A MAJORITY AT THE NEXT GOVERNORS' CONFERENCE. WARMEST PERSONAL REGARDS DICK NIXON.[25]

On November 15, one week after election night, Nancy flew to Sacramento, where she was taken on a tour of the governor's mansion, the
house she and her family would occupy after New Year's Day, 1967.

The prospect of having to move to the state capital did not fill Nancy
with enthusiasm. Although once a bustling river port that played host to
an assortment of gold seekers who poured into the city after the mother
lode was found on Captain John Augusta Sutter's farm, Sacramento now
was a mecca for politicians, political aides, and conventioneers. Nancy
was tied to her life in Los Angeles, her lunches with women friends at
her favorite restaurants, her trips to the stylish shops in Beverly Hills,
her weekly visits to get her hair done at Alida Gray (later at Saks Fifth
Avenue), and the ease of living in a city where it seldom grew cold
enough to wear a coat and the sun was visible in the sky almost every
day of the year. Sacramento is ninety miles northeast of San Francisco.
It is cold in the winter and prone to heavy fogs and a long rainy season
with fields mired in mud. The town would grow during the next few
decades into a more cosmopolitan city. However, in the 1960s, women
who wanted designer clothes had to travel the considerable distance to
San Francisco to buy them.

The city, with a population at the time of about 140,000, rested in
a loop of the Sacramento River at its confluence with the American
River. It had survived more disasters than most California cities, including three devastating floods that caused epidemics so widespread that
corpses were shoved into the swollen river to drift away, contaminating
the water for several years. There had also been severe earthquakes, a
fire that in the mid-nineteenth century destroyed two-thirds of the town,
followed by the sudden madness of gold-driven hordes seeking to become rich, bringing with their panning dishes and gold-separating para-
phernalia crime, drunkenness, and a swift rise in suicides when gold
eluded them. During the 1930s the town was hard hit by the Depression,
suffering near economic ruin. There had been hunger marches, farm
labor problems, a heavy influx of poor migrants arriving from the dust-
swept plains in overcrowded and overloaded rattletrap cars and only a
faint hope of employment. Hundreds of such refugees camped in the
fairgrounds where the California State Fair usually was held. And though

Sacramento had been the terminus of the first railroad in California and had known prosperous times, it now had an alarming budget deficit.

The people were hardy, morally upright, no-nonsense folks of mixed ethnic backgrounds—Swiss (the earliest settlers), German, Mexican, Italian, Chinese, Japanese, and Filipino, many of whom had come west as migratory farm workers or from San Francisco after the great earthquake of April 18, 1906. Sacramento was a Democratic stronghold, where the majority had voted for Brown. They were not greatly impressed by movie stars. Those who did cast their ballot for Reagan had been cheered by his promise to "clean up the mess at Berkeley [where there had taken place] sexual orgies so vile I cannot describe them to you." What they expected from Nancy was a first lady who would "not make too much of a splash for herself."[26]

For the Reagans the Christmas holidays in 1966 were filled with a mixture of joy, confusion, and anxiety. Nancy was determined that they keep the house in the Palisades. It was decided that the family would remain in Sacramento during the time that the legislature was in session and return to Los Angeles on weekends, holidays, and whatever other time could be managed, allowing for Skipper's school schedule in Sacramento. Patti had gained considerable weight, and Nancy was much agitated by it. One day when they returned from a fractious day of shopping for clothes to fit Patti, the young girl got out of the car and was told by her mother, " 'Patti, you have a fat butt.' I stopped, turned around, and faced my mother, small and slim in her perfectly coordinated outfit. She was smiling. I suddenly felt so large, so cumbersome, that I half-expected the asphalt to crack beneath my weight. I couldn't say anything."[27]

When they arrived at the governor's mansion in Sacramento shortly after Christmas, camera crews flashed their greetings. It was absolute chaos, boxes everywhere, no one knowing exactly what they should be doing, and the house was freezing cold. Nancy stood in the front hallway wrapped in a mink coat, checking boxes as to their possible contents and directing the movers where to take them. Flowers and baskets of fruit were lined up on the floor. Telephones kept ringing, and a frantic search was made to locate the instruments.

The gloomy, démodé Victorian mansion, with rusted wrought iron decoration and Italianate windows, was located in the historic section of town on Seventh and H streets, about eight blocks from the gold-domed Capitol (set amid a lovely forty-acre parkland and where the new governor would have his offices on the ground floor). The Reagans' new home was a four-story frame house with a two-story cupola. It had been built in 1877, and was modernized, but not altered greatly, shortly after World War II. On her first visit to the house Maureen remarked, "If you had to list it with a real-estate broker, you'd have to advertise it under the heading 'Handyman Special.' "

"Not exactly homey is it?" her father answered with a wry smile.[28]

The only Reagan who found the house likable was eight-year-old Skipper, who was fascinated with the highly polished wooden bannister of the central staircase. He spent the entire afternoon of their arrival racing up the stairs and shouting gleefully as he whooshed down on his backside to land with a thud at the bottom. Maureen recalled the click-click of Nancy's high heels on the hardwood floors as she ran to see if he had landed safely. He always did and, despite his mother's demand that he "stop it!" repeated his bannister act again and again.

The historic section of Sacramento had not been protected, and although there was a smattering of the old houses that had been built in the nineteenth century, the governor's mansion was hemmed in on both sides by a motel and two gas stations and was across the road from the weatherworn, dowdy railway depot. From the cupola of the house the curving form of the Sacramento River could be seen. Otherwise the vistas were bleak.

Nancy was understandably upset over the crumbling state of their new home. Wallpaper was peeling, carpets were faded. The furniture resembled the unwanted discards of a family estate. January 1967 was unusually cold and the house was drafty and damp, the scent of mold filling the rooms. The heating system needed work, she was told. But, of course, there were several working fireplaces. Nancy was rightfully concerned that the old wood house could well be a firetrap as there were no fire escapes or ladders from the upper stories, just a rope hung outside the bedroom windows to shinny down should a fire start. For the moment she contained her fear and loathing as she and Ronnie looked forward to his inauguration.

There were to be two swearing-ins, one private, one public. Reagan had decided that he should take the oath of office at exactly one minute after Brown's term ended at midnight on January 1, 1967. Nancy had taken a recent in-depth interest in astrology and the astrologer had told her that that was the moment when the stars were said to predict a brilliant future for Ronnie. (Nancy also insisted that neither she nor Ronnie should fly until the times were astrologically propitious. They would adhere whenever possible to the dictates of their horoscopes for most of their lives, changing plans for travel, appearances, and health-related appointments to coincide with the time when an astrologer informed them that the stars were in their favor.)

Reagan wanted all his family to see him take office. This desire would lead to a logistical nightmare. Patti and Skipper were in Sacramento, but Loyal and Edith Davis had to fly in from Scottsdale. Maureen and Douglas Sills came up from Los Angeles. Michael was snowed in at a ski resort and could not get there in time (a great irritation to Nancy). Neil and his wife, Bess, were present, as was Senator George Murphy. They were joined by Marshall McComb, chief justice of the California Supreme Court, his wife, Carol, and California's new lieutenant governor Robert (Bob) Finch and Mrs. Finch. A sleepy-eyed Skipper held on to his grandmother's hand as they all waited in the center hall under the darkened dome of the Capitol for the clock to strike midnight. On the balcony above stood the choir of the University of Southern California, which sang a medley of state-inspired songs.

At two minutes past midnight the chief justice administered the oath of office right where they were all standing. Then the group congregated in the new governor's office for a champagne toast. "At that hour of the night it all seemed unreal, like a dream," Maureen recalled.[29]

They did not leave the Capitol until two in the morning, Reagan radiant, seeming not in the least bit tired. Skipper had curled up in his grandmother's arms and fallen asleep while Nancy was discussing what she could do to cheer up the nearly empty, paint-peeling, dreary governor's office.

"A splash of red," her mother said, and laughed. Nancy nodded her agreement.[30]

Reagan's midnight inaugural made the formal swearing-in, which took place several days later (with his hand on Nelle's Bible), "a major news story and the subject of many jokes." As he had already taken the oath of office, the second ceremony was not needed. It was, however, a necessary public relations act. An estimated ten thousand people had arrived in Sacramento to celebrate the GOP victory. "These were the Republicans who had grumbled through eight years of the Brown administration," Bill Boyarsky, a reporter who covered the campaign, wrote, "men and women who hadn't had much to rejoice about since Eisenhower's second victory in 1956. This was their chance to yell, to forget the losing battles for Nixon and Goldwater."[31]

The climax of the week's events was the Inaugural Ball, held Thursday evening, January 5, in an ugly, barnlike building on the State Fairgrounds. A hundred thousand dollars of campaign funds had been set aside for the week of festivities and the structure where the ball took place had been "spiffied up." There were huge bouquets of flowers and balloons; chairs had been regilded, floors polished. Five bands were hired to entertain the celebrants. Programs had been designed by the artists at Walt Disney Studios, and the guest list was larded with some of Hollywood's most famous Republican celebrities. Sacramento had never seen anything quite so glamorous before. The one problem was that the heat that had been piped in was not sufficient to warm the vast, high-ceilinged room. Nancy wore a James Galanos one-shouldered white gown beaded with crystal flowers. And though most of the women spent the evening with their evening wraps and fur coats worn over their gowns to ward off the deep-freeze temperature, she prevailed coatless, beaming up at Ronnie as he whirled her around the dance floor, almost all eyes in the room on them.

A few days later Reagan wrote Mr. Elonwy Neer, his old Sunday school teacher in Dixon, Illinois: "Every once in a while I pinch myself . . . thinking 'This can't be "Dutch Reagan" here. I should still be [the life guard] out on the dock of Lowell Park.' "[32]

One morning late in January, Reagan left for an out-of-town meeting while Nancy was still sleeping. On the mirror of her dressing table he had scotch-taped a note: "I LUV U & Missed a Good Morning Kiss—GUV." Between the second line and his "Guv," he had drawn a self-profile with his lips puckered and the caption "SMACK!!!"[33]

Ronnie and Nancy seemed bound even closer than before the campaign. On March 4, 1967, their fifteenth anniversary and only eight weeks after he had been sworn in as governor, he penned a note and left it on his pillow as she lay sleeping: "My Darling First Lady I'm looking at you lie here beside me . . . wondering why everyone has only just discovered you are the First Lady. You've been the First—in fact the only—to me for fifteen years."[34]

It is doubtful that any governor's wife ever enjoyed being first lady more than Nancy Reagan did. Perhaps not the actual duties of being the governor's wife, which she often found tedious, nor the time she spent in Sacramento. The importance of the title filled her with an exhilarating sense of pride. She carried herself in an affected royal manner ("somewhere between Bette Davis's Queen Elizabeth and the Duchess of Windsor,"[35] her hairdresser commented). And while she did not seek obeisance, she did expect special privileges and received them. Her belief in Ronnie—and in herself, for choosing him as her husband—had been entirely validated. After all, he had been the host of a television program sponsored by a cleaning product only a year before his election, hardly a position that would normally give ascent to expectations of becoming the governor of California. Through her husband's meteoric ascent to power Nancy had become a woman of consequence.

CHAPTER SEVEN

THE GOVERNOR'S LADY

Bef0re moving to Sacramento, the Reagans had decided to sell Yearling Row but maintain the house on Onofre Drive so that they would have a home to return to when Reagan's term of office ended. Nancy claimed that they could not support both properties while living in Sacramento on the governor's $40,000 yearly salary. Serendipitously, the ranch abutted property recently bought by Twentieth Century–Fox, which wanted to build an annex to their Los Angeles studio for storage use and office space. The studio purchased Yearling Row with its three-hundred-plus acres for $1,900,000. The proposed Fox annex was never built, but for the Reagans the sale was a bonanza.

Nancy did not miss the ranch, preferring to fly back to Los Angeles on weekends. For Reagan, the loss of Yearling Row and its open spaces was a great wrench. Even more sobering, albeit profitable, was the sale of his horses. Then, as though a bad omen, his favorite mount, Nancy D, died mysteriously on the very day that they moved to Sacramento. "That horse just wouldn't have another rider," he repeatedly told friends. For weeks he mourned the animal's death as that of a dear friend.[1]

Nancy was immediately drawn into a maelstrom of commitments. She now had a full-time secretary, Nancy Reynolds, a much-enlarged household staff, and security personnel. There was also Lyn Nofziger, Reagan's press and public relations liaison who arranged her public appearances and had constantly to be consulted. Nofziger was an ambitious man, already at this early stage of Reagan's political career secretly plotting his boss's eventual rise to presidential candidate. "Feels kind of premature," Reagan would insist. But Nofziger, a dogged hustler, "tubby, balding, and with a penchant for Mickey Mouse ties," would never let go of a bone once he had it in his paw.[2]

It was a big transition for Nancy from actor's to politician's wife. She was not the shadow partner of her predecessor, Mrs. Bernice Brown, or of Pat Nixon, the wife of former Vice President Nixon. Nancy enjoyed the limelight, and she played her role as the governor's lady better than any character she had portrayed on the screen, where she invariably appeared dowdy. Now she had her first real chance to star. She was immaculately turned out for every public occasion, seldom seen in the same outfit twice. As California's first lady, she expected designers and shop owners to supply her clothes either gratis or at a large discount as a courtesy. The trade-off was the publicity involved for the supplier. Note of the source of the item ("Mrs. Reagan wore a John Galanos gown") might appear in published photographs or articles.

California's new first lady outshone most of the local women, but she remained aloof, a fixed smile held for the camera when it flashed. She did all the right things, supported women's organizations and education programs, attended garden club functions, and became involved in the Foster Grandparents Program, which made it possible for older people to befriend mentally retarded and institutionalized children. However, the transition was not immediate, and the Reagans' first weeks in the governor's mansion were not happy ones.

Nancy felt displaced in Sacramento, and she loathed her new home. She admitted that she cried in bed after Ronnie fell asleep. The fireplaces were inoperable; the house was so poorly heated and insulated that after dinner they both would wrap up in blankets—Nancy to watch television, Ronnie to write at the desk in the corner of their bedroom. Reagan wrote all his speeches—radio, television, those to the California State Assembly—in longhand, composing them himself as he would do throughout his political life, although in later years speechwriters would edit his first drafts or he would edit theirs, replacing their stiffer prose with his more intimate voice. He also wrote his notes for his next working day on the previous night. "I can see him sitting at his desk writing, which he seemed to do all the time," Nancy recalled. "Often he'd take a long shower because he said that is where he got a lot of his thoughts. . . . And then, when he got out, he'd sit down and write. . . . Nobody thought he ever read anything either—but he was a voracious reader. I don't ever remember Ronnie sitting and watching television. I really don't. I just don't. When I picture those days, it's him sitting behind that desk in the bedroom working."[3] All their homes contained a desk in the bedroom as well as in a den or office.

Dennis LeBlanc, Reagan's security detail during his governorship, who traveled with him wherever he went, added, "He was constantly writing [in longhand on legal pads or four-by-six cards]. . . . He would sit [in the back seat of the car or the window seat of the first-class section of a plane] with his legal pad, writing."[4]

Another of his traveling companions, executive assistant David Fischer, remembered, "I was always amazed at how hard he worked. I'd be exhausted from traveling with him; I could start reading something and quickly fall asleep, and when I woke up he'd still be working, just writing away."[5] Fischer would remain with Reagan throughout his political life, functioning as an aide and as security.

At night in the governor's mansion, sleep eluded Nancy. The house fronted the main road from San Francisco to Reno, and heavy vehicles rolled back and forth all night, coming to a screeching, grinding stop at the traffic light a short distance from the poorly insulated windows of the ground floor dining room and the master bedroom above it. "When we had people for dinner," Nancy wrote, "there were times when the traffic was so loud we'd have to stop talking." The imposingly depressing house reminded her "of a funeral parlor. When we moved in, there were purple velvet drapes in each room—so old that when we took them down, they practically crumbled in our hands."[6] The wallpaper in the reception rooms was darker in areas where paintings had hung for years and then been removed. Light fixtures were woefully old-fashioned, and three narrow, steep flights of stairs led from the first landing to the upper floors, which had no other exits or fire escape. The top floor, which housed the cupola, still contained wall gaslights; it was claimed that former governors held their weekly poker games on this floor to be far removed from familial presence and the invasive ring of a telephone. What the Browns had thought was a Victorian treasure, Nancy regarded as a Gothic horror that even lacked outside grounds where Skipper could play.

There was no way that Nancy could accept that the house was commensurate with her husband's present stature. As Reagan's political career had grown, so had the circle of wealthy friends who supported him, giving Nancy fresh insight into the way the very rich and powerful lived. The house of Lee and Walter Annenberg in Palm Springs was a palatial estate with a service wing and suites to accommodate the many guests who came for their lavish parties, including one on New Year's Eve that had become a ritual for the Reagans. The Annenbergs had a great sense of style, but it was Betsy and Alfred Bloomingdale's lush Holmby Hills (Los Angeles) home that Nancy most admired, and Betsy was the hostess whom she wished to emulate. Blond, slim, trim, and couturier-dressed, Betsy, a perennial on various "Ten Best-Dressed Women" lists, was "the queen bee of West Coast socialites . . . hostess to royalty (the European and Hollywood kinds), to artists and to world leaders."[7] A striking portrait of her painted by Cecil Beaton hung over the sofa in her library, where she would serve afternoon tea. She kept diaries of every dinner party she had hosted since 1959 "and photographs of every table setting she [had] designed," so that she would not do the same thing twice. Guests dined on the finest antique Crown Derby china. Large bowls of giant dahlias, grown in the estate's gardens, filled the Bloomingdales' Mediterranean-style house, which had been decorated by Billy Haines.

"Billy Haines," Betsy Bloomingdale later recalled, "he was such a divine man and such fun to be with. He was fabulous and irreverent about so many people. He said to Alfred, who had happily given me a diamond necklace for something, 'Wow, what a wee necklace for such a big man to give.' Alfred was so stunned and thought maybe it *was* too small," and so he replaced it with another of a more imposing size.[8]

There was no way that Nancy could envision entertaining her new friends, or other powerful and famous people whom the governor of the country's largest state might well bring home, in what she looked upon as a derelict old fossil. Finally, she confronted Ronnie demanding they rent another house until the mansion could be renovated. Nancy stood her ground over Nofziger's pleas that it would be political suicide. In April 1967 they moved into a charming two-story, white-brick, English-style country house on Forty-fifth Street, in one of the most fashionable sections of Sacramento. It had the advantage of being only a five-minute drive from the Capitol. The wide, tree-shaded street contained homes both grand and pretentious: a pink Mediterranean-style mansion "that evoked Valentino's reign in silent films," a pseudoreplica of Tara with tall columns and broad, sloping lawns, and even a turreted, gray stone, small-scale castle. Nancy was delighted, and Reagan was content that she was happy.

The Reagans paid their own rent on this house. When the landlord decided to sell, shortly before Reagan's first term ended, the Friends of Ronald Reagan, a group of the Reagans' wealthy close friends and supporters, bought it, and the Reagans' rent was paid to them. Many of these contributors became members of Reagan's well-known Kitchen Cabinet. Justin Dart, a large, gruff man, dogmatic in his opinions and a major fund-raiser for the California Republican Party, was instrumental in bringing the group into being. Dart and Reagan had been friends since Reagan's studio days. Dart, president of Rexall Drugs, was married at the time to actress Jane Bryan, one of the costars with Reagan in *Brother Rat*. "Ronnie was not the most brilliant man I ever met," Dart admitted. "But he's a real leader—he's got credibility. He can get on his feet and influence people." Dart gathered together men he knew could help Reagan politically: bank founder Charles Cook; chairman of Union Oil Cy Rubel; car dealer Holmes Tuttle; oilman Henry Salvatori; steel magnate Earle Jorgensen; businessman Jack Wrather; Diner's Club founder and department store heir Alfred Bloomingdale; and magazine magnate Walter Annenberg. These men and their wives quickly became the mainstays of the Reagans' social world.

The Reagans were not crucified for the move, as Nofziger had forecast, although there was a spate of negative articles about it in the press. Attention was directed to its location in the heart of an all-white, Republican enclave, isolated from the middle-income homes that formed the greater part of the city. But in most states, governors' mansions are situated in well-to-do sections. For the most part, Californians did not have deep ties to the state capital or the governor's mansion and accepted the Reagans' choice of homes without much notice.

Once relocated, the Reagans' life took on a more normal pattern. Skipper built a tree house (with his father's help) on the expansive, well-planted grounds and rode his bicycle up and down the long, paved, security-guarded driveway. There was a pool, patios for lounging, a well-tended rose garden, fireplaces that worked, and new central heating. In the summer the Reagans hosted large outdoor barbecues for the legislators and their families, at which their Hollywood friends—Jack Benny, Red Skelton, and Danny Thomas among them—could entertain the locals. Nancy came under fire for these large outdoor gatherings, which disallowed the members of the legislature and their families a view of the inside of the house, the bathroom off the pool being as far as anyone ever got. The size of these parties also meant that no one could command much of Reagan's individual time or attention. These issues were hotly and negatively discussed by government officials and the media. Nancy viewed the situation quite differently. As the state was not paying the rent on the house, it seemed no more than fair that she be able to give whatever kind of party she liked.

The interior of the house, for which Nancy claimed responsibility as decorator, was eclectic. She brought in whatever good furniture there had been at Yearling Row, mostly country-style wood chests and beds, and purchased additional contemporary items for the upstairs rooms. She also "took up a collection of donated items, and," she confessed, "was able to beg and scrounge some nice furniture [expensive antiques] from people who were breaking up old houses."[9] These donated pieces of furniture turned out to be quite valuable. Betsy and Alfred Bloomingdale contributed a mahogany dining table that could seat twenty-four (appraised in 1967 for $3,500), the Earle Jorgensens two Queen Anne armchairs and ten side chairs ($3,000), Mrs. Ginny (Reese) Miller an antique French Regency fruitwood secretary ($2,800). There were many other gifts and donations—paintings, rugs, and several sets of fine, antique china—most valued at four figures. These were accompanied by upholstered pieces in red and white French toile for a handsome overall effect.

Paintings were also commandeered for the walls, and as there was a good flower garden, huge bouquets of fresh flowers were ever-present.

Not only was Nancy decorating her new home, she was redoing the governor's offices at the Capitol. Red carpets were installed, and the walls covered in beige burlap that handsomely backed newly framed pictures, engravings, and documents from the California gold-rush days found in the basement of the old Sutter's Fort, now state owned. For Ronnie's office she chose red and white draperies in a cheerful floral design and had the couches recovered in the same fabric. On Ronnie's desk she placed a large apothecary jar with orders that it be kept filled with his favorite jelly beans. For the cabinet room she followed her mother's advice (and her own taste). The carpet was crimson. "Why red?" Michael Deaver asked. "Because it hides the blood,"[10] Reagan laughed.

The Capitol offices, which had looked government-issue before Nancy's redecorating, now more closely resembled the elegant English country style of Lew Wasserman's MCA Beverly Hills offices. Despite all the critics who carped at the first lady's efforts and expenditures, Nancy did more good for the image of the state her husband governed than had any of her recent predecessors. She had style, although it might not have been everyone's taste, and she made it known that whatever the office her husband might one day be elected to, his wife would be an active and eager partner. Good news, especially to the Republican Party.

On the very first day of his administration, Reagan was handed the state's fiscal audits. California had about $200 million in cash debts, and in a year's time, if current spending was maintained, it would have a deficit of more than $250 million. Its Medi-Cal program for medical assistance to the needy would be facing heavy debt and would be in serious danger of having to abandon many of its services. Reagan looked around the meeting room where his staff was gathered and asked them in dead seriousness, "Well, what do we do now?" This question at his first staff meeting was to be used by the media then (and in several books later) as displaying the new governor's lack of knowledge of state governance. In context (the notes can be read in the Ronald Reagan

Presidential Library archives) it seems a natural query for Reagan to have put to his staff, when he faced California's budgetary problems, the extent of which had not been totally revealed to him before his election.

Reagan listened for a while to his staff's discussions, but did not wait for their final conclusions, determined to cut costs by 10 percent across the board. This was not entirely practicable, and some agencies, such as health care for the mentally ill, would suffer grievously if such cuts were made.

Nancy watched anxiously as her husband was catapulted onto the front lines without much more than basic training in the tactics of a political war. As a candidate he'd had the party backing him up and an election committee doing battle for him.

Although Reagan had won the election in a landslide, the Republican Party had failed to gain control of the legislature. In the Assembly, Democrats held a four-vote lead over the Republicans, and a one-vote lead in the Senate. Reagan was seated in his Capitol office for less than a month when Democrats fought to preserve the liberal programs they had created under Governor Brown. For his tax increase and other bills to become law, Reagan needed Democratic votes. Without them, his chance for a successful term of office was in jeopardy, along with his reelection four years later and—the ultimate dream of his backers—a run in 1976 for the presidency, then held by Lyndon Baines Johnson.

Thus began the true political life of Nancy Reagan. In early interviews and books Nancy denied that either she or Ronnie had any thought about his making a bid for the presidency at this time. Lyn Nofziger, Michael Deaver, Holmes Tuttle, numerous other members of his staff, close associates, and his children—Maureen, Michael, and Patti (in their separate books)—claim this was not true. Reagan planned to mount a campaign, but not until he felt he was ready, and he did not think one term as governor of California would qualify him. Nancy went along with this, but her eye was always on a future time when Ronnie would make his move. Social and charity duties delegated to the governor's wife concerned her far less than protecting her husband's larger interests. There is no question but that she personally looked into the backgrounds of the men and women who were to be chosen for Reagan's staff and closely monitored those who were key to him. Reagan was an independent thinker and did not always take her advice. Still, he did hear her out and respected her opinion.

The gaudy red and gold room that housed the state senate quickly became a battle arena. The room, described at the time as "reminiscent of a luxurious Gay Nineties house of prostitution," had been redecorated two years earlier at taxpayer expense and to the politicians' own tastes, "which ran to shiny silk suits, two-tone shoes, and martini and steak sandwich lunches paid for by special-interest representatives," one observer wrote. With its red shutters and "red and gold columns topped by gold leaf and the big senatorial chairs covered in bright blue," the room gave credence to Reagan's campaign claim that "they've been in power so long, these professional politicians, that we're beginning to see a degeneration of moral standards."[11]

The most powerful man in the state legislature was Jesse "Big Daddy" Unruh, nicknamed for the domineering father in Tennessee Williams's play *Cat on a Hot Tin Roof*. The forty-four-year-old Unruh, Democratic speaker of the assembly, was a towering giant of a man, built like a football guard. He had just lost a hundred pounds and still remained a formidable hulk. Born dirt-poor in Texas, he had raised himself by his striped suspender straps, acquiring knowledge, polish, grace, and wily skill as a politician. He had been John F. Kennedy's strongest ally in California during the 1960 presidential campaign and was looking to the next gubernatorial election to move into the very mansion that the current first lady so scorned.

Nancy was convinced that she had done the right thing in moving out of the governor's mansion and furnishing her rented home with donated furniture. Unruh immediately turned this into a vendetta. Nancy was so incensed by Unruh's attack on her that she set up a press conference to combat his accusations, revealing how much rent they were paying, and that all items donated for their use were given, not to them, but to the state of California.

Unruh dropped the issue, but he remained a bulldog opponent to Reagan and his policies. He was too powerful for Nancy to do much about, although she most certainly would have—had it been possible. This was not the case with unfortunate staffers who she felt did not have her husband's best interests at heart. "Dismissing an incompetent aide or even dropping a consultant was anathema to Reagan," recalled Michael Deaver, his Washington-minded Sacramento aide. "Deep down, Reagan disliked personal conflict and would avoid it like the plague. . . . This quirk would have become a significant hindrance for Reagan if Nancy had not stepped in to fill the vacuum." He added, Nancy was "no Eleanor Roosevelt or Hillary Clinton. She didn't assume her strong role in politics because of a political agenda. Her only agenda was Ronald Reagan, and there was nobody alive who better knew his strengths and weaknesses."[12]

"Nancy had her own little 'secret service' going. We called it NBI—Nancy's Bureau of Investigation. She was always on the lookout for people who she thought were not giving their all to Reagan, or who she thought were duplicitous, and who she simply did not like or trust," another close staffer says. "She never fired anyone directly. She obviously did not have the authority. But she would ring up Holmes Tuttle or Michael Deaver to do the deed."[13]

"Reagan always got to don the white hat while Nancy was portrayed as the Wicked Witch of the West," Deaver countered. "I know it wounded her deeply: she never got used to reading about her alleged heavy-handedness. History owes her one, though, because if she hadn't stepped up, Ronald Reagan would never have become governor of California let alone president of the United States. He knew this better than anyone."[14]

Deaver, bespectacled, small of stature, and balding, worked closer to Reagan than anyone else on his staff. He was young and respectful, but he also held his boss in awe; he believed, as Reagan did, that his honor was beyond reproach. Reagan took this several levels higher. God, he would say, was directing his life, and it was He who had sent him Nancy to help him succeed in his true destiny. From his youth, Reagan had seen himself as a hero—as a lifeguard in Dixon notching on a log the number of lives he had saved from drowning and as a student leader at Eureka College gaining a more liberal campus life for his classmates

("I almost felt like Lincoln emancipating the slaves," he wrote his then girlfriend Margaret Cleaver, a minister's daughter who would later reject him).[15] For her part, Nancy did everything within her power to codify that idea. He trusted her implicitly. They were like two halves of the same gene that had been fused together.

Although she could get a staffer fired, Nancy could do very little to rid Reagan of Jesse Unruh or his other opponents in the state legislature. Unruh not only had control of the assembly, he held the balance of power in the Senate. Reagan's four top lieutenants were Philip Battaglia, his dedicated executive secretary, with ambitions for his own political rise through Reagan (other staffers secretly called him Governor Battaglia); Vernon Sturgeon, a former member of the Senate still bitter over his recent defeat; Jack Lindsay, an enthusiastic neophyte at politics willing to do battle whenever called to arms; and Paul Beck, Reagan's press secretary, an ex-reporter with a lot of moxie. These men would privately corner the Democrats they felt might swing their vote and promise them backing for some of their favored programs. In some cases judgeships were offered for their appointees.

There was much negotiating going on in the back of the Senate. Many of Reagan's bills were passed, but not without compromise. Hungry for victory, Reagan's lieutenants ignored his campaign promise never to make a political deal. The most problematic bill in his first year of office was that of abortion reform. A ninety-five-year-old law that allowed abortions only to save the mother's life had been redrawn by Senator Anthony C. Beilenson, a young Democrat from Beverly Hills, to include recent abortion reforms in North Carolina and Colorado that could prevent the birth of a potentially deformed child. Reagan was morally against such a bill, unable, as he told the legislature, to justify taking the life of an unborn child "simply on the supposition that it is going to be less than a perfect human being, because I don't see very far . . . from that to some day deciding after birth that we will sort out those people who should be allowed to live or not, and I don't see any difference between that and what Hitler tried to do."[16]

After much dispute and new provisions added to terminate pregnancies caused by incest or rape, or if the mother's mental health was in jeopardy, the bill was passed. At the last moment Reagan had second thoughts about this last provision, fearing it could be exploited by a pro-abortion doctor. But the bill had been rushed to the Senate for approval before he could argue this point. His tax bill was also passed after much negotiation and important alterations. "He would boldly announce a controversial program," Bill Boyarsky noted, "quietly modify it in the face of criticism and then hail the compromise as a complete victory."[17] Reagan called this "keeping an open mind," an approach that would be key to the development of his political career.

He looked amazingly in good shape, but his health suffered with the increased pressures, backroom fighting, and the working through of moral issues that his decisions would provoke. He suffered stomach spasms that appeared to be caused by an ulcer, flew down to Los Angeles in the summer to have a bladder stone removed, and had a nonmalignant growth on his lip removed as well, Nancy by his side. (This last was the first of many skin tumors, some of which would prove to be malignant, that Reagan would have removed. According to his doctors, the source of his problem had been his years of exposure to the sun. He also had testosterone shots "to boost his energy" every two weeks over the last six months of his first term.)

After the surgery on Reagan's lip, Nancy rushed home to tend to Skipper, who had been beaten up by three bullyboys because, she told the press, he came to school in a chauffeured car. Patti, who spent the summer at home, was doubtful that this was the case. She believed it had more to do with her father's stand on the antiwar marches and riots at Berkeley. Although Reagan contended that Johnson's policies in Vietnam were wrong, he held war protestors in disdain. This was not a conflict in his mind. Even if the war was wrong, Americans were risking their lives and must be supported. In one widely quoted interview he advocated the use of "the Bomb" to end the war. Patti said that Skipper confided that while the boys were punching his face they were shouting, "Warmonger!" but Nancy forbade her or Skipper ever to tell their father.

"Emotionally and physically," Patti had said, "my mother and I have been at war for a very long time, but spiritually, we've understood each other . . . Both of us have used drugs, anger, and defensiveness as a buffer against pain. And both of us have been capable of reaching out to one another for periods of time . . . That summer was one of rare cease-fires."[18]

Mother and daughter each had their explanations for what caused their lifelong combative relationship. There is little doubt that Patti very much wanted her mother's love, and when she received it was happy, although Nancy's love always came at a price. That summer Patti was accepting her mother's conditions. She did not discuss her dissenting opinions with her father on Vietnam, Berkeley, or student uprisings. She dressed appropriately and did not bring any hippie friends to the house. Nancy did not discuss drugs with Patti, but when her daughter asked her why she was taking two Valium pills, she replied, "I have a head-ache." Valium is an antianxiety medication. It appears Reagan did not realize that the pills Nancy took on a daily basis were not aspirin but a prescribed drug. She also took appetite suppressants, which she passed off as vitamins. Patti would sneak into her mother's bathroom and clip prescription pills from her medicine cabinet. It seems unlikely that Nancy was not aware this was happening, as Patti has stated that she filched rather large quantities to take back with her to school, an amount her mother most certainly would have missed. Yet, to confront Patti would have been to admit to taking drugs. Patti's great difficulties with her mother had to do with Nancy's sanctimonious hypocrisy.

The family détente was shaken when Maureen announced that she was divorcing David Sills. This could not be kept from Reagan. "He thought we could save the marriage," Maureen wrote. "He liked David. And he liked his children to work through their problems to find the best possible solution." He asked her "to at least consider going to David and trying to work things out." Maureen explained that they had grown apart, "particularly since he had made the transition into civilian life." They simply "no longer found each other interesting." Reagan could not understand this. "Six months ago you were in love with David and now you aren't?"[19] It did not make sense to him, nor that Maureen was un-willing to try to make a go of it.

She filed suit for divorce and tried to avoid any confrontation with her father. "I even avoided the telephone," she said. "It was easier for me to stay away from members of my family than to have to defend my decision every time we got together."[20]

Michael was still struggling to gain his father's attention and approval, which, now that he was governor, was even more difficult. He entered a two-day race for the Outboard World Championship, putting together a team of two assistants and himself and borrowing a boat and three Mercury engines. Reagan was much against his son's racing, certain he was bound to get hurt. Yet Michael pushed forward with his plan. During the race the boat almost fell apart and nearly crashed, but Michael won the race, a true endurance test, by a lap.

"The next day the papers read 'Reagan's Son Wins Outboard Championship.' I felt that I had finally done something significant. I was certain that when Dad read about it in the papers he would say, 'Doggone it, Mike, you're a world champion. I guess you've finally found your niche,' and he, Nancy or Mom would welcome me with open arms because of my success. I never heard from them."[21]

Reagan was not only having problems with his own children but with young people on California university campuses. What had been started in 1950 by President Truman as a thirty-five-man military advisory group to aid the French in their struggle to maintain colonial power in Vietnam had escalated by 1965 to a full-scale war as President Johnson deployed 184,000 United States troops to the area. Three years later, the war was still grinding mercilessly on; America had almost 525,000 men in Vietnam, and massive antiwar demonstrations had spread across the nation and onto the campuses of colleges and universities. A significant number of these students, Charles E. Goodell wrote, "thought that the war and the draft required to sustain it were illegal under the Constitution. Others thought it an immoral and unjust war . . . this led to civil disobedience, repressive laws, and repressive law enforcement."[22] Only a month before Reagan was elected, ten thousand University of California students at Berkeley had faced a fierce police barricade as they marched toward the Oakland Induction Center in opposition to the war. Hours passed before they were finally turned back and dispersed. As governor, Reagan inherited a period of civil disobedience and university riots that was unprecedented in California's history.

The university's president at the time was Dr. Clark Kerr. Reagan blamed him for many of the school's problems as well as some of those he encountered upon his election. Reagan had proposed cutting higher education budgets by ten percent and instituting tuition in the state university system. Kerr was publicly defiant of these proposals, "which cast considerable doubt on the credibility of the Reagan administration," Goodell added.[23] As governor, Reagan was president of the state board of regents. He attended his first meeting in February 1968 at the state-wide university administration building, which looked across the street to the Berkeley campus. Kerr believed that Reagan and a majority of the board had already decided to fire him. That was on a Friday. The following Monday, Kerr's prediction became a reality. Dr. Kerr was gone, and Charles J. Hitch became Berkeley's new president. Kerr's dismissal only fired up an already incendiary situation. Adopting a hard line toward student dissent, Reagan also continued to press for cuts in education.

"As governor," he said in one of his weekly radio broadcasts, "I am determined to maintain and protect [California's state-supported higher education] for those currently attending one of the many campuses, for those who will attend in the future and for those who foot the bill—you and I."[24]

He quickly became the symbol of everything the students distrusted in government. "He was the amazing plastic man, out-of-touch, remote, the perfect foil," former Berkeley student activist Michael Edwards explained. "He didn't precipitate it. The situation predated his governorship. Student rebellion had erupted at Berkeley in the fall of 1964. By the time Reagan took office, protest groups were already formed, forged by the civil rights and anti-Vietnam movements and the cultural, economic, and sexual revolutions. It was a time of worldwide student uprisings—Prague, the barricades in Paris. The Black Panthers were a growing force, and one of its founders, Eldridge Cleaver, ran for president in 1968 on the ticket of the Peace and Freedom Party. There were sit-ins and love-ins and an alarming number of student arrests. Young women were burning their bras while young men set fire to their draft cards."

Edwards continues: "Reagan became a welcome foil for the young intellectual groups at Berkeley. He was a B-movie actor who came across without any academic experience. To the student body at Berkeley he represented corporate interests. The regents also represented corporate interests. But they had more control than the governor or even Clark Kerr, the president. Reagan became an easy target, and he was used for that purpose."[25]

In the early months of 1968 Patti was in Arizona, "far from the fray."[26] Nonetheless, she fantasized about being "at Berkeley, protesting the war." During the idyllic summer that she spent with her mother, she was also developing a strong loathing for her father's position on Berkeley and student dissenters. When, in the fall of 1969, she was planning to apply to Northwestern University, Reagan had research done on the school. He learned that the student body president was a "radical black girl named Eva Jefferson. . . . Just be aware of that and stay away from her," he warned. Patti returned to her room and wrote herself a reminder: "look up Eva Jefferson. . . . I was standing fast against my father's politics, and I knew I would oppose him on every front."

Eva Jefferson turned out to be "soft-spoken, intelligent and seemed to be respected by everyone."[27] She was also greatly responsible for keeping student protests at Northwestern nonviolent at the time of the Kent State shootings, on May 18, 1970, when Ohio National Guardsmen fired into a crowd of students opposing the U.S. incursion into Cambodia, killing two young women and two men and wounding eight others. The incident followed Reagan's statement in his weekly press conference that "if it takes a bloodbath, then, let's get it over with." This drew fire from U.S. Secretary of Education Robert Finch, who censored Reagan for rhetoric that he claimed had "heated the climate which led to killings." Patti had to take a lot of flak from her fellow students because of her father's stand on such matters. Many of her classmates would not let her forget that Reagan had also written at an earlier time that, if America wanted to win the Vietnam War, "full technological resources should be employed"[28] and suggested that America had made a huge mistake in "assuring the enemy of our intention not to use [the nuclear bomb]."

Patti's hostility to her father's recurring statements about student dissent grew, and her summer détente with her mother began to disintegrate almost immediately upon her return to school. It wasn't helped by an incident during Patti's first year at Northwestern. A black man had entered Patti's dormitory with a box of "hot pants" (sexy shorts) that he was peddling. Another student called security, and the man was arrested, over Patti's objections. Immediately, she was called into the campus security office and ordered to remain with a woman member of the staff for "security reasons." Patti was initially furious, then desperate.

Late that night, Patti thought about slashing her wrists. When Nancy called her the next morning, she was alarmed at the distraction in her daughter's voice. Not long after, Nancy rang up again to announce that she was flying with Frank Sinatra (who had recently turned his back on the liberal wing of the Democratic Party and who believed Reagan had presidential potential) in his private plane to see her that night and for her to meet them for dinner at the Drake Hotel.

"Over dinner, Frank Sinatra said a few things about law and order, and citizens standing up for their rights. And my mother added that you can't let people influence you. . . . Then they both got tired of it and just talked to each other for the rest of the meal, which was fine with me because I thought the whole thing was ridiculous."[29]

In Kitty Kelley's 1991 scandal-oriented biography of Nancy, she suggested that Nancy and Sinatra had had an affair. "People can have dinner together, fly on a plane together and not be sleeping together. And I don't think they were. Not then, or ever," Patti countered.

Sinatra was always one to come to a friend's aid. He was almost belligerently loyal. He also made grand anonymous gestures, rescuing friends from debt and danger if he was able and believed he should. Not long after his trip to Chicago with Nancy, having learned that the late Judy Garland's remains had not been interred for over a year because funds were lacking to do so, he quietly stepped in to cover all expenses.[30] He would not have hesitated to offer Nancy assistance to ease her mind about her daughter. That was the kind of man he was. He also was not above sleeping with a good-looking woman if the opportunity presented itself. While it is true that Nancy had once had a terrific crush on Sinatra, she was unquestionably deeply in love with Reagan and ever mindful of his future and her place in it. Sinatra had recently expressed interest in supporting Reagan for future higher office if he should decide to seek it. Nancy would have found great satisfaction in his offer of help in this family matter, but it would not have suited her agenda to jeopardize her good name and Reagan's career for a night in bed with Sinatra or any other man. She was now a woman obsessed with her husband's status and his future, believing that he was of true heroic character. Her current astrologer had reaffirmed this with the prediction that, if they both remained true to each other and to their purpose, Reagan would rise to greatness.

This forecast preceded a day in the spring of the same year when, as Reagan recalled, "several leaders of the state Republican party came to see me and said they wanted me to run for the Republican presidential nomination on the California primary ballot the following June as a favorite-son candidate [to avert] a repeat of the kind of bloody battle between moderates and conservatives that split the party so badly in 1964." There were to be three major candidates in 1968—Richard Nixon, Nelson Rockefeller, and George Romney. Reagan insisted that he had been governor for such a short time "it would look ridiculous if I ran for president."

They explained that a "favorite-son candidate is not the same thing as a *real* candidate. If you enter the primary as a favorite son, the major candidates won't enter the race, so we'll avoid a disastrous primary fight; as governor, you'll win the primary, but that only means you'll head the delegation to the convention."[31]

Reagan discussed this with Nancy, who agreed that to run as a favorite son was the right thing to do. He won in the California Primary as predicted (the next day Robert Kennedy was assassinated). For the next two months he and Nancy traveled the speech circuit, sometimes in Sinatra's private jet. "Well, when the balloting took place [at the Republican national convention]," Reagan recalled, "I got a sizable number of votes behind Nixon and Rockefeller, but Nixon had the clear majority and so I ran up to the front of the hall and jumped on the platform and asked the chairman for permission to address the convention." Once on the podium he made a new motion for his votes to be cast to nominate Richard Nixon by acclamation, which was done. He claimed he was relieved because he knew he "wasn't ready to be president." But, by announcing his candidacy, he received national media coverage and bolstered his credibility for a future run for the presidency, which the Republican party assumed—believing that if Nixon won he would occupy the presidency for two terms—would be in 1976.

Reagan pressed forward with his work in Sacramento. Nancy, now nationally recognized for her campaign skills, appeared to be more agreeable to Nofziger's requests for interviews and public appearances as the governor's lady. Even if Reagan claimed he had no thoughts for the future, beyond running for reelection when his first term as governor of California ended, his Kitchen Cabinet and close staff members all believed that, in a matter of time, if they were patient and played their cards right, Reagan would follow Nixon into the White House. Maureen agreed with this. Michael had no opinion. Patti was appalled and desperately wished for it not to happen. And Nancy? Nancy smiled noncommittally and said that she could not speak for her husband, but that they were both very happy to be back in California and that she was very proud to be the wife of the governor of that grand state.

CHAPTER EIGHT

THE YEARS BETWEEN

Nancy soldiered on through Ronnie's bid for reelection, bearing the jibes of his opponent, Speaker of the Assembly Jesse Unruh, with lip-biting control worthy of a bronze medal. "Sometimes," Ronnie wrote her on March 4, 1970, the day of their eighteenth wedding anniversary, "it must seem that the world is made up of Jess Plain Jess, Campus Slobs and Legislators—but that is only the outer layer. Underneath is the place where I think about you round the clock and across the calendar. . . ."[1] Such constant avowals of Ronnie's deep love for her gave Nancy the strength to get past her hurt at the shoddy way she was being treated by the press and by her husband's political opponent.

Some help in securing the large margin of votes won by Reagan in the 1970 election for his second term as governor can be attributed to Frank Sinatra. After supporting the Democratic party for years and campaigning for Edmund Pat Brown and against Reagan in his first run for the governorship, Sinatra now became cochairman of Democrats for Reagan, appearing throughout the state at political benefits that added over half-a-million dollars in campaign funds. Sinatra's close friends were shocked by his betrayal of his earlier, more liberal loyalties. In the past he had suffered some bitter snubs by the Democratic party after he campaigned ardently for both Kennedy and Johnson. They had turned away from him after their elections because of his well-known connection to the Mafia (which in Kennedy's case was more dangerous, due to his own private brush with Mafia members through Judith Campbell, one of his mistresses). Despite this, Sinatra extended his hand to Hubert Humphrey in his bid to carry the Democratic torch for President Johnson when he decided not to run in 1968. When Humphrey lost the election to Nixon, he cut Sinatra, and again the press insinuated that Sinatra's underworld connections had been the cause. Sinatra turned fifty-five in 1970—which was not his best personal year. He was rancorous at the treatment he had received from the Democrats, for whom he had worked hard all his adult life. His third wife, nineteen-year-old Mia Farrow (actress daughter of Maureen O'Sullivan and director John Farrow), had recently divorced him. To add to his mounting depression, his father had died, his close friendships with the members of the famous Rat Pack had soured, and his last two films—*Lady in Cement* and *Dirty Dingus McGee*—had been spectacular failures.

Sinatra could not abide being a loser. He believed, as many others did, that Reagan was a winner with good odds for making it into the Oval Office. This time Sinatra *needed* assurance that he would be a favored guest. He had never much liked Reagan—"a boring man" he had said about him. But Nancy had developed a friendship with Sinatra over the years, and she was especially sympathetic to his current unhappy state of mind. Nancy was (and remained) a dedicated and compulsive telephone addict, finding it easier to discuss the most intimate matters with friends by this means than face to face, and she was at the other end of the telephone with Sinatra almost daily during this time. No doubt she was pleased that a man whom she had always admired had befriended her. If that sounds naive, perhaps it was. But Nancy was also smart enough to figure out that, despite his questionable associations, Sinatra's endorsement of Ronnie could pay off in swing votes from the Democrats and generate campaign funds.

Branded by Reagan "the tax-and-spend liberal who from the beginning had opposed our reforms tooth and nail," Unruh lost the battle forty-five percent to Reagan's fifty-three percent. "I think the [voters] made it clear that they wanted the reforms to continue," Reagan wrote. His goal for his second term was to reform "California's bloated welfare program [and to end that] cycle of dependency that robs men and women of their dignity [and to] rescue some of those people from what FDR had called the 'narcotic' of welfare."

"If California were a nation," Reagan liked to say, "it would have been the seventh-ranking economic power in the world."[2] Reagan had always been a man in need of a platform, and being California's governor gave that to him. Some men exude power simply by the way they carry themselves and enter a room. Not so Reagan. He did not become a dominant figure until he mounted a stage or spoke into a microphone. At those times he was mesmerizing, and in the age of television this was (and remains) one of the most potent means of winning political office.

Reagan's powerful stage presence never quite transferred itself onto the screen when he was portraying a role other than the one he had created for himself. His quick, retentive memory allowed him to give a speech of an hour's duration without the aid of a written text. He spoke with an earnestness and in a voice twanged by his midwestern roots, pauses always in the right places, eyes straight ahead, as though he were speaking face to face with each member of his audience, and he had a way of stopping to say something amusing that sounded as if it were completely offhand, unrehearsed, often a jape at himself. He knew how to use his hands for emphasis or to feign humility and to employ a microphone to amplify or soften his voice, so that in a huge arena he could seem to be speaking intimately and in a small space rather than pontificating. It was when Reagan found his ability to communicate to an audience in this manner that his true talent—and potential—emerged.

The one time he lost his composure before the cameras was during a weekly news conference in 1971. Rose King, a single mother and journalism student at Cal State in Sacramento, had dug up the Reagans' last two tax returns and discovered that they had paid no state tax. She tipped off a reporter. "Is this true?" the reporter asked him on camera. Reagan's face uncharacteristically sagged, and he pulled back as though to avoid a physical attack. "You know something," he finally said, in that cowboy-on-the-range voice he would often use, "I don't actually know whether I did [pay taxes] or not," and rushed on to the next question by another reporter, who seemed thrown by his predecessor's inquiry.

An explanation issued to the press later that day stated that "because of business reverses caused by losses from his cattle herd," Reagan had not owed state taxes, although he had paid federal taxes.[3]

Reagan vigorously campaigned in California for both of Nixon's presidential elections (1968, 1972), and the president showed his appreciation by sending him and Nancy abroad four times on goodwill missions during 1971–1972. Except for one short visit to Paris during her college years, Nancy had not traveled outside the United States. These overseas trips, sanctioned by the president and paid for by the government, introduced her to a wider world, and did so first class, while giving Reagan a higher foreign profile. He and Nancy met the heads of state of eighteen countries. They flew on a luxurious private jet closely resembling Air Force One. Skipper, now entering his teens and preferring to be called Ron, accompanied them on those trips that did not interfere with his school schedule. In Manila the Reagans were guests of President Ferdinand Marcos and his wife, the infamous shoe collector, Imelda. Reagan was the first foreign official other than a head of state to be formally received by Japan's Emperor Hirohito. In England the Reagans stayed with the Annenbergs, Walter having recently been appointed American ambassador to the Court of St. James's. The Reagans' other destinations as ambassadors-at-large included Ireland, Denmark, Belgium, France, Spain, Italy, and Australia.

Nancy was enjoying her role as first lady of California and as the wife of a man now looked upon with international respect. However vehement their public denials, privately Nancy, Neil Reagan, Maureen, and Reagan's staff and supporters looked upon a possible future elected stay in the White House with much enthusiasm. The remaining three Reagan children viewed such an eventuality with fear and hostility, knowing it would only further intrude upon their privacy and their lives. With their father as governor, not only were they constantly and invasively "watched" by the media, their parents seemed to have grown simultaneously more distant to them and—in Nancy's case at least—even more controlling.

During Reagan's second term as governor, Nancy's public image as "grasping," "mean-tempered," "tight-fisted," and controlling was formed by a media sharp-set for a news lead. She was being projected as the one calling the shots for Reagan, constantly pressing his lieutenants into action, responsible for firings and hirings, and expecting her position to accord her special privileges and a flow of freebies—designer clothes to wear on public occasions, household items, and beauty treatments among them. Ever-frequent swipes and outright attacks on her appeared in the press, especially the *Sacramento Bee* and *Newsweek* magazine. Jokes were made about her on late-night television. (On a Johnny Carson program satirist Mort Sahl led off with "Somebody asked Nancy Reagan if she understood poor people. 'Only if they speak slowly,' " he said she replied.) Whereas Reagan's appearance—his love of the outdoors, his ability to be charming and somewhat humble seemingly at his will—won him an advantage, Nancy's primness, her demand for perfection, her often icy tone, worked against her. Because of this, some members of the press were able to undermine Reagan by targeting his wife.

"She's been subjected to a bum rap," Reagan wrote. "She was accused of being a kind of 'shadow governor' . . . with some sort of undue influence over me. Well, that's another myth that has no foundation in reality. It's true that I'll sometimes use her as a sounding board, but Nancy has never tried to intervene on matters of policy or affect the important decisions I've had to make."[4]

Reagan's staff, as well as Nancy's, saw her in a much more manipulative light. No doubt many men in high office discuss their major job-oriented decisions with their wives. Nancy was not particularly interested in Reagan's—or the state's—welfare, environmental, education, or tax programs. What concerned her was how Ronnie's stature would be affected by an association, a viewpoint, or an appointment. There was no question of her standing by him no matter what problems might loom, but she worked diligently to dig out and get rid of any rocks that he might stumble over.

Before his second term as governor he dismissed all suggestions (and there were many) that he run for a third term (as was permitted in California); both he and Nancy believed that if he lost that election, his standing with the Republican electorate would be weakened. In 1972 Nixon seemed at the height of his power in the months before and just after his reelection, and the Reagans closely aligned themselves with him. Members of Reagan's Kitchen Cabinet and his staff, Nofziger and Deaver among them, felt strongly that the president, who had just carried the most states ever, forty-nine, in a race for the Oval Office, and just weeks after his second inaugural had overseen the peace pact between North Vietnam and South Vietnam, ending the longest war in American history, might be predisposed to endorsing Reagan as the Republican nominee in 1976. Social letters crisscrossed the country, warm notes evincing a strong friendship: "Nancy sends her love"; "Pat and I look forward to seeing you and Nancy soon." Nor did the Reagans ever challenge Nixon's complaints of the "conspiracy of the press [against him], the hostility of the Establishment [against him], the flatulence of the Georgetown set. . . ."[5]

Then, as the devastating events of 1973—Watergate and its aftermath—piled one upon the other and Nixon's authority began deteriorating—the Reagans' good-friends letters ended. "In September, 1973," Nixon's Secretary of State, Henry Kissinger wrote, "the issue of whether Nixon should surrender tape recordings from his office had moved inexorably through the courts, and was reaching a climax at the very moment war [the Yom Kippur War between Syria and Egypt and Israel] broke out. The first indictments spawned by Watergate had been handed down, including one against John Ehrlichman. Campaign aide Donald Segretti had pleaded guilty to three misdemeanors relating to 'dirty tricks' during the 1972 presidential race. On top of all this, Nixon was about to lose his vice president, Spiro Agnew, in a scandal concerning alleged payoffs when Agnew was governor of Maryland." Agnew resigned on October 10. This was followed on October 20 by the famous Saturday night massacre with the firing of Special Prosecutor Archibald Cox and the resignation of Attorney General Elliot Richardson.[6]

According to Reagan biographer Lou Cannon, despite his privately voiced and vehement disapproval of Nixon's ongoing involvement in Watergate, Reagan publicly "stuck with Nixon when it mattered." This was long after his advisers had concluded that the president was a liar and a lost cause.[7]

Reagan remained silent, as he did in public when the subject of

Watergate was introduced. He firmly believed in the worn adage that "Thou shalt not speak ill of a fellow Republican [unless they were candidates for the same office]." But he told Patti, "Nixon should have destroyed the tapes—all of them."[8]

Finally, in August 1974, Reagan publicly stated that Nixon had "deceived the country and Congress about the Watergate coverup." After Nixon's resignation and before incoming President Gerald Ford's pardon of his predecessor, Reagan urged Ford that Nixon "not be prosecuted. . . . The punishment of resignation certainly is more than adequate for the crime."[9] Reagan was fully aware that to further blacken Nixon's name would also be an assault on the Republican party—and on his own chances up the line. Some may call this hypocrisy on a grand scale, others a wise political tactic. But Reagan looked on the office of president of the United States with too much awe to willfully besmirch it.

In her memoir *My Turn* Nancy vividly recalled her last day in 1975 as California's first lady as she waited in their near-empty house for Ronnie to come and collect her so that they could start on their way back home to the Pacific Palisades. "Suddenly, I found myself sitting alone in the house. Except for our bed, all the furniture was gone. The sun was setting [and] I sat on the bed and looked out into the garden, which was so lovely, with all of the camellias in bloom. We'd come to love that old house.

"As it grew darker outside . . . I thought, So this is how it ends. Our eight years of politics are over. True, some of Ronnie's advisers were talking about Ronnie's running for president in 1976, but I didn't really expect that to happen. As we left Sacramento that night, I honestly believed we were leaving politics forever."[10]

Reagan needed time to think things out. He missed Yearling Row, the outdoor life, the horses, the closeness to nature. He discussed this with Nancy, and they agreed that they would start looking for a ranch to replace it. "The previous eight years had changed both of us," he wrote, but not his need to be able to roam free. They searched for several months and finally found what he referred to as "a new love."[11] It was originally called Tip Top Ranch and it was located a short distance north of Santa Barbara, and it was Ronnie's, not Nancy's, new love. Nancy was at heart a city girl, but she was always a willing partner in anything that she thought would make Ronnie happy.

To reach the ranch the Reagans had to drive up a treacherous, narrow, winding road high into the Santa Ynez mountains, whose granite peaks rose like a grey-white curtain above the Pacific Ocean. "The road was so steep and the area so primitive," Reagan recalled of their first trip to see the ranch with their friends Betty and Bill Wilson, "I thought, well, maybe somebody's got a house up here they call a ranch, but it sure looks like goat country to me. Where would you ride a horse?"[12]

Seven miles of precarious S-turns later, the road straightened and the car was surrounded by a stand of giant oak trees. "Then we turned off the road, went through a gate, and started down another narrow road," he added. Finally, Bill Wilson pulled to a stop at the edge of a large green meadow. There, across the great expanse, "rugged hills stretching far beyond it," was a small adobe house, more of worker's cottage really.[13] Reagan was in outdoorsman's heaven. At this elevation there were several hundred acres (the entire property consisted of 688 acres) ideal for breeding and riding horses. There was no denying the natural beauty of the place, nor in Ronnie's pure joy as he walked in long strides, yards ahead of Nancy, crossing the verdant meadow to the humble house.

They bought it and renamed it Rancho del Cielo, "Ranch in the Sky." The first records of property are dated 1872, the same year the prospering nearby oceanside city of Santa Barbara had completed construction on an elaborate wharf to which ships and side-wheel steamers could tie. One of the laborers brought in from Mexico to work on the wharf had purchased the land for thirty-two dollars and built his adobe home by transporting heavy supplies up the precipitous inclines by donkey. His expectation had been to raise cattle. But a catastrophic drought ended his dream. Despite changes in ownership, few improvements had been made until the late nineteen-forties, when modern plumbing and electricity and a workable kitchen had been installed. The original owner had been a good craftsman: the foundation of the house was strong, the adobe walls made thick enough to securely support the tile roof. The tiny building had survived a major earthquake in 1925 without so much as a crack. Reagan thought of the house as a survivor, as he often thought of himself, and he was awed by the magnificent panorama that it commanded.

Nancy saw the place with a more realistic eye. It had not been lived in full-time for many years, and the previous owners had added an unseemly screened porch with a corrugated aluminum roof and walls covered with green plastic siding. The bedroom was only nine by fourteen feet, the windows small and high up so that sunlight was mostly blocked out. Nothing daunted Reagan. He viewed their new property as a magnificent challenge and set to work almost immediately to make it comfortable enough for Nancy to want to spend time there. The monstrous porch was pulled down, and a large L-shaped room with a massive fireplace and floor-to-ceiling windows that took in the awe-inspiring view was constructed where it had stood. A new roof of simulated Spanish tiles was added to maintain the appearance of its nineteenth-century origins.

With the help of two friends, both many years his junior—his driver and personal aide Barney Barnett and former security guard Dennis LeBlanc—Reagan knocked out walls to enlarge the bedroom and added full-length windows to let in the light and the view. He finally called in a contractor to finish the work and construct an extra bedroom and bath. There was a dramatic change in Reagan when he was laboring on the ranch. He was at one with the outdoors, a truly happy man. He would strip to the waist on hot days, Western hat set on his head to screen the sun as he worked. It was hard to believe that he was a man in his sixties. His arms were muscular, his shoulders squared, his stomach flat. The sun had bronzed him, the physical work whipped him into shape. He had, indeed, found a new love, and Nancy was smart enough to add her enthusiasm to his. She even joined him in his labor on the house.

"We'd get a fire going," he recalled of Nancy's assistance in putting in the floors, "and we'd lean tiles against the screen to soften them up. They'd get very rubbery and we'd grab those and put them on the floor—feed them in while we put fresh ones up there to soften up. When the house was built I guess they didn't have square measures and things [of course, they did, but a poor man might not have been able to afford sophisticated tools]. There wasn't a square corner in the [entire] house.

So when it came to tiling, we had to figure out a way to lay the bulk of the tile and then, around the edge, cut the tile to fit the different widths that were left."[14]

During the first year of work on the house, Reagan, the two men, and frequently Nancy drove up to the ranch and back in the Reagans' red 1969 Ford station wagon for the day, a two-hour drive each way, leaving at "sun-up and returning at sun-down." Work progressed slowly without a team of professional craftsmen. Either Dennis or Barney would drive to and from while Reagan sat with Nancy in the rear seat. Going, she usually tried to get an extra hour's sleep while he would be writing in longhand on lined pads, seemingly undisturbed by the car's circuitous descent to or from the mountain and the traffic on Highway 101. He had been making speeches and contributing articles to publications.

At Rancho del Cielo, Reagan said, he felt that he was "on a cloud looking down at the world." From the house they gazed "across the meadow at a peak crowned with oak trees and beyond it, mountains that stretch toward the horizon." A short ride on horseback and you could "watch boats cruising across the Santa Barbara Channel, then turn your head and see the Santa Ynez Valley unfold like a huge wilderness am-phitheater before your eyes."[15] Despite his middle-America roots, there was something of the old Western cowboy deep down in Reagan. When he wanted to think something out, he would get on his favorite horse, a beautiful black colt he called Little Man (because he was very big) and ride out on one of the many winding trails on the property, and when he reached a plateau stop and look out at the world "God had wrought. . . . I think people who haven't tried it might be surprised at how easy your thoughts can come together when you're on the back of a horse riding with nothing else to do but think about the decision ahead of you."[16]

With Dennis and Barney he built the tack barn where he kept his extensive collection of rifles and pistols along with saddles and outdoor wear. "When we were building the place there were groundhogs and gophers out there," LeBlanc recalled. "'Round a quarter to five, when the sun starts goin' down, those guys would start comin' up and we'd go out and sit on the fence and flick them off."[17] This was done to insure that a horse would not stumble and fall if he had not anticipated a gopher hole where previously there had been none. But Reagan loved guns and was an expert marksman.

Once the house became habitable, the Reagans would spend several days at a time there. Routine seldom varied. Reagan rose at dawn because he liked to see the sun come up ("God's gift, not to miss," he would say). He often rode in the early morning. By nine he was at the tack barn to meet "the guys," Barry and Dennis. There was the work on the house and a fence to be built from old telephone poles that had to be hauled up the mountain and then axed (one of his favorite activities) into proper lengths. He helped Nancy with making a simple lunch—fruit, cheese, cold meats, fresh bread brought up by one of the guys from a bakery near the bottom of the mountain, beans, salad, occasionally macaroni and cheese (his personal favorite). At 12:15 to the second he would ring a bell hanging outside the kitchen door, and the guys would join them for lunch outdoors or in, depending on the weather.

Friends and family were excluded. In this stage of construction work, the ranch was the Reagans' retreat. Nancy rode with Ronnie at times and worked beside him, ignoring broken nails and putting aside her personal discomfort. He was enamored of the wildlife that roamed within sight—often closer than Nancy was comfortable with—deer, coyotes, bobcats. She controlled her fear of the ranch's large snake population—rattlers, water and gopher snakes. There was a telephone and a small black-and-white TV set. After a quiet dinner for just the two of them, he would sit in his favorite chair with pad and pen and write as she watched television. He had a habit of glancing up and looking her way from time to time and of smiling contentedly. By nine P.M. he was usually asleep, and she would have to wake him up to go to bed (twin beds tied together).

If Nancy was bored at the ranch, she never admitted it. The truth was, what made Ronnie happy meant more to her than her own inclinations. She still had plenty of time to spend at the house in the Palisades and with her very social circle of friends, for in 1975 Mike Deaver and Peter Hannaford, formerly of Reagan's Sacramento staff, opened a public relations firm in West Los Angeles with Reagan as their only client. They signed him to a speaking tour, a series of daily five-minute radio broadcasts, and a syndicated newspaper column. He would have to sacrifice time at the ranch, but he would be engaged in something he also loved—"communicating his beliefs about the direction in which the country ought to move." It was a warm-up for another campaign.

Edmund Morris, in his biography *Dutch*, states that Nancy Reynolds, now Reagan's forthright and lively press secretary at Deaver and Hannaford, questioned Reagan as to why a former governor would want to be heard on "hayseed radio stations." "You don't understand the ripple effect," he was said to have replied. "Only a coupla thousand might hear me one week in one signal area, but they'll get the tone if not the gist. Some of them are going to like it and talk about it, and next week I'm back with more, and more people will listen, and pretty soon all those ripples could build up into a mighty big wave."[18] Smart reasoning—and right on target—for within six months Reagan's Saturday afternoon radio slots, titled "Viewpoint," were aired nationally on 359 radio stations that reached an audience of ten to fifteen million potential voters. Why was Reagan so successful on radio? Attribution can be given in a great part to his speaking voice and intimate manner, which was immediately identifiable, familiar and, above all else, unique. Most great film and radio stars of Reagan's era had voices that set them apart: John Wayne, James Stewart, Henry Fonda, James Cagney, Peter Lorre, Edward G. Robinson, Clark Gable, Spencer Tracy, Humphrey Bogart, Gary Cooper, Cary Grant, Jack Benny, Bob Hope, and Fred Allen are just a sampling of the men; Marlene Dietrich, Judy Garland, Katharine Hepburn, Greta Garbo, Jean Arthur, Lauren Bacall, Marilyn Monroe, and Bette Davis are on a short list of the women who could be identified by a few spoken words and who the then popular professional imitators used as the basis for their acts. With his virile looks Reagan, had he been a better actor, could have commanded star roles in major films won by the likes of Wayne, Cooper, and Fonda. But he proved to be at his best only when he was playing himself, or a fantasized image of himself, like the Gipper, the football hero in *Knute Rockne, All American*, his favorite film role.

Reagan's fantasy view of himself had always been as a hero riding to the rescue (or carrying the ball over the goal line) to save those (or the game) that needed saving. He was generated by the *need* of others, which was like an ignition key that started his motor. When he spoke on the air and on the podium, he was Mr. Everyman. Well, Mr. Average Conservative Republican, let us say, answering questions he posed to himself that apparently millions of people were also pondering on. He had a natural sense of humor and a way of interjecting small witticisms into his talks, making them sound newly minted at that moment. "Status quo," he would say with a wry smile on his face and in his voice. "That's Latin for the mess we're in." And then he would go on with how he thought we, the people, could get out of it. On-screen he had never been much of a lover, but he certainly knew how to romance an audience.

Deaver, Hannaford, the members of the Kitchen Cabinet, and many other powerful and wealthy Republicans believed Reagan could talk his way right into the White House and do so in the 1976 election while his profile was at its current high. Gerald R. Ford, the incumbent Republican president sworn in directly after Nixon resigned, did not expect a race for the Republican primary vote to be of any consequence. But Ford's pardon of Nixon and his rather bumbling personality had not enamored him to voters, and there was concern among conservatives that the Democrats, with Watergate and Nixon's tapes as ammunition, stood a good chance of winning if he was the candidate. After all, Ford had never won a national election; he had spent thirteen terms in the House of Representatives when Nixon nominated him to become vice president after Agnew resigned in disgrace. "We need you," Reagan's supporters pleaded, and Reagan rallied to their battle call, challenging Ford for the Republican nomination. And so Nancy joined Ronnie once again on the campaign trail.

Nancy now admitted that she had felt for some time the inevitability of Ronnie's candidacy. As always, she went along with his decision, but this time with much greater personal enthusiasm than in the past. Her dreams had mythologized, her ambitions expanded. By the end of her eight years as first lady of California, she had begun to envision herself in a higher position. Power is not only an aphrodisiac but also a hard-core addiction. Whatever power came to Nancy did so through Ronnie. This did not lessen its potent effect on her. Staff and friends made note of how closely she observed Betty Ford. There was in her attitude an air of "I can do it better and in smarter clothes."

"That campaign was so exciting, so dramatic, and so *emotional*," she recalled, "especially at the convention—that in my mind it almost overshadows Ronnie's four victories [in the two primaries and elections for governor]."[19] Nancy's busy social schedule was put on hold, and Ronnie curtailed his time and improvements on the ranch, great wrenches in both their lives.

Reagan had a way of rationalizing almost every decision he made. "The liberals had had their turn at bat in the 1960's and they had struck out," he declared.[20] Now it was the Republicans' turn. He believed that he was the best hitter they had and that it was a decision made by God and the people and, therefore, his duty to carry the banner. He spent the weekend before he declared his candidacy at Rancho del Cielo, riding Little Man up the narrow roads to the peak of Tip Top Mountain and sitting in the saddle a long time, thinking, he said, about "the lost vision of our founding fathers and the importance of recapturing it and the voices from around the country who were pressing me to run for president. And I remembered something I'd said many years before: A candidate doesn't make the decision whether to run for president; the people make it for him."[21] This was in 1975, with the Republican convention a year away. Stuart Spencer, who had managed Reagan's gubernatorial campaigns, was now in charge of that of the incumbent president. "Ron has wanted to be president for years," Spencer told the shocked Ford. "He feels he was cheated out of his inheritance when Nixon left." Reagan also felt that since Ford had never been elected by the people, he did not have the mandate to continue as president. A great deal of bitterness arose in Ford when Reagan announced in the summer of 1975 that he was entering the primaries.

"Some of my closest advisers . . . had been warning me for months to prepare for a difficult challenge from Ronald Reagan," Ford recalled. "I hadn't taken those warnings seriously because I didn't take Reagan seriously."

The two men had met on occasion, appearing at times at the same Republican functions. "While we were always polite to one another," Ford continued, "the chemistry wasn't right. He was one of the few political leaders I have ever met whose public speeches revealed more than his private conversations. I have always been able to get to know people pretty easily. I tried to get to know Reagan, but I failed."[22]

Born in Omaha, Nebraska, Ford had attended the University of Michigan on a football scholarship and had been the school team's star center in his senior year. This had earned him a job as assistant football coach at Yale, where he studied law, graduating in 1941 in the top third of his class. When World War II came, he joined the navy, saw a great deal of action, and rose to the rank of lieutenant commander. With the war's end he returned to practice law, but then made an early run for Congress and won. In many ways Ford was a man Reagan could admire and there should have been an easy rapport between them. Yet, at the same time, Ford had achieved many of the goals Reagan had not— football star and wartime hero—where Reagan's poor eyesight had kept him on the sidelines.

Ford was a friendly guy, well liked, easy to know. A large man, he seemed at times awkward or blundering. He liked to tell stories about himself—how in his unelected term as president he had taken the family dog for a walk on the White House lawn at three A.M. dressed in his pajamas and bathrobe and found he could not get back inside. Security finally came to his rescue. He was not a man who looked comfortable holding a teacup, and his large feet often tripped him up. But he was instantly likable. There was a warmth in his smile and a genuineness in his attitude. There was nothing plastic about him. Both the vice presidency and the presidency had been thrust upon him; he had never wanted more than to become speaker of the House one day. But once in office it was natural that he would want to step out of the dark shadows left by Nixon debacle and show his worth. The Republican Party knew this and, except for Reagan, seemed ready to give him that opportunity.

"Actually," Ford confessed, "I expected to win the Republican nomination for President in a breeze . . . But several of [Reagan's] characteristics seemed to rule him out as a serious challenger. One was his penchant for offering simplistic solutions to hideously complex problems. A second was his conviction that he was always right in every argument; he seemed unable to acknowledge that he might have made a mistake. Finally, I'd heard from people who knew him well that he liked to conserve his energy. . . . I knew that you can't run for President and expect to work only from nine-to-five."[23]

Ford was not prepared for the man with whom he had to face off. He discovered that Reagan "was an extraordinarily effective public speaker who had a superb knack of exploiting a punch line." He "was far more knowledgeable about a wide range of issues than many people thought and he held deep convictions." Ford found himself in a race with a much energized Reagan who referred to his campaign stops as battlefields and entered each engagement with a fighting spirit he had never before displayed so openly. His teenage son commented with disdain on the cigar-chomping men who now filled the Palisades house with dank smoke and hard-cut words when his father was in residence. The seventeen-year-old asked his father if he really wanted to run for president. "I can do a lot for America," Reagan replied, his voice suddenly becoming more messianic than paternal.[24]

With Spencer's defection to Ford's camp, Reagan's campaign was being run by John Sears, a Washington lawyer in his midthirties who had worked on Nixon's 1968 campaign. The youthful, prematurely gray, charismatic Sears was urbane and articulate and—although not as far to the right as Reagan and his supporters—dedicated to "bring home a winner." Ronnie and Nancy trusted he would do so, even though they never seemed to get through the walls he placed between himself and the candidate (he was a little more relaxed with Nancy). "John doesn't look you in the eye," Reagan complained to Nancy. "He looks you in the *tie*. Why won't he look at me?"[25]

Sears was on a mission—winning a race—and he wanted no added emotional weight such as friendship or sympathetic bonds. "He was like a surgeon handling a life-or-death operation," a staffer observed. "Surgeons are by necessity cool to their patients and their families in such cases as they will suffer less guilt if their work fails. Sears had a job to do and someone's life was at stake at his hand. He had to insure that it was steady."[26]

Sears firmly believed that Ford's only advantage was incumbency, and even with that his pardon of Nixon and his lackluster time in office (a year at the time of the primaries) did not encourage national support. "If we can beat him in the first two or three primaries, he's dead," Sears told Reagan. He wrongly dismissed the impact of the trappings of the presidency. Ford arrived in the primary cities on Air Force One and came down the gangplank (unfortunately tripping over his feet at one point) to the sound of "Hail to the Chief."

Reagan lost the all-important New Hampshire primary by only 1,500 votes (106,500 to Ford's 108,000). With Nancy stumping right with him, he marched on to Florida and took a second loss. When Ford beat him in Reagan's home state of Illinois, it looked like the end of his candidacy, but Reagan fought on doggedly, with Nancy keeping pace with him (as did Betty Ford with her husband). The Reagans' life was a series of hotels and motels, buses and cars. Nancy got used to the smoke and gave interviews everywhere except the ladies' room, with rarely any time to change clothes or take a bath. (She claimed she learned to wear "knit dresses, which would last all day without looking wrinkled.")[27] They stopped in all the towns they could, often flying in small planes, that might have to land on short grass runways in mountainous terrain. It was exhausting, but thrilling at the same time. Townsfolk who had never been visited by a presidential candidate before came out in unprecedented numbers to greet him. And Nancy and Ronnie were doing it together, side by side, an indivisible team.

The tide turned. Reagan won in Texas, Alabama, Georgia, California, and several other states, leaving the concluding battle to be fought on the convention floor in Kansas City. The Reagans arrived on August 15, a glorious summer day of moderate heat and soft breezes, but despite their campaign enthusiasm the Reagan team was concerned. The tension was palpable on both sides. Sears was convinced that Reagan had enough support to win the required votes, but he wanted to increase the odds.

"The Reagan strategy was clear," Ford said later. "His people wanted to force me to disclose my running mate before the balloting for president. I resisted." Reagan had chosen Pennsylvania senator Richard S. Schweicker, a liberal Republican, as his running mate, an odd choice, as Schweiker and Reagan were miles apart on so many issues. But Reagan was reaching out to the other arm of the party.

"John Sears, Reagan's clever and tenacious manager," Ford explained, "drafted a proposal . . . requiring that contenders for the party's Presidential nomination name their running mate in advance of the balloting. . . . Not surprisingly, it was voted down."[28]

The most damaging blow to Reagan's campaign came when seven Republican governors released a statement calling on Reagan to withdraw in favor of Ford. But in personal terms Nancy Reagan wrote that "the biggest blow of all came when Barry Goldwater endorsed Gerald Ford . . . My mother was so furious that she called Barry and told him in no uncertain terms—and undoubtedly using *very* colorful language—that he had been to their house for the last time." The Goldwaters, Davises, and Reagans had been close friends for years. Reagan had diligently campaigned for Goldwater and given his famous "Time for Choosing" speech during Goldwater's own presidential campaign.

On August 18, 1976, at the end of the balloting (and a lot of meetings in smoke-filled rooms and in monitored corners of the convention hall), Reagan was seventy votes shy of victory and out of the race. Gerald R. Ford was the legitimate candidate. Justin Dart met privately with Reagan to urge him to approach Ford to place him on the ballot as vice president. Reagan would not consider it. Robert Dole was named by Ford, and when the winning team mounted the podium with their wives, the Reagans applauded, but Nancy found even a small smile difficult to conjure.

They returned to California scathed, exhausted, but not beaten. "Nancy and I are not going back and sit on our rocking chairs and say, 'That's all for us,'" he told the California delegation. It was his way of announcing that they would see him as a candidate at least one more time. When Democratic nominee Jimmy Carter (James Earl Carter Jr.), a fifth-generation Georgian and former governor of that state, defeated Ford in the election that November, Ford blamed the outcome in part on Reagan for deflecting power from him during the primaries.

Although losing had been bitter, Reagan steeled himself to prepare for another try for the presidency in 1980. "I think we both knew it wouldn't—couldn't—end in Kansas City," he later wrote. "After committing ten years of our lives to what we believed in, I just couldn't walk away and say, 'I don't care any more.' "[30] He then quoted from an old English ballad that he once had used as a monologue for his drama class when he was a high school student in Dixon, Illinois:

I will lay me down and bleed a while
Though I am wounded, I am not slain.
I shall rise and fight again[31]

To Nancy he confessed, "You know what I regret the most? I had really looked forward to sitting down at the table with Brezhnev [the Soviet head of state] to negotiate on arms control. He would tell me all the things that our side would have to give up. And then, when he was finished, I was planning to stand up, walk around the table, and whisper one little word in his ear, *Nyet*."[32]

CHAPTER NINE

ON THE STEPS OF
THE WHITE HOUSE

On March 4, 1977, Nancy and Ronnie celebrated their twenty-fifth wedding anniversary. Ten years earlier, at the start of their political life together, they had their first—and it seems their last—true argument. Reagan had a temper, and he often displayed it in his private offices with only close staff present. He would throw aside his glasses and slam his fist down hard on his desk; the muscles in his face would go taut, and he was capable of speaking sharply enough to cause some fear and trembling in the unlucky recipients of his anger. This was not behavior that he exhibited at home. If Nancy had seriously upset him, he would stride out of the room, slam the door—hard—and not speak for a considerable length of time. Nelle had preached to him never to go to bed "mad at your mate," and by evening he would finally sit down with Nancy and they would talk over the problem.

But one night in 1967, after an emotional disagreement, Ronnie "had to get up and take a sleeping pill halfway through the night." He had, he admitted in a letter to Nancy a few days later, gone around "feeling that you are frequently angry with me. No more. We are so much 'one' that you are as vital to me as my own heart—with one exception; you could never be replaced with a transplant."[1] According to Nancy, they never again had an angry session like the one described above. Though like other couples they had quarrels, they were able to talk them out. Often their confrontations centered on people Nancy felt were abusing his trust and whom he would defend. Seldom were they at odds about the children or money. Nancy lived within their budget, and he left the handling of the children up to her.

They hated to be apart. He claimed he got lonely when she only left a room. His hand gravitated to her shoulder, her waist, or welcoming palm when they were standing close to each other. He still found her "the most desirable woman in the world who gets more desirable every day."[2] They were so devoted to each other that it blinded them to the needs of their children, who felt themselves to be outsiders, in Patti's case "an intruder." Maureen, at least, did share a political dialogue with her father. Ron, no longer called Skipper, had found a new independence at Yale and would—against his parents' strong opposition—drop out at the end of his first term there and announce his decision to study dance.

The Reagans were shocked. Neither had suspected that their son had either the desire or the talent for that art form, although Patti was aware of his love of the dance and had encouraged him to follow his own muse. Dancing had been something of a secret rite for Ron, practiced out of sight of his parents wherever he found privacy and space. He had a lithe body, good movement, and the ability to sustain a fairly high leap. Dance might not have been the career his father would have hoped he would choose, but he did not deride it, nor did he link it to any indication of homosexual leanings. After all, his good friend James Cagney had started his career as a dancer, as had George Murphy and, of course, the screen's two greatest dancers, Gene Kelly and Fred Astaire. They were all what he called "real men."

When Ron returned to Los Angeles from New Haven, Nancy sought out Gene Kelly to ask his opinion whether Ron could have a future in dance with intense study, for, at eighteen, he would be a late starter. Ron met with Kelly who, after a long talk, put him through a few dance steps and exercises. Since the young man appeared earnest and displayed a natural ability, Kelly advised him to begin intensive study and gave him the names of possible instructors. The Reagans offered him only partial financial assistance, leaving the remainder for their son to finance himself. It was their way of determining just how serious he was about his choice.

With the 1976 campaign for the Republican nomination for president

behind him, and Nancy handling family matters, Reagan devoted himself to two things, his work on Rancho del Cielo and his writing: radio
commentaries, the syndicated column, and speeches. He wrote, as always, in longhand, no help from others. By the end of 1978, three years
after his first broadcast, he had a weekly audience of 20 million. He had
been writing regularly since his high school days in Dixon, poetry and
short stories, then articles for the Eureka College newspaper, followed
by sports stories and commentaries in his years as a sports announcer in
Iowa. While under contract to Warner Brothers he had published a series
of seventeen articles on Hollywood for the *Des Moines Sunday Register.*
His work with the Screen Actors Guild brought him into speech writing
as well as essays for their trade paper. Then came his speaking tours for
General Electric, and his contributions to the opening narratives to *General Electric Theater* and *Death Valley Days*. During the political years that
followed, he had literally turned out hundreds of articles and speeches.
One has to go through the Pre-Presidential Papers in the Ronald Reagan
Presidential Library to fully realize the extent and the expertise of Reagan's writing as he reached this stage. There are 670 handwritten radio
speeches alone, a good many of them saved by staff after he had tossed
them into a wastebasket.

"I can still see him coming into the office in LA," Peter Hannaford
recalled, "often with a sheath of yellow pages in his hand and a big grin
on his face. He would give the handwritten pages to Elaine Crispin [at
this time his chief administrative assistant], saying, "There you are,
Elaine, three weeks worth of radio scripts for typing."[3]

He had a different method for speeches, taking his longhand pages
and then translating them into a shorthand he had invented (and which
no one else seemed able to read) onto four-by-six cards that fit comfortably into his suit pocket. When placed on a lectern, they were barely
noticeable to an audience. By this time he had usually memorized the
speech, but he would occasionally glance down fleetingly, shuffling the
cards with the practiced hand of a card sharp in the event that he had
omitted an important point.

In his radio broadcasts he could be the strong-minded political commentator. His "talks" began with a hook that posed the theme of what was to follow; then there would be a break for a commercial:

"Mankind has survived all manner of evil diseases and plagues, but can it survive Communism? I'll be right back."

Or a touch of film noir:

"It's nightfall in a strange town a long way from home. I'm watching the lights come on from my hotel window on the thirty-fifth floor. I'll be right back."

Or at times the provocateur:

"How much is it worth to not have World War III? I'll be right back."[4]

About one-third of Reagan's radio broadcasts centered on defense or foreign policy issues, another third on domestic and economic policy, and the remainder on varied subjects: Tiffany & Co. (March 12, 1975), Junk Food (December 27, 1976), Basketball (November 28, 1978) are a few eclectic choices. Taken as a whole the 670 radio scripts are brilliant short essays, clearly written and put together with a master's hand. Many listeners did not agree with him, and he would personally answer a goodly number of dissenters as well as those who concurred with what he was saying.

He could sound like the home town philosopher and at the same time the professional political commentator. Losing the Republican nomination had not diminished his popularity. Intellectuals, certain someone else was writing his speeches, deplored his theatrical approach. Liberals called him a warmonger for his attacks on Communist Russia, "the Evil Empire." Still, one thing was obvious. Ronald Reagan was a major political force. Nancy had married a man she had considered a solid citizen and walked right into history.

The older he got, the tougher the campaign trail became. Nancy was fifty-seven and Reagan sixty-eight when he set out in November 1979 to win the Republican primary and face off against President Jimmy Carter. All the axing of wood at Rancho del Cielo had kept Reagan in good physical shape, but he had become testy, unable to allow things to slide off his back as he had been able to do four years earlier. Nancy, experienced now in the cutthroat tactics of such a high-stakes political race, was more protective of him than ever. The family were all informed of Reagan's decision to announce his candidacy. No one was surprised. Michael and Maureen looked at it with great anticipation, Ron was somewhat indifferent, and Patti had a difficult time controlling her disapproval. Nonetheless, she accompanied her siblings, "who were awkward and tentative in each other's presence,"[5] to New York the first week in November. There her father made his statement at a news conference at the Hilton Hotel.

Patti remained the rebellious daughter, her politics far left of center. She was running a bit wild, secretly growing marijuana in the small garden space attached to the rear of her apartment, submitting to sterilization to her parents' great sadness, and having affairs with men of whom even she did not approve. Despite this, Patti had formed a degree of détente with her parents and seemed for the time to need the family ambience. "What I remember most about [Reagan's speech the night he declared his candidacy]," Patti recalled, "is looking up at my father while he was speaking and being unable to clap at strategic points." She confided her emotional dilemma to singer-songwriter Paul Simon, a close friend. She felt she just couldn't sit back and be silent when she disagreed so vehemently with her father's political agenda. Simon told her, "Well, you're allowed to speak your mind, too. There's no gag order on you."[6]

The entire family, including Neil and Bess, regrouped at Rancho del Cielo (a rare occurrence) for Thanksgiving. The adobe cottage was overcrowded. Maureen had a new love in her life, Dennis Revell, past chairman of the Young Republicans in Kern County, California. Michael had been married for several years, and he and his wife, Colleen, were present with their towheaded toddler, Cameron, the Reagans' first grandchild. Ron, now deeply committed to dance after four years of instruction, had a steady girlfriend, Doria Palmieri, seven years his senior. Although the age difference disturbed the Reagans, they were receptive to the relationship, as it was obvious that the couple were honestly in love and that Doria was a good influence on their son, who they did not realize was struggling so hard to exist on his small allowance that he was surviving on dry cereal with water. Doria moved in with him, and her paycheck helped to support them both. Patti was also living a hard-scrabble life, writing with little success, barely scraping by. The Reagans believed that their children had to make it on their own, and their off-spring embraced this as a condition of life. Any resentment they had toward their parents was put aside at this Thanksgiving gathering.

There was no dining room at the ranch. The food was set out on Reagan's bumper-pool table with a large dining table set up in the middle of the same room. All other furniture was pushed to the side. It was a cool night and Reagan had built a fire in the fireplace because the ranch still did not have heat. He carved the turkey, which had been cooked on the outside barbecue. The conversation never steered far from the campaign. Both Maureen and Michael wanted to become involved. Reagan wasn't so sure this was a good idea. Patti remained silent throughout the meal, but Maureen challenged her father on women's issues—her main concerns were a woman's right to choose and the Equal Rights Amendment (ERA)—and received evasive replies. In a little more than two hours, dinner was over, and Nancy suggested they should all leave so that Ronnie could get some rest. Family gatherings were never the realization of the fantasies that the Reagans' children continued to spin.

Family matters were not then of prime concern to the Reagans, who were faced with serious problems in Reagan's campaign for the presidency. On board again for this run for the White House was John Sears as director of day-to-day operations. Sears was obsessed with the need for absolute power. As the campaign swung into heavy action, he railed against any interference from other Reagan forces—Nancy, Lyn Nofziger, Michael Deaver, Martin Anderson (Reagan's adviser), Paul Laxalt (general chairman of the campaign), and, of course, Reagan, himself. Unable to do anything about the Reagans, Sears moved in to rid himself of as many of his candidate's loyalists as possible. First to go was Lyn Nofziger, then Martin Anderson, replaced by two of Sears's men, Jim

Lake and Charles Black. With two of his top advisers gone, Reagan turned on key issues to another loyal old staff member, Edwin (Ed) Meese.

Sears was furious at what he considered Reagan's defiance of his authority and tried to bump both Meese and Deaver from the campaign staff. With Nancy's prodding, Reagan called a meeting of all the major players at their home in the Pacific Palisades that erupted with fiery hostility. Sears issued an ultimatum—either Deaver (whom he considered the most contentious) went or he, Lake, and Black would leave.

Reagan was in shock, face drained of color, anger mounting.

"Honey," Nancy said calmly, "it looks as though you've got to make a choice." Her glance went to Deaver, a sign to Ronnie that he should stand behind his old colleague.

Deaver immediately jumped to his feet. "No, Governor," he said. "You don't have to, because I'm leaving," and rushed from the room.

Reagan strode after Deaver, catching up with him at the front door, and tried to convince him to remain on board. "No, Governor," he insisted. "You need John Sears more than you need me." And Deaver was gone.

"When I returned to the room I was very upset," Reagan recalled. " 'Damn it!,' I said, 'You've just driven away someone who's probably a better man than the three of you [Sears, Black, and Lake]!' "[7]

Matters grew worse after Deaver's departure. Reagan blamed Sears, who further resented Reagan's interference with his authority. Nancy wanted Ronnie to fire Sears, as did Maureen and Michael Reagan, both now working actively on their father's campaign. Reagan felt it might be a mistake at this juncture, and so Sears was retained—for the time being, at least—but morale among the entire group was lowered. The explosive chemistry between Reagan and his campaign manager had an effect on everyone.

"Every night when we returned to the hotel [on tour]," Nancy wrote in *My Turn*, "Ronnie would get ready for bed, but I would go from one room to another, meeting in corridors and corners with John [Sears] and the others, trying everything I could think of to bring them together and smooth things over. When I finally got to bed, Ronnie would ask me where I had been, and I would make up various excuses. For as long as possible, I delayed telling him how much tension there was. . . . But I soon realized that we were merely putting a Band-Aid over a serious problem."[8]

The clash between Reagan and Sears finally reached a splitting point when Sears made a deliberate and underhanded move to get rid of Ed Meese. When Reagan got wind of it, he confronted Sears. "You got Deaver!" he shouted, "but, by God, you're not going to get Ed Meese!" He raised his arm, ready to take a swing. Nancy, who was by his side, grabbed it. Reagan stood immobile for a moment, his face contorted in anger. Reagan, a strong enough man to split a log with one deft blow of an axe, towered over both Nancy and Sears. When traveling by air during the earlier days of the campaign, he had become so enraged at something that Sears had done that he had "slammed his fist into the bulkhead wall with such force" that Deaver, who was standing near him, was certain he must have broken all the bones in his hand. Not only had that not been so, but Reagan seemed to experience no pain when he pulled away and opened his palm. He was a powerful man and could have, if provoked and not under control, thrown a wicked punch.

"It's late," Nancy said, still holding on to him, although obviously her grasp would not have been much of a deterrent had he decided to swing at Sears. "I think we should all get some sleep," she continued softly. Reagan's arm lowered slowly to his side and he took her hand as he turned away.[9]

Visibly shaken by Reagan's sudden violence, Sears left the room. Within twenty-four hours a press release stated that John Sears, Jim Lake, and Charles Black had bowed out of the campaign.

From the moment of Sears's departure, Reagan took full charge. Deaver, Nofziger, and Anderson rejoined the team, and shortly after that, Stu Spencer, his differences with Reagan in 1976 when he ran Ford's campaign now in the past, came on board. During the spring, the telling months in the campaign for the Republican nomination, Reagan won almost every state primary. Only George Herbert Walker Bush remained as a challenge to Reagan, and Bush's strength was faltering daily. Reagan now turned much of his concentration into a likely contest with President Carter, who had vanquished Senator Edward Kennedy on the first ballot of the Democratic convention. But Carter was still no shoo-in with American voters.

On November 4, 1979, Iranian militants had stormed the U.S. Embassy in Tehran and taken fifty-two staff and soldiers hostage. Reports of beatings, and of torture—especially of staff suspected of being CIA—had been leaked. As the Republican convention neared, the hostages had been held over six months, and Carter had not been able to free them. Secretary of State Cyrus R. Vance had failed; his successor, Edmund S. Muskie, had had no better luck in his negotiations. Carter's standing was dropping in the popularity polls, but not yet significantly, because he had managed to maintain peace during his term, with no American combat deaths, and he had helped to negotiate the Camp David accords between Israel and Egypt. He was seen as a champion of peace with his work for nuclear-arms control and his concern for international human rights. He was also untouched by personal scandal; the closest he came was his acknowledgment that he had once harbored "lust" in his heart.

Reagan wanted his good friend, the former governor of Nevada, Paul Laxalt, who had been especially helpful in the campaign, to run on the ticket with him. But demographically a California-Nevada ticket was out of the question. George Bush, who had roots in both Texas and New England, and was proving to be Reagan's strongest opponent in the primaries, seemed a natural choice, but he had no national profile. However premature this issue seemed, the campaign team was intent on being prepared. In his book *An American Life*, Reagan claimed that to his surprise former President Ford approached him through his mediators suggesting that he be placed in the second spot. Ford categorically denies that he did so. In fact, it was Spencer, who had handled Ford's successful presidential campaign, who saw him as the man who could guarantee Reagan a win and spoke to the Reagans about making the first approach.

A former president had never run for vice president before, but Reagan's staff, with Spencer's hard sell, began to see Reagan and Ford as a

Three generations:

TOP LEFT Nancy's maternal grandmother Sarah Luckett, a Southern lady of great beauty.

TOP RIGHT Edith Luckett Davis, Nancy's mother, at the start of her acting career.

LEFT Nancy, circa 1924, age three, when Edith left her with family to pursue her career.

TOP RIGHT Reagan family portrait, circa, 1913, Tampico, Illinois. Jack and Nelle flank their sons—Neil (left) and Ronald (right). Tough times and Jack's drinking caused them to move often.

TOP LEFT Ronald was called "Dutch" by his dad who thought he looked like a little Dutchman. Even at the age of three he revered the flag.

BELOW The Dramatics Society of Eureka College, 1931, Dutch is third from left, top row, wearing glasses; brother Neil is second from right, top row.

TOP LEFT Nancy and Edith, circa 1924. Nancy was still living with relatives and unwilling to leave her mother's side on Edith's brief and infrequent visits.

LEFT In 1929, when Nancy was eight, Dr. Loyal Davis, (center, Nancy wearing a hairband, her cousin, Charlotte, on opposite side), proposed to Edith and the child could finally look forward to being reunited with her mother.

TOP RIGHT Nancy, age twelve, with her stepbrother, Richard Davis.

Under contract to Warner Brothers, Reagan returned to Dixon, where he had spent his childhood and youth, on a publicity tour. (Circa 1940–1941)

TOP RIGHT With old Dixon friend, Bill Thompson.

TOP LEFT Portraying "the Gipper" in *Knute Rockne, All American* gave him the opportunity to be seen as a football hero—the fantasy of his life.

BOTTOM LEFT With his mother, Nelle Reagan.

TOP LEFT At fourteen, Nancy had already decided to be an actress, but marriage was her main goal.

TOP RIGHT Perhaps her only real glamour photo, 1943, when she was seeking stage work.

LEFT Hollywood, 1949, posing in front of her bachelorette apartment. She had just met Ronald Reagan and decided this was the man for her. He proposed to her over dinner in a booth at Chasens two years later.

BELOW They were married with only two friends present, actor William Holden and his wife, Brenda Marshall, seen here with the newly engaged couple at Chasens. The child in the sailor suit in the photograph on the wall behind Holden is proprietor Dave Chasen, age four.

The newly-married Reagans' money problems were solved when he became the television host for *General Electric Theater.* ABOVE He toured all their factories, giving speeches. At one a female employee bared her breast for an autograph.

BELOW Two photographs from the Reagans' personal album: (left) Christmas 1960, Patti with doll, Nancy, Reagan holding son Ron, and Michael; (right) with Ron at Coronado Beach, 1962.

TOP RIGHT In 1980 he won the Republican nomination for president. Pictured here are Edith and Loyal at the convention.

TOP LEFT Reading a bedtime story to Patti and Ron, 1964. The California Republican Party had already approached him to run for governor.

BOTTOM He finally ran in 1966 and won. He took the oath of office at one minute past midnight in a private ceremony on advice from Nancy's astrologer. Ron watches his father as Nancy talks with Maureen Reagan, Reagan's daughter with Jane Wyman, in the background.

TOP Patti was against her father's political career and his stand on many issues. She attended the convention, but was not happy about it.

RIGHT Son Ron was more suportive.

BELOW The Reagans celebrate with their family; (left to right) *front:* Ron Reagan, Patti Reagan, Nancy and Ronald Reagan, Michael Reagan holding his son Cameron, Colleen and Maureen Reagan, *back row:* George W., George H. W., and Barbara Bush.

Reagan won the election against Jimmy Carter in a landslide. RIGHT On inauguration night, Nancy is caught in a rare moment of shyness.

MIDDLE The Reagans are surrounded by their California friends in celebration of his seventieth birthday, February 11, 1981, at the White House. From left to right: Armand and Harriet Deutsch, William and Betty Wilson, Marion Jorgensen, Walter and Lee Annenberg, and Earle Jorgensen.

BOTTOM RIGHT Reagan's White House staff faces him for one of their first meetings in the Oval Office, January 21, 1981.

TOP March 30, 1981. A moment after this photograph was taken, shots rang out in an attempted assassination. Reagan did not know immediately that he had taken a hit. Secret Service Agent Jerry Parr, who slammed the president into the car for safety, is in a trenchcoat behind Reagan. To his left is James Brady, who was shot in the head. Michael Deaver, standing to the right of Reagan, was unscathed, but the police officer, Tom Delehanty, looking at Reagan, was shot in the neck, and Secret Service Agent Tim McCarthy, to the right of the photo, was shot in the chest.

MIDDLE Nancy raced to the hospital where the President had been taken.

BOTTOM Secretary of State Haig, seated center, in the White House basement Security Room. "I'm in charge!" he falsely insisted when he learned that Reagan had been struck down.

TOP First Dog Lucky has the President and Britain's Prime Minister Margaret Thatcher on the run at the White House, 1985.

ABOVE RIGHT Nancy used the telephone as her favorite means of communication.

LEFT Thatcher and Reagan at Camp David (1986).

TOP Staff meeting aboard Air Force One, 1986. Nancy was more than an interested bystander.

RIGHT The Reagans at work at Camp David.

BOTTOM Nancy, following her mastectomy in 1987. She had also recently lost her mother.

LEFT Reagan with his former Hollywood agent, Lew Wasserman. The President had always admired Wasserman and emulated his style.

ABOVE At Rancho del Cielo, Reagan's beloved second home. The Reagans went there for privacy, but the media found a way of photographing them from a higher point. Nancy took advantage of this by displaying a hand-drawn sign on her campaign against drugs.

TOP LEFT Reagan in the tack room at Rancho del Cielo.

TOP RIGHT In the covered terrace where they entertained guests (the living room was not large enough to accommodate more than an intimate group). Note the sign hanging from the beam: "The Reagans, 1600 Pennsylvania Avenue."

BOTTOM The Reagans and the Gorbachevs at the Soviet Embassy in Washington, 1987.

LEFT Leaving Washington shortly after George H. W. Bush was sworn in as the forty-first president. The photo was taken from inside the helicopter that would take the Reagans on the first wing of their journey back to California and a new home (January 20, 1989).

BOTTOM All the surviving presidents and first ladies, except for Jacqueline Kennedy who was under treatment for cancer, attended the opening of the Ronald Reagan Presidential Library in Simi Valley, California. In a rare photograph, the first ladies pose for the camera and later sign their names beneath their image.

Lady Bird Johnson   Pat Nixon   Nancy Reagan   Barbara Bush   Rosalynn Carter   Betty Ford

The cowboy and his lady ride into the sunset at Rancho del Cielo.

"dream ticket." It was decided that despite Nancy's misgivings the Fords should be approached.

"I recall the sequence of events clearly," President Ford told this author for the purposes of this book. "Betty and I were in Rancho Mirage [a town near Palm Springs, California, where the Fords lived for seven months of the year] when we received a call from Ron in late March [1980] saying he and Nancy would like to speak with us. I said, 'Come on down' [the Reagans were in Los Angeles at the time] and they did. Ron came in carrying an Indian peace pipe [Reagan collected Indian and early western artifacts] and gave it to me. I still have it displayed prominently, in fact. He said something to the effect that we should 'bury old grievances'—meaning the differences we had during the previous election.

"That sounded good to me. It seemed that might have been why he had come to see us, when to our shock he asked if he got the nomination, would I consider being his running mate. Betty and I were in complete accord about this. We had no desire to reenter the political scene. 'Count me out,' I told him, in very clear terms."[10]

This is easy to understand. Mrs. Ford had only recently left the care of the Alcohol and Drug Rehabilitation Service of the Long Beach Naval Hospital after courageously going public about her alcohol and drug addiction to urge others with similar problems to seek professional help. Years earlier, to dramatize the importance of regular physical examinations for breast cancer, she had also gone public when her doctors found a malignancy in her right breast and had to remove it. "When I asked myself if I would rather lose a right arm or a breast I decided I would rather lose a breast," she said in one of her many appearances before women's groups.

Betty Ford had been a popular first lady. During the 1976 campaign there were bumper stickers that proclaimed: "Elect Betty's husband; Keep Betty in the White House." She was a brave, outspoken woman, one who was not afraid to express her own viewpoints even if they were not in accord with her husband's, which to Stu Spencer seemed an advantage in winning over the women's vote. But the Fords could not be convinced, and the Reagans departed Rancho Mirage without securing him for the dream ticket.

By May, all of Reagan's opponents except George Bush had dropped out of the race, and by the end of the month, so had he. Reagan now had enough votes to win the nomination in August at the Republican convention in Detroit. When the Reagans arrived and were established in a suite at the Renaissance Center Plaza Hotel, a win seemed imminent. Still, the gathered delegates maintained a high level of convention fever. Both Maureen and Michael, who had worked diligently on their father's behalf, were situated elsewhere. For once, Michael was an insider. He had been drafted early in the campaign (when Sears was manager) to appear at rallies that Reagan could not attend and where it was thought someone carrying the Reagan name could be helpful. Michael was thrilled. He quit his job as a boat salesman and gave this new responsibility his full attention.

Although Reagan appeared unaware of it, a bitter feud existed between the Reagan offspring and Michael Deaver, who tried to keep them working for the campaign but at a distance. Maureen even had difficulty calling her father on the telephone, for Deaver had given instructions to the operator that she not be connected. Deaver was about Maureen's age, and he fancied himself as a chosen son to Reagan, whom he idolized. He was controlling the nominee's acceptance appearance with fierce propriety.

The chosen candidate always mounted the platform for a nationally covered photo op with their entire families in a show of good American family values. Deaver was insistent that the Reagans' only grandchild, Cameron, not accompany Michael and Colleen onto the stage. He cited Reagan's age and a wish not to remind voters that he was a grandfather, a fairly ludicrous consideration, for, despite the lack of gray in his hair, and his amazing physique, at the age of sixty-nine a grandchild would have seemed a natural occurrence. (Reagan himself made light of the age question. On his sixty-ninth birthday he had quipped, "I'm celebrating the thirtieth anniversary of my thirty-ninth birthday." While giving a speech in Chicago at about this time he mentioned the Roman emperor Diocletian and added, "I'm one of the few persons old enough to remember [him].") Furious at such an ultimatum, Michael issued one of his own: he and Colleen would not join the Reagans on the platform unless Cameron was included. This would have led television viewers to conclude that there was disharmony in the candidate's family, and so Cameron's presence was agreed upon. The youngster ended up being held in his grandfather's arms and was caught on camera striking him a blow on the cheek as he struggled for a moment to get loose. Reagan reacted by smiling ruefully—and somewhat proudly—holding tight to the child.

More family trouble brewed. Ron and Doria, who had joined the Reagans in Detroit, were not yet married, and Nancy did not feel that Doria should be photographed with the family. Now it was Ron's turn to rebel. No Doria, no Ron. He finally caved in to his mother's demand. Patti, still finding her father's Republican presidential candidacy difficult to accept, was in California, ensconced in her parents' house with her dog, Freebo, after a flood made her small apartment uninhabitable. She had been there for most of her father's primary campaigns, alone a good part of the time as Nancy accompanied Ronnie across the country. When her parents were at home, she wrote, "We were cautious, awkward and so polite." (It was as though everyone was fighting for control so as not to "blow up.")

While she was occupying the house in Pacific Palisades, Patti recalls wandering through the familiar rooms, checking to see whether her father still kept a gun (he did, in the drawer of his bedside table). She found a large bottle of the tranquilizer Dalmane in her mother's medicine cabinet. "I tried not to look at the spot next to the window where my mother used to hit me," she wrote in her memoir. "I always locked the bathroom door behind me even though she was miles away in another state. It was like a collision of past and present, adult and child."[11]

Yet when Nancy called her from Detroit to tell her that arrangements had been made for her to fly to the convention to join them so that they could present themselves as a family, Patti agreed to go. Smiles in place, hands joined, a happy family scene flickered on television screens across the country as Ronald Wilson Reagan was declared the Republican nominee for president of the United States, Michael holding Cameron this time and Doria still missing.

Attention turned again to the choice of Reagan's running mate. The Fords were also in Detroit, having arrived to attend the convention. After a lengthy discussion, the Reagan team asked Nancy to call Mrs. Ford and inquire how she felt at this time about the proposed dream ticket. Nancy went to the phone as asked. The former first lady, she claimed, replied that she did not think it a good idea and that she wanted her husband to withdraw from politics so that they could lead a more private life.

"I'm very clear on what happened in Detroit," President Ford told this author. "Betty and I arrived in Detroit early in the day. It was August and very hot, and we had no sooner settled in our suite when the Reagans called. He and Nancy wanted to see us between two and three P.M. They came to our suite. Ron then said that they [and their advisers] had decided that they needed me on the ballot to beat Jimmy Carter. I was shocked. I had told him in March that I would not run."

Reagan continued to press the issue. "In deference to his request [and after discussions with Mrs. Ford] I finally agreed to set up a negotiating team that would at least discuss the matter with the Reagan team."

Ford chose three colleagues who were in Detroit for the convention to represent his interests: Alan Greenspan ("a bespectacled, soft-spoken bachelor" who was chairman of the Council of Economic Advisers in Washington), Jack Marsh (Ford's liaison with Congress during his administration), and Bob Barrett (his former military aide.)

In Ford's conversation with this author, he could not recall the members of Reagan's team, but Stu Spencer and Mike Deaver were involved in the discussions, which went on for "a day and a half without an agreement. I only had two demands. I would have to be made chief of staff in charge of day-to-day operations and decisions, and Henry Kissinger, who I think is brilliant, would have to be retained as secretary of state [the office he held under both Nixon and Ford]."

Ford had been invited by CBS news anchor and news analyst Walter

Cronkite, who was covering the convention on television, to appear with him on camera. Cronkite brought up the possibility of Ford being on the ticket with Reagan and asked whether this would be a "dual presidency." Ford jumped at this, negating any inference that he was "even considering such an idea." But it was a phrase, a sound bite, that the media picked up and ran with.

"It was a figment of the press," Ford insisted. "They created an entirely false image. I had no such thing in my mind and [my representatives] knew this. A short time later, I called Ron and said, 'Thanks, but no thanks. It wasn't going to work,' that [his conditions] were unacceptable. [In essence, no Henry Kissinger, no Gerald R. Ford] Two hours later Ron announced that George Bush was to be his running mate."

In their memoirs neither Nancy nor Reagan mentions Henry Kissinger in their discussion of Ford's terms. In both, it is Ford who positioned himself as a vice-presidential choice. Reagan does say it was Ford who withdrew from the situation shortly after the Cronkite interview in which, Reagan claimed, it seemed that Ford was proposing a two-headed presidency. According to Reagan, during the negotiations with Ford's representatives, Reagan's team had pressed the importance of him having the commanding hand if a deal was to be struck between them. Ford would have only the power constitutionally invested in him as vice president. And, still according to Reagan, this was not what the ex-president had hoped for, and in their last meeting (when he withdrew) he was very clear in telling Reagan that it would not work. From his own experience, President Ford told this author, it was also clear "that the country couldn't operate with two presidents."[12] Immediately after Ford departed, Reagan reported, he then turned to the obvious choice, George Bush, to run on the ticket in the second spot.

But a third version exists. On the night that Ford was interviewed by Cronkite, Michael Reagan recalled, he was in his father's suite with Colleen, Reagan, Nancy, members of the Kitchen Cabinet and the campaign team. When the set was clicked off, everyone, except Nancy (who had already made her views clear), began "shooting opinions" at Reagan. Finally, he lifted his arm for silence. "Stop," Michael, in his autobiography, stated he said, "I'll make the decision myself. Call Gerald Ford and tell him he has three minutes to make a decision on my terms."

Michael claimed the call was made. When Ford did not ring back in the allotted time, his "dad looked directly at Ed Meese and said, 'George Bush is my man. Get him on the phone.' "[13] Whichever version one believes (I am inclined to side with Mr. Ford), Bush lost no time in accepting. In less than a half hour the two men stood side by side on the platform of the Detroit Convention Center, with Barbara Bush and Nancy at the side of their husbands. When the cheering and shouting finally subsided, Reagan promised the delegations a winning team in November.

Jimmy Carter was a country boy born thirteen years after Reagan in the small town of Plains, Georgia, and raised on a nearby farm in the even smaller hamlet of Archery. He married Rosalynn Smith, who lived on a neighboring farm, the same year, 1946, that he graduated from the U.S. Naval Academy at Annapolis. For twelve years he served in the nuclear submarine program under Admiral Hyman G. Rickover. When Carter's father, a peanut farmer and dedicated Democrat, died, Jimmy resigned from the navy and returned to the family homestead consisting of a warehouse, a cotton gin, and several thousand acres for growing seed peanuts.

Carter, perhaps due to the influence of his mother, Lillian Gordy Carter, was strongly opposed to the inequality of opportunity and conditions for black workers. Both Rosalynn and Lillian encouraged Carter to enter politics ("to make a difference"). He was elected to the Georgia Senate in 1962 and became governor in 1970.[14] At his gubernatorial inauguration he called for "an end to all racial discrimination." The Carters were not novices at campaigning. He entered the 1976 Democratic presidential primaries, won nineteen out of thirty-one—and the election. "Jimmy *who?*" people had asked, for he had seemed to have come out of nowhere.

Carter was not a great orator. His voice was that of an educated Southern gentleman-farmer, not a politician. His blue eyes were the color of a summer sky, his smile toothy, his hair the shade of sun-baked hay, and he had a courteous manner. Ford had thought he would be easy to beat—a peanut farmer-politician with a low national profile. But Carter was exactly what the country needed to sweep clean the taint of Watergate from the White House, his appeal broad to blacks and whites, liberals and conservatives, rich and poor. With Walter Mondale, senator from Minnesota, as his running mate, Carter had mightily defeated an unprepared Gerald Ford. And he had recently won renomination at the 1980 Democratic convention on the first ballot.

Shortly after the convention, the Reagans rented a house in Wexford, Virginia, an hour's drive from Washington, once owned and occupied by Jacqueline Kennedy Onassis. This served as a base of operations as Nancy and Ronnie moved into the final three months of the campaign. Thus, all media releases came from Virginia, immediately aligning Reagan demographically with a section of the country other than California, and with the Kennedy name (however tenuous the connection). There were horses on the estate, rolling hills, and verdant grassland. Whenever he could, Reagan rode to clear his mind and sort out the tangles. The house, still reflecting Jackie Kennedy Onassis's personal style, was welcomed by Nancy after the sterile sameness of the hotel suites they had occupied during the long, arduous months of the campaign.

As the two men, Reagan and Carter, set out to campaign, the odds were not overwhelmingly in Reagan's favor. Nixon's dark image still hovered over the Republicans. Unseating an incumbent president was never easy, no matter what the circumstances. People were always nervous about change. And as Reagan had found out in '76 with Ford, a president carries with him all the symbols and trappings of power. But Carter and his team were not sure of themselves, and to the surprise of many outside strategists they ran a negative, name-slinging campaign—foreign to the image that Carter had created as a gentleman during his past political outings. He called Reagan a racist, claiming he was pandering to the racists in the South when he said that he believed states should be returned the rights they had been granted in the Constitution. Based on Reagan's opposition to the Senate's ratification of the SALT II treaty, which Reagan believed "had serious weaknesses that would leave the Soviets with a dangerous preponderance of nuclear weapons," Carter said that he was a warmonger who, if elected, "would destroy the world." Reagan, on the other hand, maintained his dignity, treated such accusations with dismissive amusement, and appeared the more presidential of the two.[15]

By the time Reagan won the Republican nomination, the American hostages in Iran had been held and terrorized for nine months. Carter's appeals, the administration's economic boycott of Iran and deportation of Iranian students in the United States, and the demands of the United Nations Security Council had not brought the hostages home. The situation had worsened that April when Carter approved a U.S. raid to rescue the hostages. The mission failed. Carter was seen as a weak negotiator, and this played dramatically into Reagan's hands.

The death knell of the Carter administration was sounded when he agreed to debate Reagan on October 28, 1980, just one week before the election. Reagan's mastery of this art and his ability to create memorable sound bites ("There you go again," he said to Carter, who was reeling off incorrect figures in a somber voice) unnerved the president and conferred presidential stature on his opponent.

The Reagans returned to Los Angeles on November 2 to vote and to wait for the election returns. Patti was now back in her own apartment, and Ron and Nancy were home alone—for how long neither could (or wanted to) conjecture. Reagan knew he was far ahead in the polls but still held to the belief that nothing was sure until the last ballots were in or "the other guy conceded." Nancy, however, had been giving considerable thought to what they should do with San Onofre if Ronnie won and they were to occupy the White House for at least four years.

Nancy was against renting their home of twenty-nine years. Yet it certainly could not stand empty for such a long period, and it would never do, for security reasons, as "a second White House, as it was set apart and easily visible from a low-flying plane." Selling it seemed the only alternative, although a wrench because so much of their personal history was associated with the house. There were even discussions among the Reagans' close friends of maintaining the Palisades house as a future "museum" if Reagan was elected. Obviously, all concerned, except Reagan, who reserved judgment, expected a positive outcome.[16]

The Reagans spent most of Election Day sequestered inside the house, intermittently watching television updates. Reagan would walk into the room where the television was on, pause, check out the figures, stride back and forth for a few moments, gaze at the screen again, and then march out of the room to speak to campaign headquarters in Century City. The house was surrounded by the Secret Service and, beyond their cordon, a horde of reporters, photographers, and television cameramen. Reagan managed to go out for a haircut surrounded by security. "There was a terrible crush of people and cameras," a neighbor recalled. "I couldn't get into my driveway."[17] About four P.M. the Reagans began to ready themselves for the evening. They were to leave the house at six to be driven to Earle and Marion Jorgensen's Beverly Hills home for an early supper (now a tradition on election nights) with some of their friends, including Betsy and Alfred Bloomingdale, Harriet and Armand Deutsch, Mary Jane and Charles Wick and their son C. Z. Wick. None of the Reagans' children was to be present. About nine P.M. they would depart for the Century City Plaza Hotel, a ten-minute drive away, to wait with their campaign staff for the final results.

Nancy was relaxing in the tub at a few minutes after five, and Ronnie taking a shower in their shared bathroom when, coming from the bedroom television—turned up high so that Nancy could hear it above the sound of the water coursing through the power nozzle of the shower—came the familiar voice of news anchor John Chancellor declaring that "Reagan is going to win in a landslide victory." Nancy got out of the tub and threw a towel around herself as she pounded on the shower door shouting at him. Reagan stepped out, she recalled, "grabbed a towel, and we ran over to the television set." There they stood, "dripping wet, wearing nothing but our towels," as they listened to the announcement that Ronald W. Reagan had just been elected the fortieth president of the United States of America. Neither of them was prepared for the landslide that had swept him into the White House. He had won 489 electoral votes to Carter's 49, and had an eight million margin over Carter in the popular vote.

Reagan went back into the bathroom to dry off. Moments later the private telephone rang, and he picked up the bathroom wall extension to hear President Carter in his distinctive Southern cadences concede the election and congratulate him.

"Thank you, Mr. President," Reagan replied solemnly, "and may God be with you, as well."

It took a moment or two for the impact to hit them. "Not bad for a country boy," Reagan said as he hugged the new First Lady.

"Not bad at all," Nancy replied, tears of pride, joy, and astonishment streaking her face.[18]

CHAPTER TEN

MARCHING INTO HISTORY

A man running for president is quite a different man when elected. The battle was won. From this point in his life Ronald Reagan would be a part of America's history. Politics weren't behind him, but he would now have to ascend from candidate to president of the United States and leader of the western world. How many giant steps he could take to reach that lofty height depended not on the charismatic man he displayed on the stump but on the true inner man. Although Reagan had always fantasized himself as a hero, American mythology has rigorous standards in its choice of heroes. Few heroes become legendary; most are forgotten with the passage of only one or two generations, many within their lifetimes.

Norman Mailer wrote, "A hero embodies his time, and is not so very much better than his time, but he is larger than life and so is capable of giving direction to the time, able to encourage a nation to discover the deepest colors of its character."[1]

One can't know what deep thoughts either Reagan or Nancy had as they prepared for Reagan's inauguration. It is doubtful that even as close as these two were, they could fully express these emotions to each other. There was no way either could anticipate what to expect. Reagan had served two terms as governor of California, performing adequately with the assistance of a strong personal staff. The presidency was vastly more complex. There were issues he had never dealt with, such as nuclear-arms proliferation, the arms race, world population control, the many problems of the third world. But while his experience might not have prepared him for the role of the leader of his country and the most powerful man in the world, there was something in his makeup that might have equipped him better than most incoming presidents who had not held national office. He was a simple, confident man, secure in himself, not emotionally vulnerable, and happy in his private life. This gave him a particular strength, similar in ways to the one other nonintellectual president of the twentieth century, Harry Truman, who could make a decision to drop the atomic bomb and sleep through the night. The pressures of the presidency are great. One can watch on television a president age ten years in four. Reeling with the pressure, presidents have often become ineffective. Reagan's personality served to steer him on a steadier course.

According to one political analyst, Reagan was "a crusader, the first missionary conservative to gain the White House with the aim of reversing the liberal New Deal revolution of governmental activism and Democratic Party dominance established by Franklin D. Roosevelt nearly fifty years [before him]. He comes as a reformer preaching the gospel that 'government is not the solution, government is the problem,' promising an era of national renewal based on less government not more, and projecting that same jaunty, smiling self-confidence of Mr. Roosevelt in the teeth of public cynicism and economic despair."

Reagan would have been pleased with this last comparison. Roosevelt had always been his personal hero. He was the man who had brought the country through the nightmare years of the Great Depression and World War II by his calm manner and strength of character. During the campaign, Reagan had often evoked Roosevelt's name, reinforcing the notion of his supporters that he "could become a conservative Republican version of Mr. Roosevelt."[2]

Reagan was not a man of unique brilliance like Roosevelt. Nor was he imaginative. Yet he was able to capture the imagination of the voters and instill in them renewed hope for the nation's vitality in an age of widespread anxiety. Although Reagan identified with both Roosevelt, a Democrat, and Lincoln, a Republican, he shared only two things with them—a strong belief in the integrity of the American people and an ability to communicate his thoughts. Reagan believed that God put everyone on earth with a mission. His was to be of service. Nelle had taught him that. But Nancy's faith in him had catapulted this to another level. In Nancy's eyes he was better than he thought he was, which of necessity had to broaden his mission. The Evil Empire had to be vanquished or America would be devoured, and he was duty-bound to restore in the people "a vision for the future of a strong and just America."[3] He was a pragmatist, which could lead him to simplistic and potentially dangerous conclusions. But above all else he was a great communicator and (like Roosevelt and Lincoln) he had the *look* and the *sound* of a president of the United States. This was not a role he played. This *was* Reagan. He expressed no doubts in his ability to honor the presidency and the country, a view shared by Nancy. And since Reagan saw Nancy as his ideal woman, he believed she had all the qualifications to be a successful first lady.

Americans want to admire and emulate their first ladies, but they do not want them to have undue influence on their husbands or to meddle in government or foreign affairs. The media's insistent underscoring of the Reagans superclose marriage, along with interviews of former staff members who told of the power Nancy held over her husband (vehemently denied by both Reagans), brought a certain fear that the new first lady might feel free "to shape policy or exert power that she had not been elected to wield."[4]

Nancy was already being set up for instant criticism. Rosalynn Carter had said that she "would be criticized just as severely if she stayed in the White House and poured tea as she would be for using the influence of my unelected, unofficial, unpaid job." Nancy could expect no less. She would be constantly in the eye of the press, which would feel compelled to take a stand and explain her to their readers, who were often more interested in good copy based on half-truths or negatives than in an even-handed story. Articles in major newspapers had made harsh note of Nancy's wealthy friends, her extravagances as first lady of California, and her fierce protection of her husband. There were hints that there would be trouble ahead, and it was obvious that the press would be on duty to report it.

Nancy had about ten weeks to prepare for their final leave-taking from California and their arrival in Washington for the inauguration. Once again, the Reagans were faced with having two homes—the Palisades and the ranch—whose upkeep would be paid for out of their own pockets. This time they decided to sell the house on San Onofre Drive (priced at $1.9 million), which Nancy felt was not presidential enough and keep the ranch, because Ronnie loved it so and his image as an outdoorsman—some said "a cowboy"—was so associated with it. There were daily choices on what to sell, store, or ship to Washington. Then there was Nancy's wardrobe for the inauguration, the balls, and the many events pre-and postinauguration. She wanted to bring her own style to the White House. There would be an emphasis on elegance.

The house on San Onofre Drive was at the end of a cul-de-sac, and was once again besieged. Secret Service men swarmed the place, so many that the house next door, which happened to be up for sale, was leased by the government for several months as an added protection and for meetings. A "bridge" and a staircase had been constructed extending from the rear of one house to the other for privacy and faster access. ("What do you think it cost to put up those stairs?" Reagan asked his son Michael one afternoon. Michael replied that he couldn't guess. "Well, I just saw the bill for them. [They] charged twenty-five hundred to make those steps and they are charging a thousand dollars more to tear them down. That tells me how much waste there is in government, and I'm going to stop it because Barney and I could have done the job for five hundred dollars and had wood left over.")[5]

The premises and the street were a constant hive of activity. There were telephones in nearby trees and blinking barricades that restricted access to the street without proper identification and a reason for being there. Reporters and video cameramen, camped beyond the barricades, were stopping all the Reagans' neighbors as they came and went. The writer John Gay was one. "I couldn't even jog in peace," he recalled. "The Secret Service and the police would keep changing guards at the barricades. I would return from my running and have to stand there dripping wet while they phoned ahead to confirm my clearance."[6]

Despite a heavy load of daily meetings and briefings, Reagan tried to maintain a semblance of normal life during this waiting and planning period. Mrs. Donald Hubbs, one of the eleven other home owners on the street, recalled walking past the front gates of the Reagans' home one morning with her dog and hearing someone call down, "Hello, there."

"I looked around and the voice said: 'Up here.'

"When I gazed up I saw Ronald Reagan in the branches of one of his olive trees, pruning it." She added that there had been Secret Service men standing nearby.[7]

Shortly after Reagan won the election, Rosalynn Carter invited Nancy to "come for coffee" and to look around. Nancy was pleased to do so and flew to Washington for a tour of her soon-to-be new home. She had visited the White House in 1967, for a governors' dinner when Lyndon Johnson was president, but she had not been back since. The first lady met her in the Diplomatic Room. Nancy recalls that the temperature in the White House was being kept low, as there was an energy crisis, and that "the chill in [Mrs. Carter's] manner matched the chill in the room." She adds that she understood that "it must be painful to show the residence [which has been your home for four years] to the wife of the man who defeated your husband."

Mrs. Carter asked what she would like to see first. "Well," Nancy suggested, "I know there are two connecting rooms that can be separate bedrooms or, if you sleep together, a master bedroom and a study." She explained that she needed to decide what furniture to bring.

The first lady seemed edgy at this. She hesitated a moment and then explained that she was packing and these rooms were "so messed up." She agreed, however, to open the door and let Nancy "look in." At that point she excused herself and had Rex Stouten, the chief usher of the White House, continue the tour. Nancy was not displeased about this because she had already been told by Tish Baldrige, Jacqueline Kennedy's former press secretary who was now assisting Nancy in the transition, that the chief usher actually ran the White House: "Next to your husband, he'll be the most important man in your life." Nancy and Stouten hit it off right away. Stouten had been at the White House for thirty-one years and would become indispensable to Nancy, steering her "through landmines and traps" for all the years the Reagans would occupy the White House.

Although there were no fire hazards and the presidential quarters in the White House were immaculately kept, Nancy found them "dreary and uninviting. It just didn't look the way the president's house should look. It wasn't a place we'd be proud to bring people—our personal friends or our country friends [this last seemingly referring to the more humble folk who visited the ranch]. Frankly, the White House was a little run-down and shabby. [Son Ron, she said, at first glance, remarked, 'It looks low rent.']"[8]

This remark was made by Nancy Reagan after she left the White House in 1989, but it still seems inappropriate. The White House is a symbol of American democracy. It is the people's house, and it stands as a tribute to the history of the nation. "It wasn't a place we'd be proud to bring people—our personal friends or our country friends" is perhaps the most tasteless remark ever made publicly by a first lady. The White House was not built to impress the rich friends of one of its residents. Since Mrs. Reagan's friends were almost all American, it would seem *they* would have been proud just to be invited guests to the White House. No doubt the apartments need fresh paint at the end of an administration. Any house requires such upkeep: the White House is no exception. After the departure of each president (for at least the last seven occupants, for which there are records), the apartments have been "refreshed and repainted." The work, along with any necessary repairs, is done during the first four to six weeks of the new occupants' residence and is paid for by the government. Any costly or major renovations or restorations have to be approved. Only a portion of Mrs. Reagan's planned alterations and refurbishing were ultimately approved.

After her tour, Nancy knew exactly what she wanted to have done. A bedroom adjoining the master bedroom had to be converted into a comfortable study for Ronnie. Another room was to be fitted as an oversized walk-in closet. The living room needed new upholstered sofas and chairs and a large coffee table, and the third floor—which the Carters had not used—turned into suitable guest bedrooms to be used by the family when they came to visit. For the first time in its history, the president's apartments would be California casual. All this was not going to be easy to implement in the short time Nancy had.

As soon as she returned to California, she hired Ted Graber, a designer who was currently doing some work for Betsy and Alfred Bloomingdale and had beautifully restored the United States ambassador's residence in London for Walter and Lee Annenberg. Graber was to integrate her favored pieces (some lacquered chinoiserie) with the American antiques that predominate in the White House. The first lady she most wanted to emulate was Jacqueline Kennedy. Although the changes Nancy required were to be confidential, Graber viewed the premises twice, spending over an hour each time, and Nancy returned once while the Carters were at Camp David.

There were unfortunate leaks of these visits. Hostile press reports appeared claiming that Mrs. Reagan wanted to redo the White House *before* the inauguration and knock down a wall in the Lincoln Bedroom. Nancy was appalled, the latter she claimed was inconceivable and the former simply not true. She had, she said, consulted a designer (Graber) to start work *after* they were in residence. Still, Nancy Reagan was believed to be the first new occupant of the White House with plans in progress for physical changes to the presidential apartments before her husband's inauguration. It obviously would have been much more politic to wait until the Carters had moved out.

The Reagan family gathered together at San Onofre for the last Christmas they would spend together in the house where they had lived for twenty-nine years. Doria and Ron, who was now dancing with the celebrated Joffrey Ballet Company, had recently married in a private ceremony in New York. (A Secret Service agent was best man.) "Putting an end," Michael wrote, "to the gossip [of Ron's] sexual preferences."[9] Maureen was present with her fiancé, six-foot, seven-inch Dennis Revell, and they were talking about the possibility of a spring wedding.

Nancy wanted Maureen to marry *before* the inauguration as she had reservations about the propriety of the couple being photographed together at the swearing-in and staying at Blair House with the rest of the family before they were wed. She eventually weakened on this, and both Maureen and Dennis appear in the official family photograph taken in the White House the first day of the Reagans' residence.

Patti came accompanied by her dog, Freebo, who was placed in a confined area of the backyard, as he never seemed able to control his bladder when he was excited. Neil and Bess arrived carrying shopping bags filled with presents. There was a Christmas tree, but not all the ornaments collected by Nancy over the years were hung on it, as she had already packed the best ones away to be shipped with their other household belongings to Washington. A heightened air of excitement hung over the gathering. The only calm person in the group was Reagan, who carved the ham with a surgeon's expertise. A Christmas dinner was also served in the adjoining house to the Secret Service men who were on duty that day.

Nancy received a $10,000 floor-length Maximillian mink coat from Ronnie and a Christmas letter that had become a tradition, wherein he thanked her for all the love, togetherness, and happiness of the past year. Another Christmas ritual was the gift of a half of a frozen steer from the ranch for each of their family members. This year Michael complained that he and Colleen still had a quarter left from the previous year—and so he received two baskets filled with local Santa Barbara wines. Years before Nancy had stopped buying individual gifts, personally selected.

Throughout most of December and the first two weeks in January, Nancy was engaged in the almost full-time occupation of gathering together a new wardrobe, while Tish Baldrige worked to set up Nancy's social schedule for her first weeks in the White House. (Along with Jacqueline Kennedy, Baldrige had also helped Lady Bird Johnson, Pat Nixon, and Rosalynn Carter during their first weeks in the White House.) Nancy convinced James Galanos, whose gowns she had often worn, that he would be doing California designers a great service if he gave her a gown for the inaugural balls, since the dress was sure to be credited and described worldwide by the press. Galanos came up with a striking, white crystal and bead gown that took his workers six weeks to complete and cost him as much as Nancy's Maximillian mink. Most of her shopping was done in private rooms at the expensive shops on Rodeo Drive, where she assembled over $25,000 in clothes, at highly discounted prices, or free. Only Barbra Streisand, a dedicated Democrat who would not attend the inauguration, was as nimble at securing "free-bies" or discounted purchases for her wardrobe (and household). Arrangements had been made for Nancy's current hairdresser, Julius, who had also had Betsy Bloomingdale as a client, to fly to Washington to do her hair for all the events.

The Reagans began their journey to Washington and into the unknown on January 14, the inauguration just six days away. Their housekeeper of many years, Anne Allman, remained in the house on San Onofre to oversee the moving and cleaning-out operations. Early that morning, Patti had arrived to wish her parents luck and to "mend fences." Her refusal to change her attitude toward her father's candidacy had wounded them, even though Patti claims that, aside from her political differences with her father, she had a deep-seated fear that he would be assassinated if elected. For the moment past differences were set aside and mother and daughter clung together in a long goodbye.

All their neighbors, none of whom had really been friends with the Reagans, were grouped at the barricades to wave to them as their limousine pulled out of the cul-de-sac for the last time. Their car was led and flanked by a convoy of police cars and motorcycles flashing their lights and honking their horns as the motorcade wound through the curving roads of the Palisades to Sunset Boulevard, flag-wavers lining the streets until it turned off and headed for the private government airfield where Air Force One, the president's gleaming blue and white private plane, the American flag emblazoned on its tail and the presidential seal on either side of its nose, waited for them.

Nancy admitted that she could not contain her awe as she stepped into the plane, carrying a hatbox with Nelle's Bible, which Ronnie was to use at his inauguration, nestled safely within. There was a private presidential suite containing a study, bedroom, and bath, furnished luxuriously. They were taken on a tour of the airship, into the cockpit to meet the pilot and copilot, and to the kitchen, where the chef advised them that on future flights they could order anything they wanted in advance and it would be prepared for them. This time there was a menu. For security reasons, supplies came from a different source with each flight, and the suppliers did not know in advance that they were for Air Force One. The Reagans kissed as the plane lifted off, then Reagan sat at the desk in their suite and went over the sheaf of paperwork that he had brought with him, including some notes for his inaugural address, while Nancy wrote letters on stationery embossed with the Air Force One letterhead to her close friends. It was her way, she admitted, of saying, "Look at me! I'm riding on Air Force One!"[10]

After arriving at Andrews Air Force Base, they were driven to Blair House, situated across Pennsylvania Avenue from the White House, consisting of four houses connected together, each offering privacy and comfort to presidential guests. "Blair House *really* needs fixing up," Nancy wrote in her diary on January 14, 1981, the first day of her stay there.[11] Blair House had been acquired by the government during the Truman administration when major repairs were being made to the White House, and in all fairness to Nancy, it had not had much done to it in the intervening years. (It would take six years and nearly ten million dollars to renovate Blair House while Reagan was president, during which time foreign dignitaries were housed at commercial hotels, causing many security problems to the establishments.) Within forty-eight hours, the rest of the family, including Nancy's parents (neither of whom was entirely well), Richard Davis, his wife Patricia, and their family, and Neil and Bess, as well as the Reagan's housekeeper, Anne Allman, and Reagan's driver, Barney Barnett, stayed at Blair House, while their many California friends established themselves at various top hotels.

Washington had not seen such lavish festivities since Dolley Madison's golden days. There would be 103 Republican-hosted, extravagant galas in the four days leading up to the inauguration. The display of diamonds and other jewels was dazzling. Dinners and after-theater parties were Edwardian in their abundance of food. Tickets for the various inaugural balls were priced upward of $100, whereas four years earlier Jimmy Carter had insisted during his inaugural that no ticket should cost more than $25 and Rosalynn wore a dress she had worn six years previously at a governor's ball in Atlanta.

The press was hard on the Reagans, even as they took glee in covering every overindulgence. All this lavish consumption came at a time when unemployment was at an almost forty-year high of 7.5 percent, inflation and bankruptcies were rampant, and the fifty-two American hostages were, after more than 440 days, still being held by terrorists in the American embassy in Tehran where some had been subjected to the horror of mock executions. Despite the elegance of the participants and the infectious gaiety of the events, this would not seem an intelligent way to start a new presidency. But there were many who disagreed, who thought the country needed a "business-man fantasy" instead of the "common-man fantasy" symbolized by Jimmy Carter and that the Republicans' lavish inaugural plans were a sign of renewed presidential power.

While Carter desperately tried to get the hostages released before his term came to an end, and Mrs. Carter supervised the moving of the family's personal belongings, and teen-aged Amy Carter said goodbye to the friends she had made during the family's four years in Washington, Reagan and Nancy partied. Reagan had never enjoyed large formal gatherings and receptions or wearing a tuxedo; "they're made for those slim, graceful fellows like Fred Astaire," he once said.[12] But he was in high spirits and enough of his California friends attended each party to make him feel at ease. The first evening, an elegant dinner was held at Merrywood, Jacqueline Kennedy Onassis's childhood home across the Potomac from Washington. There were "parties within parties, before-the-party parties, after-the-party parties, state parties, cocktail parties, and receptions. The only thing to do after the brunches and lunches," one witness wrote, "was to head out in the late afternoon already formally dressed." The flaunting of wealth so disturbed Barry Goldwater that when asked in a television interview on NBC what he thought about the celebrations, he blurted, "Ostentatious! I've seen seven of them [parties]. And I say when you've got to pay $2,000 for a limousine for four days . . . the women wear different jewels and dresses for every party, at a time when most people in this country can't hack it, that's ostentatious!"[13]

The Reagans did not let Goldwater's chastening words stop them.

In the four preinaugural days they attended as many parties as they could, stopping at each for a limited time, driven in the $2,000 limousine and accompanied by a bevy of Secret Service men. On Saturday night, January 17, with the thermometer at a frigid 26 degrees and snow crusting the earth and roofs, the Reagans stood on the steps of the Lincoln Memorial while the Mormon Tabernacle Choir sang "God Bless America" and "laser beams laced through the sky linking the Lincoln Memorial with the Washington Monument, the Capitol, the White House and the Jefferson Memorial."[14] On Sunday (after a brunch, an afternoon tea—for Nancy—and three cocktail parties, departing each after exactly ten minutes), the Reagans attended the extravaganza in the John F. Kennedy Performing Arts Center, spending twenty minutes at each performance in the three theaters within the center, catching snatches of the National Symphony in a program of movie music (including the theme from *Kings Row*, one of Reagan's early films), Mikhail Baryshnikov dancing in a new ballet, *Push Comes to Shove*, and Lorin Maazel conducting a Schubert symphony. They ended the day with a brief stop at a late supper party.

Until sundown Monday Reagan had remained secluded at Blair House, working on—and rehearsing—his inaugural speech, consulting with his transition staff, including Richard V. Allen, his senior foreign policy adviser, and Alexander M. Haig Jr., his designated secretary of state, while waiting anxiously for news about the hostages. Meanwhile, Nancy continued her marathon pace in the festivities, attending a reception in honor of Vice President-elect George Bush and acting as cohonoree with Barbara Bush for a "Distinguished Ladies Reception" at the Kennedy Center. As the day progressed, it looked as if the hostage crisis would not be resolved, making a clean shift of power difficult. Reagan directed Haig to set up a special interagency task force, consisting of aides to both himself and Carter. Dressed nattily in a dark brown hand-tailored suit, the president-elect walked jauntily from one part of Blair House to another to meet with his staff.

As sunset approached, on the night before the inauguration, there still had been no word from Iran about the hostages, and seemingly no breakthrough. At 7 P.M., Julius having done Nancy's hair for the second time that day, Nancy and Reagan were taken by helicopter to the Capital Center in Largo, Maryland, where Johnnie Carson, host of NBC's *The Tonight Show*, would emcee a two-and-a-half-hour televised inaugural gala put together by Frank Sinatra with entertainment provided by Sinatra, Dean Martin, Bob Hope, Ethel Merman, Jimmy Stewart, Charlton Heston, opera star Grace Bumbry, and Broadway song-and-dance man Ben Vereen, among many others. The Capital Center is a huge, shell-shaped sports arena that seats twenty thousand (this night at a ticket high of $500 to $2000). The Reagans were seated in blue velvet thronelike chairs on a raised platform at one end of the arena. Nancy wore a regal gown with a black velvet bodice with exaggerated puffed sleeves, wasp waist, and a full black satin skirt, the hem etched in jet. Reagan was splendid in black tie and tux. Carson opened the show with cracks about the expensive, exclusive parties being thrown in the Reagans' honor. "I went to the men's room at the Shoreham Hotel," he quipped, "and found it was by invitation only."

Merman sang "Everything's Comin' Up Roses," changing the lyrics to "I had a dream, a dream about you, *Ronnie* [baby]." Jimmy Stewart brought laughter when he repeated the oft-told story of how when Jack Warner, Reagan's former studio boss, first heard about his presidential hopes, he quipped, "No, Jimmy Stewart for President, Reagan as his best friend." Then he gave a short, moving speech to introduce the country's only living five-star general, Omar Bradley, who was helped out on stage and saluted the president-elect from his wheelchair. For Nancy, the high point came when Sinatra took the microphone and announced: "I should like to do something special for our new first lady. This is one of my favorite songs and we've had just a little change in the lyrics. And I hope you'll like this, Nancy." The song, "Nancy, With the Laughing Face," had originally been written when his first child, Nancy, was born and it had been a top hit.

"I'm so pleased that our First Lady's Nancy,
Also pleased that I'm sort of a chum.
Bet the eight years all will be fancy,

As fancy as they come . . .
Nancy, Nancy, Nancy, with the smiling face."

At the end of the show (later criticized for what the critics felt was an outrageous lack of taste), the president-elect and his lady, to thunderous applause, walked down from their platform and onto the stage, the black-suited Secret Service men, looking like Wall Street traders at the opening bell of the stock market, scurrying to surround them, then lining up across the foot of the stage facing the audience. Reagan stood at the microphone, Nancy beside him. He spoke with well-felt emotion, ending with: "Almost every day for a long time now people have said to Nancy and myself, 'Has it really sunk in?' And we've looked at each other and said, 'Well, no, it really hasn't.' Well, tonight there was a part in the program when I leaned over to her and said, 'It's sunk in.' Thank you." The ovations continued, and the program closed with the Reagans waving back at the audience.[15] They had played the scene like the conquering heroes. Republicans loved them for it, while the Democrats found the evening a galling taste of the crass theatrics that certainly would follow. Some Democrats, however, thought that might not be too bad, because it was sure to bring their party back to power in four years.

The Reagans returned to Blair House late that night, both looking tired and yet exhilarated. Reagan went straight to the desk in their apartments and began to edit some small points in his inaugural speech. He had been in touch with his transition team all during the day—the 443rd day since the hostages had been taken—and it looked at this moment as if the crisis would be left over for his administration to solve.

Less than three weeks short of his seventieth birthday, he was the oldest man elected president. He would laugh this off. "You know I've already lived twenty years longer than my life expectancy was at birth." A pause, and then, "And that has been a source of annoyance to a number of people."[16]

Nancy rose early on January 20. Ronnie was sound asleep, his snores a low buzz. She decided not to wake him and went into the adjoining room, where she was served her breakfast on a tray. At half-past seven Julius arrived to do her hair. A half hour later, a breathless Michael Deaver appeared, certain he would find Reagan rehearsing his speech. "Where's the governor?" he asked. Nancy replied that he was still in bed. Deaver indicated that he thought it might be wise for him to be awakened. There was the question as to whether he should mention the hostages in his speech. Carter had been up all night, he had been told, trying to get them freed while he was still president. Nancy nodded her agreement for Deaver to go into the bedroom.

Darkness greeted him when he entered. He picked his way to the windows and opened the drapes a little. A swath of morning sun rushed across the room and onto the king-sized bed that dominated it; its appearance was a surprise, especially to the weathermen who had predicted partially cloudy skies.

"Governor?" Deaver called rather loudly from a distance. "It's eight o'clock."

Reagan grunted and pushed himself up. "Yeah?"

Deaver reminded him that in less than four hours he would be inaugurated as the fortieth president of the United States and gave him the latest bulletin on the hostages—which was no news, really. Deaver was overwhelmed at the man's calm. It seemed to be "business as usual." After Reagan had eaten breakfast, he read all the latest briefings and decided that he would not make any mention of the hostages in his address.[17]

The Reagans then got dressed for the day's long-awaited swearing-in. A morning suit was traditional for the president-elect, but Carter (as had Lyndon Johnson, the last Democratic president before Carter) wore a business suit to signal his desire for a common-man approach. Nancy had convinced Ronnie that a more formal choice was preferable out of respect for the occasion. After some research on past swearing-ins, it was decided that he would opt for a club coat, striped pants, and a gray vest, but unlike Lincoln or Roosevelt, who wore top hats, he would go bareheaded. Nancy wore a cardinal red dress and coat ensemble by Adolfo. Thus, dressed splendidly by nine-thirty, they collected their family and, joined by the Bushes and a cordon of Secret Service men, attended a brief service at nearby St. John's Episcopal Church, seated in George Washington's onetime pew in the small eighteenth-century building.

The Reagans then returned to Blair House, where they were joined by Senator Mark Hatfield, chairman of the Joint Congressional Committee on Inaugural Ceremonies, who escorted them to the White House. It is a tradition that the incoming and outgoing presidents, along with the vice presidents and their wives, meet for coffee in the Blue Room before the swearing-in.

"[President Carter's] face was pale and he looked exhausted. It was impossible not to feel for him," Nancy recalled. "Rosalynn was visibly uncomfortable and unhappy. She said hello, but aside from that we barely spoke to each other."[18]

Carter told Reagan that he had secured the hostages' freedom, but the Iranians had not yet released them. (Later, in the holding room at the Capitol before the swearing-in, Reagan told Deaver to pass him a note, "even if it's during my speech," if the hostages had been released, so that he could announce it.)[19]

They drove to the Capitol in two cars—Reagan and Carter in the lead car, Nancy and Rosalynn and John Rhodes, the House minority leader, in a second car. The day had grown overcast, but the temperature was a moderate fifty-five degrees and the air clear. Inside the cars, it was a bit more chilly. "As we drove up Pennsylvania Avenue," Reagan wrote, "the limousine was very quiet. The president and I were seated side by side. Although he was polite he said hardly a word to me as we moved slowly toward the Capitol, and I think he hesitated to look me in the face. Perhaps he felt drained after being up most of the previous night. . . . Whatever the reason the atmosphere in the limousine was . . . chilly." Reagan added in a kindly way that "to be forced out of the White House by a vote of the people. . . . It must have been very hard on him [Carter]."[20]

The motorcade arrived at the Capitol at 11:15 A.M. where the presidential party was greeted by the House and Senate sergeants at arms and escorted to two separate holding rooms—the Reagans in one, the Carters in another—which would seem to have been a sizable relief for both families. However, the hostage crisis was a continuing concern and threatened to overshadow what was now almost regarded as "the day's other event." The three major networks were forced to cut back and forth from Iran to Washington. "If we can just get those planes off the ground," said Walter Cronkite. "It certainly hangs over this event."[21]

"They did it deliberately," ABC's Frank Reynolds said of the Iranians.[22] The hitch was supposedly caused by escrow funds that had been frozen and were now to be transferred to Iran but which the Iranians claimed they had not yet received. "He's not even the lead story in his own inauguration," Phil Jones of CBS complained.[23] Syndicated columnist George Will, acting as a contributing commentator on ABC, added, "This is just the final episode of Iran's manipulation of us through television . . . planning this to rain on our parade."[24]

Since James Monroe's 1817 inauguration, it had been established tradition, broken only by unexpected circumstances such as FDR's death, Kennedy's assassination, and Nixon's resignation, that the new president and vice president were sworn in on the East Portico of the Capitol. Reagan had requested the site be changed to the West Portico, which faced out across the city and had an open view to the monuments to past presidents. It was a panoramic scene, one that Reagan with his film background knew would play better on television, and a stroke of public relations genius. To a military fanfare the participants and their honored guests entered onto the glass-protected speakers' stand from opposite sides at exactly 11:45 A.M. The platform had been erected on top of the tiered marble and granite steps leading to the freshly painted Capitol.

In his left hand Reagan held his mother's Bible, crumbling and bandaged with tape. Inside the front cover, in Nelle's flowing script was written "You can be too big for God to use, but you cannot be too small." A folded paper also inside contained a sonnet, composed by her but paraphrasing (at least the first line) Milton's sonnet "On His Blindness."

When I consider how my life is spent
The most that I can do will be to prove
'Tis by his side, each day, I seek to move
To higher, nobler things my mind is bent

Thus giving of my strength, which God has lent,
I strive some needy souls' unrest to soothe
Lest they the paths of righteousness shall lose.
Through fault of mine, my maker to present
If I should fail to show them of their needs
How would I hope to meet him face to face
Or give a just account of all my ways
In thought of mind, in word, and in each deed
My life must prove the power of his grace
By every action through my living days.

Inside the back cover of Nelle's Bible were listed the births and deaths of her family, the Wilsons. Reagan had placed a marker in the Bible at a passage in Chronicles quoting the words of God to Solomon: "If my people, which are called by my name, shall humble themselves, and pray, and seek my face, and turn from their wicked ways, then will I hear from heaven, and will forgive their sin, and will heal the land." As soon as he was seated, Reagan passed the Bible to Nancy.

The program began with a band selection of patriotic music, with the thousands who lined the streets singing along with those on the speakers' platform. After the invocation, George Herbert Walker Bush took the oath of office as vice president, administered by associate justice of the Supreme Court Potter Stewart on a Bible held by Barbara Bush (it had been given to Bush by the Reverend Billy Graham). Both the outgoing vice president, Walter Mondale, and Carter sat expressionless while helicopters wheeled overhead and as if at a light director's command, the winter sun broke through the clouds and splintered off the newly gilded dome of the Capitol.

Reagan's step was sure, his posture proud, as he approached the microphone preparing to take the oath of office administered by Warren Earl Burger, chief justice of the United States. Nancy was by his side, holding his hand on the Bible, an ever-so-faint nervous twitch at the corner of her mouth as she gazed lovingly up at him. In a strong voice he said: "I, Ronald Wilson Reagan, do solemnly swear that I will faithfully execute the office of the President of the United States, and will to the best of my ability, preserve, protect and defend the Constitution of the United States, so help me God." Immediately, he leaned down and kissed Nancy and then shook hands with Chief Justice Burger. The crowds on the mall cheered and applauded, and Reagan, Nancy beaming at his side, waved at them for several moments before stepping to the microphone.

He spoke for exactly nineteen minutes. It was an impressive speech, delivered in Reagan's inimitable style, beginning with the country's current economic ills. "We must act today, to preserve tomorrow," he advised. "And let there be no misunderstanding—we are going to begin to act, beginning today." The speech began truly to build about halfway through, when Reagan said, "Let us renew our determination, our courage, and our strength. And let us renew our faith and our hope.

"We have every right to dream heroic dreams. Those who say that we are in a time when there are no heroes just don't know where to look. You can see heroes every day going in and out of factory gates. Others, a handful in number, produce enough food to feed all of us and then the world beyond.

"You meet heroes across a counter—and they are on both sides of that counter. There are entrepreneurs with faith in themselves and faith in an idea who create new jobs, new wealth and opportunity. . . . Your dreams, your hopes, your goals are going to be the dreams, the hopes, and the goals of this administration, so help me God. . . . How can we love our country and not love our countrymen, and loving them, reach out a hand when they fall, heal them when they are sick and provide opportunity to make them self-sufficient so they will be equal in fact and not just in theory?"

He was very much Nelle's son in this speech, especially so when he continued: "I am told that tens of thousand of prayer meetings are being held on this day, for that I am deeply grateful. We are a nation under God, and I believe God intended for us to be free. It would be fitting and good, I think, if on each Inauguration Day in future years it should be declared a day of prayer.

"This is the first time in history that this ceremony has been held . . . on this West Front of the Capitol. Standing here, one faces a magnificent vista, opening up on this city's special beauty and history. At the end of this open mall are those shrines to the giants on whose shoulders we stand.

"Directly in front of me, the monument to a monumental man: George Washington, Father of our country. A man of humility who came to greatness reluctantly. He led America out of revolutionary victory into infant nationhood. Off to one side, the stately memorial to Thomas Jefferson. The Declaration of Independence flames with his eloquence.

"And then beyond the Reflecting Pool the dignified columns of the Lincoln Memorial. Whoever would understand in his heart the meaning of America will find it in the life of Abraham Lincoln.

"Beyond those monuments to heroism is the Potomac River, and on the far shore the sloping hills of Arlington National Cemetery with its row upon row of simple white markers bearing crosses or Stars of David. They add up to only a tiny fraction of the price that has been paid for our freedom.

"Each one of those markers is a monument to the kind of hero I spoke of earlier."

The speech did not have as great a sound bite as Roosevelt's famous "All we have to fear is fear itself" or Kennedy's "Ask not what your country can do for you—ask what you can do for your country." But it was of presidential quality and it defined the man to the world.

Reagan had written the first draft of his inaugural address on January 8, while flying from Washington, where he and Nancy had spent a few days, back to Los Angeles. It was based on fifty pages (10,000 words) of material assembled for him by Kenneth Khachigian, who had worked in a similar capacity with Richard Nixon. From the material given to him, which included subjects his advisers had thought should be mentioned, Reagan had fashioned a three-thousand word speech. But certain things continued to worry him. There was a phrase "no barriers born of discrimination." Going over this draft with Khachigian, he said, "There's been such an increase in anti-Semitism around the world—let's include the word bigotry." The line finally delivered was "no barriers born of bigotry or discrimination." He had put the draft aside until the flight on Air Force One, at which time he'd changed a few things, cut others, and added the memorable line "How can you love your country and not your countrymen?" (which might seem sexist today). The day before the inauguration, he trimmed the address further, so that its final length would be just over two thousand words. The speeches of most presidents-elect, including Jimmy Carter's, were largely the handiwork of professional speechwriters.

Reagan's original draft was written in longhand on nine legal-sized lined pages. He trimmed it and added the final paragraphs later and suggested to his secretary, "You may have trouble reading my writing, so let me read this to you." Earlier presidents-elect also distributed their speeches widely before delivery. Reagan did not. Aside from Khachigian and a secretary, he showed the speech to only five people: Deaver, Meese, Nofziger, his press secretary James S. Brady, and Nancy.[25]

After the speech, Reagan heard a band playing "Hail to the Chief" to him for the first time. Then a man in the crowd nearest the stand jumped up, his arm extended, a small radio in his hand, and shouted, "They're in the air!" Everyone knew what that meant. The hostages had lifted off and were on their way home by way of a U.S. base in Germany. It was a dramatic moment. People rose up from their seats, crying, hugging each other. Reagan, Nancy, their family, and close friends left the speakers' stand and went to a room off the Senate chamber to hear the latest news. Reagan's first decision was that Carter should fly to Germany to welcome the freed hostages. The presidential party was served lunch in the Capitol amid great excitement. There were California roses on each table, and women guests received small silver-plated boxes containing jelly beans. Reagan stood up and announced, "With thanks to Almighty God, I have been given a tag line, the get-off line everyone wants at the end of a toast or a speech. Thirty minutes ago, the plane bearing our prisoners left Iranian airspace and are free of Iran."

After formally signing papers nominating members of his cabinet, the Reagans were escorted to an open-top limousine for the inaugural parade from Capitol Hill to the White House. The car moved at a slow speed, Secret Service men walking beside it and the new President and First Lady waving and throwing kisses to the cheering crowds; Nancy, the press reported, "looking bright as a beacon" in her colorful red

Adolfo outfit. Through all the excitement and the din and brass of the many bands (including the Dixon High School Band, strutting proudly and marching in front of the Reagans' car), Nancy claims her thoughts were on the transfer of their baggage from Blair House to the White House, which was being supervised by Anne Allman and Ted Graber. Her fear was that in the confusion—for the Carter staff would be moving the last of their belongings out at the same time—her ball gown and accessories for the gala events that night might be lost.

Suddenly they were at the steps of their new home. The household staff stood waiting to greet them as the elevator doors opened to the White House family quarters. Rex Stouten led them to their private suite. All the suitcases that had been labeled "President's Bedroom" had been unpacked. Nancy's gown was hung in the closet with Reagan's evening suit and dress shirt, creaseless, ready for them to wear.

She felt "awed," she said, "coming *home* as the new president and first lady. You think of all the families who have lived here before. It's very humbling."[27]

At 5:15 P.M. the Reagans stood hand in hand in the winter dusk on the Truman Balcony of the White House and watched the magnificent fireworks display in their honor. Then, after a light supper, they dressed for the evening's festivities. Nancy excitedly fastened around her neck the $450,000 diamond necklace loaned to her for the evening by Harry Winston Jewelers. They were scheduled to appear at a record ten balls between 9:00 and 12:00 P.M. They set out in a limousine followed by a cortege of Secret Service men, who were amazed at the Reagans' stamina as they breezed in and out of the celebrations, each one a mob scene of opulence and high spirits. Midway through the evening they reached the Kennedy Center, where their family was seated in a long box (Patti in a flapper-style ruffled red chiffon that contrasted dramatically with her obvious discomfort) surrounded by their California friends, patiently waiting for the guests of honor in a tier of boxes festooned with patriotic bunting. Ten thousand Californians, some representatives from neighboring states mixed in, pushed and shoved to get a glimpse of the president and the first lady as they were escorted through the crush of well-wishers and the just-plain-curious who wanted a close look at

Nancy's gown before it went on display some time later at the Smithsonian, as was the custom.

The clothes and jewels were spectacular. Many women wore full-length fur coats of chinchilla, mink, or Norwegian blue fox. With not enough safe places to leave them, they carried them around. Rubies and diamonds appeared to be the favorite gems of the evening, Nancy's necklace was outvalued by many, and "bouffant hairdos of almost architectural stature" were much in evidence. The Reagans danced once around the floor at three of the galas, spending no more than fifteen minutes at each, and still managed to look fresh at midnight when they were whisked back to the White House.

Their king-size bed had been assembled and made up, the linen and covers turned down. Fresh flowers scented the air. Whatever else of historic magnitude had occurred during this day, the moment the Reagans closed the door to their new bedroom, turned off the lights, and lay back on their pillows, spending their first night in this room, in this house filled with the ghosts of presidents and first ladies past, must have seemed overwhelming.

Here Franklin Roosevelt had been helped from his wheelchair into bed, the fate of a world at war depending on decisions he had made that day and would make in the days to come; here John Fitzgerald Kennedy spent the last few nights before his assassination; and here Richard Nixon, his words rambling and incoherent when awakened, dressed to make his emotional exit after his resignation.

If he survived, no president, or his wife, ever left the White House unscathed and unchanged. The Reagans had dared the fates. Now their fates were in the balance.

CHAPTER ELEVEN

MEET THE PRESS

W hen asked by a reporter what it was like to be the wife of a president, Eleanor Roosevelt replied, "It's hell."[1] Nancy quickly discovered that this was true and that the responsible parties were the members of the press. First ladies lived fairly sheltered lives in the nineteenth century, when the press was not so predatory. Still, a few were publicly censured, vilified, and only occasionally praised by the newshounds. Dolley Madison, hostess extraordinaire, was one who was well liked. She was known as Queen Dolley and reigned as the *grande dame* of the nation's capital during and after Madison's presidency. Mary Todd Lincoln was the victim of slanderous attacks by the popular press, which called her variously "vulgar," "vain," "pretentious," "greedy," "wasteful" and "corrupt," and, during the Civil War, "at heart a traitor . . . in communication with the Confederate authorities."[2] But it was Eleanor Roosevelt who learned to use the press for her own purposes.

There is a story, perhaps apocryphal, that Mrs. Roosevelt went missing the night Franklin was first elected president. She was found weeping in a secluded corner of a hallway in the hotel in New York City where they were listening to election results. When asked what was wrong, she sighed and said, "Now, I'll have no identity." To the contrary. She became a standard-bearer for women's rights, gave lectures, and wrote a popular newspaper column, "My Day," often citing her husband's views along with her own. She was a highly intelligent, dynamic woman, who it was rumored had a lesbian relationship for several years with an Associated Press reporter, Lorena Hickok (not revealed until many years after both were dead), while Franklin carried on a long-time affair with Lucy Mercer Rutherford. Eleanor was the most lionized and the most controversial first lady until Hillary Clinton, who claimed a psychic connection with Mrs. Roosevelt. Eleanor understood politics, kept up with foreign affairs and domestic policy, and voiced her views. In 1940 there were those who thought she could run in Franklin's place if he were denied the opportunity for an unprecedented third term— and that she would win. He ran and won, and in 1945 was inaugurated for a fourth term, dying only weeks later, on April 12, 1945. Eleanor was the one to call Harry Truman, her husband's vice president, to inform him, "Harry, the president is dead," in her usual forthright manner. Truman was overcome for a moment and then asked, "Is there anything I can do for you?"

"Is there anything *we* can do for you," she replied. "You are the one in trouble now," the *we* referring to herself as one of the people.[3]

Eleanor Roosevelt chaired the United Nations Human Rights Commission after her husband's death and was one of the original drafters of the Universal Declaration of Human Rights and then fought to ensure it was adopted by the General Assembly. She became an international spokesperson for her beliefs and was on the board of the newly formed Peace Corps when she died of a rare blood disease in 1962, having completed the last of her many books, *Tomorrow Is Now*, the title from her oft-repeated phrase "We cannot wait until tomorrow. Tomorrow is now."

It was not Mrs. Roosevelt, but Jacqueline Kennedy whom Nancy most admired, perhaps for what some might consider shallower achievements: her sense of elegance and style and her ability to win the hearts of both the people and the press. Jackie carried herself with grace and dignity. She epitomized the American idea of royalty. "Jackie is superb in her personal life," Kennedy said of his wife at dinner with friends, "but do you think she'll ever amount to anything in her political life?" To which Jackie snapped back, "Jack is superb in his political life, but do you think he'll ever amount to anything in his personal life?"[4]

Nancy had become a member of one of the smallest sororities in the country—that of the first ladies of the land. The most recent ones could be immediately identified by their first names—Eleanor, Bess, Mamie, Jackie, Lady Bird, Pat, Betty, Rosalynn, and now Nancy. "They're the second-biggest story in the White House every day," Helen Thomas, dean of the White House press corps, claimed, "and there have been days when they've taken the top spot from their husbands."[5] Nothing in the Constitution defines the duties, if any, that might be ascribed to the wife of a president. The term *first lady* was first used in 1834, but was popularized when Lucy Hayes, wife of President Rutherford B. Hayes, described herself as "the first lady of the land." Lucy was a true woman of the nineteenth century, a time in America when it was believed that "a lady's name should appear in print only three times: at her birth, marriage, and death" and in the case of the president's wife at his inauguration, social events, and her husband's funeral. The media explosion and the emancipation of women in the twentieth century gravely altered that perception. Eleanor Roosevelt's activism showed how far-reaching the first lady's services to the country could be.

Nancy's twentieth-century forerunners had mostly chosen to concentrate on causes or projects meaningful to them—except for Mamie Eisenhower, who famously stated, "Ike runs the country and I turn the lamb chops." Jackie will be remembered for her efforts in historic preservation, especially that of the White House itself; Lady Bird for her attention to the country's flora and fauna; Eleanor for her dedication to women's rights, health care for the poor and elderly, and her efforts for international peace. Betty Ford strove to make women more aware of their bodies in order to detect early signs of breast cancer. In the first weeks of their husbands' terms of office, however, these aims had not yet been formed. All of the first ladies had needed time to adjust to their new position. Nancy was dealing with the same indecisiveness. What really was her role—or "unpaid job" as Rosalynn Carter had called it? There had never been a caucus of first ladies. And although, like Nancy, several of them had been a first lady of a state when their husband was a governor, it did not necessarily prepare them for their new place in the global scheme of things.

The question arises, in this day of the enlightenment of women, whether first ladies deserve to be treated as employees of the government in the same manner as their husbands. As is, she receives no benefits that do not come through her husband. Her staff, in fact, receives more employment benefits than she does. Her unpaid job hours extend far past the accepted forty-hour week of workers. Before Reagan's election, Mrs. Reagan stated that her job was "looking after Ronnie." But, in point of fact, a modern first lady has to be wife and official hostess to the White House, is expected to make frequent public appearances (at which she must look her best) and to contribute a good portion of what little extra time she has to travel for matters related to her husband's job. She is expected to reply to hundreds of letters each week and answer requests. She does have a press secretary and a personal secretary, their salaries paid by the government. But she has to decide which letters deserve personal replies, which requests to satisfy, which to turn down. This takes many hours of personal time. The first lady is also expected to be gracious, stand on her feet for hours in reception lines, remember the names of hundreds of people, who they are and by what title they should be addressed. There are interviews, speeches, honors to be received, ships to be christened, heroes welcomed home, funerals to attend. In Great Britain the queen's husband, Prince Philip, is paid a yearly fixed amount for his services, and the prime minister's wife is able to maintain her own paid job if she so wishes, which is not an option for our first ladies, and in the case of Prime Minister Thatcher, her husband was not expected, or called upon, to execute any of the tasks expected of a first lady. In the eighteenth and nineteenth centuries a president's wife had few official duties. That is no longer the case.

One first lady, Woodrow Wilson's second wife, Edith Bolling Wilson, was suspected of secretly taking over her husband's job after he suffered a massive stroke and was paralyzed on one side. She vehemently called it her "stewardship" of her husband. His mind was as good as ever and the doctors had assured her that he would make an excellent recovery, regaining most of his muscle control, but that it would take much care. The decision was made for him not to resign. No one was allowed into his bedroom during his recovery period, and Edith was his only liaison with his staff, the cabinet, Senate leaders, and diplomats. "I never made a single decision regarding the disposition of public affairs," she later wrote. "The only decision that was mine was what was important and what was not, and the *very* important decision of when to present matters to my husband."[6] Wilson's health improved, though not wholly, and for the remaining eighteen months of his term he was confined to a wheelchair but could walk a few steps. Edith was extremely protective of him, shielding him from becoming stressed or overtired. Her actual stewardship had lasted several months. Both the Wilsons denied that Edith had ever truly acted in his place. But the speculation continues to this day.

One title all first ladies had to share, like it or not, was that of the country's most renowned hostess. Nancy, like her more recent predecessors, would have a large staff at her disposal, but she would have to be fully involved and make the final decisions. And, although she wasn't sure of much else in her job classification, Nancy believed this was one area in which she could shine. The other was as a style-setter, a category that had defeated many first ladies—certainly Mamie, Bess, and Eleanor, who once, in the face of undue attention by the press to her often dowdy attire, said, "Sometimes I feel like I'm dressing the Washington Monument."[7]

White House press doyenne Helen Thomas, a fixture from the time of the Eisenhower administration, said, "Of all the first ladies I have covered this one [Nancy] got off to the worst start."[8] It was Nancy, not the host of wealthy friends she had wanted so to impress, who was most in awe of her new position and home. She was at first overwhelmed by the sudden change in her life. Despite the governorship and the many campaigns and Nancy's penchant for rich friends, the success of the Reagans' marriage was based on simple, mostly shared pleasures; never had they lived, so to speak, "over the store," where privacy was hard to come by. As there was no fixed precedent for the role of first lady, Nancy made her own rules. Instead of taking the time to find her way, she lost herself in the one activity that she had always enjoyed and that she thought could raise her profile equal to her new position—she would redecorate her home.

There was a $50,000 limit imposed by the White House budget

department for the refurbishing of the family quarters of the White House for incoming presidents. This was far short of the funds Nancy's improvements would cost. She had no problem in raising the additional $800,000 to implement her plans, which involved some expert restoration as well as modernization. In return for their generosity, the contributors (mostly her California friends) received a tax deduction, the satisfaction that they had helped beautify the White House, and the assurance of becoming "favored guests." The Reagans' friends were not part of an established old-money class or numbered among society's four hundred. Most came from working-class families and had accumulated their personal fortunes. Friendship with the Reagans greatly raised their social status to insiders at the White House. It also elevated Nancy's position to Queen Bee among the women she most admired.

"I believe very strongly the White House is a special place and should have the best of everything. I think people want it that way," Nancy announced in one of her first White House interviews.[9] She had just discovered that there was a jumble of White House china, due to breakage over the years, which had not been replaced since the Kennedys' tenure. She had her office contact Lenox china company and request that they submit presidential patterns with their best price, implying that it should be significantly lowered in consideration of the publicity and honor the company would receive should they be purchased for the White House. The final figure for the accepted design was for 4,324 pieces at a cost of $209,000. Though highly discounted, this price was far in excess of what the office of the White House would approve, so the Friends of Reagan picked up that cost as well. As the china would not be delivered for nine months, the order was kept for the present from the press, who were already referring to her in the tabloids as Queen Nancy.

Two days after the inauguration, she hosted—in honor of the people who had helped finance the spectacular inaugural festivities—a late-afternoon thank-you champagne (California's finest vintage) reception at the White House for more than eight hundred guests. The party was put together in rather a hurry, and many who thought they should have been invited were not. As Mary Jane Wick, whose husband Charles co-chaired the inaugural committee, explained, "We did the best we could [but] there were some people we couldn't reach."[10]

This was the first reception of Reagan's presidency, and the party was covered nationwide, along with a list of the rich and famous who attended: the millionaire donors and powerful businessmen (including Fred Hartley, president of Union Oil, whose limousine license plates were OIL on the front and UNION on the back), movie stars, and those who graced the Reagans' inner circle. The press assumed the champagne party to be a signpost for the future, and it did not rest well with them at a time when there was double-digit inflation and the hostages, having arrived in Germany after fifteen months of pain, torture, and indignities—inflicted only because they were Americans—were about to board planes to be reunited with their families at home. "A thanksgiving service would have been more appropriate for the President and the First Lady to host as their first outing," one critic carped.[11] Unfortunately, the "good reviews" were printed in the society pages by columnists who took great joy in listing every guest who was "anybody," whereas the searing comments appeared on the front pages and editorial pages of the same newspapers.

While Nancy found the adjustment to becoming first lady more difficult than she had anticipated, Reagan moved comfortably into his new role. He told one very personal story about himself that reveals much about the man. He recalled that about the same time as he became governor of California, he began having a recurring dream. "I'd find myself in a big old house that had huge rooms—not always the same house, but always one with huge rooms. Each time somebody would take me for a tour of the house; usually it was up for sale at a bargain price. I'd wander around, walk from room to room, stare up at high ceilings and great staircases and balconies above me." This description bears great similarities to the Charles Walgreen house in Dixon, Illinois. Walgreen was the richest man in town, but the house was far more modest than Reagan recalled. It did, however, have a grand central staircase, a bannistered balcony overlooking the high-ceilinged living room, and many luxuries that Reagan had never before seen at the time.

"Although the house in my dream might be run-down," Reagan continued, "I'd see a great potential for it as a place to live, and I'd want to buy it. . . . Funny thing: Once I moved to Washington, I never had that dream again. Somehow, living in the White House, with its ceilings that reached up eighteen feet, cured me. . . . I guess something inside me said: 'You've made it.' "[12]

It was not true of Reagan that what you saw was what you got, for what you got was never the real man. On the exterior he seemed relaxed, cool to the point of laziness—but how could a man of seventy be lazy when he could split wood with a heavy axe for an hour with few pauses and saw no reason not to engage in such strenuous exercise? A gregarious man in public, Reagan's natural inclination was to be a private person. Whenever possible, he chose to eat a meager lunch (usually soup or a sandwich, seldom both) alone in his office so that he could go over papers. While president, Reagan greatly missed his time at the ranch, when he would ride by himself for hours up into the Santa Ynez mountains. Being alone, for even a few hours, was necessary, he repeatedly averred, because he needed time "to think about things," and it would make him so happy "when he came home and found" Nancy there waiting for him.

Reagan quit work 5:00 P.M. sharp, but he carried a satchel of material up to the family wing of the White House and spent two hours or more each night reading and writing notes. His brain just worked in its own way and at its own time. No one on his staff seems to have ever seen him take a nap during working hours—even on long flights. Commentators often jibed about his "falling off" during meetings. This had only occurred once after a protracted international flight followed immediately by a lengthy, dull conference. Reagan tried to make a joke of it and even had a small sign printed that he placed in his chair in the Oval Office: "The President slept here." In at least five memoirs written by close associates it has been noted that during all flights on Air Force One, he would sit at his desk, engrossed in material that needed his attention. He had the unwelcome habit of waking up others if there was something he wanted to discuss, leaning over them, finger nudging their shoulder, no polite "I'm sorry," and no time given for them to awaken fully before he threw a complicated question at them. Nancy's image of him remains that of a man seated, head bent, shoulders square, at a desk late at night in pajamas and robe, writing or reading. He would pause momentarily, remove his tortoise-shell glasses, dangle them, as he tried to clear something in his mind, and then thrust them back onto the bridge of his nose as he returned to the matters before him.

Nelle had taught him that wasting time was a sin of graver consequence than wasting money. President Carter recalled that during his one-hour briefing with Reagan the day before the inauguration, he was disturbed to see that his about-to-be successor took no notes and seemed to be listening abstractedly. The next day Deaver and Meese were impressed by how much Reagan had absorbed at that meeting and how quickly he had assimilated and analyzed what Carter had told him. From his early schoolboy days, before his visual problem was discovered, Reagan had had to listen harder than most of his classmates so that he could keep up his grades, which were in the top 10 percent. On this occasion, his amazing memory had retained his opinions of what Carter was saying as well as the president's text—something he called "brain-noting."[13]

Although his early years were a hardscrabble life, Nelle had taught him that it was his duty to help those less fortunate. So deeply had she drilled this into him, he found it impossible to give to his own children, who, despite their personal struggles, he felt had much more than most. Deaver, his secretary Helene von Damm, and his press spokesman Larry Speakes all tell stories of how he read all the "begging letters" filled with despair that arrived at the White House and would privately send personal checks to those recipients who he thought were truly in need. (Many of these checks have turned up at autograph auctions through the years, the recipients so in awe of having received them that, despite their need, they found it impossible to turn their presidential check into cash, either for sentimental reasons or because the signed signature was worth more than the face value of the check.)

He continued to tithe to the church, but due to the security it involved, which he thought was disruptive to the congregation, he did not often attend. Instead, he spent private time each day in prayer. This, too, came from his childhood. Nelle's congregation was so poor that for many years they had no real church, only a place to gather. Time was allotted at home for praying. This was done, until he entered college, on his knees in the front room of wherever they might be living, with Nelle reading dramatically from the same crumbling Bible on which he had taken his oath as president.

He once said, "The first time I tried to swim across the Rock River near my home [in Dixon] I thought I would never make it to the shore. Life sometimes feels like that. I kept swimming and I made it. Then I practiced my stroke and breathing. I knew I could make it, but I wasn't so sure others could. That was one reason I became a lifeguard."[14]

Another was his desire to prove himself worthwhile, a hero, to be the man for Nelle that his father's weakness had disenfranchised. "Small and less" had been Nelle's unstated credo. Nelle, who had an evangelistic manner of persuasion, believed too much ambition was also a sin, especially if the person's aim was for self-aggrandizement and earthly pleasures. Reagan had always had the need for bigger and better things than Nelle imagined for him. He rationalized his ambition by shrouding it with good intentions. He felt certain that God had led him to the presidency and that He had allowed him to come this far so that he could help others safely to the shore, as he had done on the Rock River.

From their earliest years, Nelle insisted her sons never exhibit in public their emotions regarding the difficulties within their family— Jack's drinking and job losses, the often bare cupboards of their kitchen—which accounts greatly for Reagan's "invisible wall," which acted as a shield behind his charming, easy-going façade. He never questioned the rightness of anything Nelle had taught him. It simply *was*, that was all. And he never doubted Nancy in the rightness of what she did. Reagan had gone from *momism* to *wife-ism*. Nancy once said, "We were like a circle—you know, each one a half—and we completed each other." Reagan believed this, too.

While Nancy was engaged in activities that were being labeled extravagances, Reagan embarked on ways to shrink federal spending. He arrived in the Oval Office the first morning of his presidency at half-past-eight, startling a staff who expected, due to the late hours of the festivities the previous night, that he would be delayed. There was much activity for everyone on his immediate staff. "Is he on his way?" Deaver asked on the telephone of Helene von Damm. "He's *alrh*eady here!"

she responded in her distinctive Austrian accent. His desk (once used by Kennedy) was cleared and polished till it shimmered. The California flag that he had carried with him on Air Force One when he departed Los Angeles was furled in a corner ready to be placed wherever he chose. There had been a light snow during the night, and the bare arms of the giant tree outside the Oval Office windows glistened as it melted in the winter sun. He was nattily dressed in a dark blue suit, white shirt with French cuffs, and a red-and-off-white striped silk tie; his thick brown hair Brylcreemed smoothly back from his face (shades of Lew Wasserman). He looked rested, although his staff, who had also returned late from the festivities of the previous evening, did not.

His first day was a full one. He stood by as thirty-eight members of his White House staff were sworn in by Chief Justice Warren E. Burger. Many had served him in California or on the campaign trail. Among those sworn in were Elizabeth Dole, assistant to the president for public liaison; Edwin Meese III, counselor to the president; James A. Baker, the president's chief of staff; Michael K. Deaver, deputy chief of staff; Richard V. Allen, national security adviser; Martin Anderson, domestic policy adviser; and James S. Brady, press secretary. "We have a new kind of loyalty now," he told them. "Our loyalty must be only to this nation and the people we represent. . . . every judgment must be made on the basis that no one's going to be seeking office ever again. Now I don't say that we won't seek office ever again, but the decisions will be made on what is good for the people, what is right as against what is wrong, and with no political considerations being discussed."[15] From this first day a "troika" was formed—Deaver, Meese, and Baker—and the first order of the day would be a meeting with them in the Oval Office. Seldom did the president have a one-to-one meeting with anyone when a member of the troika was not present, apparently to bear witness if there was ever a misunderstanding of what the president had said.

Nancy's first direct influence on White House affairs had occurred before the inauguration when Reagan discussed with her the possible choices for his cabinet. The transition team had suggested William Simon as secretary of the treasury, the same post he had held in both the Nixon and Ford administrations. Nancy was vehemently against him.

She had met Simon and disliked him intensely, sensing what she believed was the man's "greed for power." True or not, Reagan abided by
her judgment and requested other names. Donald Regan, the chairman
of Merrill Lynch, was finally selected, although neither of the Reagans
knew him well. Nancy had also "put her foot down, when it came to
Lyn Nofziger" for the position of press secretary to Reagan. "It was one
thing when Reagan was only a governor, but now that [Reagan was pres-
ident] Nofziger did not fit her image of what a press spokesman should
be. He was rambunctious, profane, and rumpled," Larry Speakes recalled. (He would later take over this office himself.)[16] Nofziger had
served Reagan well and loyally for fifteen years. It was Nofziger who
had believed from the start of Reagan's political life that he was headed
for the White House, who had worked slavishly for him to this end, and
whose own ambitions were finally about to be realized, he thought, as
press secretary to the president, and then—well, who knew how far he
could go? It was a crushing blow when he was bypassed.

Reagan tried to convince Nancy that she was wrong, that maybe
Nofziger could clean up his act, dress more conservatively. Nancy won
out. Nofziger has written that he and Nancy were on good terms and
that he does not believe she was responsible for his not being named
press secretary. Others hold to the opposite view. The rumor was that
"she wanted someone young and handsome," and when James Brady
was selected for the post, she would kid around and call him "Y and H"
"for young and handsome, just as within the White House Reagan was
called 'O and W,' 'oldest and wisest.' " Exhibit one, perhaps, of Nancy's
power within the Oval Office even in these early days of her husband's
presidency. Rumor also placed her in meetings—not in the Oval Office,
but in the family quarters, where staff were gathered to discuss important
decisions to be made, and perhaps held there so that Nancy could have
her say.[17]

Only one member of the Kitchen Cabinet was brought into the *real*
cabinet—William French Smith as attorney general. This created some
grumbling among the Californians, several of whom had considered re-
locating to Washington (in fact, the Wicks did have an apartment in
Watergate). When they saw that their power had been diminished, Tuttle

Holmes is quoted as saying, "Well, guys, it looks as though we're not wanted here. We might as well go home."[18]

Betsy Bloomingdale recalled that Alfred was asked to "find a black for the Cabinet and he came up with a lawyer he'd worked with in New York, Sam Pierce. A very nice man, but soft, as it turned out."[19] (This last is a reference to the scandal in Reagan's second term over corruption at the Department of Housing and Urban Development under Pierce's management.) The most controversial choice, because of his role as chief of staff in the Nixon administration, was Gen. Alexander Haig as secretary of state.

"On the day [when he was to appear before a Senate committee for his confirmation hearings as secretary of state]," Speakes relates, "a group of us were in a conference room waiting for Haig when the door sprang open and practically slammed back against the wall and in walked two of Haig's people—John Lehman, wearing an ascot, and Richard Perle. The two of them announced, 'Gentlemen, General Haig.' And Haig strode in, ever the commander-in-chief. He pounded the table and shouted, 'All right, we're going to go up on the Hill and win this thing. We're going to show those sons-of-bitches how the game is played."[20]

Nancy did not like Haig, but her evaluation of him was purely instinctive. She hardly knew him. The troika thought he was the best qualified for the job, Reagan agreed, and he was confirmed by the Senate. Within a few weeks Nancy's dislike of the man grew. Haig was "obsessed with matters of status—with exactly where he stood on a receiving line, or where he was seated on a plane or helicopter. If he didn't think his seat was important enough, he'd let you know. He had a prickly personality and was always complaining that he was being slighted." She sums up her feelings about him by adding, "He was too power-hungry. He saw himself as the only person in the administration who should be making decisions on foreign policy."[21] This last statement fairly sets out how deeply Reagan drew Nancy into the machinations of his administration, making her—at that time—the most powerful, and best informed, first lady since Eleanor Roosevelt.

Reagan fell quite naturally into his job; "comfortable" was his word. On February 18, 1981, after he had addressed a joint session of Congress for the first time, he wrote in his diary, "I've seen Presidents over the years enter the House chamber without ever thinking I would one day be doing it. It was a thrill and something I'll long remember."[22] This was on the same day that he had announced a program for economic recovery, which contained sweeping budgetary cuts of close to $55 billion, measures for defense increased by $7.2 billion, and taxes cut thirty percent over the next three years. Congress had been stunned. Spending billions and cutting taxes seemed an impossible task and totally unworkable. Main programs would be forfeited, although Social Security would not be touched. Reagan was claiming that less revenue now would build the economy later. The speech received even greater enthusiasm from the public, who, when polled, approved his proposal by a two-thirds majority.

There were not many in Congress, no matter how strongly they disagreed with Reagan's views and measures, who did not like the man. He would have meetings with his opponents or members of the press, often in the anteroom to the Oval Office, where champagne flowed and where he was in his element telling stories, many raunchy, sometimes downright dirty, but somehow never offensive. He was, according to the men (he never told an off-color joke in front of a woman), an "irresistible story-teller, seeming to have invented a joke that very moment, and laughing just as hardily at them as his listeners."[23] No one can recall ever seeing him in the Oval Office without his jacket and tie, French cuffs perfectly creased and stiffly starched, and with the faint scent of spicy aftershave lotion wafting to anyone within five feet of him.

The Reagans missed California, which he would say was "not a place but a way of life." He loved his adopted state and told Margaret Thatcher when she came to Washington in early March (they had met previously in London during one of the Reagans' ambassadorial trips for the Nixon administration) that the British people "should have crossed the other ocean to get to this continent. That way the capital of the United States would have been in California."[24] He got on well with Thatcher. They shared many views and Britain's first female prime minister, not known to be a coquette but rather a flinty figure, the "iron lady" some called her, was certainly a bit flirty around Reagan, who admitted that she had great legs but admired her intelligence above her feminine charms. Happily, Nancy liked Thatcher, too. Ronnie always had a gentlemanly deference where women were concerned. He "enjoyed looking at a pretty woman as much as any other man."[25] But since his marriage to Nancy there had never been even the vaguest rumors of his engaging in a flirtation, never mind an affair. Nancy was his whole life, and he still let her know it on a daily basis. There were loving notes on her breakfast tray. Occasions were never forgotten. For example on March 4, 1981, the date of the Reagans' twenty-ninth anniversary, Reagan wrote in a letter accompanying his gift: "[My Nancy has] made one man (me) the most happy man in *the world* for twenty-nine years. She has done this in spite of the fact that he can't find the words to tell her how lost he would be without her. He sits in the Oval Office from which he can see (if he scrooches down) her window and feels warm all over just knowing she is there."[26] He wrote in his memoirs how reassuring it was when he was in the Oval Office to know she was nearby, that he somehow could feel her presence and that it got him through many a difficult day.

Nancy was determined to turn the White House into a *home* where Ronnie would feel that he belonged. She was not only a dedicated nest-builder; she also wanted affirmation that she was contributing, as had Jackie, to the beauty of the people's house. She did this, with Ted Graber's help, by having the floors stripped and refinished, having new and lighter carpeting laid, the walls covered with wallpaper recreated from an eighteenth-century pattern. She interviewed some of the oldest members of the White House staff to see whether they could recall what might have happened to "lost" pieces of furniture or china or paintings. Then, with a host of helpers, she went on a treasure hunt for the best of these, often priceless English antiques that current owners (if the pieces were given as gifts) or the keepers of government buildings were not easily persuaded to part with. Some other pieces had to be ferreted out of storage rooms in the basement of the White House, where they had been kept for fifty years or more. She furnished Ronnie's sitting room–office in the family quarters with newly upholstered pieces, and rugs, red predominating. Photographs of the family, celebrities, and royalty were displayed. She left alone the president's bathroom, "where Lyndon Johnson had installed a telephone, a very elaborate shower, bright lights, and enough electrical power to run a small country."[27] They entertained personal guests in the Yellow Oval Room, with its spectacular view of the Jefferson Memorial. It had contained several dozen carved wood chairs with gold damask seats set rather formally amid a scattering of tables. Most of the chairs were moved to storage, and with the addition of sofas, wing chairs, and several large coffee tables, the room was transformed into a welcoming place for dinner guests to gather for cocktails beforehand and coffee later.

The third floor was reserved for guest rooms. The billiard room so enjoyed by Teddy Roosevelt was transformed into a California-style den with two massive sofas, movie posters, and an array of family photographs. Displayed prominently was "a gag poster of *Gone with the Wind* starring Ronald Reagan and Margaret Thatcher."[28] The family quarters also contained a solarium and a family dining room that Jackie Kennedy had made from an old bedroom and bath into a charming room with a "nice historical feel to it." It had been altered to its disadvantage by the Nixons and the Carters. Nancy restored it to Jackie's original designs. She also managed to put her hand into some redecorating of the Oval Office, which was repainted, refloored, and recarpeted. Rumors abounded that Nancy was turning the president's apartments into an East Coast San Simeon. The first press tour of the rooms belied that. Although the quarters might not have been to everyone's taste, they were in *good* taste, beautifully done, certainly more comfortable and livable than previously. The revamp might not have brought a swell of pride to the chests of the American public (few of whom would ever enter the rooms), but it made the current president a happy man and filled Nancy with a sense of having contributed to the improvement of America's most historic house.

Still, the media would not let up. Nancy Reagan was good press, better if the stories derided her, proving once again that everyone loves to cheer a hero, but prefers to read about his or her errant ways and clay feet. Nancy was having a severe image problem. A story in *Newsweek* referred to her as one of the "idle rich, a queen-bee figure." And even though public sympathy shifted in her favor after the inconceivable happened and she responded gallantly, the criticism and barbs of the media could not be silenced.

CHAPTER TWELVE

"OH, GOD!
IT'S HAPPENING AGAIN!"

Monday, March 30, 1981, Reagan's seventieth day in office, began routinely. The White House telephone operator rang and said cheerfully, "Good morning, it's seven-thirty." Nancy said "thank you" and pressed the buzzer on the bedside table that alerted the second-floor kitchen staff. A minute later a White House butler knocked and entered; Rex, the Reagans' frisky King Charles spaniel, given to them by Bill Buckley and named after Rex Stouten, leapt in front of him and onto the foot of their bed. The butler pulled the curtains and handed them the morning papers—Reagan the *Washington Post* and Nancy the *New York Times*. He always turned to the comics first. "You need a laugh to start the day," he would say disarmingly. He read "Peanuts" and one or two other strips and then went to the front page, after which, as was their custom, they switched newspapers. He flipped to the *Times* financial section and glanced at the sports section while she read the style and arts pages.[1]

The Academy Awards were scheduled for that evening, and they were both speculating on the possible winners. One of their favorite actors, Henry Fonda, was to be given an award in recognition of his "enduring contribution to the art of motion pictures" and Ronnie had videotaped a congratulatory message to be shown during the presentation at the Dorothy Chandler Pavilion in Los Angeles. At 7:40 breakfast was brought in on a tray—fresh juice, dry cereal with milk, and decaffeinated coffee. To Nancy's surprise, after their first month's residence in the White House, she was presented with a bill for their groceries. They could have anything they wanted and the staff would secure it for them, but they paid for their own food (as had all presidents before them).

These few early morning minutes alone were a favorite time for them, when they could discuss things—their take on the news and family matters. Maureen was to be married to Dennis Revell in three weeks at the Beverly Wilshire Hotel in Beverly Hills. Maureen had agreed to a traditional wedding, a white gown but a pared-down guest list. The Reagans were picking up a good portion of the costs, and Nancy was pleased that the marriage would legitimize Maureen's relationship. The Reagans were both looking forward to the trip to the coast, which they had been able to schedule as a stop before continuing on to Mexico, where Ronnie was meeting with President José López Portillo. What the Reagans wanted to avoid at the wedding (besides a confrontation with Jane Wyman, the technicalities of which were being delicately worked out), was an invasion of the press and the Secret Service. Reagan agreed that he would discuss this with James Brady to see what could be arranged.

He rose to dress at 8:10, leaving Nancy to relax and read the rest of the papers. At 8:35 he returned, "leaned over the bed, and kissed [Nancy] goodbye" and then, as usual, took Rex back to the kitchen, where someone would then lead him onto the grounds for his morning walk. Reagan stepped out of the elevator on the state floor punctually at 8:40 and was greeted by Dave Fischer, his personal Secret Service bodyguard.[2] Fischer, a former aide from Reagan's Sacramento days, was a youthful man of good humor. He wore a neatly trimmed mustache, possessed a firm physique, and had somewhat piercing eyes. He was by Reagan's side every day, from the moment the president left the family quarters in the morning until he entered the elevator to return there in the evening. Together, the two men, walking briskly in the cool of the early morning air, crossed to the colonnade on the side of the Rose Garden, strode along it and into the West Wing, where Reagan greeted Helene von Damm before entering the Oval Office. The troika, who had arrived before him, stood as he appeared. A few words of greeting were exchanged before Reagan sat down behind his desk to begin their daily morning briefing. It was exactly 8:45. Much programmed—for all his California casualness—Reagan was never late to a meeting. This morning there were some pointers on the twenty-minute speech he was to deliver at two that afternoon at the Washington Hilton before 3,500 union delegates of the National Conference of the Building and Construction Trades Department of the AFL-CIO. Talking to trade unions was always "a piece of cake" and brought him back to his long tenure as president of SAG.

Security measures had to be placed in position whenever the President was to appear anywhere. A dry run had been made and plans set for him to arrive and leave by the hotel's private side entrance. The troika did not anticipate a large press turnout as it was rather a routine engagement, despite the large numbers of union workers he was to address. "Any of the regulars?" Reagan asked, referring to the media. "Maybe, Sam [Donaldson]," Deaver said. But as Reagan had a meeting with David Rockefeller (former Vice President Nelson Rockefeller's brother) of Chase Manhattan Bank in the Oval Office at 2:45, he suggested that it would be better after the speech to leave the building and get into the limousine without delay. No question time.[3]

Next on the agenda was General Haig. Nancy's negative presentiments were proving to be right on target. In the troika's view, the secretary of state was overplaying his authority, acting as though he were in charge and Reagan nothing more than a ceremonial president. Something had to be done. Haig's egomania had manifested itself early on during his confirmation on the Hill. Immediately afterward he had submitted to the president a charter that would have given him unprecedented control of foreign affairs. Reagan refused to sign it and had been so irritated by Haig's appearance on the Hill and the broad scope of the charter that he had named Vice President Bush, not Haig, as the man who would be in the situation room in emergencies ranging from "an isolated terrorist incident to an armed attack on U.S. territory and . . . Bush was to get into forward planning for emergency responses, develop options for Presidential consideration and take the lead in the implementation of these decisions."[4]

Reagan had always believed that if you brought someone on board because you thought he was the best, which had been the case with Haig, then that person could be trusted with a certain leeway of power. Haig, however, had gone far over the line and continued to do so, leaking word to the press that he had persuaded the president to keep an embargo on grain to the Soviet Union and grousing publicly about "an encroachment on a Secretary of State's special area of responsibility" by Defense Secretary Caspar Weinberger.[5] "In the perfect Al Haig world," one of the troika complained, "the Secretary of Defense would be a mechanic."[6] Haig tangled with Agriculture Secretary John Block on the Russian grain embargo and "bumped heads" with budget director David Stockman. For two months he had been a constant thorn in everyone's side as he accelerated his effort to accumulate power. The previous week a political cartoon had appeared in the *Washington Post*, with a uniformed Haig standing in a Napoleonic pose as a reporter asked, "And it's not true, then, that you asked for the resignations of Reagan and Bush?" In fact, it was Haig who had threatened to hand in his resignation. He set up a meeting with Reagan to do so and then backtracked when an adviser warned him that the answer might be, "Fine. When can we expect it?" He was a man driven by his ego. The troika did not trust him and went so far as to indicate that his egomania "frightened the shit out of them." In a small confrontation over the hiring of an assistant, Haig— his steel-blue eyes flashing—shouted at Deaver, "How dare you talk to me like that. I have served six presidents!" and called the troika "the gorillas in the White House." For two long days, Haig had pitted himself against the troika in a corridors-of-power conflict, and had gone public with his grievances, wading deeper and deeper into lèse-majesté.[7]

Reagan disagreed with Haig's "tone, tactics and timing," but he had acceded to his choice as secretary of state because Haig, like himself, held a hard-line approach to the Soviet Union. Haig's foreign policy was to contain Russian expansionism in the third world and to help weaker nations defend themselves against Russian aggression. This, too, went along with Reagan's thinking. Despite Haig's troublesome personality, Reagan believed he had the right slant on foreign affairs and that to force a resignation of a secretary of state this early in his administration would present a picture of confusion in the Oval Office. Nonetheless, "Haig may have seriously misread his President," ventured a member of the White House staff. "While Reagan sometimes appears relaxed to the point of inattention, he is acutely attentive to any insubordination on the part of his staff. He abhors internal feuding and prefers a collegial harmony that will present him with a consensus on the issues, or at least clearly defined alternatives." Haig was now considered to be a nonteam player by Reagan and the troika, who were also concerned about the damage Haig could do to the president if he became a loose cannon.[8]

At the moment Haig was needed, for trouble was brewing in Poland, where Lech Walesa and Poland's Solidarity unionists had issued their stiffest ultimatum yet to the government: protect reform or face a general strike. A final showdown could bring Poland to its knees and Soviet troops across Poland's borders. The troika left at 9:35 when Richard Allen, the national security adviser, went over the morning cables with the president. Then Max Friedersdorf, Reagan's top congressional lobbyist, filled him in on Congress's schedule for the day. On his departure, Reagan settled down to read and answer mail, the most important red-tabbed and at the top of a tall, bulky pile. Helene von Damm sat down across from him. "Well, here we go again," he smiled as he picked up the first letter. It was from Haig.

While hard issues were being debated in the Oval Office, Nancy went into her dressing room to get ready for what was to be a fairly unstressful day. She loved the peach-and-white, totally feminine boudoir with its gracefully flowered print curtains and upholstered pieces. On the wall, facing her when she entered the room, was a charming nineteenth-century painting of an aristocratic young lady with her dog, "a scene so peaceful it sometimes made me feel that I was born in the wrong century, [and] outside the window was a magnolia tree that had been planted by Andrew Jackson."[9] Pat Nixon had installed a mini-sized beauty parlor adjoining the dressing room and bath, and Nancy had fallen into the habit of starting her day by having her hair and nails done by the local professionals who came early every weekday, while Julius would still fly in from the West Coast if there was a special occasion.

The transition from the Palisades to the White House had been a fantasy come true for Nancy. When you live there, she wrote, "the world is yours." Baths are drawn for you, laundry and dry cleaning whisked away for instant care. At night the bed is turned down, curtains drawn, a thermos filled with ice water is placed conveniently at bedside. The White House telephone operators handle all calls in and out. As first lady, Nancy never had to deal with a busy signal or a wrong number, and room service was available twenty-four hours, seven days a week. It was, Ronnie told her, "like living in an eight-star hotel,"[10] but with a ghost, that of Abraham Lincoln, who most of the White House domestic staff believed haunted the Lincoln Bedroom, down the hall from the Reagans' suite. Many had claimed to have seen a tall, narrow, phantasmatic figure by the fireplace in the Lincoln Bedroom. So far, Nancy had not come upon it, or it upon her. "If it is Mr. Lincoln's ghost, at least it will be Republican, which ought to be safe enough," Ronnie had joked.[11]

Midmorning the sun disappeared and the sky grew leaden gray. Nancy dressed in a comfortable Adolfo wool ensemble and went into her office to attend to her mail. She was having some worrying staff problems. A young woman who had come highly recommended as an assistant secretary was not working out. As everything Nancy did quickly became a public issue, firing this woman had to be handled carefully. Nancy was to attend a luncheon at the Georgetown home of Michael Ainsley, president of the National Trust for Historic Preservation. She was never too pleased about having to make a luncheon appearance, because noon was the time she usually set aside to call her friends in California and her parents in Arizona. Nancy spoke to her mother daily. Both the Davises were failing, especially the doctor, who was fighting a losing battle against cancer. She talked to Betsy Bloomingdale several times a week and, with the wedding drawing closer, to Maureen almost every day. Calls to and from Patti were infrequent, but Nancy kept in weekly touch with Ron and somewhat less often with Colleen and Michael to inquire about Cameron.

Nancy was planning to return to the White House at 2:30 for a meeting with Rex Stouten and Ted Graber. Most of the construction work on the second floor was either completed or well on the way, although the rooms still waited for pieces to be refinished, recovered, and delivered. The third floor was to be tackled last, but decisions had to be made to set things in motion. At 3:30 she had an interview with a photographic session to follow, and there was a dinner that evening that she and Ronnie were to attend.

At 12:15, after a brief call to Betsy, she left for the luncheon with her Secret Service man and a follow-up car with two more men. Nancy now accepted this as normal practice, although she hated not being able just to go someplace on her own if she so wished. Curious, she remarked to a close friend, now that she was first lady, she had less freedom than other citizens. She smiled her most radiant smile as she was escorted into the Ainsleys' elegant, antique-filled home, where the luncheon was being held. Her handshake was warm as she greeted people, her eyes directed at the person's face in personal recognition. She never looked away until she had been moved on to the next person. This was called "the royal greeting" she was told; all members of Britain's royal family had been trained in this art, and Nancy quickly adapted it as her own style.

As press assistant, Larry Speakes—"a down-home Mississippian," forty-one, earthy, ambitious, with homely good looks and well-honed shrewdness—was to have accompanied the president to the Hilton along with Deaver. Shortly before they were set to leave, however, Reagan's spokesman in chief, White House press secretary James Brady, decided he would go instead. Nobody didn't like Jim Brady, a gentle bear of a man, balding early at forty, a gourmet cook, and a host known for his talent for telling a good story. For all that, he had almost been passed over for the job he now held. He had not been a Reagan intimate, and he had yet to gain the access to the president that he felt was necessary. "The joke was that Reagan had access to Brady, instead of the other way around," a veteran reporter complained. Brady's sense of humor had seen him through the difficulties with Haig. "Whatever happened to foreplay?"[12] he cracked when at a press conference a reporter threw him a loaded question about the secretary of state's recent temper outbursts. He had not been influenced by the buttoned-up,

1940s style of Reagan and his troika: he had shown up recently for the rather formal president's lunch wearing a Chicago Cubs cap. The gesture was meant to humor Reagan, who had covered the Cubs' games during his radio days.

Brady had decided that he should make more of an effort to get close to his boss. A routine outing like the Hilton speech, with fewer staff in attendance, seemed a good opening. He and David Prosperi, an aide in the press office, joined the multicar motorcade, at 1:45 P.M., getting into the vehicle behind Reagan's limousine, the Secret Service car, and the control car. With him were Deaver; Dr. Daniel Ruge, the White House physician, a stately, graying sixty-three-year-old and longtime friend of Loyal Davis; a military aide who carried the so-called Black Box containing the codes that would enable the president to activate a nuclear response; and a fourth passenger—the senior staff member who would be responsible for making a decision at the civilian level if the president was incapacitated. All this was normal procedure. Everyone expected the afternoon to be uneventful and had no reason to think otherwise. But since Kennedy's assassination, and that of his brother, Robert, and of Martin Luther King Jr. followed by two attempts on Ford's life, such precautions had been mandated.

Reagan had changed into a brand-new dark blue, pinstriped suit at lunchtime, when he also took off his best wristwatch and "for reasons I'll never know, put on an old one Nancy had given me that I usually wore only when I was doing chores outside at the ranch."[13] Secretary of Labor Raymond Donovan joined him in the Oval Office at 1:30 P.M. to escort him to the Hilton. The two men greeted each other warmly. Donovan had played a crucial role in helping Reagan in the 1980 New Jersey primary. Both men had Irish roots and were tellers of good stories. They exchanged a few as they got into the president's limousine for the five-minute ride to the Hilton. With them in the car were Secret Service agent Dave Fischer, seated in the front with the driver, and Jerry Parr, the fifty-year-old head of the White House Secret Service unit. Parr was the approximate height of Reagan, but somewhat broader in build and outweighing him by perhaps twenty pounds. He wore his light tan raincoat open, and the sleeves were about an inch too long. His thick brown hair was tousled and brushed unevenly with gray. He gave a laid-back appearance but was well known for his quick reflexes and his firmness of character.

The motorcade pulled up at the hotel at 2:00 P.M. Secret Service men in two cars got out first and blocked the way for Reagan. Parr exited the limo before Reagan stepped out. There were red velvet ropes on both sides of the entranceway from curb to door, a distance of about twenty-three feet. A small crowd had gathered behind the ropes, reporters filling the front area to the right of the president and his party as they moved toward the building. Reagan smiled as he took long strides toward the door, now open and guarded by uniformed policemen. Deaver followed with the other riders from the control car, Brady and Prosperi behind them.

Once inside, the President, Donovan, Deaver, and Brady went into a VIP holding room. At 2:05 Reagan was escorted onto the stage of the gargantuan, downstairs ballroom of the Hilton, which had been set up to accommodate the huge numbers of delegates from the Building and Construction Workers Union, a group—mostly Democrats—not sympathetic to Reagan's views. This did not seem to bother Reagan, who appeared confident and began his speech with a humorous baseball story, going on to "extol the virtues of the work ethic," then segueing to an attack on big government and a call for more military spending. His speech ended twenty minutes later with the words, "Together we will make America great again." The audience's response was only mildly enthusiastic.[14]

Parr, Fischer, and several other agents surrounded him as, smile set, waving to the audience, he left the platform. Donovan, Deaver, Brady, and Prosperi followed them along a back route, down a long corridor, to an elevator that took them to the ground floor, where they navigated another dark hallway to the door through which they had entered. Reagan stepped out into a misty rain, smile in place, noting the television camera crews. He paused for a moment as Brady, Prosperi, and Deaver started toward their cars. He recognized Sam Donaldson, waved at him, and then, with Parr beside him, headed for the limousine, the door already open, a Secret Service man beside it.

"Mr. President! Mr. Reagan!" Mike Putzel of the Associated Press called out. Donaldson also tried to get his attention, shouting something about Poland. Deaver tapped Brady on the shoulder, a signal that meant Brady should take the questions. As Brady advanced toward the red velvet rope, Deaver crossed to the far side of the control car and Reagan continued on to his limousine. Suddenly, a crouching, blond-haired young man, who had somehow managed to infiltrate the press section, raised clenched hands in which he held a .22-caliber pistol. Reagan was only about ten feet away. Someone shouted and a policeman started toward the gunman as Secret Service agent Tim McCarthy stood, spread-eagled, arms outstretched, a human shield, in the path of any bullet directed at the president. There were six shots. Secret Service men plunged over the rope and were joined by a burly union representative from Cleveland in an effort to wrestle the assailant to the ground. "Eight or nine people were leaping on this one guy," a bystander recalled. "It seemed like forever before they got him under control."

Pandemonium raged. A man screamed, "Oh, God! It's happening again!" The smile on Reagan's face twisted in shock.

"It was like looking at a person who has seen death reflected in his eyes," Mickey Crowl, another bystander recalled. "All I can remember is [the president's] expression. It was like a guy saying 'I'm in a moment of helplessness.' "[15]

"I was almost to the car," Reagan wrote, "when I heard what sounded like two or three firecrackers over to my left—just a small fluttering sound, *pop, pop, pop.*" He turned and said, "What the hell's that?" Parr grabbed him around the waist from the rear, "doubling Reagan over to reduce his target profile, hunched over him as a human shield" and hurled him forward into the back seat of the car. "I landed on my face atop the [center] arm rest across the backseat and Jerry jumped on top of me."[16] The door was slammed shut and the limousine shunted forward and sped away up T Street to Connecticut Avenue toward the White House on Pennsylvania Avenue. The six shots had been discharged from the would-be assassin's gun within two seconds. Reagan's limousine was on its way within five seconds. Seeing that Reagan had made it safely to the car (or so it was thought), Dr. Ruge, Reagan's physician, stayed behind to oversee the wounded, Brady being the most seriously hurt.

In a rare moment of profane speech, Reagan shouted for Parr "to get the fuck off me!" He was furious and thought Parr had broken his rib. "When he landed [on me] I felt . . . the most excruciating pain I had ever felt," he recalled.[17] But Parr had done his job. Years of training for this moment had prepared him to "cover and evacuate. You hear a shot you don't go for your gun, you don't curse, you don't yell, you don't go after the assassin—you cover the president with your body and you get him out of there."[18]

By then the car was already in motion. Parr rolled off the president and called the Secret Service command post at the White House and told them that *Rawhide* (Reagan's code name) had not been hit and that they were heading back to *Crown* (the White House), a distance of about half of a mile. Reagan managed to get to an upright sitting position although he felt "paralyzed with pain."[19] Then he started to cough. He covered his mouth, and Parr handed him a clean handkerchief, which within moments turned deep red. Reagan was bleeding profusely from his mouth, sure now that his rib was broken and that it had punctured his lung. "There was something about the way he looked," Parr remembered. "He was growing pale, grayish, not looking well."[20] They were now on Seventeenth Street, the White House clearly in view ahead of them. Parr ordered the driver to turn onto Pennsylvania Avenue and go directly to the emergency entrance of George Washington University Hospital, six blocks away. Then he called the command post again with his change of plans and instructed them to alert the medical staff. No one in the cars behind them knew what was happening, but they switched routes as well.

Three ambulances screeched past them, sirens blaring, going the other way. At the Hilton the struggling gunman had finally been subdued and handcuffed. The smell of burnt gunpowder still peppered the air. James Brady lay face down, "bleeding into a steel grating and tended to by a Secret Service agent who laid his gun to rest next to Brady's wounded head."[21] Police officer Delehanty lay on the ground "groaning in agony." Agent McCarthy was bleeding profusely, but silent. Blood, somewhat thinned by the light rain, spread quickly across the sidewalk and spilled over the curb into the street. It only took three minutes for the medics to reach the crime site, but for those there it seemed an hour.

Reagan's car arrived at the emergency wing of the hospital at 2:35 P.M. A nurse came running toward them, but a stretcher had not yet appeared. Parr and Fischer got Reagan out of the car. He insisted on walking the distance—about fifteen yards—to the door. With a man on either side of him and the nurse hovering close, he managed to get just inside the door when his "eyes rolled upward, his head went back, his knees buckled and he started to collapse." Fischer and Parr hoisted him gently under his arms, "faint but still conscious," to the code room, where the worst emergency cases were treated.[22]

Moments later Deaver arrived and was informed that Reagan had not been shot. The medics at the hospital who examined him first, not finding a wound or evidence of external bleeding, initially believed that he had suffered a possible heart attack, and that he might have also had an internal hemorrhage. Deaver called the White House. Nancy had returned to learn that an attempt had been made on Reagan's life and was about to leave for the hospital. Deaver assured her that the president had not been shot and that it would be better if she waited so as not to alarm the press. He did not inform her of the medics' other concerns. When he returned to the trauma section, he was informed that the president had indeed taken a hit. At this stage the doctors were not sure where the bullet was lodged, but he was at present orally losing a lot of blood, indicating profuse internal bleeding. This was a life-threatening situation. When Deaver ran back to telephone Nancy, he was told she was already en route.

Reagan, hemorrhaging internally, his mouth and teeth bloodied, his face drained of color, was stretched out on a gurney. His outer clothing had been cut off him as tubes were being connected to his arms, the slow drip of plasma having begun. An oxygen mask was attached as he was having trouble breathing. Larry Speakes, alerted by Prosperi (who had been left behind at the crime scene) of the seriousness of Brady's injuries, raced from the White House to the hospital emergency room "and found the President in the emergency suite just to the left as you walk in the door. I started taking notes, which still give me shivers when I read them. 'Doctors believe bleeding to death. Can't find a wound. Think we're going to lose him [one doctor said]. Rapid loss of blood pressure. Touch and go.' " Dr. Ruge had arrived about the same time and was conferring with the medical staff.[23]

Dr. Wesley Price, a surgical resident, finally located a small puncture just below Reagan's armpit and covered by strands of his underarm hair. There was no exit wound and only a trace of blood around the narrow slit where the bullet had entered his body. The Secret Service, in contact with the operatives still at the crime site, had just learned that the gunman had used Devastator exploding bullets. This meant that the bullet inside the president's chest could explode at any moment, splintering and damaging other organs. They were later to find that the bullet had not been a direct hit but had ricocheted off the limousine. It had struck Reagan, his arm raised, as he was about to enter the vehicle, so the bullet's initial impact was lower, and it flattened into a razor-thin shape just before it sliced into the president's chest. Deaver recalls at about this time turning to see Jim Brady, "his head split open," blood gushing as medics worked furiously to staunch the flow, being wheeled by on a gurney toward an operating theater, and, at the entrance of the emergency room, agent Tim McCarthy lying under a bloody sheet on still another gurney and moaning in pain.[24] "God! It looks like Vietnam!" one intern cried. Speakes recalled that he realized Brady was close to death. "I thought to myself that he was only forty, almost exactly a year younger than I. And I might have been [dying] there instead of him but for his decision to accompany the President that day."[25]

There was an oxygen mask over Reagan's face, his lips caked with blood beneath it. "Who's holding my hand?" Reagan thought he asked. But it could have been in his head and not on his lips. No one answered. He caught a glimpse of a nurse in a white uniform. Her hand was warm and comforting, and his thoughts went to Nancy, wondering whether she knew what was happening. Reagan later wrote, "Although I tried to learn afterwards who the nurse was, I was never able to find her. I had wanted to tell her how much the touch of her hand meant to me, but I never was able to do that."[26]

Nancy arrived at the hospital at 2:50 P.M. not yet knowing that Ronnie had been shot. Deaver said she was near hysteria when the doctors informed her of what they suspected. A team of expert surgeons was now on the way for consultation. "Will they operate?" she wanted to know and was informed that X rays had first to be taken to see if they could locate the bullet. Nancy's hand was shaking as she raised it to her mouth to hold back her inclination to cry. Her high heels click-clicked and echoed as she raced down the tile floors of the hospital corridors to where Ronnie still lay on the gurney. The moment she was by his side, she straightened and tried to smile as he looked up at her through the oxygen mask, which the nurse lifted for a moment. Nancy saw the blood on his mouth and she took his hand. "Honey," he said weakly, his words coming in small gasps, "I forgot to duck." Reagan would eventually write: "As long as I live I will never forget the thought that rushed into my head as I looked up into [Nancy's] face. Later I wrote it down in my diary: *'I pray I'll never face a day when she isn't there . . . of all the ways God has blessed me, giving her to me was the greatest—beyond anything I can ever hope deserve'.*"[27]

A few moments later they were surrounded by a team of specialists. X rays were taken, more blood plasma given. One of the doctors signaled Nancy, and she leaned over, kissed Ronnie, and stood there as he was wheeled away down the tunnel-like hallway surrounded by equipment and medical staff and by Dave Fischer, who remained on duty despite the attending doctors' strong objections. As he was wheeled past Baker, Deaver, and Meese, Reagan said in a raspy voice, "Who's minding the store?"

Nancy appeared small and vulnerable as she stood in the clinical coldness of the hospital corridor—shoulders narrowed, hands clasped, in shock as Ronnie's gurney disappeared behind a pair of green doors. Deaver came up close to her side. Her hand was trembling again. "There's a little chapel upstairs," he said. "Why don't we go in there for a while?" After she was assured that she would be kept constantly informed, she took Deaver's arm for support and, with the Secret Service surrounding her, made her way to the chapel via a nearby elevator.[28]

Luckily, there had been a major conference of the hospital's top surgeons in session at the time the president was brought in. As soon as they were alerted that the president had been shot, they rushed to Reagan's side. By 3:00 P.M. they had set their medical course. The bullet had to be removed, but first they had to be sure that the internal bleeding was not coming from any of his abdominal organs. Dr. Benjamin Aaron, chief of thoracic surgery and head of the surgical team who would operate on the president, determined that a peritoneal lavage should be performed immediately. Reagan was losing blood fast and Doctor Aaron "didn't want to get into a situation where [with the president on the table to remove the bullet from the chest cavity, where it had lodged], they'd have a major blood transfusion to deal with [caused by bleeding elsewhere]." The result was negative, and by 3:24 P.M. the president was wheeled into the operating room to be prepared for the delicate surgery—to locate and remove the bullet, which they could only hope had not entered the heart chamber.[29]

When Doctor Aaron informed Reagan that he was about to begin surgery, he replied, "I hope you're a Republican."

The doctor answered earnestly, "Today, Mr. President, we're all Republicans."[30]

A nurse, wanting to know if the anesthesia was taking effect, inquired how he was feeling. "All in all, I'd rather be in Philadelphia," he quipped, quoting an old W. C. Fields comedy line.[31] Reagan's mind, the medical team were reassured, was still sharp. Only a few minutes passed before he was completely anesthetized.

Nancy was joined in the chapel by Tim McCarthy's wife, Carolyn, and by Sarah Brady, whose husband was also in surgery. Brady's chances for survival seemed even slimmer than the president's. The women embraced, although they had never before met. Having had to arrange care for their two-year-old son and travel from her suburban home, Sarah Brady had not arrived until her husband was in surgery and so had not seen the extent of his injuries. She was a young woman of aristocratic bearing and much grit. "They're strong men," she told Nancy. "They'll get through this."[32]

"Yes," Nancy said, "yes." But the images of Brady as she had passed him on a bloodied gurney, the top of his head apparently missing, and of Ronnie, so pale, blood caked on his lips, made it impossible for her to be optimistic.

A short time later the three wives of the stricken men were ushered to a private office on the second floor, which had windows overlooking the front court of the building, where a crowd had gathered. Nancy went to glance out and was pulled sharply away by a Secret Service man. At this stage no one knew whether this was the work of a lone assassin or a conspiracy, and they wanted to be sure that the first lady was never in the line of fire.

With Brady incapacitated it was decided that Speakes would return to the White House and deal with the press there, while Lyn Nofziger would set up a press area at the hospital, with easy access to expert medical updates about the president, Brady, and agent Tim McCarthy. Police officer Thomas Delehanty had been taken to the critical-care tower of the Washington Hospital Center.

Every twenty minutes or so a nurse reported to the women with an update on their husbands' condition. Sarah Brady had been informed that if Jim should survive there was no certainty that he would ever be able to walk, speak, or even regain consciousness.

Tim McCarthy, the Secret Service agent who had stepped deliberately into the line of fire, was the first of the injured quartet to complete surgery. The bullet, which had penetrated his lung but missed his heart, had been removed, and it was a Devastator. About 5:00 P.M., McCarthy was transferred to the recovery room. At 5:30 police officer Thomas Delehanty came out of surgery to remove a bullet that had gone through his neck and lodged not far from his spine.

After tearful goodbyes to Nancy and Sarah Brady, Carolyn McCarthy left. The two remaining women waited for news of their husbands, held hands, and prayed.

It was just past 6:00 P.M. when a nurse came in to tell Nancy that the bullet had been located in the president's chest. It had missed his heart by one inch, "penetrated to the seventh rib, where it deflected to the left lower lobe of the lung." He had been "that close" to death. It would be an hour and a half before Nancy would be allowed to see him. She went to call the family. For Sarah Brady, left alone in the room, the vigil was not yet over. James Brady would be under the knife for three more hours.

While Reagan was in the operating room, Vice President Bush was on a plane en route from Fort Worth, Texas, where he had given a speech at a convention of cattlemen, to Austin, where he was scheduled to address the state legislature. A coded teletype message reached Bush on Air Force Two with the news of the attempted assassination and the gravity of the president's condition. The pilot was ordered to refuel in Austin and continue on to Washington.

It would take Bush several hours to reach the White House, where, at that moment, Ronald Reagan's cabinet gathered in the protected underground Situation Room to try to figure out who, indeed, "was minding the store." Suddenly, Haig jumped to his feet and bolted from the room. "What's he doing?" one aide cried. Another shouted out, "Where's he going?" There was fear and trembling around the power table. No one knew what Haig was up to, but most of them now felt the man was unstable. There was a television in a corner of the room so that the events at the hospital and the crime scene could be monitored. To everyone's shock, less than three minutes after Haig's departure, a television commentator in the White House pressroom announced in an excited voice, "Here comes the secretary of state!" Haig strode out in front of the live television cameras as an update on the president's condition was going out across the nation. Haig bounded onto the podium, a look approaching delirium in his steely eyes. The reporters in the room were not sure what to expect, but seeing the secretary of state so distracted, they feared the worst. Haig, his voice quavering, his face ashen, proclaimed that with Bush in flight he was the next in the succession, then blurted out, "I am in charge here!" After a short improvised statement, Haig rushed out of the room before anyone had time to contradict or question his unfortunate blunder, for in fact, the secretary of state is behind the vice president, the speaker of the House, and the president pro tempore of the Senate in the line of succession.[33]

The evening had turned thunderous. Lightning flashed across the dark skies and a heavy rain pummeled the ground. Larry Speakes, his coat soggy, rivulets of water from his hair sliding onto his face, entered the Situation Room moments after Haig's return and heard him repeat his gaffe, still seeming to be unaware of his terrible mistake. The men at the table, who included Secretary of Defense Caspar Weinberger, National Security Adviser Richard Allen, Edwin Meese (who had returned from the hospital), Attorney General William French Smith, Secretary of the Treasury Donald Regan, CIA director William Casey, and Interior Secretary James Watt, looked startled. "With the President disabled and the Vice President in flight, the Secretary of State is next in the succession," Haig explained, appearing to think that *they* were the ones who were confused. "No, sir," an aide solemnly ventured as he rolled off the true order of the succession. The men in the room were all staring at Haig. "You're sure?" he asked. "Yes, sir," the aide responded. Haig paled. A vein on his left temple pulsed visibly. He held his military bearing, but he had to grasp the edge of the table to do so. "To see the man, a four-star general, who had steered Richard Nixon through his final crisis on the edge of an emotional collapse," an aide recalled, "was surreal."[34]

In fact, the Twenty-fifth Amendment, which passed the president's powers to those next in the succession, had not been invoked; Reagan was technically still in command. (See appendix 4 for the text of the amendment.) The troika had decided this at the hospital before Reagan entered the operating theater. While he was under the knife, Nofziger, handling the press station at the hospital, was reporting Reagan's humorous quips to assure the public that he was of sound mind. To invoke the Twenty-fifth Amendment, they believed, would have given the impression that the president was incapacitated. Weinberger, who had information that Soviet submarines were not far off the Atlantic Coast, although supposedly with "no hostile intentions," did not want the Russians to know the real situation. And with no knowledge of who the gunman's associates might be, or if there were any, the troika had taken what they thought to be the safest course.

Air Force Two set down at Andrews Air Force Base at 6:30 P.M. Bush was met by Meese, who fully apprised him of Reagan's condition and the problems with Haig at the White House. They went directly to the Situation Room at the White House. "[Bush] took his seat at the head of the table in the Situation Room at six-fifty-nine," Speakes recorded, "and presided over a crisis-management meeting that lasted half an hour. The seal of the President hung on the wall behind [him], and a wooden-paneled wall was opened to reveal the now-silent television set. . . . I was never so impressed with Bush as I was that night, the way he instantly took command." A much chastened Haig sat stoically at the other end of the table.[35]

The president had been in the recovery room for about forty-five minutes when Nancy was finally allowed in to see him at 7:15 P.M. She was led through a rear door to the room where he was concealed behind screens. When she gazed down at him for the first time since he had been wheeled into the operating theater, emotion overwhelmed her and she could not control her tears. Her beloved Ronnie looked almost skeletal, bone-white with the loss of so much blood. He was still woozy from the anesthetic and not really sure where he was or what had happened to him. Nancy reached down and touched his arm and amid her tears told him that she loved him. He seemed to be struggling to say something. A nurse handed him a pencil and held a pad for him to write on. "I can't breathe," he managed to scrawl. Nancy started screaming, "He can't *breathe*! He can't *breathe*!" A medic assured her that the respirator was doing his breathing for him, that he had not yet become used to it.

Ron was the first of the children to arrive, having chartered a plane from Lincoln, Nebraska, where he had been on tour with the Joffrey II Ballet. The other children were in California and would not be able to get there until early morning. He leaned over his father and said, "It's okay, Dad. What you're feeling is the tube down your throat. . . . They're getting air to you, and you'll be fine."[36]

The doctors insisted that Nancy leave the recovery room at about

8:00 P.M. They were giving the president morphine to ease his pain and wanted him to rest. Nancy returned to the White House with Ron and Doria. Rex Stouten and Ted Graber were there to meet her. Ron and Doria went with her to the master bedroom, where Ron started a fire in the fireplace because she was chilled. When she left the hospital, a wind had risen and it was pelting rain. Despite being under a huge umbrella, she had gotten damp. Supper was served on trays in the room as they all watched the television coverage. About ten P.M. Ron and Doria retired to a nearby room (formerly Amy Carter's bedroom). Unable to sleep, Nancy watched the repeated replays of the attempted assassination that she now knew had almost succeeded: Ronnie as he exited the Hilton, smiling; arm raised as he waved to the press and those who had gathered to see him; the popping of gunshots and the look of shock on his face; Jerry Parr literally hurling him into the back seat of the limousine. When, she wondered, had the bullet hit him? They had told her at the hospital that it had first struck the car, then sped through the opened hinge of the door and caught him just as he was about to take his final steps toward the car's open rear door.

So many thoughts rushed through her head. So many what-ifs? caught at her heart, so many images from the past rose before her. Jackie Kennedy in Dallas with her husband's bloodied head resting against her body in the back seat of the open car; Ronnie saying as they watched with horror the tragedy unfolding on the television screen, "Why doesn't she change her dress?" concerned at how distressed the public would be at the sight of their dead president's blood. Nancy understood that for Jackie this was her husband, the man she loved, not the president, and the red streaks on her clothes were reminders of his life—not his death— that she could not let go of so soon.

Only three weeks before this terrible day, the Reagans had visited Ford's Theater and had stood looking up at the flag-draped box where Lincoln had been shot. Nancy had no way of knowing that Ronnie was recalling that visit during this same long, rain-throbbing night, the morphine only partially easing his pain. "With all the protection in the world," he later recalled thinking, "it is probably impossible to guarantee completely the safety of the president."[37]

"Nothing can happen to my Ronnie," she wrote in her diary that night. "My life would be over."[38]

The Academy Awards had been canceled. All the major television stations kept broadcasting updates from the hospital, new information on the gunman, now identified as twenty-five-year-old John Warmock Hinckley. He was in police custody. Nancy called the hospital every twenty minutes or so. James Brady had pulled through the operation but remained in grave condition. Agent Tim McCarthy was stable, as was Officer Delehanty. Ronnie was restless, but all the signs were good. He continued to write notes that seemed to indicate some confusion. "Where am I?" His agent told him he was in the recovery room. "How long have I been here?" Then, when he was told, "How long will I have to stay here?" The agent replied, "Not long."

At 2:35 A.M. the doctors took off the respirator and he began breathing on his own. At 2:50 A.M. the endotracheal tube was removed. When this was completed, one of the medics commented, "This is it." Reagan grabbed a pad and scrawled, "What does he mean—*this is it?*"[39] He calmed down after it was explained to him that the doctor had been referring to the tube in his throat. When Nancy called at 4:00 A.M., she was told that the president was more comfortable with the tube removed and was dozing. He would be transferred to the intensive care unit at 6:00 A.M. and, if all went well, to a private suite by midmorning.

Nancy scooted over to Ronnie's side of the bed and finally found a few moment's rest as she nestled into his pillows.

CHAPTER THIRTEEN

AFTERMATH

The troika appeared at Reagan's bedside the next morning, Tuesday, March 31, at 6:45 A.M. Although still connected to several machines, he had been propped up and was brushing his teeth. He suddenly looked his age. Framed by the sickroom pallor of his face, the dark circles under his eyes gave him an owl-like expression. He had lost over fifty percent of his blood and still was being fed plasma. For security, the curtains were nailed tight and the room lit surrealistically by fluorescent tubing. Reagan's hand moved slowly and wavered as he stopped what he was doing and wiped his mouth on a cloth. He was in pain, but he cracked a smile when he glanced up and saw Deaver, Meese, and Baker in their de rigueur dark business suits and looking somber. "I should have known I wasn't going to avoid a staff meeting," he quipped.[1] That broke the ice. They all laughed.

As a youngster with an alcoholic father and a mother who preferred martyrdom to charity, Reagan had learned the fine art of badinage to mask his true feelings. Through the years he had honed it into a militarized defense ploy, shielding his private thoughts and feelings, protecting others as well as himself from the truth in a way he believed to be noble. He had been in the courtyard of death. Others had suffered because they had protected him. His debt weighed as heavy as his pain. Ronald Reagan's earliest teachings had been to give, not to take.

The troika had come with a congressional bill that needed his signature: a cutback on federal price supports for dairy products. This was not an emergency bill that required immediate attention, but the men wanted to show the press and the public that the president was able to function. Deaver asked if he felt strong enough to sign the paper. "You bet I do!" he replied. He took the pen Deaver offered and did so in a "weak and wobbly" hand. "If I had seen [the signature] under different circumstances," Deaver wrote, "I might have called it a forgery. But it was his. And the significance of that fact was not lost on any of us."[2]

Reagan, isolated from any news since he entered the hospital, immediately wanted to know what had really happened? How was Jim Brady? Who were the other men who took a hit? Did they have the gunman? Baker told him that the police had the shooter in custody and that at present they thought he was not part of a conspiracy. Reagan's other questions were bypassed, the troika having been warned by the doctors not to discuss Jim Brady or the others yet. "The vice president is back and everything is going well at the White House," Meese quickly interjected.

"What made you think I'd be happy to hear *that?*" Reagan cracked. He pressed his inquiry again about Jim Brady just as a nurse and a doctor entered. The troika, the signed document now safely in Deaver's attaché case, took the opportunity to leave.[3]

Reagan had floated in and out of consciousness during the night, but he remembered being told by a nurse in the emergency room as Jim Brady was wheeled past him on his way to the operating room that Brady might not make it. "I quickly said a [silent] prayer for him," Reagan later recalled. "I didn't feel I could ask God's help to heal Jim, the others, and myself [at that time he did not know who else had been hit], and at the same time feel hatred for the man who had shot us, so I silently asked God to help him deal with whatever demons had led him to shoot us."[4]

Nancy arrived a little later in the morning with his bathrobe, slippers, a large jar of multicolored jelly beans, and a pocketbook filled with get-well telegrams passed on to her by Helene von Damm, who had not left the White House until long past midnight and had returned with the light of day. One telegram was from Reagan's good friend, actor Jimmy Stewart: "I would have taken that bullet," he wrote.[5]

Ronnie was dozing when Nancy entered the room. Dr. Kraus, who was in charge of postoperative care, had given him a small dose of narcotics to ease his pain. Nancy spent about twenty minutes with him, holding his hand. It all still seemed so unreal to her. She left the room when the medics came in to turn the president over on his stomach, preparing to pound on his back to keep fluids from building up in his lungs. The sound of the *whacks* on his body unnerved her. She knew the beating was necessary, but Ronnie was already in so much pain that just one look at his face had telegraphed the message to her. It was an expression she had never seen before.

A secure suite was being readied for him, but the doctors wanted him to remain in intensive care at least until late that evening. Meanwhile the area was surrounded by Secret Service agents, and the small, hot, windowless room nearby, where Nancy waited until she could return to see him, was equally well guarded.

A staff member gave Nancy the numerous notes Reagan had scrawled during the night. "There is no more exhil[arating] feeling than being shot at without result," he wrote, quoting Winston Churchill. "Send me to L.A., where I can see the air I'm breathing!" was another. In the recovery room he had scribbled, "If I'd had this much attention in Hollywood, I'd have stayed there," and "I'd like to do this scene again—starting at the hotel." As he began to remember what had happened, the notes took a more serious tone:

"How is Jim Brady?"

"Was anyone else hurt?"

"What happened to the guy with the gun?"

"What was his beef?"

"Will I still be able to work on the ranch?"

All of his questions received pat answers. "Well, we don't know right now."[6]

In Los Angeles on the day of the shooting, Patti, Michael, Colleen, Maureen, and Dennis had been informed by the Secret Service of the assassination attempt within ten minutes after it occurred. Patti was pulled from a therapy session. Not yet knowing whether there was a conspiracy that might place the president's family in danger, the Secret

Service dispersed numerous agents to bring them to Washington in an army transport plane. By the time they boarded, the sun was going down; in Washington it was already late evening, and the president was out of surgery after the removal of a bullet. More than that none of them knew. The only one of the children whom Nancy had contacted directly had been Ron. One of the agents informed the others that Ron was already in Washington at the hospital with the First Lady. "People reach out to each other at times like this only if they know how, and we didn't," Patti remarked. "I thought about that as I took a seat on the plane. None of us had called each other. No one had gotten through to my mother, nor had she called any of us. No one had spoken to [Ron]. 'What kind of family is this?' I wondered. 'Even a bullet can't bring us together.'"[7]

Even in this time of great concern they sat separated in the plane, Patti toward the front, Michael and Colleen in the center, and Maureen and Dennis in the last two seats.

Patti was certain that they were being taken to their father's bedside only because his staff was conscious that the world was watching. There might have been a desire to maintain an image of "the American family," but having their children near them was not important to either parent as long as they had each other. The army plane set down at Andrews Air Force Base in the middle of the night, and Reagan's children were taken directly to the White House, where sleeping accommodations had been arranged. Despite the hour, Patti went into her mother's room, and sat on the edge of her bed. Nancy was still awake and looked as if she were "crumbling," eyes red from crying, hair in disarray, her hands icy to the touch although the room was warm. Patti had seen her in many attitudes—angry, edgy, distant, sad, loving. But never in such despair. There was a tearful reunion, with the terrifying events of the day retold before Patti left to spend the remainder of a sleepless night in one of the third-floor bedrooms. She did not see Ron and Doria until after their mother had left for the hospital earlier that morning. Then she, her brother, and Doria were escorted to a White House car and taken to join her. When Maureen and Michael and their mates arose somewhat later, they were told that on Mrs. Reagan's orders they could not go to see their father yet. They were furious and insisted a car take them to the hospital or they would get there on their own. Calls were made and their request was granted.

When Patti entered her father's room in the intensive care unit, she noted that "his skin was pale, almost translucent."[8] When Maureen and Michael arrived, "Patti and Ron were already in his room," Michael recounted, "but [we] were told he was too weak to see us, too. When Patti and Ron came out of the room, they walked by us without a word. In fact we never saw them till the following Thanksgiving."[9]

Nancy had left the area to see Sarah Brady, so Michael ran in search of Dr. Kraus who he'd been told was the doctor in charge. He and Maureen were, at first, refused permission to see their father. He finally succeeded by issuing dire warnings that he would force his way in. Dr. Kraus doubted he could or would do so, but did not want a disturbance to occur that might prove damaging to the president. He therefore agreed to their seeing their father. Maureen, Michael, and Colleen (Dennis remained in a waiting area) went into Reagan's room together. The drapes remained nailed shut, and the room was dimly lit to afford the president a more restful environment. It was hard to tell what time of day it was. Reagan was propped up on pillows "obviously in pain, but he managed a smile" when he saw them. "I'm told the parents of the kid who shot me are well off," he said, trying for an upbeat tone. "You'd think they would at least buy me a new blue suit." They were with him for only a few minutes as they could see he was uncomfortable.[10]

When they returned to the waiting room, Nancy was sitting alone, crying, seeming fragile. Nancy would admit later that what she had been feeling was terrible guilt because she had not been with Ronnie at the Hilton. This was irrational, of course, but she somehow believed that if she had been there it would not have happened as it did.

Nancy was not the only one who suffered a personal guilt for some imagined infraction at the time of the shooting. Dave Fischer blamed himself for not being next to the president as he always was when he had stepped momentarily away and toward the back of the limousine. He had nightmares for months and refused to leave Reagan's side in the hospital. Michael Deaver was emotional for many weeks after the shooting because he felt he had, however inadvertently, placed James Brady in harm's way by directing him to take the questions of the reporters. "I had weeks and weeks and weeks of anguish. I would break down," he recalled. "I was in such anguish over Jim. I'd think, 'My God, I'm the guy who put him there.' "[11] The neurosurgeon would later draw a diagram to present the alternative. As Deaver was only five feet nine inches tall and Brady over six feet, had Deaver been in Brady's place, the bullet would have gone over his head and struck the president in his head. Mike Putzel, the reporter who had called out to Reagan and caused him to turn for a split second, was saddled with the thought that if he had not shouted to him, the president might not have paused and so would have made it safely to his car.

As always, Nancy was doing all she could to protect Ronnie, which included insulating him from visits that would exhaust him. She had not been happy that Maureen, Michael, and Doria had been to see him. She now left instructions that no one be allowed into his room without Mike Deaver's approval. She fully realized that Vice President Bush or a member of the cabinet might require immediate access. What she wanted to do was to shield him from well-wishers among the staff, knowing he would force himself to appear "on the mend," and so further erode his strength.

Late that first morning, after the children had left, Reagan's personal secretary, Helene von Damm, arrived. Ronnie had been resting and Nancy had gone to speak to the wives of the other injured men. Deaver, who was a friend of von Damm's and who also knew better than most others how much the president relied on her, assumed that the no-visitors order did not include her. When Nancy returned, von Damm was still in Reagan's room, "talking nonsense, keeping him awake when he should have been sleeping."[12] Despite her twelve years as a hard-working Reagan staff member, this was the beginning of a serious rift between von Damm and Nancy, who had never been too keen on the much younger von Damm, an attractive though certainly not glamorous woman. Nancy considered von Damm pushy and disapproved of the fact that she had been divorced twice and was planning a third trip up the aisle. She was also piqued that von Damm was socially courting some of the Reagans' old friends, such as the Annenbergs and the Wicks. As there was no denying von Damm's strong loyalty to Ronnie, or her efficiency, and as he seemed at ease with her, Nancy had tempered her disregard. Certainly now was not the time to make an issue about Helene von Damm. But Nancy did not entirely put aside her anger that von Damm had not had the good sense to wait before paying what Nancy considered to be a strictly self-serving visit, designed to demonstrate her VIP standing in the administration.

At 9:00 P.M., Reagan was moved to a secure eight-room suite (consisting of his room, a room for Nancy, a consultation and a press room, as well as space for the Secret Service) on the third floor of the hospital opposite the ICU wing. "We pushed to get him out of the ICU," Dr. Kraus said, "because we knew he'd be better some place that was quieter. The environment [in ICU] was getting him a little disoriented [and the suite would be more secure]."[13] Although the room was large and comfortably furnished, its windows remained tightly concealed so that day slipped into night. Nancy spent the late evening of March 31 with Ronnie watching the Academy Awards. He slept intermittently (it is always a long show, and this night it seemed excessively so), but he was cheered when the audience rose to its feet and loudly applauded his taped message to Fonda after it was announced that he was out of danger. Because he kept dozing off, however, he did not learn until the next day that the winners included *Ordinary People* as Best Picture, Robert Redford as Best Director for *Ordinary People*, Sissy Spacek as Best Actress for *The Coal Miner's Daughter*, and Robert DeNiro as Best Actor for *Raging Bull*.

Bush was doing an excellent job of handling matters at the White House. Still, there were papers that required the President's signature and attention. On the third day he managed to tend to these by working in short segments of time. Those who saw him that morning, mainly cabinet members, were shocked at how ill he looked, color blanched from his gaunt face, a tremor in his hands. He was fully informed about the events that led up to his being in a hospital bed. He shed tears when told about the seriousness of Jim Brady's injuries. Unlike the bullet that had hit Reagan, the Devastator that entered Brady's head had exploded in his brain. Nancy told him that Brady was fighting gallantly and that Sarah was constantly with him, repeating over and over, "You can make it! You can make it!"

He felt guilty that Brady and the others had taken hits because of him, and he apologized to Jerry Parr for chewing him out right after it happened. He now realized that Parr, too, had put his life on the line for him. "I thanked God for what He and they had done for me," he said. Later he would vow, "Whatever happens now I owe my life to God and will try to serve Him in every way I can."[14]

On Thursday morning, April 2, he appeared to be progressing so well that he agreed to have a photograph taken of him as he took a few steps down the hospital corridor on Nancy's arm. Late that afternoon the unexpected happened. His temperature suddenly soared to 103 degrees and his white blood count rose alarmingly. "For the first two days we were living in a dream world," Dr. Aaron confessed. "We were talking about getting him out of the hospital within a week. I thought to myself, 'That doesn't seem very realistic, but let's hope anyway. Of course, it didn't turn out to be very realistic.' "[15]

X rays were taken. The President had some haziness in the left lower chest area. Dr. Aaron's concern increased when his patient began to spit up blood. "I had the thought that he might be bleeding down in the bullet tract [and that it might be infected]. So I had to consider that he might begin to bleed briskly intrabronchially [which meant Dr. Aaron might have to return to surgery and remove the lobe, a part of the lung]." Aaron surmised that the bullet had tumbled through the lungs. "The pleural gap was huge; it was like a ball had gone into the lung—perhaps two cm in diameter. And I thought, 'There is going to be a lot of destroyed lung in that lower lobe.' "[16] The situation was grave; the president was once more in mortal danger, perhaps even more dire than when he had first been shot. A decision was made by the troika and the White House press staff that this information would not be given to the media.

The medical staff carefully monitored Reagan's condition for the next twenty-four hours. When things did not improve, an X ray of his chest (taken after the Secret Service "swept the department for security [and] cleaned it out of unneeded personnel")[17] revealed that the left lower lobe had collapsed. Reagan had pneumonia and a possible infection caused by the bullet. Given the President's weakened condition, Dr. Aaron decided that to perform a second surgery so close to the first was too chancy and placed him on a heavy dosage of antibiotics.

Reagan had lapsed into unconsciousness, though statements were still being released by Nofziger at the hospital and Speakes at the White House that painted quite a different picture. Nancy was on the point of collapse but managed a restrained smile for the cameras, as it had been impressed upon her that it would be a serious problem if the public believed the president was in crisis. It was not until April 8, the tenth day after being hit by Hinckley's bullet, that Reagan began to show some definite progress and was able to meet individually with members of his cabinet and discuss prevailing issues. On Saturday, April 11, he left the hospital, insisting on getting up from the wheelchair that had brought him down from his room and walking without assistance from the exit to his car.

He repeated this test of his endurance when he reached the White House. Smiling and waving, he walked from the limousine to the entrance and then to the elevator to the family quarters, displaying "his strength" to a select group of photographers allowed to take pictures. He had even agreed to being made up before he left the hospital. His staff was doing everything possible to avoid what they called "a Woodrow Wilson episode—[the perception of] a sick president remaining in office beyond his time," and he was adding to it his best effort.[18]

Once inside the family quarters, he slowed down "walking with the hesitant steps of an old man [and when he started to sit down] he fell the rest of the way, collapsing into his chair."[19] His concentrated efforts to appear well had exhausted all of his strength. The following day he wrote in his diary, "The first full day at home. I'm not jumping any fences and the routine is still one of blood tests, X-rays, bottles dripping into my arms but I'm home." Nancy hardly left his side. She, above all others, really knew how weak he was. A hospital bed was set up in the Lincoln Bedroom for his recuperation. ("President Lincoln's ghost never paid me a call," he later remarked.)[20] He was on medication and got through the nights better than Nancy did. Although there was a nurse on duty, Nancy had forfeited her own pills so that she could be alert if he needed her. Every minor advance Ronnie made was a small victory for her as well. He saw his cabinet members, met with George Bush, and answered letters to concerned close friends.

Most of the rooms in the family quarters, except for the master bedroom and the den, did not have television sets. However, one had been installed in the Lincoln Bedroom during the last days of Richard Nixon's presidency. Nixon would go into the room (an almost holy place for many presidents) and sit alone watching the drama of his fall from grace unfold on the screen before him.

On April 14 Ronnie and Nancy watched on television as the space shuttle *Columbia* returned to earth after a successful maiden voyage. He was moved by the wave of patriotism it had aroused in the country, something that had been sadly missing through the Vietnam War, the Nixon debacle, and the hostage crisis. Reagan was convinced that the country wanted to feel "proud and patriotic again."[21] That was now to be his mission.

While Ronnie was in the hospital, Nancy managed in her few free hours to supervise some cursory redoing of the White House solarium, which had once been Franklin Roosevelt's favored retreat, a beautiful room situated on the third floor with a large bay window that overlooked the Washington Monument. Dr. Richard Davis, Nancy's stepbrother, recalled her taking him up to the room just a few days after the shooting. "Now, Dick," she said, "my job this week is to really go over this room and renovate it so the President can recover here. It will make him feel like he's outside once again and, you know, we want to keep all that sunshine and happiness in his life."[22] And it was in the solarium—fresh slipcovers swiftly replacing old, worn ones, window boxes filled with bright yellow daffodils, sun filtering through the wide glass windows warming him to his bones, easing the tension in his body—that he spent his mornings during his convalescence. Spring had finally come to Washington. The snow was melted, the cherry trees about to bloom. But although the summerhouse ambiance eased his body, his mind went back to thoughts he had had the day before the shooting.

It had been a Sunday, and he decided, quite impulsively, that he would like to attend church services. Despite his reservations about the need for requiring so many Secret Service men and the possibility of placing innocent people in harm's way (a thought that disturbed him more now than it had previously), he and Nancy had gone. His need to go to church had grown out of a conversation a few days earlier with Helene von Damm. She had given him a Defense Department memo that stated that if Russia dropped a nuclear bomb on the United States, 150 million people could suffer the consequences. The sheer numbers had haunted him, and he had not been able to put from his mind "the future of America and the MAD policy."[23] Perhaps he thought that God's word as to what he could do to prevent such a catastrophe would be better relayed to him in church; or perhaps he simply needed to pray for guidance.

The acronym MAD stood for "mutual assured destruction," the United States' only shield against nuclear annihilation. The country had stockpiled and kept at the ready enough nuclear weapons to destroy the USSR in the event that the Soviets either attacked or were known to be about to attack the United States. Reagan likened this to "two spiders in a bottle locked in a suicidal fight until both were dead. As president, I carried no wallet, no money, no driver's license, no keys in my pockets—only secret codes that were capable of bringing about the annihilation of much of the world as we knew it." At all times, he carried a plastic coated card (much like any credit card) with the codes that he was to issue to the Pentagon for proof that it was the president who was "ordering the unleashing of our nuclear weapons."[24] The decision would be entirely his, and he would have six minutes in which to make it. When he was on that hospital gurney, his clothes being stripped from him, the card had been in his inside pocket. He did not know, nor would he ever learn, who removed it. But he had been assured that it was a Secret Service man.

The idea that anyone could believe that the United States could fight and win a nuclear war was sheer madness. He felt neither side could be the victor, but, he wondered, "how do we go about trying to prevent it and pulling back from this hair-trigger existence?" He set his mind to trying to find some way the country could end this "nervous

standoff" and start up a process of peace. "During my watch as president," he vowed, "there is nothing more I want than to lessen [the risk
of nuclear warfare]."[25]

Patti returned to Washington to see him while he was still recuperating. She asked her father "[in the hours after the shooting] if he ever
feared that he would die?"

"No," he replied. And then added, "I prayed for that young man
when I was lying there. . . . I prayed that God would forgive him. And
that he would ask for God's forgiveness."[26]

There was nothing within the Hinckleys' family structure to account
for the violence perpetrated by John Jr., the third and last child of Jack
and JoAnne Hinckley. The family had moved several times during their
youngest child's early years as Jack's oil-and-gas-drilling business pros-
pered. All three of the Hinckley kids possessed "good, natural looks—
a big smile, a big set of teeth, blond hair, blue eyes."[27] John Jr. had been
popular enough in seventh and eighth grades to be elected president of
his homeroom. That had been in comfortable Highland Park, Illinois,
where the Hinckleys had lived from 1966 until 1974. But his popularity
seems to have faded by the time he entered Highland Park High School.
Despite the background of his oil-money privilege, he had few friends
and was a low achiever, while his sister was an A student and a nominee
for homecoming queen and his brother scored well both scholastically
and athletically.

John wanted to go to Yale, but his grades were not good enough,
and he wound up at Texas Tech in Lubbock where he slid into heavy
drinking and "hell-raising." He left school in 1976 and for a while lived
in Hollywood with some fantasy of becoming an actor or a producer and
winning the love of Jodie Foster. Before leaving for Hollywood, he had
seen the movie *Taxi Driver* about a teenaged prostitute and a crazed taxi
driver's descent into violence. When the protagonist is scorned by Foster's character, he mails her a letter telling her he is going to kill a
presidential candidate. Hinckley wanted to meet and "save" Foster, in
his mind believing her to be the character she had played. But it never
happened. He was drifting, living in a seedy, dangerous neighborhood
and just about out of money. His parents were distressed about him but

did not at the time suspect that he might be suffering from a mental disorder. On the insistence of his father, who agreed to send him $2,000, he returned to Texas Tech, where he walked around the campus "a glum, seedy figure in beltless blue jeans and a T shirt . . . in a continual trudge," recalled one campus merchant who sold him the doughnuts on which he survived, along with hamburgers from McDonald's.[28]

During this time he became a member of the National Socialist Party of America, a Nazi organization, and participated in a rally where he joined the rest of his group in shouting racial invective. "Outside of being a Nazi, he was a pretty ordinary fellow," the party chief recalled. "After the rally he was like a different person. He was very agitated. He said we needed something more dramatic [than rallies]. I took that to mean like shooting people. When somebody comes to us and starts advocating shooting people, it's a natural reaction: the guy's either a nut or a Federal Agent."[29] He was dropped from the party in 1979 and started on a gun-shopping spree that would last nearly two years.

His father, although unaware of his son's recent connections, had become alarmed at his disheveled appearance and lack of ambition. It was a pattern. When John Jr. got down to rock bottom financially, he would call upon his father for help. For what he warned his son would be the last time, Jack agreed to give him a substantial amount if he returned to Texas Tech and completed his education. He took the money, promising to be the good son. But he was still fixated on winning Jodie Foster's love. She was a student at Yale, and so he bought a bus ticket to New Haven, Connecticut, telling everyone he met that he and Foster were lovers. Once there, he left several notes for her at her dormitory. They seemed harmless enough, love notes from an impassioned fan. They went unanswered and ignored. He left New Haven, greatly frustrated, ending up in October 1980, in Nashville, Tennessee, where President Carter was making a campaign appearance. There are some unconfirmed stories that he stalked but never came in direct contact with the president and others that he changed his mind once he was in Nashville and decided to move on. He was arrested at Nashville Airport as he attempted to board a flight for New York City: he had three handguns and fifty rounds of ammunition in his carry-on luggage. His arsenal and the president's presence in the city apparently did not send up a red flag to airport security or the FBI. Since he had a gun permit, he was released and told he could not carry firearms on board a flight. He left the airport, bought a bus ticket, and continued on to his destination without any further interference.

The Hinckleys now believed their son was emotionally disturbed and needed help. They demanded he return to their current home, a mini-estate in a suburb of Denver, and begin therapy with a local psychiatrist, Dr. John Hopper. Young Hinckley was diagnosed to be a victim of erotomania in one of its forms: obsession with a celebrity. In the six months that followed, he avoided his sessions with Dr. Hopper whenever he could—flying briefly to Los Angeles, to Salt Lake City, and back to New Haven, where he again left notes for Foster without success. Whether he had firearms with him is not known. He managed to reach her by telephone in her dormitory, and Foster told him to stop contacting her.

In November 1980 the FBI received an anonymous warning that was later identified as having been written by Hinckley: "There's a plot underway to abduct actress Jodi Foster from Yale University Dorm in December or January. She's being taken for romantic reasons. There is no joke! I don't want to get further involved. Act as you wish."[30] Apparently the FBI believed this was not a substantial threat, and it was not investigated thoroughly. In retrospect, it reveals a great deal about Hinckley's state of mind. It can be seen as a cry for help to stop him from causing harm—at this time, perhaps, to Jodie Foster.

Hinckley was drifting aimlessly, frustrated, unable to rid himself of thoughts of the young movie star, and desperately trying to think of ways to gain her attention. He returned to Denver and his sessions with Dr. Hopper when he ran out of money and realized he needed his father's help. But on March 25, five days before his violence erupted, he returned to Salt Lake City. From there he took a bus to Washington, D.C., with a virtual arsenal of firearms, arriving on March 29 and checking into the Park Central Hotel, across the intersection from FBI headquarters. On March 30 he wrote a letter to Foster that began "Dear Jodie: There is a definite possibility that I will be killed in my attempt to get Reagan. . . ." (See appendix 5 for the full text of the letter.) Leaving the letter behind in his hotel room, and armed with a .22-caliber pistol and Devastator bullets, he set out across town to the Hilton Hotel, where it had been announced that President Reagan would be giving a speech. In his diseased mind Hinckley believed that assassinating the president would make Foster love him even if (and perhaps because) he died during the attempt. He could just as well have decided to walk a high wire between two of Washington's tallest monuments. His aim was for instant fame, a show of bravado. He wanted Jodie to notice him—dead or alive. He was happy that she knew the sound of his voice. And he still had her confused with the character she had played in *Taxi Driver*. He wasn't particularly political; he would have assassinated Jimmy Carter, a Democrat, if his first attempt had not failed, mainly because he still had hopes of seeing Foster in person. Gaining Jodie's attention was more real to him than the fear of dying to obtain it.

Jack Hinckley, when told that his son was being held as the would-be assassin of the president, "scowled in disbelief: 'It has to be a stolen ID.' "[31] When he and his wife realized it was true, they were overcome with grief and sent Reagan a letter of deep apology. They had known their son was troubled but never seemed to suspect he was a danger to himself and others.

How was it possible that Hinckley had slipped through so many nets on his wild race to kill a president? Family, school, the FBI's lack of vision when he was arrested in Nashville: so many lost opportunities to have saved the president, Brady, McCarthy, Delehanty, and the nation their terrible ordeal. *The Times* of London wrote: "The United States was born out of the violence of conquest, rebellion and civil war. Its myths are those of the frontier where the fastest gun was king and every man had his fate in his own hands. The U.S. has risen to become a major industrial and military power claiming universality for its values while seeming unable to shake off the darker elements of its tradition."[32]

Hinckley had not been one of his country's have-nots. Mean streets and drug dealers could not be blamed for his horrendous crime. He was twisted, sick, and everyone who was a part of his life had cotton in their ears and a blindfold over their eyes, unwilling to see the truth. Could he have been an assassin if there had been tighter gun control? Such laws are certainly called for. But the madness that drives a person to the act of murder can not be eliminated by constitutional or state law.

Reagan stood in the late April sunshine, Nancy glossy-haired and shiny-eyed beside him, as they took a short, slow stroll in the Rose Garden and allowed photographs to be taken. It was just eighteen days since the President had been shot. He was still experiencing considerable pain. Although he had increased his workload to four or five hours a day, he had not gone down to the Oval Office to do so. His breathing was slow, his pace not yet normal. It would be several months before he would be "up and charging" and able to live the active life he had known before the shooting. Nancy had initiated plans to convert the bedroom near their own (the one once occupied by Amy Carter and other presidential offspring) into a private gym with a Nautilus machine and barbells—for both of them to use, she assured him. Nancy, however, had little need of exercise at this time. She had lost over ten pounds from her slight frame.

They had been forced to cancel their trip to California for Maureen's wedding and Reagan's meeting with the president of Mexico. But on Friday morning, April 14, falling back into routine, he met Dave Fischer as he stepped off the elevator that brought him down from the family quarters and walked slowly but surely along the usual path to the West Wing for his first public appearance since the shooting. From his manner the country assumed that he had rallied because he had exceptional recuperative powers. This was deliberate. The administration did not want the country to feel nervous about their president's ability to govern and made as few references as possible to his age in health bulletins. At seventy he was the oldest president to ever hold office. His rendezvous with death, and his humor and bravery throughout the ordeal, had endeared him ever more to the public, and would grant him a lengthy grace period in which it would seem he could do little wrong.

Nancy, on the other hand, dropped in the ratings, to the lowest of any first lady since such polls were taken. It was difficult to fathom exactly why, as she had carried herself no less valiantly, if perhaps less publicly, than Jackie Kennedy during her time of crisis. There was the ongoing negative coverage of her extravagances and her determined work on the White House, and then, in October, when the Lenox dinnerware set was finally delivered to the White House and its cost became known, she was crucified. Little mention was made of the fact that it had been paid for by private funds. Unfortunately, the dinnerware arrived on the same day that the Health and Education Department announced that catsup could be considered a vegetable and so a healthy addition to school lunches because it contained puree of tomatoes.

The year that should have been the highlight of her life had been a nightmare for Nancy. Ronnie had almost died. Her mother and father were both failing. Although Ronnie had returned to their king-size bed, she slept restlessly beside him, her pill taking diminished, a close aide concluded, by fear that she would not hear him if he woke up in pain or need. She was always apprehensive that something could happen to him when he left the White House. He had a bulletproof vest that he hated and had not worn at the time of the shooting, but now agreed to wear on future outings. He was putting himself back into shape by working everyday with weights and was beginning to look even more "strapping" than before that terrible day. (Nancy never could bring herself to say the word *assassination* or to watch television when any part of that day was replayed.) Their home was now a comfortable place for them, and one the nation (she believed) could be proud of. But she was treated poorly by the press, and it hurt deeply.

She had to do something to change her image. She needed a cause. Her staff convened daily to discuss what this could be. Why not the foster grandparent program she had given so much time to in Sacramento? Not powerful enough. An antidrug campaign aimed at stopping youngsters from using illegal drugs? She did not have to think about that for long. It was a problem she had seen close up during her years as first lady of California when the drug problem among college students was exploding. There was Patti's dalliance, which she had always tried to ignore but could not. She refused to think of herself as having a drug problem. After all, the pills she had taken for so many years had been prescribed to her by a qualified doctor—to help her sleep or calm her nerves or monitor her weight. No matter how she classified her own intake, she was conscious of how easy it was for young people to gain access to illegal drugs, how peer pressure could prevail and a child be lost. And so Nancy Reagan's "Just Say No to Drugs" campaign was set in motion.

CHAPTER FOURTEEN

JUST SAY NO

Power in a man, especially a politician, is respected. If it is feared, it can lift him to great heights. Men who exude an aura of power, that ability to command attention, are raised by those whose own power can only be elevated by close association with others. They flock around a power figure like hungry feeders. Without protection, he might be consumed. A leader like Lyndon Johnson was an exception in politics, a man already devoured lean by ambition, leaving nothing over for his rapacious followers.

Reagan never possessed Johnson's blind ambition. What he had was a mission that he believed to be his destiny, divined for him by a higher power. An evil empire was menacing the world, and it was his charge, his duty, to uproot it without deracinating mankind. He had always seen himself as a rescuer: saving incautious swimmers from the undercurrents of the Rock River, saving Hollywood from the Red Menace, saving the Republican party from the rash liberalism of the Democrats. He went at this with a kind of detachment that was often incomprehensible to those he led and those who wrote about him. He lacked the passion of men who feel driven to change the world. But Reagan's quest was to *save* the world, not to change it.

He also felt himself to be a Washington outsider. Unlike Kennedy, Johnson, Nixon, and Ford, he had not served time in the House or the Senate or in any position under any other president. No one in Congress owed him favors. He knew none of the powerful lobbyists. Congress was not like the State House in Sacramento where his staff could lobby in the hallways. His onetime Washington connection, Richard Nixon, was disgraced, and his money-powered friends had mostly returned to California after the inauguration. Haig had been brought in partly because of his Washington know-how, but he had become a liability. The only other Washington insider on Reagan's staff and cabinet was James Baker.

It was at this point that Lew Wasserman reentered his life. Wasserman was still all-powerful in Hollywood, but his resourceful work in the campaigns of Lyndon Johnson and Jimmy Carter, and his friendship with Katharine Graham and many other Washington insiders, had made him an important political power as well. The Reagans were aware that their old friend and adviser could be indispensable in helping Reagan to bridge differences between the two parties. Shortly after the assassination attempt, the Reagans received a warm, moving letter from Wasserman. Their rift had been deeply felt by Reagan, who was pleased to welcome his former agent into his life again. There is no evidence that Wasserman advised him on government matters, but he did discuss with him the social structure of Washington and, according to Nancy, always gave them good advice. (In fact, Lew Wasserman would retain both Hollywood and political power, as a Democrat, to the end of his life in 2002. He would be one of the first to recognize the potential of Bill Clinton when he was a first-term governor of Arkansas and to raise Hollywood's consciousness of him in giving their financial support when in 1992 Clinton ran for president.)

By the press and by the public, Nancy was perceived as powerful— the woman behind the man in the Oval Office—and what American woman in the twentieth century could be more powerful than that? Nancy could disclaim her influence as often and as loudly as she wished—and she did so frequently—but no one was closer to him than Nancy, and there was no one he respected more or listened to more closely than Nancy. Her belief in him validated everything he did, and there was no way he was ever going to chance losing it. He never dismissed her opinions and only on the rare occasion cut her out of a discussion in which she cared to be part. He had no private life that did not involve her. Both gossipmongers and legitimate reporters were

known to have used their sharpest tools to ferret out information that
Reagan had strayed away from his connubial ties. Nothing. Nowhere.
No one. Not even a hint of a mild flirtation in the nearly thirty years
since he and Nancy were married.

In the United States, power in a *woman* comes with a lot of baggage.
Men are threatened by it; women, if they want a share for themselves,
or if they are resentful of it, are afraid it will upset the status quo. In
the early 1980s Washington was almost exclusively a men's club. There
was really only one powerful woman in Washington at the time: Katharine Graham, the publisher of the *Washington Post*, and a Democrat.
Nancy's social wooing of Graham in the days before the inauguration
did not go unnoticed by the media or by the city's Democratic population. When Graham hosted the first dinner party for the new first couple,
fists were raised—and Nancy was the chosen target.

Her extravagances were a handy weapon. In fact, Jackie Kennedy
was far more extravagant than Nancy Reagan. Jackie's clothes were also
from top designers, but she did not seek special consideration or expect
them to be provided gratis for the prestige of dressing the first lady. Nor
was Jackie known for wearing the same outfit more than once. She was
written up flatteringly as being a meticulous woman who had her "maid
hand-wash and press her silk stockings" before each wearing, despite
the fact that the statement revealed her to be as much a spoiled woman
as a meticulous one.

Jackie did attract controversy when she undertook the redecoration
of the State Floor of the White House, working furiously to raise private
funds from wealthy supporters to do so. But because Jackie's extensive
efforts to locate authentic antiques associated with the White House and
its history turned it into a museum of Federal style, she was ultimately
lauded rather than excoriated for her contribution. Actually Jackie had
secretly hired Stephane Boudin, a leading French decorator who spe-
cialized in sophisticated interiors for royalty and wealthy Europeans, to
supervise the redecoration of the White House, hiring at the same time
"as a beard" Sister Parish, a well-known American decorator, whose contribution was minimal. Boudin's presence was kept under wraps until
Washington Post columnist Maxine Cheshire got wind of who was actually

doing the work and revealed it in her column. The Frenchman "may be all right as a decorator but he has absolutely no knowledge or respect for American furniture or paintings," William Voss Elder III, the registrar of the White House collection, offered in criticism. Jacqueline Kennedy had given the White House a definite French look, but the eighty million Americans who took a televised tour through the White House, narrated by the First Lady, loved it.[1]

Jackie had also raised over $200,000 for new china and was not chastised for it. In Nancy Reagan's case, it seems, the public believed that they were footing the bill, which was not so. (Updating the scenario to 1993, First Lady Hillary Clinton ordered three hundred twelve-piece place settings from Lenox, to be paid for by the White House Historical Association with the understanding that first ladies—like Jackie and Nancy—would never again have to go begging for private funds to pay for White House china. It is worth noting that Nancy Reagan was attacked for doing exactly what Jackie Kennedy did without causing a fury, and what Hillary Clinton did without attracting much notice.)

Then there was Jackie's wispy, come-hither voice and her nonseeing, approach to her husband's many sexual liaisons. Jackie Kennedy was admired because she spoke French (which she had studied in school) with a good accent, and for restoring a part of the White House (with government funds). But she represented an image of royal stature that much appealed to the American people.

Lady Bird also looked the other way where Lyndon's dalliances were concerned and endured his public parading of Helen Gahagan Douglas during the years she was his mistress. She was applauded for her efforts to beautify America's parks and animal sanctuaries—worthwhile efforts to be sure, but also an acceptable feminine endeavor that broke no new ground. In the first months of Reagan's presidency, Nancy had a difficult time finding a niche for herself that would heighten her popularity. Reagan, on the other hand, was now looked upon as a hero for having survived the assassination attempt with so much humor and manliness.

He was determined to restore himself to health as quickly as possible, or at least give evidence that such was the case. He worked for hours each day blowing into a Respirex, a breathing therapy aid used by hospitals for postoperative patients. Breathing into it causes a Ping-Pong ball to rise to the top of a plastic tube and exercises the lungs. A therapist worked with him for an hour every day with easy stretching and lifting exercises. He increased his work hours and his self-imposed body-building regimen using weights in their new home gym to strengthen his arm and chest muscles.

Before the shooting, he had been scheduled to speak at prime time in front of a televised Joint Session of Congress on April 28, an appearance that could have been canceled or postponed with full understanding by both sides of the House. He refused to do either. As he appeared at the wide doorway to the House, standing tall before staff and cabinet members, he looked as robust as ever and surely not a man of seventy who had fought off death only four weeks earlier. The doorkeeper shouted out, "The president of the United States!" As Reagan started down the wide aisle, all members on their feet as protocol demanded, there was an overwhelming ovation that went on for several minutes. One commentator called it "the most dramatic presidential appearance in Congress since Franklin Roosevelt's return from Yalta," where the Big Three—Churchill, Stalin, and Roosevelt—had planned the final defeat of Germany in February 1945.[2]

Reagan's speech detailed his program for economic recovery, "a program that will balance the budget, put us well on the road to our ultimate objective of eliminating inflation entirely, increasing productivity, and creating millions of new jobs."[3]

On three separate occasions during his speech the ovations lasted for over two minutes. "In the 3rd part of these [ovations]," he wrote later that night in his diary, "about forty Democrats stood and applauded. Maybe we are going to make it. It took a lot of courage for them to do that, and it sent a tingle down my spine."[4]

On May 1 Prince Charles, returning from a royal tour, stopped in Washington and paid an unofficial call at the White House. Reagan had not yet returned to a full schedule in the Oval Office, although he was planning his first trip, a visit to Notre Dame University on the seventeenth. Nancy had much objected to this, but he refused to be swayed. Notre Dame had a special place in his heart. His favorite film had been

Knute Rockne, in which he had costarred with Pat O'Brien as the university's famed football hero, George Gipp, and the last (and perhaps only time) he had shared a father-son outing with Jack Reagan had been at this most Irish of all American universities. Reagan was determined to show the country that he was well on his way back to full health. The excursion to Notre Dame would prove this, and the prince's visit also offered a fine opportunity to exhibit his return to his old self. The Reagans—he in a tuxedo and black bow tie, and she in an elegant black and silver gown with a blouson top—entertained the prince in their private quarters for a dinner in his honor that included his entourage and a number of highly selected guests, including Lee and Walter Annenberg (the former American ambassador to the Court of St. James's), Audrey Hepburn, Cary Grant and his wife, Barbara Harris (not the theater actress), William and Pat Buckley, Betsy and Alfred Bloomingdale, James Galanos, Jerry Zipkin, Ted Graber, songwriter Sammy Cahn, and former *Vogue* editor Diana Vreeland. They discussed horses and the game of polo, which Reagan had never participated in, preferring "the freedom of the range," he said. Charles later confessed a certain admiration for the American president and his amazing stamina.

Shortly after Charles's visit, the Reagans received an invitation to the July 29 wedding of Prince Charles and the Lady Diana, accompanied with another invitation to the Queen's Reception and Ball being held on the previous evening at Buckingham Palace. Reagan knew he could not go, but insisted that Nancy accept the invitation. She had been under considerable strain and was badly in need of a change. She agreed to do so, and went about the happy task of gathering together the clothes she would need for the gala doings. The Reagans believed this would give the public another indication that things in the family quarters of the White House were back to normal. Neither the press nor the public, however, viewed Nancy's prospective trip in this light. Once again they said she was being extravagant, playing the social scene—this time on a grand, royal scale. The Reagans were shocked, the president completely noncomprehending.

"I could never get over the gap in perceptions between Ronald Reagan and the rest of the world when it came to Nancy," Helene von

Damm said. "We [the staff] all thought of her as a demanding and some-what aloof person. But in his adoring eyes she was the sweetest, gentlest, most wonderful person in the world. It wasn't just that he loved her . . . Ronald Reagan didn't even seem to see the same person the rest of us saw. [If someone complained about her attempt to interfere in office matters] he was utterly incredulous and completely unbelieving. ('You must be wrong. My Nancy wouldn't do that.') He was infinitely patient with her and only on the rarest of occasions would blow up at her. . . . Only once was I witness to it in the White House. She was relentlessly pursuing the ouster of a person and badgering the President mercilessly. I don't remember who it was—it might have been [Secretary of Labor] Ray Donovan. RR blew his stack and laid down the rule once and for all: he would no longer tolerate her debating any controversial member of the Administration. The rule stuck for some time. Of course, this didn't mean she wasn't discussing such matters with Mike Deaver and others [who would then relay it to Reagan]."[5]

Reagan worked to control his temper with his staff. But then he would "just blow," Robert Higdon, presidential aide and soon-to-be good friend, remarked. Most often, Reagan held himself in until he was up-stairs with Nancy. "He would put up with a lot . . . and then finally he'd go boom. And he'd do it in front of her. And she'd listen, and the lis-tening, helped him. 'I know, honey, I see, honey, calm down, we'll take care of it.' " She would tell him to rest and when she was alone with the staff she would say, "Why is this on the schedule, . . . what the heck's going on here? . . . She didn't swing the bat for him, he did that. But she tried to make it so he was pitched to the right."[6]

People on both staffs were afraid of her. That was because they "didn't get to see the tender side, the real Nancy Reagan," Secret Ser-vice agent Dave Fischer contended.[7] Fischer, however, had a longer per-sonal history with the Reagans, having spent considerable time with them in Sacramento and at Rancho del Cielo in Santa Barbara before guarding Reagan in the White House.

Her role as first lady of California "was nowhere near the level of influence she came to exert in the White House," von Damm added. "In some ways her ambition was stronger than his."[8] In fact, her ambition was *for* him. She was obsessed not only with her husband's political life but with their social life as well.

"Nancy wanted to be with social Somebodies," Peggy Noonan, a Reagan speechwriter and one of his special assistants, wrote. Nancy wanted to have fun, "but there was another reason she chose the Somebodies in Washington. She had judged the town with a practiced eye and wanted to help her husband." Robert Higdon added: "She was the one who made friends with Kay Graham . . . who had Bob Strauss [former Democratic chairman and a powerful figure in Washington] in the White House and said, 'What do you think, what's your view, you've been here a long time, ol' man, tell us.' "[9]

As was true with most husbands, Reagan let Nancy organize their social life. She wanted it to serve two purposes: people she could call on for support if she needed something, and people with whom they could relax and have some fun. This meant holding on tightly to their California ties. In addition to this small group, there were also the droll author and commentator William (Bill) Buckley and his wife, Pat, and Jerry Zipkin, the New York socialite with whom she loved to gossip on the telephone. Sinatra would show up from time to time and be welcomed into the family quarters. Though she lunched occasionally with Katharine Graham, their friendship never moved to an intimate level.

Nancy was not a deep thinker. She liked stories about politics and politicians but was uninterested in discussing the policies they espoused. She had an intuitive intelligence that only went so far, and she was uncomfortable when a conversation grew beyond her means to understand and comment upon.

Reagan enjoyed more original thinkers. His enthusiasm was fired for hours when he spent time with Margaret Thatcher, whom he would meet again when he attended his first foreign conference in Ottawa on July 19. He had almost memorized the texts of Winston Churchill's histories and autobiographies. He liked to joke, exchange a few "good ones." But when a serious historian or academic crossed his path, he hungrily questioned them. It is somewhat of a mystery why people thought he was shallow. He had the ability to go straight to the heart of the matter. His easy charm, his penchant for cracking a joke at a serious time, and his history as a film actor may have seemed to indicate that that was all there was to the man—that he was playing a role, a theory many of his critics and a few of his biographers have espoused. Prime Minister Margaret Thatcher and Mikhail Gorbachev, the political leader of the Soviet Union, had quite different opinions of the man. Both found him not only intelligent but politically canny. But Reagan's intellectual capacity would always engender diverse views.

Lou Cannon, one of the reporters who attended the Ottawa session and flew with Reagan on Air Force One, claimed Reagan held up well during the conference but collapsed from exhaustion the moment he boarded his plane for the return home. His perseverance and ability to endure a difficult and perhaps even painful lengthy meeting without giving public evidence of his discomfort was astonishing to all who traveled with him during this time.

After the Ottawa conference, François Mitterrand, the new president of France, was to comment to chancellor Helmut Schmidt of Germany, "This is a man without ideas and without culture . . . but beneath the surface you find someone who isn't stupid, who had a great good sense and profoundly good intentions. What he does not perceive with intelligence, he feels by nature."[10] Reagan's image, as well as some of his choices, might have been different if he had cultivated more intellectual friendships in Washington. Pleasing Nancy was always paramount, however, and so it was not to be. Nor did she ever reach out for the friendship of any of his cabinet or staff members, except perhaps to Michael Deaver, whom she needed. Such personal alliances came with a high price: It was much more difficult to get rid of someone who was not doing his job in the way she thought would best benefit Ronnie if that person was also a friend.

Nancy stepped lightly at the start of Reagan's presidency, trying to feel her way, learning how to use her power. After the assassination attempt, just nine weeks into his first term, she trod with a heavier step, protecting him by not allowing the outside world to learn how physically weak he was. Now, when he began to show true signs of recovery, she attended to the task of polishing her image. She sincerely believed her appearance in London for the royal wedding would enhance her world profile and make Americans proud that she was representing them. Instead, the press on both side of the Atlantic wrote hostile articles. The American press lambasted her extravagance, for, besides her numerous suitcases, hat boxes, and jewelry cases (Bulgari Jewelers had lent her jewels to match each of her outfits, including a magnificent sapphire necklace and perfectly matched diamond earrings with an estimated worth of over $800,000), she arrived in London with sixteen security men, her three top aides, her hairdresser, a White House photographer, and Betsy and Alfred Bloomingdale—none of whom were to be guests at the wedding.

The *Times* of London nastily wrote that she had managed to schedule "more engagements before the wedding [she arrived five days beforehand] than Alice's White Rabbit," while the *Guardian* snippily referred to her as "the one time starlet of B films." A tabloid added insult by describing her as "an aging film star." The press also made much of the fact that she arrived at a polo match, in which Charles was playing, accompanied by a motorcade of black limousines, while the queen made her entrance via a "Vauxhall station wagon with her corgis in a basket in the back seat." This last was certainly not Nancy's fault. The Secret Service had decreed that she needed extra protection. Nonetheless, the carping of the media hurt. Nancy was learning that Britain's press corps was even more brutal than those at home due to the rivalry created by the large number of English newspapers.[11]

Despite these shortcomings, Nancy very much enjoyed her royal wedding excursion. On the serious side, she placed flowers at the foot of the memorial to Britain's Unknown Soldier and visited a veterans hospital. She shared one thing with the future Princess Diana—her ability to face deformity and decaying flesh with great equanimity and much empathy. She was, after all, a surgeon's daughter, no newcomer to such things, for in her youth she had accompanied her father on his hospital rounds. In California, when Reagan was governor, she had spent many hours at the Veterans Hospital in Los Angeles, sitting by the side of young men severely injured and deformed in the Vietnam War, holding their hands, and looking straight into their eyes, her own ofttimes misty.

She would ask them for telephone numbers of their family members, then would call and speak to their wives, mothers, and sisters.

Galanos had dressed her most elegantly, and she was handsomely bejeweled for her royal debut. The prewedding reception was not anything like what she had expected. There were 1,500 guests, with music by Charles's favorite pop group, the Three Degrees. As the evening progressed, so did the heightened gaiety and reveling of the guests. Diana, beautiful in a pink shell ball gown, with an exquisite diamond and pearl necklace that was a gift from her future mother-in-law, "danced and danced and danced." There was something *veddy* Noel Coward about the evening. Charles Spencer, Diana's brother, recalled that "Princess Margaret tied a balloon to her tiara; Prince Andrew tied one to the tails of his dinner jacket [and] I bowed at a uniformed waiter because there were so many royals there, I was in automatic bowing mood. I bowed and he looked surprised. Then he asked me if I wanted a drink. Everybody got terribly drunk—but not the Queen, Charles or Diana and certainly not First Lady Nancy Reagan! It was a blur. A glorious blur!"[12]

Not for Nancy, who found the wedding next day more memorable. It was attended by more royalty and world figures than had been gathered together for many a decade. She was seated in the sixth row in the cathedral, surrounded by foreign diplomats and lesser royals. Invitations had included a notice of suitable attire; men were expected to wear a regimental uniform, afternoon suit, or Scots kilts. Trousers were banned for women, who were allowed outfits only in colors outside the hues worn by the female members of the royal family. These included yellow (Princess Anne), turquoise (the queen), light blue (the queen mum), and rose (Princess Margaret)—the royal ladies all looking very much like an English garden bouquet. Nancy chose a navy blue afternoon ensemble by Adolfo.

All of the 2,650 guests in St. Paul's Cathedral stood as Big Ben struck the last count of eleven and, at the sound of a fanfare, the queen led the royal family to the right of the altar. Then came a procession of foreign sovereigns who occupied a block of front seats. After a second fanfare, Charles, dressed in uniform and flanked by his brothers Andrew

and Edward, took measured steps down the aisle. Three and a half
minutes passed before the third fanfare brought Diana supporting her
father, the Seventh Earl Spencer (patriarch of a family that figured prominently in the history of England), who had been weakened by a serious
stroke. Diana's face was heavily veiled. She wore the famous Spencer
diamond tiara, her bouffant ivory gown a splendid recreation of one worn
by an illustrious Spencer ancestor. The beauty of the cathedral, of the
ceremony, and of the bride was almost overwhelming. An augmented
sense of history enveloped the massive interior.

Of course, Nancy was impressed, and, *of course*, the press made snide
remarks about her own suspected royal-like aspirations. "*Queen Nancy* of
the U.S.A." the tabloids captioned more than one photograph of her. She
returned to Washington excited by the experience but feeling bruised
by both the American and the British media.

The importance of finding a new image for herself took on greater
immediacy. Photographs taken of her in London visiting war veterans
had revealed her more womanly and human side as she was caught off
guard, moved by the suffering and resignation of these men. But these
were not the pictures that turned up in newspapers and magazines that
had already set out to portray the first lady as a cross between Lady
Macbeth and Joan Crawford, whose daughter had recently published the
devastating memoir *Mommie Dearest*.

"Just Say No," the name for Nancy's newly begun antidrug program,
was decided upon in one of the weekly Monday morning meetings of
her executive staff, which included her new press secretary, Sheila Tate,
and five others. Except for Tate, who would remain with her for the next
five years, and James Rosebush, her chief of staff, there was a rather
frequent turnover in Nancy's personnel. These two, and Michael Deaver,
were the people she counted on the most, and whose suggestions she
most respected. They all agreed that her new endeavor should bring her
in contact with the people with drug-related problems, not just the agencies. Above all, her staff wanted to humanize her and her program. Nancy
claimed the slogan had come to her during a visit to a class of fifth-

graders in Oakland, California, during the Reagans' years in Sacramento when a youngster asked her, "What do you do if somebody offers you drugs?"

"Just say no," the first lady responded. And so the program was christened.[13] The idea was that Nancy would go to schools, hospitals, and drug centers, give a short speech, and then interact with both children and young adults. A camera crew would go with her to film these encounters, and the best ones (meaning the most moving) would then be circulated to the news agencies.

There was no small irony in the program's name. Few people ever dared to "just say no" to Nancy Reagan. If she told von Damm she had too many plants in her office, von Damm got rid of them. If Nancy told Deaver she felt a certain staffer wasn't performing up to her standards, Deaver talked to Reagan about replacing the person. Over and over again, in speaking to those who worked either for her or for Reagan during his presidency, one hears the phrase, "She is a tough lady." Visitors to the White House, on the other hand, most often came away extolling her warmth and graciousness. She was exceptionally kind and openhearted to anyone with a disability or serious illness, as she was to most artists. The composer-lyricist Jerry Herman (*Hello Dolly!*, *Mame*) and musician Miles Davis recounted fond stories of how she welcomed them to the White House, and they are just two among many, many others this author has spoken with.[14]

When she returned from London, Nancy was faced with an exhausted Ronnie, who had been under great stress while she was away. Without her constant presence, she felt that his staff took advantage of him, so on August 8 the Reagans flew on Air Force One to Santa Barbara. They were then driven to Rancho del Cielo. Reagan brought a stack of work with him, but being at the ranch, in the open air, able to ride up into the mountains (albeit with a somewhat grumbling Secret Service detail not as comfortable in the saddle as their charge), revitalized him. There was something of the long-gone frontier cowboy that lurked in Reagan's psyche. He trusted his mounts as much as he did the men who loped behind and—unhappily—ahead of him. "Nothing up ahead but more of God's wonder," he told them to no avail.[15] They wanted to make damned sure that was the case. But he refused straight out to wear what he called "the iron vest."

While they were at the ranch, Maureen decided to declare herself a candidate for senator from California in the coming election. She called her father before doing so, and he "sounded pleased, but also tentative. . . . One afternoon, with the splendor of the Santa Ynez Mountains as a backdrop," Reagan held a press conference in front of the house as he signed the 1981 tax bill that he had worked for ever since his campaign. After the bill was signed, the reporters were allowed some questions. "Is Maureen going to run for the Senate?" one of them asked.[16]

"I hope not," her father replied. As he said it he realized that it would be "misinterpreted," so he called Maureen straightaway. "Mermie," he said, "I think we have a problem. . . . What I meant to say was that having campaigned myself, it was not something I would wish on someone [especially my daughter]. I was trying to be facetious, but I don't think it came out that way. I just want you to know I'm sorry."[17] This would not be the only Reagan slight Maureen would suffer. Her uncle Neil Reagan would decide to support another candidate, Pete Wilson, and appear in a television commercial for him. Although she would never forgive her uncle, she managed to rationalize her father's position, obviously because she needed his presence in her life and would not do anything to jeopardize it. In the end, Maureen received only 5 per cent of the vote.

The Reagans remained at the ranch until September 3, when they returned to Washington. Unwillingly, but with Nancy's nudging, he put the "iron vest" on whenever he was away from the White House attending a meeting, giving a speech, dining out or horseback riding in Rock Creek Park, only a stone's throw from the White House, where he went several times a week for an hour's ride. With all the Secret Service men who accompanied him it looked like a parade. Joggers got used to the intrusion, and people walking their dogs quickly scrambled from underfoot. Rock Creek Park is an eighteen-hundred-acre natural wilderness sanctuary. One could hear the roars and squawks of the caged animals at the National Zoo, but in the upper reaches of the park deer, fox, and other wildlife roam freely. It wasn't the ranch, but it was a touch of the country life that Reagan felt at one with.

Just Say No was beginning to shape up into a solid campaign. It would begin slowly after the first of the year so that Nancy could ease herself into it. She would visit some schools, a treatment center, and give several interviews to the press stating her views on young people and drugs. She had seen Ronnie through the difficult times that followed the shooting. It was the lowest point in her life and nothing would ever quite be the same again. It had also been a time of personal strength for her and she knew that her strength had been a boon to Ronnie. By the beginning of October, six months had passed, and he looked and felt almost his old self. His hearing was not good, and they were talking about fitting him with a hearing aid that would not be visible. Whenever she thought about Jim Brady, she knew how lucky they both had been, for he would never really recover; one side of his body had been paralysed and the injury to the brain had affected his speech and motor movement. Brady was only forty-one, and it was extremely doubtful he would ever be able to hold down a job again. Since Reagan refused to take his name off the payroll, Larry Speakes filled his position without the title of press secretary, which Brady retained.

The Reagans' first Christmas in the White House was approaching. With it came the realization that Nancy's beloved Dr. Davis, the only father she would acknowledge, was dying. She spoke to him on the telephone every evening, cried a lot, and was suffering depression. It made her temper shorter. She became more demanding of her staff, and not all of them understood why. A group of kindergartners was invited to attend the annual televised tree-lighting ceremony in Washington. Reagan lifted a towheaded five-year-old boy in his arms and said into the camera, "I only wish my grandson Cameron was here to celebrate Christmas with us." And the youngster flicked a switch, which produced a blaze of light. Michael and Colleen were watching the ceremony on television in California, and were dismayed by Reagan's comment. The next morning Michael called his father and reminded him of a conversation they had had earlier in the year. Michael had offered to bring

Cameron to Washington so that he could turn on the lights to what was regarded as the national Christmas tree.

Reagan appeared surprised that Michael had actually considered flying to Washington and questioned his ability to pay for the plane trip. There would always be this "money thing" between the Reagans and their children. None of the Reagan offspring ever expected their parents to pay the airfare to have them join them for a holiday unless it came under the heading of public relations. Michael later told his father that he would have borrowed the money.

Reagan would write a personal check for $100 to a needy child who had written to him, but he was tightfisted when it came to anyone in his family other than Nancy. Although he enjoyed personal wealth, he was not in the financial bracket of many of their friends, which might have accounted for the Reagans' view of themselves as not being rich. Nancy still had a closet fairly crammed with unwanted gifts that she would recycle. Cameron was sent a teddy bear that, to the shock of his parents, was one they had accidentally left behind during a previous visit.

The Reagans spent Christmas Eve, 1981, with Charles and Mary Jane Wick and their son, C.Z., in their luxurious Watergate apartment. The next day the Wick family went to the White House for Christmas dinner. This would become a tradition while the Reagans were in Washington, with one of them dressing as Santa Claus, "coming into the living room on the cue of 'Jingle Bells,' . . . and sitting in a big high chair and having everyone in the room sit on your knee and tell you why they should get everything they want for Christmas." Both Nancy and the president would take their turns as Santa and, C.Z. said, "We all had a great time." Christmas morning Nancy received her annual holiday letter from Ronnie—a long one equating her laugh to "twinkling bells," singling out her innate "class, grace and charm," and her ability as a "nest-builder." He called her "a peewee power house and . . . [yet] the little girl who takes her [ba]nana to bed in case she gets hungry during the night." He signed it "Lucky Me."[18]

Ron and Doria would occasionally join the group at Christmas. None of the other children came to Washington for the holiday, and it does not seem that Nancy ever pressed them to do so. Yet as she began her campaign against drug abuse, she was out there telling other parents, "Money doesn't buy love or affection or attention or involvement, all those things that have to be there [to combat the use of drugs by minors]. Only people provide those things, and, particularly, parents."[19]

She made a serious effort with Just Say No. Her aides felt she needed a significant and meaningful project, and there is no doubt that drug abuse was very much her own personal choice. There was some doubt by her advisers that the program was the right one, but it was more startling and more of a wake-up call than, say, the foster grandparents program. From the moment that she appeared at the first school to ask the kids to "just say no" to drugs no matter who offered them or how much peer pressure was exerted, her team knew she had been right. This was the program for her.

When she could sit with a child, Sheila Tate recalled, "those big eyes focus on a kid and the kid finds himself telling his whole life story to her, and they both sit there and cry, but when she leaves, the kid can say, 'You know, here's someone so important, and she cares about me. And that's the feeling they got from that. That started building. . . . And she was taking that camera, that media spotlight, and turning it around and focusing it on the issue, which is something she cared about."[20]

Perhaps the campaign was only a means to improve Nancy's image, but stormy winds of dissent rose behind the scenes. Insiders in the antidrug movement found her Just Say No campaign, and the clubs that were being formed with that name, without any substance. At the same time as the first lady was proselytizing against drugs, the president was whittling the budgets of drug rehabilitation programs and cutting funds to other programs that might have reduced the quantities of illegal drugs entering the country. The Reagans had the naive idea that wagging a finger and lecturing on self-control was the cure for the disease of drug abuse.

Still, the campaign did have an impact. To her staff's delight and her own pride, Nancy's popularity with the public began a slow but steady rise.

CHAPTER FIFTEEN

A DEATH IN THE FAMILY

R ancho del Cielo would always be Reagan's first love, but early in his presidency Camp David came to occupy a special niche. Built in 1938 and chosen by Franklin D. Roosevelt as a retreat during the years of World War II, it has since become an historic venue for presidents to meet with heads of state during momentous times, allowing them to relax their dress and formal attitudes. Originally it was called Shangri-La, after the fictional, idyllic, Tibetan land in *Lost Horizon*, James Hilton's bestselling novel, which was filmed successfully in 1937. When the media asked him about the new presidential retreat, which had been cloaked in secrecy, Roosevelt, who had enjoyed the movie, referred to it as *his* Shangri-La. The name stuck for nearly twenty years until Dwight D. Eisenhower, in honor of his first grandson, renamed it Camp David.

Shangri-La might not have had a presidential sound to it, but it was well chosen. The setting is spectacularly beautiful, nestled as it is in the rolling Catoctin Mountains, a part of the Blue Ridge range, and hidden by thick forests of century-old trees of magnificent variety—laurel, aspen, oak, poplar, ash, locust, hickory, pine, and maple. Although it was only a twenty-five-minute helicopter flight from the White House to Camp David, Nancy always preferred the longer one-hour drive by car through the historic Maryland towns of Frederick and Thurmont. It was never announced when the president's cortege might be heading through the main streets of these towns, but still "a handful of people would wave" to the Reagans from curbside. The final ascent by car of the circuitous mountain road, no less difficult than the one leading to Rancho del Cielo, was equally picturesque, a new view coming into sight at each sharp curve. Partway up, a small bridge crosses Big Hunting Creek, which feeds the various trout streams where the early Indian population had once fished. The road keeps ascending until the cottages at Camp David can be seen, "snuggled on top and down one side of the mountain and sheltered by a thick growth of [trees]."[1]

The hand-hewn, craftsman-designed cottages that originally occupied the site, most of which were still standing and in use during the Reagan administration, were built under the direction of the Works Progress Administration, an agency created by Franklin Roosevelt during the worst years of the Depression to put many of the country's unemployed artists, artisans, architects, and technicians to work. Schools were built by the thousands, roads paved, parklands created, and theater, art, and literature funded through the WPA. Shangri-La began as a project of the Catoctin Recreational Demonstration Area, which had suffered a tree disease that had affected thousands of trees. Afflicted trees were cut down, and with such a mass of lumber close and available, the National Park Service, in conjunction with the WPA, decided to build crude cottages and clear picnic areas to be used by federal employees for summer outings, as its high elevation kept it cool even on days of soaring temperatures. Mountain sandstone was crushed into stone for fireplaces and fences; crafts people and blacksmiths were employed to fashion iron lighting fixtures and hinges; furniture was carved by expert carpenters from the same wood as was the interior of the cabins with their high beamed ceilings and paneled walls.

During World War II, with Roosevelt's approval, the government decided to convert the area, which had not been much used by government workers, into a presidential retreat. Not only was it cool in summer, it had the advantage of being within easy communication range of the War Room and was sited so that it could be secured both from above and below. Its transformation from rustic parkland to presidential retreat was kept secret for a year or more while the main lodge and presidential quarters were being constructed anew. Cabins were built without steps, and walkways between the cabins were paved to accommodate Roosevelt's wheelchair. In his day there were only enough cabins to house the White House staff, domestic help, and one or two guests. The Secret Service was put up in tents.

By the time the Reagans arrived, the retreat had transmogrified into a rustic estate with vast private parklands. Each succeeding president after Roosevelt had redesigned the cottages and added more, all within a few hundred yards of Laurel Lodge, the main meeting accommodation, producing an atmosphere, according to President Carter, "of both isolation and intimacy, conducive to easing tension and encouraging informality." With Truman's occupancy, more cabins were built so that the Secret Service could sleep beneath roofs. Eisenhower made room for a three-hole golf course and a putting green. The Kennedys enlarged Aspen, the president's cabin (all the cottages were named after trees), to include a modern kitchen and a second bedroom, and the nearest cottage was turned into a nursery with rooms for their two young children, a nanny, and a playroom. This accommodation was later converted by Lyndon Johnson into suitable housing for his two teenage daughters. Johnson also built a two-lane bowling alley and a heliport, while Lady Bird oversaw the planting of magnificent gardens. (In the second volume of *The Years of Lyndon Johnson: Means of Ascent*, Robert Caro wrote that from her youth Lady Bird "loved nature, boating on the winding bayous of Lake Caddo [in East Texas] or walking along its shores." Lady Bird described "drifts of magnolia all through the woods in Spring—and daffodils in the yard. When the first one bloomed, I'd have a little ceremony, all by myself, and name it the queen.")[2] Richard Nixon, while keeping the materials and design authentic, supervised the construction of a fully equipped office with a high-security telephone system. Pat Nixon never took much interest in Camp David, nor did the next two first ladies. But the Reagans, equally charmed by the privacy it offered and by the beauty of its natural setting, made immediate plans for work to be done to accommodate their individual agendas.

Nixon had paved many of the riding paths so that he could travel about the vast area in a golf cart. Reagan ripped these up, extended them, cleared the brush on higher ground for riding trails, and enlarged the stables. None of the former presidents had been horse lovers, and so the stables had been used mostly for the mounts of the rangers and groundspeople. Nancy, this time with no outside criticism, refurbished Aspen, being faithful to its heritage and retaining all its original rustic appeal: the wooded interior, the old wagon-wheel chandelier over the dining area, the two stone fireplaces in the bedroom, the lounge with the presidential seal embedded in one wall, the handsome, wide-planked floors, handcrafted furniture, and iron fixtures. A large projection movie screen was installed so that they could watch current and old films (which they enjoyed more). On those winter evenings when they did not have guests, they often curled up reading a book before a warming fire, which provided the only heat. When the Reagans were not in residence at Camp David, Vice President and Mrs. Bush were given access.

While past occupants had made a concerted effort to enhance and preserve the natural beauty of the wilderness of Camp David, perhaps no one enjoyed it more than Reagan, who was always happiest riding the range. His favorite trail wound high up on the pine-wooded hillside that overlooked the deep cleft of the valley beyond and in the general direction of Keysville, the birthplace of Francis Scott Key, author of the "The Star-Spangled Banner." The Reagans would take long walks through the woods together, and although Nancy, never a confident horsewoman, would often accompany Ronnie on his rides, Reagan never minded getting on to the back of his mount and going out alone—although he could not actually do so, for the Secret Service still grumbled ahead and behind him. In earlier years, swimming was done in a brook; now there was a pool that the Reagans put to good use.

Unable to go to California more than a few times a year, and then only for short stays, they put Camp David on their schedule twice monthly when possible. The Reagans were to use Camp David more days than any presidential couple before them—571 days during their eight-year tenure, or an average of 61 days a year. They were resident at Rancho del Cielo an average of 45 days a year, always difficult for their staff and the Secret Service, who were housed in rented premises at the foot of the mountain; as there was no helicopter pad, travel to and from the nearest government airport was a long drive.

With them they brought to Camp David (which also had a permanent staff): Reagan's press aide, Mark Weinberg; his chief steward, Eddie Serrano; his doctor, John Hutton (Dr. Ruge retired in 1982); Reagan's personal assistant, Jim Kuhn; the helicopter pilot; the chief communication officer (the officer, rotated weekly, who carried the black box manacled to his wrist); and the Reagans' Secret Service officers. Hutton and Kuhn often came with their wives and children, as did Michael and Carolyn Deaver. There were never more than three or four women at Camp David, which lent it somewhat of a men's club ambience despite Lady Bird's gardens and the occasional sound of children splashing in the pool. Ron and Doria visited from time to time, as did Dr. Richard Davis and his wife, Patricia. The other Reagan children and members of their close circle of friends did not. Camp David had been created as a strictly private retreat for the president and the first lady, and the Reagans respected that mandate. They also enjoyed each other's company so thoroughly that the limited time that they could manage to be alone was vigilantly guarded. Saturday noontimes at Camp David were reserved for the broadcast of Reagan's weekly five-minute radio commentaries, which he gave from a cabin that had been converted into a sound studio. Nancy was almost always in attendance.

The Reagans had visited Camp David once during Richard Nixon's administration, and again when a member of Carter's staff gave Nancy a tour of the premises and grounds just five days before Reagan's inauguration. But they arrived at the retreat for the first time as official occupants on January 30, 1981, ten days after the inauguration, remaining from Friday evening until early the next Monday morning. Camp David would make Reagan's years in the White House a much less anguished time for him. No past president had ever been so attuned to the sound and silence of nature as Ronald Reagan. Just to be able to open the front door of Aspen and walk wherever he choose around the vast grounds, which he could not do in Washington, was a cherished freedom.

On the weekend of June 8, 1981, President José López Portillo of Mexico, whom Reagan had originally been scheduled to meet in Mexico before the assassination attempt, visited Camp David. Like Reagan, he was an avid horseman, which gave them an immediate rapport. The two men held their working sessions while traversing the winding, challenging horse trails. Reagan found Camp David, where dress was casual and talk flowed freely, a perfect venue for meetings with pressured heads of state. He came to use it more and more for high-powered meetings that might have been stiff and unproductive in the formal atmosphere of the White House. A superb host, he always had his staff investigate his guests' likes and dislikes beforehand, and he joined in whatever they enjoyed—riding, swimming, fishing, golf, skeet, long walks (taken through the blazing autumn colors of Camp David's majestic forests or the brilliant display of wildflowers bordering the winding paths in the summer), or cowboy movies. Nancy hosted lunches on the large tree-shaded patio of Aspen. Toys and special movies were arranged for their young visitors, pony rides, too.

Perhaps the most desirable aspect of the retreat was that it was completely off-limits to the press. In Washington Reagan felt attending church services on a Sunday created too many security problems. At Camp David that would not be true. So early on in their occupancy, Nancy initiated plans to have a chapel built, though it would not be completed until George Herbert Walker Bush succeeded Reagan.

However much the Reagans looked forward to weekends at the compound, they knew that their days would never be carefree. The presidency is a seven-day-a-week, twenty-four-hour-a-day job. Wherever the president goes he takes with him a briefcase stuffed with urgent papers that he must study. There is no weekend freeze on shattering events, domestic or global, that require the attention, and often the immediate action, of the American president. On October 6, 1981, Anwar el-Sadat, president of Egypt, was assassinated in a hail of automatic gunfire at a military parade in Cairo; ten other people were killed and nearly forty wounded, including three U.S. military officers. Sadat had made peace with Israel at Camp David just three years earlier, on September 18, 1978, in a groundbreaking agreement between Egypt and Israel that Carter had helped to broker.

Over the winter of 1981–1982, not only were there explosive situations within Egypt, but dangerous hostilities erupted between Israelis and Palestinians when Israel annexed the Golan Heights. In Iran, revolution was raging while that country was still engaged in a bloody war with Iraq. Reports of 1,800 executions of suspected Iranian revolutionaries without trials shocked the West, along with word that the Soviets, engaged in a bitter war with Afghanistan, had caused 3,000 deaths by chemical warfare. With terrorism blatantly on the rise in Libya, Reagan asked all Americans to leave that country. Meanwhile, Italy's leftist Red Brigade had kidnapped U.S. Brig. Gen. James L. Dozier, a NATO attaché, in December 1981. Forty-two days later, General Dozier was freed when Italian police (working with American security) stormed the Padua apartment where he had been held captive. When the police broke in, a Brigade member was holding a gun to the general's head.

Reagan's problems were not all an ocean away. On the home front his economic program was in great difficulties. Although the president refused to accept the resignation of his budget director, David Stockman, differences between them over the president's economic program would persist. Staff problems loomed larger on January 4, 1982, when Richard V. Allen, the national security adviser, resigned and was replaced by William P. Clark, who found himself immediately in conflict with Secretary of State Haig.

Policy clashes with Haig continued throughout the spring of 1982. Reagan seemed unready to abandon his secretary of state, rationalizing that, "despite his outbursts, Haig was both well-informed and well-meaning. . . . Al hasn't steered me wrong yet."[3] Haig was working hard to head off a war between Argentina and Great Britain over possession of the Falkland Islands, a confrontation in which Reagan strongly supported Margaret Thatcher. Britain's prime minister was adamant in her decision to defend her country's sparsely inhabited dependency, whose main income was derived from the herds of sheep that grazed on its promontories. The English captain John Strong had discovered and claimed the Falkland Islands for Great Britain in 1690, but in the next 130 years the islands were won over by France, Spain, and Great Britain alternately. In 1833 a British force took over the islands without a shot ever having been fired. In 1892 the Falklands were granted colonial status by the British. Since that time Argentina had made numerous unsuccessful incursions to regain its long-lost claim, and on April 10,

1982, it invaded the islands (population 1,806), an event Alexander Haig was attempting to forestall by persuading Britain to mediate Argentina's claim. Haig's personal mission failed. The war was fought for ten weeks, ending with the surrender of the Argentine forces at Stanley (the capital) to British forces.

Haig also tried to negotiate a solution to a raging pipeline dispute with the Soviets. Badly in need of hard currency, the Soviets had made an agreement with the West to construct a $10 billion pipeline that would transport natural gas from Siberia to western Europe. Reagan was against the proposal, but "Haig sought a compromise under which the United States would acquiesce to the pipeline in return for an agreement of allied consultation on future technology transfers."[4]

As Lou Cannon suggests, "It was his personality more than his policy advocacies that kept getting Haig in trouble."[5] Haig's tenure finally ended in a blaze of supposed insults by the Reagans during their first overseas trip together as president and first lady, accompanied by Haig and by Clark and Deaver.

The eleven-day European tour, from June 1 to June 11, 1982, began in Rome, with the Reagans meeting the Pope almost immediately after a nine-hour flight from Washington. Much has been made of the fact that Reagan nodded off for a moment during his audience with the pope. It is true, but he had just come from a tedious flight during which he had had no chance to rest because he was working on his speeches. Nancy, who nudged him awake as discreetly as she could, said that the time difference was a factor, and that the room was airless and the pope's voice a soothing drone.

That same night they continued to Versailles, where Reagan attended the annual economic summit of industrialized nations. He then flew to West Germany, and from there to Great Britain to address both Houses of Parliament. On the second day of the summit, the Israeli ambassador to Great Britain was shot and seriously wounded by Arab terrorists. The Israelis instantly retaliated by bombing an empty sports stadium in Beirut. In response, the Palestine Liberation Organization bombed towns in Galilee. The summit ended on June 6, the day Israel launched a full-scale invasion of Lebanon. In the midst of all this, Reagan did not have the patience to humor his secretary of state's misplaced pride and "repeated displays of temper over what seemed to the President to be minor matters of protocol."[6]

Problems with Haig had begun only moments before Air Force One's takeoff for Europe. The secretary of state loudly complained about his seat, which was next to Deaver in the third compartment. He insisted he should have been in the second compartment, directly behind the Reagans' presidential quarters. He made a terrible fuss, refusing to sit down until orders to do so came from Reagan. By then he had delayed takeoff for ten minutes and greatly irritated both the Reagans. In England he repeated his poor behavior when he was assigned to a helicopter other than the president's on a fifteen-minute flight from London Heathrow Airport to Windsor Castle, where the Reagans were to spend two days as guests of Queen Elizabeth and Prince Philip. During those two days Haig was overheard directing a loud and intemperate outburst at Clark. The last straw came when, at a luncheon at 10 Downing Street, Haig took it upon himself to stand in the reception line with Margaret Thatcher, her husband, Dennis, and the Reagans. Both Clark and Deaver tried to get him to step away, but he refused to do so until Thatcher herself, a compressed smile thinly veiling her own irritation, "whispered to him that he was not supposed to be there."[7] Almost immediately upon their return to Washington, Reagan asked for Haig's resignation. His replacement, George Shultz, who had served as secretary of the treasury under Nixon, was already waiting in the wings. Nancy, who greatly respected Shultz, had been much in favor of his selection. Called prior to Haig's resignation, Shultz had agreed to accept the post and to hold his peace until his selection was announced to the public.

Reagan had worked long and hard on the addresses he gave to the foreign parliaments. Concerned about his image, he later wrote, which was "fired up by demagogues depicting me as a shoot-from-the-hip cowboy aching to pull out my nuclear six-shooter and bring on doomsday. . . . I wanted to demonstrate that I wasn't flirting with doomsday. I told the Europeans how I felt: A nuclear war cannot be won and must never be fought, but before we could persuade the Russians to take their finger off the trigger, we had to make them realize that there was a boundary beyond which the Free World would not accept criminal behavior from another state—and to do that we had to be able to negotiate with the Russians from a position of strength."[8] To the British Parliament on June 8, he said, "Our military strength is a prerequisite to peace." He also expressed his opinion that "Communism's struggle against capitalism would be resolved by market, not military forces."[9]

Nancy was thrilled at being a guest of the queen at Windsor Castle. Elizabeth and Reagan formed a rapport, not over politics (which the queen seldom discussed), but over horses. They walked the grounds of Windsor together, Reagan dropping the more formal modes of address for the respectful but friendlier "Ma'am" and rushing to take the queen's arm, strictly against protocol, to help her up some high stone steps. Elizabeth smiled almost coquettishly, apparently pleased at this bow to her femininity, however incorrect the gesture. (She called him "Mr. Reagan.")

Windsor is beautiful in June, its giant oaks a majestic backdrop for the sweeping floral display that formed a colorful tapestry of the grounds. Nancy could not help but be impressed with the castle, even as the massive gates swung open to allow their limousine and escorting cars to pass through them. The brilliance of the guards' uniforms, with Nancy's favorite red predominating, offset the grayness of the ancient stone walls and turrets. While Reagan walked the grounds and visited the stables with the queen, Nancy toured the castle, redolent of what has been known for centuries as the special Windsor Castle smell—ancient furniture heavily polished and musk-scented flowers. An *aura* pervaded the interior that extended to the dignified staff. A vast and magnificent collection of paintings hung in the long corridor that connected one part of the castle to another and where, for centuries, royal children have been allowed to play. Austere Gothic corridors were lined with bookshelves filled with ancient volumes. There were elaborate carved doors, royal apartments rich with gilded woodwork and plaster and sumptuous crimson and shimmering green silk-brocade walls. Even in June, with a gentle sun dappling the grounds, the corridors of Windsor were arctic, and in the reception room where the Reagans, the queen, and Philip had afternoon tea (one of over three hundred rooms served by an equal number of uniformed staff), there was a vigorous fire burning on the hearth.

On June 10 the Reagans flew to West Berlin and were driven to Checkpoint Charlie. East German soldiers with submachine guns stood in little knots around the guardhouses, prohibiting passage from West to East Berlin. Above the forbidding gray wall were gun towers laced together by barbed wire. Guard dogs yowled on the eastern side of the wall that had kept families separated for so many years and confined East Berliners as surely as if they were prisoners. What could be seen of the Communist side of the divided city from Checkpoint Charlie was a choppy sea of gray rooftops atop dingy gray apartment complexes barren of any trace of greenery to alleviate the grimness.

When asked his opinion of what he was seeing, Reagan replied through an unusual furrowed scowl, "It's as ugly as the idea behind it."[10]

The Reagans' lives had changed dramatically in a year and a half. Both were under increasing pressures. Still, Reagan remained the same man, calm in times of crisis and seldom, if ever, allowing his temper to overcome reason. Nancy's attitude became more imperious. As late as March 1982, when her antidrug campaign was winning over a slowly growing percentage of the public, her relationship with the press, who found her aloof and caustic, remained strained.

Knowing something had to be done to improve the situation, Sheila Tate approached Nancy with a daring plan for her to make an unscheduled appearance as a performer during the show at the annual elegant white-tie Gridiron Dinner. The dinner was sponsored by the Gridiron Club, which was composed of about sixty journalists who comprised the White House press corps. It was an important event attended by the members of the Supreme Court, the Cabinet, top White House aids, and leading members of Congress, including the Speaker of the House.

"One day in March, 1982," Helen Thomas recalled, "I got a call from Tate, who sounded me out about the possibility of the first lady appearing in a skit [at the dinner]. I quietly passed the word along and what happened later made no small number of headlines."[11]

The Gridiron event contained appearances by various members of the White House press corps in skits satirizing White House luminaries. Tate had managed to learn in advance the content of one of these skits. At the dinner, Nancy was seated at the same table with the president, who knew nothing about what was to follow. Neither did the rest of the gathering, including Maureen Ribble, who sang a sharp-edged parody of "Secondhand Rose," a song made famous by Fanny Brice in the early years of the century and revived popularly in the 1960's by Barbra Streisand. Tate had learned that Ribble would sing the parody dressed and coifed outrageously as a 'Nancy clone':

Secondhand clothes,
I give my secondhand clothes
To museum collections and traveling shows
They were oh, so happy when they got 'em
Won't notice they were ragged on the bottom.
Secondhand dress
Good-bye you worn-out old mess,
I never wear a frock just more than once
Calvin Klein, Adolfo, Ralph Lauren and Bill Blass
Ronald Reagan's mama's going strictly first-class
Rodeo Drive, I sure miss Rodeo Drive
In frumpy Washington.[12]

When Ribble finished the song, everyone glanced nervously over to Nancy. Her face was expressionless, her wide brown eyes two vacant circles. The president was flushed. No one knew quite what to expect. Nancy pushed her chair back, got up, and walked quickly and unsmilingly from the room. A murmur spread from table to table. The first lady had taken offense. The press corps looked to Reagan, who, uneasy but unmoving, sat through the next number with an impenetrable expression. Then the curtains opened, and to the shock of everyone (except Sheila Tate and the piano player to the right of the stage), there Nancy stood, looking even more outrageous than Ribble, "decked out in an aqua cotton skirt with red and yellow flowers, a navy polka-dot blouse

and short-sleeved red sweater, white pantaloons decorated with blue but-
terflies, a big feathered hat, white feather boa, yellow rubber boots and
big red earrings."[13]

With the piano backing her, Nancy began (in a clear, pleasing voice,
tinged with a Brooklyn accent), to sing a self-deprecating version of
"Secondhand Rose" that she had written with Tate:

Secondhand clothes
I'm wearing secondhand clothes
They're all the thing in
The spring fashion shows
Even my new trench coat with fur collar
Ronnie bought for 10 cents on the dollar
Even though they tell me that I'm no longer queen
Did Ronnie have to buy me that new sewing machine?
Secondhand clothes, secondhand clothes
I sure hope Ed Meese sews . . . [14]

Everyone except the President jumped up, applauding wildly and
screaming for an encore, which Nancy seemed only too happy to give
them. When she was finished, she picked up a nearby plate and threw
it to the floor. It didn't break, and there was a chorus of laughter with
the applause as she ran off the stage. She had cracked the ice, and the
press, who had been ruthless before the Gridiron dinner, suddenly toned
down their criticism and snide remarks.

"I came as a happy husband," Reagan told the crowd, "and am leaving as a stage door Johnny!"[15]

Personally, 1982 was a difficult year for Nancy. Dr. Davis was gravely
ill with congestive heart disease. In January she had celebrated his
(eighty-sixth birthday with him in Arizona, calling him by the name she
had used when she was a child—*Bapa*. Since then his health had steadily
declined. Edith was frail and not well either, and Nancy was handling
their affairs, medical and financial, from Washington. She called the Davises individually every day. "It was a curious reversal of positions," a
close associate remarked. "It seemed that Nancy had suddenly usurped

her mother's place, making decisions that really should have been Edith's to make, and she did this without consulting the doctor's son, Richard, who, after all, was a credible medical authority."[16]

To further darken this time for Nancy, Alfred Bloomingdale, husband of Betsy ("Bets," as Nancy called her lovingly), was not only dying of cancer, but being exposed and dragged through the tabloids in a lurid scandal. He was said to have attended sadomasochistic rites where he beat up prostitutes and to have paid blackmail for years to cover up his alleged Mafia connections. (He had been friends with Izzy Glasser, who represented the notorious Mickey Cohen.) The headlines grew uglier. For the past twelve years Alfred had been keeping a mistress, Vicki Morgan, with a past said to connect her to drugs and sadomasochistic sex orgies. During the summer of 1982, Nancy shuttled between Arizona and California to be with her father and to support Betsy. While Alfred was on his death bed, he signed a new will transferring all assets into a Bloomingdale Family Trust, with her as chief executor.

Nancy, who had always dissociated herself from anyone who might bear the slightest tinge of scandal, stood by Betsy. "Just remember," she admirably told other friends, "Betsy's still my friend."[17] Nancy even ended friendships with some of the women who turned their backs on Betsy during this terrible time. Betsy had not done anything wrong, and Nancy was furious that people who had enjoyed her gracious hospitality through the years and had never been shy in soliciting her successfully for funds for their favorite charities would turn on her as they had.

In early August Loyal Davis's condition worsened, and Nancy flew down to Arizona to be with him. Kitty Kelley gives a devastating portrait of this period in her scandal-ridden biography of Nancy. In Kelley's scathing version, Nancy refused to pay for her father's nursing care, and so the attending physician, who Kelley claims was a former student of Davis's and a family friend, called Colleen Moore—Edith's old colleague (eighty-three at the time)—in California and requested that she pay the nursing expenses for Loyal. The physician said Moore had agreed to do this. Colleen Moore died in 1988, and the doctor's name is not given in Kelley's book, so this story cannot be verified. However, it seems highly unlikely—and would be highly unethical—for a doctor to solicit funds for a patient in his care from a private source. Also, Nancy's parents were affluent (there was, in fact, a million-dollar estate), and Nancy was paying for their care out of their own checking accounts, having been entrusted with power of attorney. Moreover, the Davises were covered by Medicare for the major portion of the bill, the remaining amount payable almost fully by the personal medical insurance which Davis carried as a member of the American Medical Association. Many policies do not include out-of-hospital private nursing shifts. Perhaps that was the case with Dr. Davis's coverage and the crux of the dispute that Kelley includes in her version of the events that preceded his death.

Dr. Davis took a turn for the worse on August 9. He developed serious breathing problems and was in a semiconscious state. "Nancy in tears," Reagan wrote in his diary on the ninth. "Her father is back in the hospital. She's going out there [Arizona] on Wednesday [August 11]. I wish I could bear her pain myself."[18] By the time Nancy flew to Phoenix, Dr. Davis was home again and semicomatose. Believing it to be in his best interest, Nancy took him back to the hospital. According to Kelley's published interview with the anonymous doctor, Davis at an earlier time had expressed his wish to him to die at home, and that was why the physician called Nancy to authorize payment for twenty-four-hour nursing care. Nancy considered that ill advised. Even with full-time care, her father would not have immediate access to the lifesaving equipment in the hospital. There was also her mother to be considered. Edith, Nancy feared, would not be able to cope with the painful experience of helplessly watching the life of her beloved husband ebb away. The decision to take Dr. Davis to the hospital was her own; she told Edith that "Bapa was going to have some tests."

The next day Nancy was joined by her stepbrother, Dr. Richard Davis, and Ron and Doria. By Sunday, August 15, Reagan was even more distressed at Nancy's having to deal with her father's last days without him. "Talked to Nancy. She's very low, thinks the end may come to Loyal in the next few days. How I wish I could be with her and help her."[19]

Nancy spent hours at the hospital by his bedside in the next few days, Dr. Davis in an unconscious state as she held his hand. An early call from the hospital on the morning of August 19 informed Nancy that death was imminent. She rushed to her father's side, sat beside him, talking to him, and was stroking his hand when she felt life leave his body. "No! No!" she was heard to cry. Ron and Doria ran into the room and stood beside her. She would not let go of her father's hand for several minutes and had a difficult time controlling her emotions. She had never seen anyone die before. This was the man whose love she had wanted since childhood, and thought she had, but who can ever be sure?

She went back to see Edith as soon as possible. "I was afraid that my mother would hear it on television or the radio, and I didn't want that to happen. So I had to leave the hospital and go to my mother and tell her that he was gone."[20] Edith appeared to have been expecting the end and was stronger and more resilient than her daughter.

"It was when her father died that I saw her at the lowest period I've ever known," Nancy Reynolds recalled of Dr. Davis's death. "I think she felt the loss more keenly than she ever believed she would, even though he had been quite ill. I think the President was deeply concerned about her. . . . the loss certainly affected her greatly. He was a tremendous influence in her life."[21]

"Dr. Loyal died this morning," Reagan recorded in his diary on August 19. "Nancy wasn't alone, thank heaven. Ron and Doria were there. But it seemed awful to be here and not be with her. All day I sat at my desk phoning Congressmen on the tax bill and tonight it passed with 103 Republicans and more than half the Democrats. . . . Tip O'Neill made a speech to Republicans telling them why they should support me. It seemed strange. Both of us [Democrat and Republican] on the same side. . . . Now I am packing to leave for Phoenix and my sweetheart."[22]

Larry Speakes accompanied the president with the usual contingent of Secret Service agents. By the time they arrived, Nancy and her stepbrother had had a serious argument over Dr. Davis's burial and Nancy's proprietary takeover of the arrangements and of matters concerning the estate "that threatened to rupture their relationship permanently," Speakes wrote. "On the evening before Dr. Davis's memorial service, the two got into a loud argument at the family home. Dick Davis, a calm, orderly man, left on the next plane back East, missing his father's service. Although we [in the Reagan company] heard of the spat between the two, we never knew what caused it."[23]

Nancy and Richard Davis would mend their fences within a few years of Loyal's death. Nancy would, in fact, lean heavily upon her step-brother in matters of her own or Reagan's ill health. They had been close as children. Davis warmly recalled a time when he and Nancy were very young: "We played some outrageous games. We had one called 'Help, Murder, Police!' This was a very precarious game. We'd both get on the highest piece of furniture and then jump on a sliding stool. And this went on and was very carefully timed for Dad's return home. By that time, we were totally exhausted, feigned broken arms and legs, and, of course, the great surgeon had to heal us."[24] There was sibling competition, however, throughout their father's life. Nancy always felt the pain of being "the adopted child," and Richard that of the son who was often outside the loop of his father's second family.

Perhaps Nancy had some unresolved questions she wanted Loyal to answer. Why had he waited so long to adopt her? Did he view her as a true daughter in the same way he saw Richard as a son? She knew, because of Michael and Maureen Reagan, how difficult this was to answer. This knowledge, however, did not bring her any closer to the children she and Reagan shared by blood and by marriage.

CHAPTER SIXTEEN

THE POWER AND
THE GLITTER

B y the spring of 1983, only two years into Reagan's first presidential term, Nancy was being viewed in quite a different way. In
Washington the buzz had spread. The first lady was not just a
California parvenu with a taste for extravagantly spending the money of
others, she was fast becoming a shareholder of the presidency. She had
her eyes and ears everywhere, it was said. No one got to the president
without having Nancy on their side. Ironically, given earlier concerns
over the possibility of Reagan and Ford forming a two-headed presidency, Nancy Reagan had slipped past the voters' scrutiny and into an
unelected role in the Oval Office. Nancy dismissed such rumors as ridiculous. Of course, she and Ronnie often discussed issues that weighed
heavily on his mind. What loving, intelligent wife would do otherwise?
When reporters dared to question her about her so-called power over
the president, she vehemently denied that she could influence him in
any executive decision. Nevertheless, the rumors of Nancy's power became common talk in the capital and were beginning to spread from
ocean to ocean, substantiated by those as close to the sources of power
as one could get in a political town like Washington.

"I'd go so far as to say that Nancy Reagan was the most powerful
First Lady of the last 40 years," Richard Burt, under secretary of state
and a confidant of the Reagans, said in 1998. Burt would thus have
included all first ladies from Mamie Eisenhower through Hillary Rodman
Clinton. Moreover, since his wife, Gahl Hodges Burt, was the first lady's

social secretary for nearly two years, he had been privy to Nancy's position both from a political and a social prospective. "[Nancy] had a tremendous influence on people close to Reagan," he professed. She could get staff members hired and fired. Those in her favor found their stock rise; those not so lucky found that it fell. "She read the polls. She read the newspapers. She watched television. But more importantly, she had her network. She talked to [key players] on the phone all day long and she knew what [they] were saying. And so, if Ronnie was screwing up in one area or another," she would telephone the person closest to the situation and butt him into action to correct it. "For anybody outside to break into that inner circle, Nancy had to approve," Burt contended, and that had not been an easy matter.[1]

After her father's death, Nancy's thirst for power increased dramatically, encouraged by Reagan, who felt he was now her sole protector and must try harder than ever to keep her happy. Certainly, there were times he resisted Nancy's positions. For example, in Helene von Damm's case. Nancy made it clear that she wanted her out of the White House. Reagan tried to compromise by removing von Damm from her position close to the Oval Office in the West Wing, placing her in charge of foreign diplomatic posting with an office in the East Wing of the White House. Then, when Nancy remained unappeased, he named von Damm ambassador to her native country, Austria. Nancy's dislike of von Damm was satisfied only when the longtime, faithful Reagan supporter was asked a year later to resign this post.

Nancy's vendetta against von Damm could well have been caused by personal pique. The first lady thought Helene (who, although a confidante to Reagan, was not a major, or even a minor player in the corridors of Washington power) was trying to push her way into her own private circle. Von Damm was Reagan's old friend, one who had been with him since his first day as governor of California. The fact that he ultimately put Nancy's feelings about von Damm ahead of his own reinforces the rumors about the balance of power between them. "There was more than pillow talk between the Reagans," an insider confirmed, "or wifely interest. Nancy was always concerned with what Ronnie's place would be in history. She wanted to be sure that he would be revered, respected, one of the great presidents every schoolchild grows up learning about. One can't fault her for that. But very often it was as though she were writing the script *and* directing the action. She was kept fully apprised of his schedule and knew where he was and with whom he was talking every minute that he was not with her."[2]

It was Nancy, more than Reagan, who held on to her early training as an actor. She was adept at playing two roles almost simultaneously—the weaker-than-her-husband-and-must-be-protected wife and the authoritative woman staunchly taking on the tough world of power politics. Had she had greater perspective and been able to rise above her personal animosity, she might have helped Reagan to achieve the Olympian goals she had set for him.

"She was *much* more influential than she ever let on," Muffie Brandon, who would later become her social secretary, added. "And she didn't *want* to be perceived as being influential. I once asked her. 'Don't you ever think about *your* place in history?' She looked at me and she said, "Oh, no. It's Ronnie. And Ronnie's place in history."[3] But, of course, they were one and the same. As long as Reagan remained on top, so then did she. He was her conduit to the power she enjoyed and wished to hold on to. With Dr. Davis gone, she now even controlled her mother who, although she had always loved her, had held Loyal, not Nancy, first in her life.

The fact that Nancy could make the really tough and distasteful decisions regarding close associates allowed Reagan to be Mr. Nice Guy. It was a situation that he not only allowed but encouraged. At the same time, there is conclusive proof that Nancy worked to moderate some of his hard-line conservative views, especially in his negotiations with Russia, where she believed his unique persuasive powers as a communicator could win more points than would a confrontational approach. What is tragic is that she was not curious or passionate about those things that she believed had little to do with Reagan's figures in opinion polls or his place in history. It was on Reagan's watch that the first indications of the AIDS plague appeared, but funding for research was slow to materialize. At first AIDS had the unfortunate onus of appearing to be associated only with homosexuals, a group not considered much of a voting block and whose endorsement would have offended the religious right, Reagan's strongest supporters. And despite the assassination attempt, James Brady's sad condition, and Sarah Brady's valiant efforts to secure gun control, the Reagans were not ready to buck the powerful gun lobby, who were also large contributors to Republican candidates. This applied as well to the tobacco lobby.

Nancy was a fierce defender of her husband's policies, which were not much different from those of her late father. "During Reagan's first year in office, his tough talk and military buildup frightened so many people that a spontaneous nuclear-freeze movement broke out all over Europe," political analyst William Schneider wrote. The western world was "shocked by Reagan's 'evil empire' speech to the British House of Commons [June, 1982], when he denounced the Soviet Union as a tyranny, relegated Marxism-Leninism to 'the ash heap of history' and asked, 'Must freedom wither—in a quiet, deadening accommodation with totalitarian evil?' Reagan's policy was 'Talk tough, and carry a big stick.' "[4]

This is true. It is also true, as Nancy advised, a little diplomacy if interspersed with his combative attitude might have yielded better results. And it would be this sweetened version of hard principle that would, in the end, so incredibly win out. Reagan believed in a huge military buildup so that the Soviets would understand the consequences of threatening such a powerful nation as the United States. At the same time he wanted to be thought of as a peacemaker, and that was what Nancy desired his legacy to be. To Reagan the Soviets were the school bully who terrorizes all the younger and smaller kids—until someone bigger steps in, someone the bully knows he can't beat, and so he backs down, withdraws. Although Reagan was not loved and admired abroad (except perhaps by Margaret Thatcher), he was respected internationally far more in the early days of his presidency than he was at home. He was restoring a sense of power to the presidency that had not been there since Nixon's dramatic fall, and he was rescuing patriotism from an overlong lethargy and raising it to flag-waving exuberance.

At the age when many men are hunched, he stood unbowed, hair sans silver ("Ask my barber. He'll tell you it's never seen dye," he would say), the glint in his eyes revealing the boyish mischievousness that he had carried with him since his Dixon days. Age had impaired his hearing, but his voice was strong, and with his new soft contact lenses he was able to read for even longer periods without suffering the eyestrain he once had experienced. He worked out assiduously and preened proudly as he showed off the muscles in his arms to Michael Deaver. Although in awe of some of his predecessors—Washington, Adams, Jefferson, Lincoln, and FDR—he felt touched by greatness. Peggy Noonan wrote that "he was possessed of an intuitive sense of the purpose of royalty, the need for people to flee the normal petty tyrants and tell their story to 'the king' and be heard . . . and that they know that they have at least a chance to make it through to the top guy."[5] No other president ever answered as many personal letters as did Ronald Reagan, and he gave the same respect and care to letters from ordinary people as he did to those from world leaders. He often would write a follow-up letter to someone who had written him about a troubling family situation. Anne Higgins, director of his correspondence, recalled that he wrote the mother of a Vietnam veteran, "I haven't heard from you. How is your son, please let me know and keep me posted." He shared private experiences—"When my mother died . . ."; "My father also had a drinking problem . . ."; "I've known depression, but never despair. There is always room for hope . . ."—with correspondents he had never met and probably never would.[6] Nelle's teachings and his Disciples of Christ education certainly contributed to his need to help others. But there was also his sense of who he now was, how high he had risen, and the responsibility that came with such elevation.

He did not flaunt his power, as had Richard Nixon. He never wielded it in a manner that humbled or humiliated others, as Lyndon Johnson had done. His role models were Abraham Lincoln and Franklin Delano Roosevelt, not such an odd couple as they might seem. Lincoln was a president known to be a compassionate man, accessible to the people who wrote to him of their private concerns, and FDR was idolized for his art of communication, which included his famous fireside chats. He also greatly admired Theodore Roosevelt, perhaps the only other man who fit the bill as a cowboy-president. Reagan did not deny his position—ever: He was the most powerful man in the world and he knew it. But he never forgot his Bible stories, especially that of the powerful Goliath and the seemingly weaker David. "Beware of the power of the weak" was a self-created maxim he respected and followed.

Without question, the new dynamics of their situation altered the Reagans' lives, but not their attitude toward each other. Whereas the presidency had stressed the marriages of the Kennedys and the Nixons, it bound the Reagans ever closer. "As far as he was concerned," Nancy wrote of these years in the White House, "Ronnie always was my husband first, Mr. President second. He never took himself too seriously. His letters, once signed 'Your Ranch Hand,' now were signed 'Prexy.' "[7] With her Just Say No campaign she traveled rather extensively. Before one such trip, he set out her vitamin pills in small vials with a note that they would make her "healthy wealthy & wise—you're already beautiful. Your Resident Dr." Into the mid-1980s, he continued to leave mash notes on her breakfast tray or dressing table: "I can never get enough of kissing you. You are the light of my life. I just worship my Roommate— Your husband." Or "Dear Glamour Puss ... I love you mucher and mucher every day. Your Roommate."[8] What sixty-two-year-old woman, married over thirty years, could hope for more? Nancy did, and received it. *Power*, a chance to be an integral part of her husband's career as well as his life. And she was.

Did the Reagans have bad times, disagreements, misunderstandings? Sure. They were human. But Nancy always knew when to give in. The closest members of Nancy's staff, with access to the family quarters, recall seeing her momentarily depressed, on occasion in tears. She was well known for using tears to win points in discussions not going her way. Members of the White House domestic staff who served during several administrations could recall terrible arguments between the Nixons, "but never a raised voice between the Reagans. He was sometimes more emphatic than usual. 'No, Nancy!' could have a hard sound to it but was never a shout. He would go into his study alone, and she would come knocking at the door a short time later. They seemed always, sincerely in love. They were very relaxed together. Laughed a lot. And in all the time I worked for them, I don't ever recall seeing Mrs. Reagan look frumpy. She always looked well dressed even in a sweater and slacks, which she often wore in the evenings when they were not going out. And her hair—curious—it shined, *always*."⁹

The previous June, while the Reagans were guests at Windsor Castle, they had invited Queen Elizabeth and Prince Philip to visit them at Rancho del Cielo. Nancy had followed this up with a more formal written invitation, and the queen, a fine horsewoman, had enthusiastically accepted. The visit was set for early March, overlapping the Reagans' thirty-first anniversary on March 4. Nancy was in a high fever of excitement. Everything was meticulously arranged—riding trails cleared, horses prepared for the queen's selection, along with saddles. Nancy planned a barbecue with mariachi singers and other outdoor entertainment. The weather had been glorious for all of February. Then, on the day the royal yacht *Britannia* anchored at Santa Barbara, the skies opened up with biblical lightning and torrential rain. The royal party, not to be deterred, made it up to the ranch in a Land Rover, chugging through mud that deepened with each twist in the mountain road, in a fog of near-zero visibility.

Nancy was in a state when the royal party finally arrived. But Elizabeth, scarf tied tightly under her developing second chin, umbrella held high over her graying head, seemed unperturbed. "Don't be silly," Nancy reported Elizabeth said, smiling. "This is an adventure!" Of course, life in Britain brought many heavy rainfalls, whatever the season, and the queen seldom went anywhere without an umbrella. "She seemed genuinely disappointed about not being able to ride," Reagan said. "The Queen is an expert horsewoman. But we managed to enjoy the afternoon."¹⁰ It was spent inside the ranch house before a roaring fire without mariachis. When the royal couple left, Nancy, on their insistence, went with them to spend the evening on the *Britannia*, the rain somewhat lighter, but the road, which had turned into a virtual mud slide, was more difficult to navigate. The ride was bumpy and at times the driver of the Land Rover had to avoid a serious skid. Through it all the queen sat unperturbed as she chatted with a rather nervous first lady.

Boarding the *Britannia* was an impressive experience, even for the first lady of the United States. Night had come. Hundreds of lights glistened from its decks, which were the ultimate in seafaring elegance. Nancy was given a suite in which to freshen up before dinner, and then she was taken on a tour of the yacht before meeting her royal hosts for cocktails. Aboard was a staff of 277 crewmen, a great number of them standing at attention as Queen Elizabeth, Prince Philip, and the first lady came up the gangplank. There were two tennis courts, an indoor and an outdoor swimming pool. Handsomely marbled fireplaces graced the reception rooms, which also contained magnificent French rugs, exquisite antique mahogany furniture, and crystal chandeliers. A vast garage housed the queen's Land Rover and Rolls-Royce, along with other cars that might be needed for land tours when the yacht was in dock. The state and private dining room both gleamed with great displays of polished silver and the gold of the royal crest emblazoned on the wall that faced the entrances to the rooms. Bedroom suites were furnished in bright chintzes, and fitted with gold-plated hardware, adding a lighter touch. But walls and ceilings on the royal deck were pristine white, the upholstered furniture a rich carmine red, and the carpets dove gray, achieving a stark look; and the somber sea paintings throughout the quarters did nothing to relieve the air of austerity.

Philip excused himself directly after dinner in the private dining room and the two women spent the rest of the evening in the informal (but by most standards grand) reception room "talking about our children like old friends."[11] One wonders what that conversation might have entailed, as the offspring of both the Windsor-Mountbattens and the Reagans had difficult relationships with their parents. Diana and the Prince of Wales were already having serious marital problems—Diana fighting depression, bulimia, and suicidal thoughts and Charles finding comfort in the arms of his longtime mistress, Camilla Parker Bowles. Princess Anne's marriage was also in trouble, and there were rumors that she was having an affair (this marriage would ultimately end in divorce).

Nancy sailed with the royal couple to San Francisco the next day while the president flew to Florida "to make a pair of speeches," one at the EPCOT Center, the other at the annual convention of the National Association of Evangelicals. In San Francisco Nancy and the royal couple had dinner at Trader Vic's, known for its campy Polynesian food and decor. For security purposes they ate in a well-guarded private dining room that lacked even the vaguest atmosphere of the South Pacific. Philip did not appear pleased (but then Philip seldom did), while the queen took it in her usual gracious way, seeming to find the strangely named poo-poo platter with its assortment of pseudo-Polynesian finger foods both tasty and amusing. Despite Nancy's trepidation about the success of the royal visit, on Reagan's return later that week Elizabeth (who did, indeed, consider her California visit an adventure) hosted an anniversary party aboard the *Britannia*. "I know I promised Nancy a lot of things thirty-one years ago," Reagan said as champagne glasses were raised, "but I never promised her *this*."

"It was an unforgettable evening—," Nancy wrote, "to be on the queen's private yacht, celebrating our anniversary."[12] The Deavers and Chief of Protocol Selwa "Lucky" Roosevelt joined them. The queen's chef made a special tiered cake somewhat bridal in appearance, and after dinner, with some coaxing, and with Deaver accompanying her on the piano, Nancy sang Gershwin's lush ballad "Our Love Is Here to Stay," in tune and fair voice. The queen presented the Reagans with an engraved silver box. The Reagans had to report this gift, as they did all gifts, to the government. Presidential couples are not allowed to keep any presents given to them over a cost set by Congress ($180 at the time). The president is permitted to "purchase" an item at an assessed price if he desires to keep it. As this was a special gift, engraved to them, the Reagans did pay to keep the queen's anniversary present. It is difficult to put a price on such an item, as the provenance adds greatly to its value. It was quite a good size and sterling silver. It is believed Reagan paid something in the neighborhood of a thousand dollars, a concession in price no doubt due to its sentimental value.[13]

The Reagans returned to Rancho del Cielo shortly after Christmas 1983 in order to attend the ritual New Year's Eve party hosted by the Annenbergs at their Palm Springs mansion. It was also a time of great decision for them: If Reagan was to run for reelection, he needed to announce his candidacy shortly after the first of the year. During the rest of their holiday their evenings at Rancho del Cielo were filled with discussions of whether this was what they should do. Reagan felt he had many things yet to accomplish in his presidency, but Nancy had great misgivings. She still feared the possibility of assassination, despite the fact that there had been no further incidents since Hinckley's attack, and she was concerned for his health. She has never said that she noticed any signs of the memory lapses that would lead a decade later to a diagnosis of Alzheimer's disease, but others close to them felt she sensed some problem. She claimed she missed her friends and California and yearned for more privacy. This is certainly likely. Still, she seemed too comfortable with her new power, too alive with it, and possessive of it, to ever turn her back on it unless there was some strong motivational factor. Reagan would soon be seventy-three. The pressures of the presidency were intense, and although he was in good shape, his body had suffered quite a shock in the assassination attempt. Nancy noted things others did not—the increase in his loss of hearing, the small diminishment of his former high levels of energy. Presidential campaigns were tough. Didn't she know? Hadn't she watched him push himself through three of them already? Being the incumbent might help to win votes, but it did not lessen the hard work, the long hours, and the grueling travel involved in a campaign. The thoughts kept returning: What if the worst scenario happened? What would she do if Ronnie was taken from her? (Questions she asked in several ways in her diary.)

Had she had her way, Reagan would have served only one term. But Reagan was determined. They argued back and forth every night after dinner until Nancy reluctantly agreed. One point that might well have helped sway Nancy to concede was a look at recent history. Presidents with high ratings at the end of their first terms had all sought a second—and won. Johnson, feeling defeated by Vietnam, had decided not to run, but he had already served out Kennedy's unfinished term as well as one elected term.

Reagan announced his intention to run for a second term on January 29, 1984, in a televised broadcast from the Oval Office with Nancy, Maureen, her husband Dennis, Chief of Staff James Baker and speechwriter Ken Khachegian in attendance. Once Reagan had made his announcement, Nancy devoted herself again to the rigors of a presidential campaign. Maureen had taken her defeat in the race for U.S. Senate hard, but was working diligently in a job to promote American exports abroad. In her spare time she continued to speak on women's issues and party concerns and work in local elections. She was the only one of Reagan's children who had business reasons for coming to Washington, and when she did, she stayed at the White House. Nancy developed a new rapport with Maureen. Michael Deaver recalls that they would have stay-at-home evenings "when a good deal of girlish giggling could be heard," and Nancy was grateful to have a close family member to share her concerns and help relieve the tensions of her dual role as first lady and campaign supporter.

The campaign was kicked off on February 6, 1984, with a visit to Dixon, Reagan's fourth since he had moved to California to begin his career in the movies. Dixon (1934 population, 10,757; 1984 population, 15,144) had remained mostly unchanged in those fifty years. Main Street looked pretty much the same. The housing boom in the rest of the country had not affected the town; new housing was concentrated on the outskirts, where there was also a state prison and an asylum for the mentally unstable. Lowell Park still provided shade from the harsh summer sun and a place where families could picnic, and the town glowed in the aura of having once been the home of the president of the United States.

Reagan had a soft spot for the town where he first nurtured his dreams and always looked forward to these rare visits. Whereas Nancy, except for her parents and stepbrother, dissociated herself completely from the people who had been a part of her pre-Hollywood years, Reagan was fascinated with his roots. He had kept in touch with several of his Dixon friends, corresponding frequently with them, as well as with his old coach at Eureka College, Ralph McKinzie, and his former Sunday school teacher, Elonwy Neer.

One of Reagan's friends back in Dixon was Bill Thompson. Six years Reagan's junior, Thompson had set Dutch up as a hero from the time he was nine and sat with his feet dangling in the Rock River at Lowell Park, watching the fifteen-year-old lifeguard dive into the icy waters to retrieve those he thought might be in trouble. Thompson remained in awe of Dutch through his rise from sportscaster to movie star to governor of California to president of the United States. In 1941 Thompson had proudly driven him around Dixon when Reagan, then a B-movie star, returned to a week-long, conquering-hero's welcome to publicize his then current movies. (There were four that year, all fairly forgettable: *The Bad Man, Million Dollar Baby, Nine Lives Are Not Enough*, and *International Squadron*, which was the most successful.) Reagan was not alone on this tour: Another former Dixonite, powerful Hollywood columnist Louella Parsons (who had once sold corsets in Geisenheimers, Dixon's only department store), headed the small group of coming players that included Susan Hayward and Jane Wyman on a cross-country tour that had Reagan's and Parson's hometown stop as a highlight. It was one of the most glamorous weeks in Dixon's history and a great thrill for Reagan. Years later Thompson was instrumental in setting up arrangements for campaign stops in Dixon and active in turning one of Reagan's boyhood homes (the Reagans had had to move several times for financial reasons) into a museum. The house rented by the Reagans had been built and lived in by Thompson's grandfather.

In one of the letters Reagan wrote to Thompson from the White House, he discusses the books to be placed on the shelves in the "Ronald Reagan Boyhood Home." He recalls discovering "knights in armor . . . *King Arthur*. (Even named a cat King Arthur until *he* had kittens.) Another book that impressed me to the point of reading it several times was called *Northern Trails*. It planted deep within me a love of the outdoors and nature.

"At least twice a week in Dixon . . . beginning at the age of ten, I would hike down to the public library for books. My reading was undirected and went through phases. There was *Frank Merriwell at Yale*, which convinced me playing football was my goal, then came Zane Grey, *Horatio Alger* and of course, Mark Twain. The names of books come to mind like a montage, but, all in all, as I look back I realize that my reading left an abiding belief in the triumph of good over evil."

In another letter to Thompson, dated July 13, 1983, Reagan recalled his mother's cooking. "There is no recipe for my mother's oatmeal meat. She would just mix oatmeal with ground beef (as much needed to make enough for a meal, depending how much beef there was), and then she would just make a gravy to pour over it. I'm afraid I don't remember any other ingredients or proportions."[14]

Reagan's faith, as much as his small-town roots, had an important effect on the man. He had been baptized at the age of ten, as the Disciples of Christ do not believe in infant baptism. After his immersion before the congregation, as he rose from the waters, Reagan remembered hearing the minister say, "Arise and walk in newness of faith." At a Southern Baptist Convention in 1980, he told the Reverend Adrian Rogers that he had felt "called" at the time of his baptism, adding, "I had a personal experience when I invited Christ into my life." The Reverend Rogers asked him if he knew the Lord Jesus or just knew about him. Reagan replied, "I KNOW him."[15] His mother's faith was so ingrained in him that he claimed he did not realize until he departed for college that his father was Catholic, even though Jack never accompanied his wife and sons to their services. He taught Sunday school at the church at the age of thirteen and earned money doing janitorial work in an adjacent building to help pay for the plastering of the classroom.

The town of Dixon sat on land as flat as the bottom of an old iron. It was and remains a small, dusty town (except when the Rock River overflows) with rows of working-class houses, lace curtains at the windows, and, more recently, television antennas attached to shingled roofs. Lowell Park offered a green oasis. Otherwise, there was not much life or beauty to the place. However, a strong and heartwarming sense of community pervaded. Dixon might be "no frills," but it had the comforting feeling of a town where children could safely play in their backyards, where neighbors thought it was their duty to help each other, where church on Sunday was a ritual, church socials a fond mode of entertainment, and senior-citizen dances and the high school play were always well attended. If Reagan appeared in the oft-told stories of his life to be the All-American boy, it is due to the fact that he was raised in an All-American town.

Here in Dixon Reagan would always be known as Dutch. Banners reading WELCOME HOME DUTCH flew above the DIXON arch at the entrance leading into town from the narrow highway. Reagan, with Nancy and

Neil, rode through the arch in a limousine waving like a synchronized royal trio at the crowds who lined the street shouting, "Hi, Dutch!" The high school band that had performed at his first inauguration was on hand, the sprightly baton twirlers ready to step out in front with high kicks even though the day was gray, clouds threatened rain, and a dampness in the air went straight to one's bones. But Reagan was a happy, beaming man. He hugged an old friend, Apple Crabtree, then slapped him on the back and winked. He and Apple had been through some well-remembered, adolescent adventures together, stories Reagan liked to recount. Reagan walked slowly and thoughtfully through his boyhood home, stopping to examine everything, exclaim, ask questions. A local group had restored the interior as nearly as possible to what it was when he lived there. Nothing fancy about the Reagan's household goods. Most of the furniture looked as though it had been purchased from a Sears, Roebuck or Montgomery Ward catalog circa 1930.

Nancy was gracious although not exactly thrilled to be there. Dressed in a trim red Adolfo suit, she sat on the bed in the boxy room that Dutch and Moon had once shared (when there were no boarders). She smiled for the photographers, but otherwise remained in the background. "You can't imagine Nancy wanting to go back to her Aunt Virgie's house in Bethesda," a longtime friend of hers remarked. "Nancy always chose to bury the past. Ronnie was happy to relive it—except for those years with Jane Wyman. He reveled in hearing and repeating the same stories about his youth over and over again, facts changing some in the retelling, but always retaining their down-home charm."[16]

He returned to Washington, spirits high, determined to triumph in this campaign by his biggest margin ever. At his request Maureen took an active part in helping him win over women voters. She began by convincing him that he had the wrong people dealing publicly with the issue—"all white males between the ages of forty and sixty. Nobody's listening to them," she told him one night as they were relaxing together in his private study in the White House, her father in a sweater and slippers. "We were on Dad's own turf, and we spent the rest of that evening banging out a strategy, talking all about form and substance, about perceptions and deeds." The room put both of them at ease,

Nancy having made sure that their private rooms provided a comfortable retreat from the museum-like confines of the national shrine that was their home. Reagan settled back into the homey, red-floral-print over-stuffed chair that was his favorite, his feet up on the matching ottoman, while Maureen stressed her belief that Deaver wasn't doing an adequate job of dealing with such sensitive women's issues as "child care for working mothers, equal pay for equal work, equal pension benefits, availability of credit, and enforcement of civil-rights statutes." She told her father, "When a woman is discriminated against, her children are discriminated against, her husband is discriminated against, her community is discriminated against."[17]

At that time Reagan had two women in the cabinet (Margaret M. Heckler, secretary of health and human services, and Elizabeth H. Dole, secretary of transportation), and one woman, Sandra Day O'Connor, sat on the Supreme Court. Reagan listened attentively to Maureen's suggestions. He was well aware that he was plagued by a gender gap and that a recent Gallop poll showed that fifty-seven percent of all men endorsed his performance, but only thirty-nine percent of women. Maureen suggested they might start by planning a Susan B. Anthony celebration in the early months of his campaign. She was given an office with the National Republican Committee and "began shuttling back and forth from Los Angeles to [her] temporary quarters in the Lincoln Bedroom of the White House," Maureen recalled.[18]

Reagan was facing a multitude of problems other than reelection. American, British, French, and Italian peacekeeping forces had been sent to Beirut, Lebanon, following a harrowing massacre of hundreds of Palestinians in two refugee camps, which the PLO attributed to the Israelis, who adamantly denied any knowledge or participation. Islamic Jihad struck back at the peacekeeping forces with suicide bombings that killed 220 American marines and another 21 other service personnel. Reagan had to make a difficult decision. He withdrew American forces from Lebanon, eliciting strongly mixed feelings from our allies and from voters about to make up their minds as to whether they wished to have Reagan in the White House for another four years, at the end of which he would be seventy-seven years old.

Iran's sporadic war with Iraq had also gained momentum, as had covert funding of the Nicaraguan-based CIA army known as the Contras. These two complex situations would become almost inconceivably entwined and would ultimately produce a crisis for Reagan's presidency. But as he swung into campaign mode, he did not anticipate such a result. His mantra had always been to fight Communism, and that was exactly what he believed his administration and the CIA were doing. In fact, the CIA was raising cash for secret illicit operations—to buy arms for rebel forces fighting against the left-wing Sandinista government of Nicaragua and then to sell arms to Iran. This was accomplished through illegal weapons deals, narcotics smuggling, and money laundering, all in the name of fighting Communism. The clandestine operations exploded into scandal two years later. But in 1984 Reagan knew about the operation, as did the highest members of his administration, and most of them became silent or active coconspirators. The exceptions were Secretary of State George Shultz and Secretary of Defense Caspar Weinberger. (Weinberger would later go along, leaving Shultz as the sole dissenter.)

The president had come in for his share of condemnation as early as April 10, 1984, when Congress rebuked him for using federal funds to mine Nicaraguan harbors. He battled Congress all through the year, intensifying his efforts not to abandon "the Nicaraguan freedom fighters," as he called them. "I felt we had to do everything we legally could to keep the force in existence. I told the staff: We can't break the law, but, within the law, we have do whatever we can to help the Contras survive." He was, he told America's allies, "fighting for the survival of democracy."[19] Throughout the future investigations he would claim that he was never aware of any covert operations or illegal activities.

"As president, I was at the helm, so I am the one who is ultimately responsible. But . . . Central America was only one of many things that occupied me at the time. Besides trying to end the recession, we were working on modernization of our military forces, trying to get a new nuclear arms reduction initiative off the ground, trying to cut federal spending, trying to end the fighting in Lebanon and the Middle East— and many other things were on my plate as well, [winning reelection certainly being one of them]. A president simply cannot monitor the day-to-day conduct of all his subordinates. . . . had I attempted to involve myself in the details of the [Nicaraguan situation], I would have been unable to attend to the other wide-ranging issues before me at the time."[20] With or without true knowledge of the CIA's Central America activities, which included condoning drug smuggling as a means to supply funds to the rebel forces, by his silence Reagan made a farce of his own vitriolic feelings about drugs and of Nancy's Just Say No campaign.

The distinguished American historian Barbara W. Tuchman once wrote, "For the chief of state under modern conditions, a limiting factor is too many subjects and problems in too many areas of government to allow solid understanding of any of them, and too little time to think between fifteen-minute appointments and thirty-page briefs. This leaves the field open to protective stupidity."[21] At election time voters go to the polls with the eternal hope that the man or woman of their choice will be endowed with a high degree of moral courage, which Montaigne described as being "not that which is sharpened by ambition but that which wisdom and reason may implant in a well-ordered soul." In 1984 Reagan was guided by Potomac fever—understood better, perhaps, as the lure of high office, of reelection, at a time when a candidate, even an incumbent, has to please as many and offend as few supporters as possible. Ambition for a second term controlled many of his reactions and took up much space in his thoughts. Perhaps Nancy had been right in wanting him to quit while, as she saw it, he was still ahead. But Reagan had finally been recruited by the arrogance of power and a belief that he alone could save the world from the Evil Empire.

Once having agreed with Reagan's decision to run again, Nancy threw herself wholeheartedly into the campaign that Stuart Spencer was managing. There were those on the team who thought Nancy should keep a low profile. Spencer was not one of them. "Nancy has very good political instincts," he explained. "In the latter part of '83 and the early part of '84, she reviewed with me at length how she viewed the potential Democratic contenders, and gave me as good and helpful and clear an analysis of [Walter] Mondale [vice president under Carter], [Senator

John] Glenn, and [Senator Gary] Hart as any of the political so-called pros. In fact, her judgment and her instincts in some ways were even more closely attuned to what the realities turned out to be than some of those who are paid for their political judgment.

"In October, 1983, she felt that Glenn would not get the nomination, and she . . . tagged Hart who could give Mondale a run for his money. She felt that Mondale would likely be the opponent. She believed his biggest vulnerability was his tendency, his penchant to attack, and do it in a way that would alienate rather than gain support. She was right on target on that particular judgment. . . . [She's] a realist and she's also very willing to make some tough decisions on personnel. . . . She [also] has a good deal of sensitivity about communicating messages."

Reagan, of course, was known as the Great Communicator. But it was Nancy who had a handle on "what kinds of messages can be communicated clearly and which cannot," Spencer added.[22]

Despite Reagan's declaration that the office sought the man, not the other way around, it was clear to Nancy, as well as to Spencer and others close to the president, that he had wanted the office since his first term as governor of California. He had gone after the presidency from the moment he realized he might have a strong chance of getting it, and when he failed, he went out and tried again. Now a septuagenarian, he would have found the campaign trail harder even had he not faced the day-to-day pressures of the office. Nancy was often accused of wanting the presidency for him more than he did. Her pat answer was "I married an actor. . . . And when the governorship came along, I went along with it. But that wasn't something I had carved out for our future."

The night that Reagan announced over national television that he had decided to run, Nancy wrote in her diary: "I think it's going to be a tough, personal, close campaign. Mondale is supposed to be an infighter. . . . Ronnie is so popular that they [Mondale's campaign team] might be desperate. I'll be glad when the next nine months are over."[23] More was demanded of Nancy during this campaign than ever before, as Reagan could not spend as much time on the campaign trail. She traveled the country on Air Force One with Stu Spencer and the staff, speaking at women's clubs and fund-raisers, hospitals and Young Republican organizations. She became pretty expert at bowling with oranges during takeoffs as Willie Nelson's "On the Road Again" played over the plane's public address system. She made notes on everything and kept in close touch with Reagan's political adviser, Ed Rollins.

"She was very concerned [in California] . . . that the people out there were probably not being as effective as they could have been and that Mondale was making a very heavy effort in the state, and she wanted to make sure that we were alert to it," Rollins recalled, remembering as well that he immediately went out and "rechecked everything again and made a few changes."[24]

A strong anti-Reagan feeling was rampant among Hollywood liberals. A Democratic organizing committee was formed by Andy Spahn, Jane Fonda, and her then-husband, Tom Hayden, with funds provided by the Democratic National Committee and the senatorial and congressional Democratic committees. Over fifty celebrities were organized into a group called the Democratic Entertainment Industry Project and went to work actively raising funds and speaking out in support of Mondale.

As summer approached, bringing with it the two political conventions that would decide the final candidates, Mondale became the opponent who would face Reagan and Bush in the election, but it was still not known who he would choose for vice president. Maureen reiterated Nancy's sense that Mondale's desperation to win could cause him to team up with someone unexpected, perhaps Jesse Jackson, whose chances had been crushed early in the presidential race. It was believed that Jackson would bring in the black vote but might prove a liability otherwise. Mondale, twenty-two years Reagan's junior, was a crafty politician, well seasoned for his years. A liberal Democrat from Minnesota, protégé of former vice president Hubert Humphrey, Mondale had been Carter's vice president and two-time running mate. He was an attractive, knowledgeable candidate and a good debater, and he was being handled by an excellent team who had brought him through the primaries unscathed. He was the indisputable leader.

Michael Reagan was not working in this campaign. Now the father of the Reagans' first granddaughter, eighteen-month-old Ashley (whom they had yet to see), Michael was devoting his time to selling boats to increase his growing family's income. Ron had abandoned his career in ballet and was working as a journalist for a Dallas newspaper. Patti, of course, had never been one of her father's supporters; her political alliances were far, *far* to the left of his policies. She was also seriously in love with Paul Grilley, her yoga instructor. In early May she called her mother to announce their intention to marry. To Nancy's surprise, she requested a traditional wedding.

Before she met Grilley, a young man who was into both yoga and spirituality, Patti wrote that she felt her life was "slipping in ways" that made her nervous. "The man I was seeing liked life in the fast lane— late-night parties, coke," and she found herself in the passenger seat.[25] At the age of thirty-one she was also broke, with few acting or modeling jobs on the horizon. Her final humiliation, as she had never been able to approach her parents for money, came when she had to ask to borrow $5,000 from her father to meet current debts and living expenses, and was required to sign a note, proffered by a lawyer, to repay the loan in monthly installments (a manageable amount of $25 until she could afford a larger figure).

Even though the Reagans were not exactly thrilled by Patti's choice of a husband, they were relieved that she was getting married to a young man who seemed to be stable. Patti's monthly loan payments were not canceled, but her parents happily took on the responsibility of giving their daughter a lovely wedding. Despite the pressures of the campaign, Nancy took over and made all the plans.

The détente between Patti and her parents would not last more than a few months. At the same time the Reagans were not on speaking terms with Michael, who had been quoted in *Redbook* magazine as repeating some of his past unpleasant epithets about them. Nancy was deeply hurt. She saw the children as being more to blame for their problems than their parents, who had paid for their care and education.

A new twist was added to the campaign when Mondale chose a congresswoman from New York, Geraldine A. Ferraro, as his running mate at the Democratic National Convention in San Francisco on July 19. The following month the Republican convention in Dallas, although lacking in suspense, gave rousing cheers to the Reagan-Bush reelection ticket.

Despite early enthusiasm by women's groups, Ferraro's candidacy did not energize Mondale's campaign in the way that he and his team had imagined it would. Perhaps Ferraro was the wrong woman, one not well known enough or from the wrong sector of the country. Or maybe, the country, still struggling with the issues of the Equal Rights Amendment and abortion rights, was not yet ready. By September, the election less than eight weeks away, the Reagan-Bush ticket looked like a sure winner. Then, on October 7 in Louisville, Kentucky, came the first debate between Mondale and Reagan.

Giving a stirring speech is one thing—and Reagan was a master—but four years had passed since he had debated Carter. For weeks Mondale had been primed to "combine aggressiveness with occasional expressions of deference to Reagan and his office—sort of the way one might treat a valued uncle who was no longer up to the job," Lou Cannon suggested.[26] Mondale sought to throw Reagan off stride, and he succeeded. The president had come prepared with a head full of figures intending to show Mondale up as being ill-informed. This backfired, as Mondale strode out belligerently onto the podium and began his opening remarks by first attacking the Republican record and then battered away at the president's "age problem."

"Right from the start," Nancy remembered bitterly, Reagan "was tense, muddled, and off-stride. He lacked authority. He stumbled. This was a Ronald Reagan I had never seen before. It was painful to watch. There was no way around it; that debate was a nightmare." Later, Reagan confessed to Nancy that the debate had been a disaster, that he had been "terrible." She consoled him, but both of them were too politically astute not to see the facts as they were. He had lost the debate, and his rattled demeanor had been harmful to his image.

Reagan was better prepared for the second, and last, debate in Kansas City on October 21. Nancy had insisted that the team let "Ronnie be Ronnie" this time around. The format was that each candidate would have a limited period of time to respond to questions posed by a group of noted political journalists. Only moments after the debate began,

Henry Trewhitt of the *Baltimore Sun* asked Reagan about the age factor. "Well," Reagan replied in an unscripted riposte, "I will not make age an issue in this campaign." He paused knowingly, the wry smile, the famous Reagan arched eyebrow. "I am not going to exploit, for political purposes, my opponent's youth and inexperience." Reagan relaxed. Mondale tensed. The audience laughed. And from that moment the debate—and the election—was won by the president.[27]

CHAPTER SEVENTEEN

FACING THE DEMONS

The Reagans' traditional election-eve festivities were held at the Beverly Hills home of Earle and Marion Jorgensen in Beverly Hills, where Reagan received a call from Mondale conceding the race. The next morning, a warm winter sun streaming through the windows of their car, the Reagans headed for their beloved Rancho del Cielo. He had won forty-nine states and fifty-nine percent of the vote, but was concerned about Nancy, who had taken a nasty fall a few days earlier, missing a platform step that surrounded their elevated, four-poster-bed in the Red Lion Inn in Sacramento, where they had appeared at a rally. Still bruised and stiff, she welcomed the three days of relaxation. Reagan rode happily every morning and split wood from downed oak trees in the afternoon. He viewed the landslide victory as approbation of his first term and a mandate to continue the things he had set in motion. Nancy immediately began to plan for the second inaugural and called Joan Quigley, her astrologer for the past three years, at her home in San Francisco.

Nancy had long held a belief in astrology, with which Edith had also dabbled. As early as Reagan's first inauguration as governor Nancy had consulted various practitioners of the science at times of crisis or impending major events. But in the days following the assassination attempt, she had been overwhelmed with fear for Ronnie's safety and shaken by the thought that if he died she would not be able to cope on her own. She resorted to nerve-calming medication to see her through the initial emotional impact, but it had not been enough to quell all of her fears. Astrology had worked for her in the past, and so she turned to it once again.

Her first contact with Quigley had taken place in the summer of 1973, a particularly difficult time for Reagan in the governing of California, where he fought a deep recession, and for Nancy in her fractious relationships with the four Reagan children and in growing problems with her public image. One of Nancy's closest friends, Merv Griffin, who was then a successful television talk-show host, shared Nancy's birthday, July 6. Quigley had become a frequent guest on his show, and Merv, who consulted her personally, believed in the astrologer's ability to chart a safer, more rewarding life with the stars as a guide. He suggested that Nancy call her.

The telephone was Nancy's favored means of communication. She prided herself on being able to tell a lot about a person by their voice and vocal reactions. The telephone also enabled her to discuss intimate and private matters more easily. Daily telephone calls to her friends lasting one hour, or even longer, were not unusual. From her initial contact with Quigley, Nancy felt a natural empathy. As they spoke at length, Nancy confided to the astrologer some of her most personal concerns and gave her the full information she needed to draw up her horoscope. The next time they spoke, Quigley told Nancy that she had not seen "so superlative a stellium since Jackie's [Kennedy]," and explained that a "stellium was a collection of planets in the same signs, or adjacent signs, very close together."[1] She would be internationally known, a power figure, a great hostess. Quigley also devoted much time to listening to Nancy's problems. On their next call she would have answers, and apparently they were what Nancy wanted to hear. She was hooked.

Reagan never personally consulted Quigley. She prepared his horoscope from the information provided by Nancy. (He would, in fact, meet the astrologer only once, and in a cursory manner, in a reception line where he whispered a few words of appreciation to her, Quigley reported.) For the next few years, Nancy called Quigley two or three times a year for an update and consultation. They met for the first time, in 1976, at a San Francisco fund-raiser, a public meeting, lasting no more than a few minutes. Quigley was a handsome, well-groomed blonde, hair lacquered in perfect waves, makeup carefully applied, nails impeccably manicured. She possessed a melodious voice and a gracious manner. In her several television appearances with Merv, she never seemed to be at a loss for words and had the ability to pick up immediately on any opportunity to air her views.

In the early summer of 1981, shortly before she flew to England to attend the wedding of Prince Charles and Lady Diana Spencer, Nancy entered into a far more intense arrangement with Quigley in which the consultations could be increased a hundredfold to daily sessions if necessary. Knowing that public knowledge of her reliance on astrology for both herself and the president might draw strong criticism, Nancy devised a plan to conceal her affiliation with Quigley. First, there was the matter of charges and billing. Nancy initially felt that she was such an important client that Quigley should waive her fee. Quigley refused to do so but said she would charge Nancy less than her other clients.

"Nancy always seemed pinched for money," Quigley remarked.[2] Mary Jane Wick was chosen as their intermediary. The bills, which amounted to many thousands of dollars a year, were sent to Wick. Nancy in turn forwarded her personal checks (written and sent without the help or knowledge of her staff) to Mary Jane, who deposited them to her account and then paid Quigley with her own check. Calls, too, often were routed through Wick when, Quigley says, "I needed to get back to [Nancy] at a time not scheduled at the end of our most recent [consultation]. Later, my liaison was Betsy Bloomingdale. Once in a while, I called Elaine Crispin, Nancy's social secretary [in the late eighties], at the White House."[3] More often, Nancy telephoned Quigley daily and often on weekends when the Reagans were at Camp David or Rancho del Cielo.

These frequent astrological consultations had transmuted from agreeable dates for the Reagans' individual and dual schedules to more involved concerns. Nancy was now frantic to find a way to improve her image. Quigley states that she was central in the decision the First Lady made to inaugurate her Just Say No campaign to create a more caring, softer public face, Quigley also claims that she advised Nancy to arrange photo sessions hugging an "endangered" child and to visit hospitals and schools to further enhance this image. Nancy's judgments on the performance of Reagan's staff members were now based in great part on Quigley's astrological work, which grew to include charting the best times for Reagan's speeches and "the hour and minute of his departure on Air Force One." Quigley later boldly professed that she "wielded considerable influence in the creation of major U.S. policy, [the various summits] . . . and the President's historical shift from viewing Russia as the Evil Empire."[4]

Reagan knew Nancy was talking with an astrologer and would inquire, "What does Joan say?" There is every evidence that he took seriously the advice Quigley passed on to him via Nancy and did not dismiss astrology as a science. Quigley's counsel seemed to meet with a fairly high rate of success. While she may have been wrong in briefing him on the date of that almost disastrous first debate with Mondale, he had made several hundred flights on Air Force One without incident, there had been no further assassination attempts, and his "numbers" were moving upward in the polls. Obviously, however, there is no way to prove that these results might not have been the same without Quigley's computations.

Except for Michael Deaver and his assistant, William Sittman, Nancy's astrological consultations were concealed from everyone at the White House, including the Secret Service, who apparently believed Quigley was just another of the First Lady's telephone buddies. (Later, Donald Regan, who made the switch from secretary of the treasury to Reagan's chief of staff, was taken into Nancy's confidence on this matter.) The president was not aware of the multiplicity or depth of the consultations, nor of the lengthy telephone conversations Nancy devoted to the scheduling and rescheduling of events to comply as best she could with Quigley's advice.

"What a shock it must have been to the agents," Donald Regan later wrote, "who so carefully guarded the President, to learn [later] that a total stranger—to them—knew not only intimate details of presidential movements, but could actually set the time of these movements! Surely they would think that posed a security risk."[5] This obviously did not occur to Nancy, or if it did, she quickly brushed the idea aside. For all she knew, the astrologer could well have been conspiring to place the president in harm's way. But she trusted Quigley's integrity, and that seemed to be all that was necessary. Curiously, according to Quigley, once Nancy was first lady, her questions and queries for help never involved family problems, such as her relationship with the children. Her only interests were in her image, Reagan's health, his place in history, and ferreting out those people or elements that could be detrimental to these aims.

As the second inauguration drew close, Nancy consulted Quigley about the most beneficial time for Reagan to take his vows. There was little leeway in this, as the government sets noon (or a few minutes before or after) on January 20 as the time for a new or an incumbent president to be inaugurated. Quigley chose three minutes to noon. Even so, she forecast "trouble ahead," adding the balm that Reagan would leave office as one of the most successful presidents ever; like fellow presidential Aquarians Lincoln and Franklin Roosevelt, he would retain the public's esteem in history.

Washington, D.C., was bitter cold, with heavy snow on the ground, when Reagan and Bush took their oaths of office in the crowded rotunda of the Capitol, the weather disallowing an outdoor venue. Only ninety members of Congress, the Cabinet, and the Reagan and Bush families were able to attend. Bleachers on Pennsylvania Avenue stood empty, crusted with ice. Most outdoor activities had been canceled because of a predicted chill factor of twenty degrees below zero, along with warnings that exposed skin could experience severe frostbite within fifteen seconds. Earlier in the day, Reagan and his grandson, Cameron, wearing layers of clothes beneath their outer garments, braved the freezing weather to pose briefly for photographers on the White House lawn building a snowman, while in the family quarters there was a gathering of the Reagan clan. This was a reconciliatory visit with Michael and Colleen, the first time that the Reagans had seen Cameron's entrancing toddler sister, Ashley. Michael Deaver and the press staff had encouraged a détente believing—rightly, perhaps—that the nation wanted to embrace Reagan as a father figure. Michael and Colleen were only too happy to oblige. Patti was not so enthusiastic when asked to attend the ceremony but had grudgingly agreed. The only missing members were Edith, who was too frail to travel, and Patti's husband, Paul Grilley, his reasons not fully explained. ("Surely he could have taken one day away from work to see his father-in-law inaugurated as president!" Nancy complained.)[6]

The guest bedrooms in the White House were completely filled. It seemed a time for celebration. Reagan's first term had ended with the economy on the upsurge, inflation reduced along with unemployment. Abroad, 1,900 American forces, along with a small military presence from nearby islands, had succeeded in eliminating Soviet and Cuban influence in Grenada, and the *Challenger* had made a successful maiden voyage, which included the first U.S. space walk in nine years. A new sense of pride and patriotism was sweeping across America. And in the Reagan family, during these chilly days in January 1985, with the patriarch riding high, there was harmony. It did not last long.

Shortly after the inauguration Patti signed a book contract for an autobiographical novel about a woman growing up as the daughter of a governor of California who becomes president of the United States. The novel would be written with the help of Maureen Strange Foster, a fiction writer who lived in Los Angeles. The publishing effort was to serve several purposes for Patti: to prove she had a talent to write, to raise needed money, and to be able to express (under the guise of fiction) the way she felt her parents had failed her. She did not tell her parents about the novel.

When *Home Front* appeared in the spring of 1986, Nancy was aghast. The Reagans had only learned about it a short time before its publication and had assumed it contained no autobiographical references or incidents. To her shock, Nancy later wrote, it painted a bitter, "thinly disguised, self-pitying" picture of Patti's relationship with her parents, and she was of the opinion that Patti's publishers would never have considered contracting the book, which portrayed the fictionalized Reagans as a seriously dysfunctional family, if it had not been written by the daughter of the president, who, with members of the family, had been made easy enough to identify.[7]

When asked in a press conference about the book, Reagan said simply, "It's fiction." But *Home Front* contains too many personal details and descriptions of the Reagans to be accepted as pure fiction. The Reagans, especially Nancy, whose portrait was the most unsympathetic, were pained by its publication. Nancy considered it a great betrayal on Patti's part, written mainly for financial gain. Silence was chosen by the Reagans as the only course to follow. Neither parent contacted Patti. She had been waiting expectantly for a call, and when this did not occur, she telephoned her brother to convey her disappointment.

"I don't think you should expect kudos from anyone," Ron snapped. He, too, was portrayed in an unflattering way in *Home Front.* "You've trashed our folks."[8] Patti slammed down the telephone in response. It would be years before the two would speak again.

To intensify the anger of all involved, her publisher sent Patti out on a national book tour. She appeared on some of the most viewed talk shows in the country (not Merv Griffin's, however), where she admitted only a slight autobiographical nature to the book. "After all, being the daughter of a governor with presidential expectations was what I knew to write about," she told an NBC talk show host. Reviewers found *Home Front* lacking as literature, mean-spirited, and not shocking enough to be worth all the fuss made over it. Nonetheless, it sold well, and Patti Davis (who had chosen to use her mother's maiden name) became an infamous figure. Many thought her an ungrateful, privileged young woman who had besmirched the president they had come to regard as embodying the American spirit. By 2002 Patti Davis had written numerous other books, as well as essays published in the *Los Angeles Times* and various magazines. Once on her own, without a coauthor, her style improved. She continued to use her life and that of her parents as material. She also published an autobiography, *The Way I See It*, that contained far more condemnatory portraits of the Reagans as parents then had the novel, but it also contained important insights into the Reagan family structure.

Reagan was considered now to be "the Great Communicator," and a good part of that was traceable to his raising Americans' pride in their land. It had eroded under the impact of Vietnam and Watergate. He accomplished it through patriotic speeches, and in his second inaugural address, delivered inside the Capitol: "Now we're standing inside this symbol of our democracy, and we see and hear again the echoes of our past. A general falls to his knees in the hard snow of Valley Forge; a lonely President paces the darkened halls and ponders his struggle to preserve the Union; the men of the Alamo call out encouragement to each other; a settler pushes west and sings a song, and the song echoes out forever and fills the unknowing air. It is the American sound. It is hopeful, bighearted, idealistic, daring, decent, and fair. That's our heritage. That's our song."[9]

Bill Thompson and his wife, Jean, were among the privileged few who attended the second inauguration. "Dutch called us on the telephone to invite us," Thompson recalled. "Then he sent us an invitation that was marked 'Friends of the Family.' He called again and asked what events or activities we wished to attend. The White House sent us a list and we marked off the ones we thought we would like the best. We had reserved parking and a police escort. We felt like celebrities."[10]

On February 12, 1985, Reagan wrote on White House stationery: "Dear Jean and Bill: It was good to hear that you had a good time at our 'option renewal' ceremonies. I'm glad we at least could say a hello but sorry there was no time for a visit. We really were on a fast track." The letter ended with regards to several friends in Dixon and was signed "Sincerely, Dutch."[11]

Reagan's second term started off well enough. His rating was at its peak at eighty-five percent after twenty-five consecutive months of economic growth. Secretary of State George Shultz had just reached a new agreement on arms reduction with the seventy-six-year-old Soviet foreign minister Andrei Gromyko in a ninety-minute meeting in Geneva. More pertinent to Nancy was the renewed strength she had observed in Ronnie's health. But immediately following the election, he began to tire easily, and there was a certain listlessness in his demeanor. She prodded him to submit to a full medical check-up. On Friday, March 8, he dutifully went through a series of routine tests at Bethesda Naval Hospital which included a colonoscopy. Monday morning brought the news that for the third time in two-and-a-half years a Soviet leader, Konstantin

Chernenko, the successor to Leonid Brezhnev and Yuri Andropov, had died. The new leader, Mikhail Gorbachev, at fifty-four, was the youngest man since Stalin to take charge in Moscow. He appeared to have been handpicked for the job by Chernenko, who warned those who might think his comparative youth and his pleasant manner signaled détente with the West, "Comrades, this man has a nice smile but he's got iron teeth."

"How can I be expected to keep peace with them if they keep dying on me?" Edmund Morris claims Reagan commented.[12]

Shultz urged Reagan to attend the funeral in Moscow later that week. Reagan refused (Bush was sent as his representative), but consented to go to the Soviet embassy to sign the condolence book. Upon his return to the White House, he was informed that the colonoscopy indicated that he had an "inflammatory pseudopolyp" in his colon. A few days later, after further tests, the polyp was found to be benign. A cautious medical team insisted he be checked again in a few months. He laughed off Nancy's concern. "I've got twenty years on those guys [the doctors] and I'm in better health than any of them."

Plans were being readied for the Reagans to fly to Germany to attend the Bonn economic summit scheduled for early May. As part of his state visit to Germany, to mark the anniversary of the end of World War II and "the beginning of forty years of peace and friendship between two former enemies," he was to lay a wreath on a monument to the dead at the military cemetery in Bitburg and to stop at Bergen-Belsen, the site of a horrifying Nazi concentration camp where thousands had died, half of whom were Jewish.[13] These events were arranged to enhance the image of Chancellor Helmut Kohl, whose government was in danger of collapsing. It was important to the United States that Kohl was committed to allowing U.S. missiles to be based in Germany. Lou Cannon writes that Reagan's agreement to speak at Bergen-Belsen "was in political compensation for his participation the same day" at the ceremony at the German military cemetery near Bitburg. Reagan had deep feelings about the Holocaust and had great trouble returning to "the scenes where this crime of crimes had been committed." But Shultz was adamant that if he went to Bitburg "where forty-nine members of the SS were buried amidst two thousand German soldiers," he had to view Bergen-Belsen.[14]

Shultz pressed on, and finally the visits were arranged and announced. Four hundred members of the House and fifty-four senators called on Reagan to cancel the visit to Bitburg. There was a great outcry and protest by Jews in America and in Israel, led by Elie Wiesel, the Romanian-born writer and lecturer, who would be awarded the Nobel Prize for Peace in 1986. Two days before their planned departure, Reagan called Kohl and asked him to arrange an alternative to Bitburg. Kohl refused on the grounds that it would make him look like a puppet of the United States.

Nancy was furious at Kohl and at Elie Wiesel, who she thought was creating a hostile atmosphere, and jittery about the upcoming events. With only a few days to go until their departure, she called Joan Quigley to chart the best time for each event. Quigley came back with 11:45 A.M. for Bergen-Belsen and 2:45 P.M. for Bitburg. Mike Deaver went ballistic when Nancy informed him of this. It was impossible. An hour-long picnic lunch with Bitburg villagers had been arranged and would conflict with that timing. Nancy put Deaver on the telephone with Quigley. He insisted the events had to be at the times already scheduled. She retorted that he would have to reschedule them for her chosen times. In Quigley's version of the events, she took on a self-appointed role as a political adviser.

"I said [the picnic at Bitburg] was absolutely out of the question as it made Bitburg far too important and called attention to something I felt should be glossed over [that the American president was laying a wreath in a cemetery where members of the SS were buried]" Quigley claims. "Mike was so eager to get out of the mess he was in, he was willing to do anything I said. I told him that the picnic had to be cancelled. [In truth, Deaver, a nonbeliever in astrology, intensely disliked Quigley and referred to her out of Nancy's hearing as Madame Zorba.] I suggested that the Reagans' plane fly around in circles as long as it had to in order to land at Bitburg at my chosen time." Quigley further claims that Deaver did as she demanded. "The Bitburg visit was brief and the controversy soon died down. I had diffused Bitburg for all intents and purposes. Kohl was re-elected and the missiles were installed in Germany," she boasts.[15]

Deaver confided later to Lou Cannon that Quigley's demands, sanctioned by the first lady, created an intolerable burden on him. "All of a sudden we would have to change our schedules at the eleventh hour. We couldn't fly at night. We couldn't fly on a Monday." He would have to try to invent "rational reasons for irrational changes in the schedule, explanations that most who heard them found singularly unconvincing." After a while he "stopped trying to explain the changes and refused to answer any questions about them.... People would come in with perfectly reasonable ideas, and I would say to them, 'That's crazy, are you out of your mind?' I couldn't talk about why we were doing what we were doing, so I insulted people. I'm not proud of it, but that's what I did."[16]

There is no record of Air Force One circling over Bitburg for an hour. Nancy does say they were there for only a few minutes while Reagan laid the wreath. The Reagans stood in the freezing cold—a sharp wind blowing Nancy's usually disciplined hair across her face— the American president, red-cheeked and grim-faced, paid homage to the dead of all nations who had fought in the war for the world's survival. Standing by their side was ninety-year-old General Matthew Ridgway, commander of the U.S. 82d Airborne Division during World War II. His participation, a brainstorm of Deaver's, diminished some of the public's and Reagan's own distaste at the thought of an American president laying a wreath near Nazi graves.

There was a moment earlier that day, at the site of the former Bergen-Belsen concentration camp, when Reagan appeared almost Lincolnesque. He had just gone through the small museum with enlarged photographs of the horrors committed there, and "walked past the mounds planted with heather each being a mass grave for 5000 or more people, largely Jews but also many Christians, a number of Catholic priests and gypsies who had been slaughtered there or who were just starved to death."[17] As one watched the moment caught on television, there was a far-off tortured look in his eyes that conjured the image of honest Abe staring across the battlefield at Gettysburg where thousands of America's brave men had been slain. "Here lie people—Jews—whose death was inflicted for no other reason than their very existence. Here—death ruled," Reagan solemnly intoned.

It was a great and moving commemorative speech. He read a short passage from the diary of Anne Frank, the young Jewish girl forced to hide in a concealed attic room with her family to avoid being taken by the Nazis to a death camp, a fate, in the end she did not escape. Then he raised his eyes from the text before him and, in a voice much touched by emotion, continued:

> Everywhere here are memories—pulling us, touching us, making us understand that they can never be erased. Such memories take us where God intended His children to go—toward learning, toward healing, and above all, toward redemption. They beckon us through the endless stretches of our heart to the knowing commitment that the life of each individual can change the world and make it better.
>
> We're all witnesses; we share the glistening hope that rests in every human soul. Hope leads us, if we're prepared to trust it, toward what our President Lincoln called the better angels of our nature. And then, rising above all this tragic and nightmarish time, beyond the anguish, the pain, the suffering for all time, we can and must pledge: Never again.[18]

An aura surrounded Reagan as he braced himself against the cold wind. He seemed every inch a man capable of heading the free world, of possibly one day achieving a mantle of greatness. One could hope for that, at least. Against such a bleak background of inhumanity, hope for mankind seemed a much-needed emotion. As he turned away and started back to his car, he appeared shaken. He put his arm around Nancy, each seemed to be supporting the other.

Air Force One brought the Reagans home on May 9. That Sunday, the eleventh, was Mother's Day, and Reagan gave what had become an annual radio address on that occasion. After a long, moving tribute to Nelle, he closed with "She was the greatest influence on my life, and as I think of her this weekend I remember the words of Lincoln, 'All that I am, or hope to be, I owe to my mother'."[19]

On July 12 Reagan went as scheduled to Bethesda Naval Hospital to have the benign polyp found in March removed. The forty-five-minute procedure was believed to be routine. Reagan requested that he not be given an anesthetic in order to avoid having to transfer power to Vice President Bush. Reagan would then rest for two or three hours before going home. Having been assured there was no reason for concern, Nancy was relaxed as she waited with Larry Speakes for him to be taken to his room. When she joined him he was in his usual good humor, spouting hospital jokes. She was about to sit down beside his bed, when the doctors asked if they could have a word with her outside. Once she was in another room and surrounded by a team of white-jacketed medics, she was told that a "large suspicious mass, the size of a golfball had been found on the lower right side of [the President's] colon, where it goes into the intestines. Although they weren't sure it was malignant, they thought it probably was. At best," they confessed, "it was precancerous."

The growth had to be removed. Their recommendation was that the president remain at Bethesda and have the surgery the following morning. Once Nancy overcame the immediate shock of this unexpected news, she asked the doctors not to use the C word when they spoke to Ronnie. After all, they were not sure it was cancer, and it seemed wiser to wait until they had more information. She also insisted she be the one to go in and tell him that he had, once again, to face surgery. They agreed to both her requests. She walked back into the room by herself, sat down on the bed, and put her arms around him. When she told him about the impending need for surgery, she disguised the truth by saying that the polyp that was found was too large to be removed during the colonoscopy, especially without anesthesia.

"Let's get it done," he agreed. Then, with a small grin, he asked, "Does this mean I won't be getting dinner tonight, either?" He had not been allowed food for sixteen hours before the colonoscopy.[20]

At 10:30 A.M. the following morning, a half hour before Reagan was to go under the knife, Fred Fielding, the White House counsel, had him sign the papers authorizing the vice president to act in his name for the next eight hours. The documents were immediately delivered into the hands of Speaker of the House Tip O'Neill and to Strom Thurmond, president pro tempore of the Senate. Nancy states unequivocally that she did not consult Quigley on the timing of this, a crucial event in Reagan's life. Donald Regan's memoir, however, gives credence to Quigley's claim that she "delayed President Reagan's first operation for cancer from July 10 to July 13."[21] (She also claims to have done the same for future surgery.) The facts do not support her assertion. Reagan checked into the hospital on Friday, July 12, with no idea that he would have to undergo surgery, which ultimately took place on July 13. Nancy had not lost faith in Quigley, but there was an urgency to the operation and a surgeon's schedule cannot be rearranged in accordance with someone's whim.

At seven o'clock on Saturday evening, while Reagan was in recovery, Fielding returned with the paper for him to sign to take back his power as President. This was a weekend and George Bush had not had any official duties to perform in the brief period when he was technically in charge of the executive branch.

Reagan's first few postoperative days were difficult. The growth had been malignant. The surrounding area had to be cleaned and a large section of intestine removed, leaving him in a good deal of pain. Nancy spent as much time as she could with him at the hospital, but she also took over some appearances that he was originally scheduled to make, including a short speech before a concert on the White House Lawn to celebrate the Boston Pops' hundredth anniversary. She decorated his room with family photographs and other personal items that she thought might cheer him up. He worked two or three hours a day from his hospital bed, reading reports and signing papers. He did his lung exercises religiously and walked around his room and the adjoining area as much as the medical staff would let him. He was determined to be back in the White House for a scheduled meeting with President Xiannian Li of China on July 23.

The Chinese president was frail and himself in poor health, but Reagan—only ten days removed from major surgery—greeted Li at the White House and helped him up the steps to the room where they were to appear together for the press. Reagan managed to stay throughout the state dinner for President and Madame Li that evening but had to excuse himself before the entertainment as the strain of the day had finally taken its toll on him. On July 31 the doctors noted that a mole on Reagan's nose that had been there for years was inflamed. They removed it. A biopsy proved it to be malignant. It was a low-level carcinoma, not as serious as the first cancer, and the doctors were certain that they had gotten all of it as well.

Reagan explained in *An American Life*, "It was a result of a lifetime spent outdoors. From the day I started those summers working as a lifeguard, I'd enjoyed being outside and getting a tan. I tanned easily and seldom got sunburned. When I got into pictures I *had* to stay tanned." He was warned by the doctors that he would have to wear a hat and covering clothes when out in the sun from this time forward. "First I have to give up popcorn [because of the intestinal surgery] and now sunbathing," he complained in his diary on August 5, 1985.[22]

In mid-August the Reagans flew to California for a three-week hiatus at Rancho del Cielo. He could fully recuperate there. They had always looked forward to the privacy the mountaintop ranch gave them, but on their first night they turned on the television to see pictures of themselves walking about the grounds. Photographers had learned how to approach the mountain from the opposite side, and from its top, just beyond the Reagans' boundaries, plant a zoom camera that looked down on the grounds. From that vantage point they were able to photograph them quite clearly. At first Nancy was furious. Then she took a large board and wrote on it with bright red paint JUST SAY NO and held it up toward the intrusive camera, a wide grin on her face.

To add to the stress of this time in Nancy's life was the departure from the White House of Mike Deaver, Reagan's trusted aide and Nancy's steadfast friend. Deaver found himself running on a treadmill, his private life and health suffering and his use of alcohol spiraling down into serious abuse and addiction. Shortly after the inauguration, he had told Nancy of his intention to leave and of plans to open a private public relations practice. She implored him to remain at least until after the Bitburg trip in May. He agreed. On their return from Germany he departed as planned. The Reagans were not aware of his drinking problems at the time. His health—he had a heart condition being treated with beta blockers—had been stressed, and Nancy agreed he should remove some of the tensions in his life. For Nancy, whose private confidant and frequent conspirator he was, there could be no real replacement. The Reagans never saw the side of him that Maureen did, the manipulation, arrogance, and self-promotion that she found so despicable during the campaigns in which they both had worked. Deaver had been Reagan's deputy executive secretary during his years as governor, and from the very beginning he had been as indispensable to Nancy as to Reagan. They had—putting it simply—"hit it off." Reagan had lost a reliable aide. Nancy had lost her closest White House ally.[23]

Bitburg and Nancy's frenetic behavior, the constant back and forth with Quigley, changing dates, and having to cover the real reason to the rest of the White House staff, had brought Deaver to the breaking point, from which it would take him several years to recover. Reagan's trip to Bitburg (which Deaver had arranged) would greatly tarnish Reagan's reputation. Because of Bitburg, and despite his sincere and moving speech at Bergen-Belsen, Reagan had sacrificed the trust of the Jewish community that he had so enjoyed previously. Within the White House, by her meddling in the Bitburg scheduling, Nancy became "a force to be avoided rather than consulted," an attitude that made her task of protecting Reagan more difficult and gave further credence to how difficult and demanding she was.[24]

Worse was yet to come. No sooner had Reagan returned to Washington after the summer holiday at the ranch than his administration became enmeshed in a covert initiative to trade antitank and antiaircraft weapons to Iran for their influence in gaining the release of six American hostages who had been held in Lebanon by Shi'ite rebels for over a year. The six hostages were William Buckley (already murdered, but this was not known during the negotiations), claimed by the kidnappers to be a CIA agent (which, in fact, he was); Benjamin Weir, a missionary and the first to gain his release; Father Lawrence Martin Jenco, former head of Catholic Relief Services in Lebanon, the second hostage to be released (after nineteen months of captivity); and James Southerland, David Jacobson, and Terry Anderson, who was the last to be released. All suffered torture at the hands of their captors. Jacobson reported being kept chained and nude in a dark cell during much of his long incarceration. His observations during this ordeal proved the most helpful to the CIA upon his release.

These covert dealings violated U.S. government policy on withholding arms from countries engaged in or supporting terrorists, including a specific embargo prohibiting the sale of weapons to Iran. Engineered by Oliver North, a marine officer who had served with distinction in Vietnam, the negotiations would turn into a fiasco, and money from the arms sale was diverted to help the Contras in Nicaragua "in defiance of congressional restrictions specifically designed to prevent such assistance."[25]

North was known for perpetuating many ambiguities and deceptions about his actions, but his leadership abilities were never in doubt. Reagan consistently denied he had any knowledge of the diversions. John Poindexter, the president's national security adviser, later would state before a congressional committee that this was the case. But there was too much contrary testimony later to substantiate this. Either way, the buck stopped, not with his advisers, but with Reagan. If he had not been informed of a move so important and so potentially dangerous, then why not? Who was running the store—Reagan or his advisers? And if he did know, why had he not stopped it when he was fully aware that it violated the law? As Reagan's chief concern was getting the hostages home safely, it is conceivable that this was the reason. After all, he had criticized Carter for his failure to end the Iran hostage crisis more speedily. On a human level bringing these men home to their families loomed as his major responsibility as president—above and beyond attempting a rapprochement with Iran, which others in his administration considered a much larger objective.

Since the overthrow of the shah of Iran by Islamic militants in January 1979 and the establishment of an Islamic theocracy after the exiled cleric Ayatollah Ruhollah Khomeini's reemergence—returning women to the veil, banning alcohol and western music, closing universities and eliminating political parties and a free media—there had been a break in diplomatic relations between the two nations.

To add to Iran's domestic problems, a war with neighboring Iraq over a territorial dispute had dragged on for five years, depleting Iranian resources. Iraq, with its vast oil deposits, had been able to build up a supply of arms, said to include poison gas. The United States was playing a dangerous game on two fronts: on one side, efforts were in effect to win over Iran and obtain the release of the hostages; on the other, through the CIA, the government was providing Iraq "with satellite photography of the war front." American officials were "desperate to make sure that Iraq did not lose" to Iran; at stake were the rich oil fields in the states bordering the Persian Gulf. At the time, Saddam Hussein had been president (i.e., dictator) of Iraq for only five years, and his regime had not yet gained its grim reputation for repression, human rights abuses, and terrorism. Still, the Reagan administration surely knew the potential for these aberrations was there; they knew they were, at best, playing with fire. For example, members of Reagan's administration knew that Iraq used chemical weapons later in their war with Iran. Colonel Walter P. Lang, then a senior defense intelligence officer, asserted that the CIA and the Defense Intelligence Agency "would have never accepted the use of chemical weapons against civilians, but the use against military objectives was seen as inevitable in the Iraqi struggle for survival . . . what Mr. Reagan's aides were concerned about was that Iran not break through to the Fao Peninsula and spread the Islamic revolution to Kuwait and Saudi Arabia." A former DIA official, under the shield of anonymity, told a reporter that having "gone through the 440 days of the hostage crisis in Iran [during the last days of Carter's term], if Iraq had gone down it would have had a catastrophic effect on Kuwait and Saudi Arabia and the whole region might have gone down. That was the backdrop of the policy."[26]

The strategy of the Reagan administration appears to have been to help Iran until the hostages were released, then to assist Iraq in stopping the march of Islamic fundamentalism from spreading to the Persian Gulf states and overrunning the oilfields. No one in the administration, including Vice President Bush, Secretary of State George Shultz, Secretary of Defense Caspar Weinberger, Oliver North, or the top officials in the CIA and the DIA, seems to have realized that Reagan saw the hostage situation as the major tragedy while they considered it the minor concern in comparison to the overall global issues.

The Iran-Contra affair, when it became known, would hang over Reagan's head for the next two years. It would diminish the people's regard for him at a time when he had the highest rating of any president since Franklin D. Roosevelt. However, as November 1985 approached, so did Reagan's first meeting with the new Soviet premier, Mikhail Gorbachev, which was to take place in Geneva. This was the one time that Nancy's strong views on policy (as opposed to staff and scheduling) had preinfluenced him. Nancy was pressing for as honorable and safe a détente as could be accomplished, urging him constantly to soften his approach. Both had high hopes that he could make some headway with the new Soviet leader.

Gorbachev was a comparatively young man, the first Soviet president who wasn't part of the Stalin era. From all that the Reagans knew about him, he was not only highly intelligent but also reasonable. He would be coming to Geneva with his wife, Raisa, which was unusual for a Soviet leader. (It was not even known that former Soviet president Yuri Andropov was married until his wife appeared at his funeral.) There was little that could be found out about Mrs. Gorbachev. She had been a schoolteacher and lectured on Marxist philosophy at Moscow University, but she had never given an interview and was, therefore, something of a mystery. In fact, the Gorbachevs were closely bonded, in much the same way as were the Reagans. Raisa was a strong woman, not unlike Nancy, and unlike any of her predecessors, she was attractive and well dressed. The meeting of these two couples would be historic. But for the mission of peace that hung in the balance, it was fortunate that Reagan and Gorbachev got on so well, because the two women seemed at war from their first interpreted greeting.

CHAPTER EIGHTEEN

THE BEST OF TIMES AND
THE WORST OF TIMES

" I felt it was ridiculous for these two heavily armed superpowers [Russia and the USA] to be sitting there and not talking to each other," Nancy says of the influence she had on Reagan to take the initial steps to meet with Gorbachev at Geneva in November 1985. "I encouraged Ronnie to meet with Gorbachev as soon as possible, especially when I realized that some people in the administration did not favor any real talks."[1] She was referring to Weinberger and Shultz, who along with other members of his staff wanted Reagan to get tough with the Soviets. Nancy, Deaver says, persuaded him to take "a longer view of history." She kept at him, insisting that he make an overture to the new Soviet leader, who was already "preaching the openness of glasnost and the reforms of perestroika." The other woman who had Reagan's ear (albeit not on a pillow at night), Margaret Thatcher, concurred, saying that although Gorbachev was no pushover, "he is a chap we can do business with." It took a while before Gorbachev agreed and the arrangements were made. Reagan was delighted. He was always at his best with foreign leaders when they could talk on a one-to-one basis.

A month before the scheduled meeting, Reagan had ordered a pair of gold cufflinks to present to Gorbachev in the spirit of friendship. "He doesn't wear French cuffs," his advisers insisted. Reagan was adamant. *He* wore French cuffs. It would make a more personal statement. "For all you know," he said to one adviser, "he might well have a shirt with French cuffs and no cufflinks."[2] When they were finally on Air Force

One en route to Geneva, he told Shultz that he believed the use of first names broke the ice in these summit meetings. On first meeting with Thatcher, he suggested she call him Ron. Using the same approach had worked well with the leaders of France, Mexico, and Canada. He was going to ask Gorbachev to call him Ron as well, and he hoped that Gorbachev might reply in kind. Shultz tried to discourage him. Reagan was determined.

During the summit the Reagans were to have the use of the Maison de Saussure, Karim Aga Khan's palatial eighteenth-century home in Geneva. This was not in any way odd, as the Reagans had previously met Karim and his begum, Princess Salimah (born Sarah Croker-Poole, daughter of a retired English officer, former fashion model, and ex-wife of Lord James Crighton-Stuart), in London during Reagan's first term and had seen them socially several times since then, the two women seeming to enjoy each other's company. For generations the Aga Khans had been internationalists, working toward the betterment of relationships between nations. Karim's grandfather, Aga Khan III (famous for the jubilees at which his Ismaili followers offered him his hefty weight in gold, platinum, and diamonds), had unanimously been elected president of the League of Nations in 1937. The Ismaili sect is the smallest of three Muslim groups—Sunni, Shi'ite, and Ismaili. They are also the richest and the most progressive, believing strongly in education for women as well as for men. Although the Aga Khans through the centuries have all been fabulously rich, it is because their followers tithe and are in the main quite successful in business, the arts, medicine, and science. The Aga Khan Foundation is one of the largest in the world, globally funding universities, hospitals, museums, and housing for the poor.

Karim Aga Khan's Geneva estate, one of several Geneva properties owned by Karim, was magnificently furnished and decorated, had park-like grounds, and was well secured. Nancy, delighted with the luxury of it all, immediately extended an invitation to Raisa Gorbachev to have lunch or tea with her on November 19, the day their husbands were also meeting for the first time. It took Raisa two days to respond, which infuriated Nancy. Her acceptance came on the very morning of the tea.

Nancy was extremely nervous (as she assumed her counterpart might be) about what she would talk about with Raisa through interpreters. Her concerns turned out to be unnecessary. Mrs. Gorbachev "talked and talked and *talked*—so much so that I could barely get a word in, edgewise or otherwise," Nancy reported, adding, "my fundamental impression of Raisa Gorbachev was that she never stopped talking." Raisa seemed intent on taking Nancy on as a student of the "Soviet Union and the glories of the Communist system . . . [and on the] failings of the American political system."[3]

The Soviet leader's wife, dressed in a smartly tailored dark suit (she had shopped in Paris before coming to Geneva), her hair tinted a rather bright red, also exhibited an imperiousness that shocked the few other Americans present (the translator and members of the embassy staff). She would snap her fingers to summon her staff (KGB guards) whenever she wanted anything. Twice she moved to a different seat from the one she had originally been offered, a guard rushing to her side to assist her. After tea and light refreshments, Nancy led Raisa into the drawing room where a fire was burning in the fireplace. Though in a warmer, more intimate setting, Raisa continued to lecture about the fine values of Marxism. When she chose to leave, she once again snapped her fingers and two KGB guards rushed to her side as she perfunctorily thanked her hostess, turned, and departed, a degree of rudeness never before observed by Nancy at any meeting of world leaders and their wives.

Plans had been preset for Mrs. Gorbachev to return the gesture with a tea for Nancy at the Soviet mission to the United Nations the next day. This time Raisa was dressed in a starched white shirt and black skirt, the required uniform of a teacher in the Soviet Union. "It made her look like a prison matron," Nancy commented. Photographs of her in this outfit would be the only images of Mrs. Gorbachev to be published in the Communist press. She still commanded the conversation with propagandizing lectures. "I wanted you to see what a typical Russian tea looks like," Raisa told Nancy as they were ushered into a reception room dominated by a long carved-wood table. Tea was almost a full meal. Caviar and blini, cabbage rolls, and pastries were set out on beautiful china. Tea was served from a large, ornate silver samovar—

hardly, it would seem, a typical tea in Communist Russia. ("It was a beautiful spread, but if that was an ordinary housewife's tea," Nancy wrote, "then I'm Catherine the Great.")[4]

Reagan was doing much better in his talks with Gorbachev. The president did ask the Soviet leader to call him Ron, but Gorbachev never did so, nor did he suggest that Reagan address him by his first name, or a diminutive thereof. This, it was explained to Reagan, was not meant as a slight. In Russian culture, a man twenty-plus years younger than another would not address his elder in that fashion. It was a matter of respect. Nevertheless, after the second meeting at the Fleur d'Eau, the château overlooking Lake Leman, where the conference summit was being held, Gorbachev himself noted a "chemistry" between them.

"When I was told his car had arrived," Reagan recalled of their first meeting, "I hurried out to the porch and walked down several steps to greet him. He was dressed in a heavy topcoat and wearing a hat [the weather was quite cold, and there was a sharp wind off the lake]; I was hatless and in a suit. Why the press made a point of the fact that he was bundled up and I wasn't, I don't know. . . . I hadn't planned it that way; the next time we were outdoors, I was wearing a topcoat—I didn't want to rub it in [that he might be hardier than the younger man]."[5]

As Reagan had insisted, they adjourned to a boathouse on the property, separated from the main building by about a hundred yards, and sat, as their wives had done for close to an hour, before a roaring fire, only the essential interpreters present. Reagan immediately liked the man, who seemed so unlike Soviet officials he had previously met, warmer, absent the cold look and tone of Gorbachev's predecessors.[6] At the plenary meeting that followed, each gave long speeches on their views of the obstacles to peace between the nations. After this, Reagan suggested they return to the boathouse for more private talks. Their second meeting was to have lasted fifteen minutes. They conversed for an hour and twenty minutes seated across from each other in stuffed chairs before the crackling fire on the hearth.

These were two men born and raised in quite different cultures and political attitudes. Yet they could still meet on common ground. Gorbachev's roots were in the small Russian village of Privolnoye. His family, like the Reagans, had been poor. What he had attained he had done through his own means. Yet, here they were, two basically simple men, who controlled the destiny of their countries, and possibly peace or war for the world. As the men walked back to the main building, Reagan paused and turning to the Soviet leader invited him to Washington for another private meeting. Gorbachev replied by extending an invitation for a second meeting in the Kremlin. The ice between the two countries—although not yet cracked—had been pierced at the crust.

The next day the two world leaders met privately again, this time in a small room at the Soviet mission. The bargaining was to begin. Reagan's past experience in negotiating across the table for SAG and in meetings with Hollywood studio executives came in handy. "I'd learned a few lessons about negotiating," he recalled. "You're unlikely to ever get *all* you want; you'll probably get more of what you want if you don't issue ultimatums and leave your adversary room to maneuver; you shouldn't back your adversary into a corner, embarrass him, or humiliate him; and sometimes the easiest way to get some things done is for the top people to do them alone and in private."[7]

Gorbachev was certain at this time that Communism was a form of government superior to democracy. But the two men had found it possible to talk, a first between an American president and a Soviet leader. This made news worldwide and spawned some hope for the future. Certainly that was the greater news story of the summit, yet the popular press gave equal coverage to their warring wives.

On January 1, 1986, Reagan broadcast New Year's greetings to the Soviet Union, and Gorbachev did the same for American audiences. This was not the first time the leaders of these two countries had exchanged good wishes on the holiday; Nixon and Leonid Breznev had conveyed the same goodwill in 1973, with no effect on their relations. But this time there seemed real cause for optimism. On January 15 Gorbachev announced a plan to eliminate all nuclear weapons by the year 2000.

The year seemed to be starting off well for the Reagans, but within a few weeks a series of tragic events, illnesses, and personal difficulties would plague them. As noon approached on January 28, Reagan sat at his desk in the Oval Office with Larry Speakes and several other staff members. They were preparing him for questions he might be asked during a press lunch scheduled for one o'clock. It was a bleak day in Washington. Gray skies dispensed dark shadows through the large window behind the president, snaking across his shoulder onto the desk. Suddenly, George Bush, John Poindexter, and Communications Director Pat Buchanan burst into the room and Buchanan cried out, "The [space shuttle] *Challenger* just blew up!" Reagan gasped, "Oh, no!" Speakes recalled that Reagan cradled his face in his right hand, a look of horror on his face that turned almost immediately into despair. "He had the saddest look on his face I have ever seen. He also [suddenly] looked extremely old."[8] They all went into the adjoining room to watch the events unfolding on a large-screen television. Reagan remained in shock, his face drained of color, his lips pressed hard together as the explosion was replayed. Somebody asked what they should tell the press.

"Tell them," Reagan said, regaining his composure, "what we will do is we will fix it [the space program] and we will keep on going. These people [the seven who had died] were dedicated to this program. We couldn't do more to honor them than to go forward."[9]

Along with the experienced six-man crew, the first ordinary citizen to travel into space—Mrs. Christa McAuliffe, a high school teacher and mother of two from Concord, New Hampshire—had died in the explosion. The launch, the twenty-fifth shuttle mission, had been postponed for three days due to inclement weather. Liftoff was delayed two hours owing to unusually low temperatures that had caused ice to form on the shuttle and its support structures. When a beaming Mrs. McAuliffe strode toward the shuttle with the six-man crew earlier, she had waved a triumphant goodbye. She considered herself one of the luckiest women in the world because she had won the spot on the shuttle through a lottery.

Challenger lifted off flawlessly to great cheering at 11:38, rose spectacularly for seventy-four seconds, and exploded in a tremendous ball of fire. Two vast white streamers erupted from the blast as debris scattered the sky. What was to have been the busiest year in shuttle mission history was brought to a standstill, and a nation that had been in such high spirits was catapulted into one of deep mourning. No one could forget those seven astronauts in their white space suits striding out to the shuttle before takeoff; the image of smiling, waving Mrs. McAuliffe was burned forever into the memory of the people of her country.

That afternoon at five o'clock Reagan spoke to the nation on radio and television from the Oval Office. He had worked for about an hour with Peggy Noonan, his speechwriter since 1984, on this address to the nation, which Noonan had drafted earlier. It was surely one of the finest speeches of Noonan's two-year stint with Reagan. She seems to have zeroed in to the inner Reagan and caught the man as well as the office. Reagan always contributed much to his speeches, going along with his writers' content and form but changing words and phrases to suit his own style. This was true of this speech. Still, Noonan had constructed a masterpiece and filled it with images that soared.

Addressing the families of the *Challenger* seven, he said:

"Your loved ones were daring and brave, and they had that special spirit that says, 'Give me a challenge, and I'll meet it with joy.' They had a hunger to explore the universe, and discover its truths. They wished to serve, and they did. They served all of us. We've grown used to wonders in this century. It's hard to dazzle us. But for twenty-five years the United States space program has been doing just that. We've grown used to the idea of space, and perhaps we forget that we've only just begun. We're still pioneers. They, the members of the *Challenger* crew, were pioneers . . . The future doesn't belong to the faint-hearted; it belongs to the brave . . . The crew of the *Challenger* honored us in the manner in which they lived their lives. We will never forget them, nor the last time we saw them, this morning, as they prepared for their journey and waved goodbye and 'slipped the surly bonds of earth' to 'touch the face of God.'" (This quote comes from a poem written by John Gillespie Magee Jr., a nineteen-year-old American volunteer with the Royal Canadian Air Force, who was killed in training on December 11, 1941. See appendix 7 for the text of the speech.)

The address was delivered so movingly that Reagan was quickly perceived as a wise, all-knowing father figure by the nation. Tip O'Neill admitted that he cried, as he was sure nearly anyone listening to the president must have done. O'Neill, one of Reagan's chief critics (who had known eight presidents and wrote in his memoir that Reagan was the worst," but added that "he would have made a hell of a king"), conceded that he was "the best public speaker" he'd ever heard, and that he was beginning to think "that in this respect he dwarfs both Roosevelt and Kennedy."[10]

On October 11 and 12, 1986, Reagan and Gorbachev met for talks at Reykjavik, Iceland, that were meant to be preparatory to a 1987 summit meeting in Washington. When the talks were originally scheduled, their wives were not to accompany them, a direct attempt to avoid the adverse publicity Raisa and Nancy received in Geneva. Three days before the meetings, Moscow announced that it had been decided that Mrs. Gorbachev would travel with her husband to Reykjavik. This threw the Reagans and their advisers into a frenzy of pros and cons as to what Nancy should do. Raisa was playing a game of one-upmanship, and it was finally decided that for Nancy to rush off to Iceland, too, would be to allow Raisa to call the shots, and so she remained in Washington while Reagan flew off to Iceland. When asked by the press why Mrs. Reagan had not come to Reykjavik, Raisa replied with a flip of her hand, "Perhaps she has something else to do. Or maybe she is not feeling well."[11]

The momentum Reagan had started in Geneva was badly stalled in Reykjavik. The main cause of dispute was Reagan's Strategic Defense Initiative program (or SDI), which he viewed as insurance for the national security of the United States. Gorbachev was on the verge of agreeing to a nuclear ban for both countries by 1996 but insisted on a ten-year ban on SDI. Reagan was furious. There had been no such conditions discussed at the start of the talks. The U.S. having SDI technology "scared the daylights out of the Russians," Larry Speakes insisted. "Reagan believed in the dramatic possibilities of [SDI]. I am convinced that his insistence on retaining [SDI] did more than anything to cause an about-face in the Soviet approach to arms control."[12]

Reagan came home from Reykjavik empty-handed. Each man immediately sent strong messages blaming the other for the failure to come to an agreement on arms. But Reagan softened his somewhat by adding: "The door is open and the opportunity to begin eliminating the nuclear threat is within reach." Gorbachev shot back, "Only a madman could go forward with arms control if SDI is developed."[13]

Reagan had only been home a few weeks when his administration was plunged into the worst crisis of his presidency with the disclosure in early November that the United States had been selling arms to Iran and siphoning off money from the sales to assist the rebels of Nicaragua. By the end of November Reagan found himself confronted with accusations that his administration had violated its own policy by selling arms to Iran and "that it had attempted to circumvent a congressional ban on aid to the Nicaraguan contras through diversion of funds." The most damaging questions were: Who was conducting the secret diplomacy with Iran? And what was known and approved by the president? Reagan, who never had the stomach to fire members of his staff, was forced to dismiss Poindexter as national security adviser, as well as Lt. Col. Oliver North, a Marine officer assigned in 1981 to the National Security Council staff who was deputy director of political military affairs. Reagan used an apologetic tone in his weekly broadcast and stated unequivocally that he had no knowledge that money from the sale of arms to Iran was being diverted to the Contras. Congress moved to set up an inquiry of its own; it was not satisfied with a three-man panel appointed by Reagan and headed by former Senator John Tower to examine the role of the National Security Council staff. Reagan was suddenly engulfed in an explosive, threatening scandal, possibly impeachment.

Nancy grew more fearful by the day. She had not wanted Ronnie to run for a second term. Lou Cannon, covering the story on a daily basis, believed that Nancy was "more politically astute than her husband, and took the threat of impeachment seriously. She also realized that Reagan could not survive without his credibility. But Ronnie would never be the villain in Nancy's eyes. Her first remedy for repairing the damage to his presidency was a top to bottom housecleaning in the White House, starting with the chief of staff [Donald Regan]."[14] Reagan resisted. Deaver (actually no longer working for Reagan but summoned by Nancy to make Ronnie see that this was what had to be done) and Stu Spencer came to talk him into agreeing to fire Regan. The Reagan presidency was "falling into a black hole of undetermined depth," Spencer insisted. "Someone had to be sacrificed" to save the president, Deaver added.

"I'll be goddamned if I'll throw somebody else out to save my own ass," Reagan was claimed to have angrily responded.

"It's not your ass I'm talking about," Deaver countered. "You stood up on the steps of the Capitol and took an oath to defend the Constitution and this office. You've got to think of the country first."

"I've always thought of the country," Reagan said, exploding in fury as he threw his pen so hard onto the carpet that it bounced up about a foot before landing again.[15]

Reagan was under pressure not only from his advisers but also from Nancy. She was determined that Regan was an albatross that Ronnie had to cast off. It had perhaps been ill-advised for Reagan to switch Regan from his job as secretary of the treasury, which he had handled well, to chief of staff, where he was not as effective. Nancy believed Regan had led Ronnie into an abyss that might lead to disaster. She might well have been right, but her crusade to get Ronnie to fire his chief of staff nearly backfired. For the first time there was a true standoff between Ronnie and Nancy, and he angrily turned on her. She broke down sobbing in the presence of members of his staff. In the end, Regan was fired, and on February 27 Howard Baker was appointed chief of staff. But Nancy's interference in what was essentially an Oval Office matter had made Reagan appear weak. Although she was never able to concede that she had done the wrong thing, believing that she had acted in Ronnie's best interests, she immediately regretted her handling of the situation. Within a few days after their rather public spat, the couple appeared to have made amends. Nothing made more points with Reagan than seeing Nancy cry.

It was hard for Nancy to believe that things could get much worse. But on January 6, during the height of the Regan arguments, Reagan was operated on for prostate problems. Fortunately, his condition this time was diagnosed as not cancerous. Once again the power of the office was turned over to George Bush while Reagan was in surgery and rescinded shortly after he was moved to recovery. Neither Reagan and Bush nor Nancy and Barbara Bush could be said to have the kind of close relationship that the Clintons and the Gores enjoyed in later years. Like most presidents and their vice presidents, and their respective mates, they played on the same team, but the president and the first lady were the stars and were treated accordingly. Privately, the Reagans and the Bushes had very little in common. The Bushes were family oriented and motivated. They had an entirely different circle of friends and quite diverse interests. Reagan respected Bush's professional attitude, trusted him implicitly to do his job, but seldom called upon him for his opinion.

Larry Speakes recalled a crisis meeting in February, 1986, in the Situation Room in the White House during the last days of Ferdinand Marcos's dictatorial reign in the Philippines. Serious violence seemed imminent, and a crowd of thousands was being held back by Catholic nuns, "their arms interlocked as they stood in the front ranks."

"With his background as CIA director and ambassador to mainland China and to the United Nations," Speakes wrote, "Bush was uniquely qualified to be of help in a situation like this, yet he had offered no insightful opinion, no sage advice. It was disappointing that Bush had come to believe that it wasn't his place to offer his opinion to the President."[16] Barbara Bush learned early on that there was only one star and no female supporting players in the administration. All the wives, from Barbara Bush on down the ranks in the Reagan era, knew and accepted this. Nancy Davis might not have been able to control the casting of her movies at MGM, but Nancy Reagan was the "studio head" of the White House.

Reagan's recovery from the prostate operation was exceptionally slow. It took him a long time to regain even a portion of his old strength. He worked hard not to show any weakness in public, but those on his staff were aware of it, and Nancy obsessed over it. "Don't work him so hard" was her credo. But it had always been difficult for Reagan to say no when staff members piled on meetings, appearances, and travel agendas. An economic summit to be held in Venice was charted for early June, and Nancy did not feel that he was up to the strenuous plans for him on the trip. Baker was adamant about the schedule, which included several stops at which Reagan was to give speeches. He was the good guy, and Nancy—who would ask "Why must he do this?" or declare more boldly, "He can't do this. You'll have to reschedule"—was the "witch of the West." Sometimes her tactics worked. This time they did not, and the Reagans flew off together on Baker's itinerary.

Reagan was to speak on June 12 in Berlin at the Brandenburg Gate that separated East and West. It would be the most memorable speech—partially unscripted—of his presidency. "I met with my West German hosts in a government building not far from the wall," he recorded later. "From the window, I could see the graffiti and prodemocracy slogans scrawled on liberty's side of the wall." A West German official leaned in close to him and warned him to watch what he said as in the government building they could see KGB men monitoring their conversations on the other side of the wall. This infuriated Reagan, who strode out on the landing where microphones had been set up, and sounded "off about what I thought about a government that penned in its people like animals."[17]

"Behind me stands a wall that encircles the free sectors of this city, part of a vast system of barriers that divides the entire continent of Europe," he began.

"From the Baltic, south, those barriers cut across Germany in a gash of barbed wire, concrete, dog runs, and guard towers. Farther south, there may be no visible, no obvious wall. But there remain armed guards and checkpoints all the same—still a restriction on the right to travel, still an instrument to impose upon ordinary men and women the will of a totalitarian state. Yet it is here in Berlin where the wall emerges most clearly; here, cutting across your city, where the news photo and the television screen have imprinted this brutal division of a continent upon the mind of the world. Standing before the Brandenburg Gate, every man is a German, separated from his fellow man. Every man is a Berliner, forced to look upon a scar. . . ."

He ended with his famous declaration: "General Secretary Gorbachev, if you seek peace, if you seek prosperity for the Soviet Union and Eastern Europe, if you seek liberalization: Come here to this gate! Mr. Gorbachev, open this gate! Mr. Gorbachev tear down this wall!"[18]

Reagan glowed in what would be his finest hour, and Nancy was moved to tears in his reflection. Still, as the summer of '87 sizzled steaming hot, so did the Iran-Contra probe. It was turning swiftly into Reagan's Bay of Pigs, "Something," as Larry Speakes said, "that he got sucked into and then it simply got out of control."[19] In a televised hearing in July, Colonel North told a congressional panel "in a slightly raspy mixture of gung-ho Marine commander, preacher and salesman" that his involvement in the Iran-Contra affair was directed by officials inside the White House. "I have never carried out a single act, not one, in which I did not have authority from my superiors," he said on oath. He was at times cocky and defiant, his posture rifle-stiff, his uniform impeccable— one lonely cowlick over his forehead defying his command. North added that he assumed, but was not certain, that the president was aware of the diversion of arms profits to the Contras.[20]

Nancy rode out to Bethesda Naval Hospital on October 6 for her annual mammogram. She had been under tremendous pressure with her fears of the effect of the Iran-Contra scandal on Ronnie's presidency and his place in history. Otherwise, she felt in good health. When the test was done, she was asked to wait a few minutes. Then apologies were extended. They were sorry but they had to take some additional X rays. She says her stomach sank with the thought that something was wrong. It was. There was a malignant tumor in her left breast. She drove back to the White House in disbelieving silence with Dr. John Hutton, the current White House physician. The impact of what this meant had not yet hit her. Hutton saw her up to the family quarters and then offered to go down to the Oval Office to tell Reagan. She argued with him, but he insisted that she should not be alone at this moment and the president would want to be immediately involved.

Hutton said that when he informed Reagan of Nancy's condition and the recommendation that an operation be performed as soon as possible, the president "had an expression on his face" he would never forget. "I think [he] has always believed nothing could ever happen to you," he told Nancy.[21] After Dr. Hutton left the Oval Office, the president's secretary went in to find him breathing hard, his hand across his face as he fought off tears. She asked if he would like her to call Dr. Hutton back. He said he just wanted a few minutes to himself. About ten minutes later he left the office and went upstairs to Nancy, who reassured him that she felt fine and that she wanted to carry on with her schedule until the date of the operation, which was set for October 16. A decision was made—by Nancy and Reagan—that although she had two choices, a lumpectomy or a mastectomy, she would have the latter. This way, they decided, the results would be conclusive and she would not have to submit to a second surgery. During the next ten days she entertained the Crown Prince Akihito and the Princess Michiko of Japan, flew to Chicago to receive an award from the Ronald McDonald Foundation, and then spent a gray, overcast weekend at Camp David. She longed to talk with her mother, but Edith was slipping away day by day, and no longer could remember or recognize Nancy. She confided in her stepbrother and told Ron and Doria and Maureen (who then called Michael), but held off making a public announcement until October 15. No one in the family was speaking to Patti, who learned of her mother's condition from a news report. Patti's uncle, Dr. Richard Davis, was the only member of the family to contact her. "It would mean a lot if you phoned your mother," he told her. "This is a terrible thing to go through." But it was not until after the operation that Patti was able to do so.[22]

On October 16, the night before the operation, the surgeon came up to see Nancy, who was in the same vast seven-room presidential suite where Reagan had been for his previous colon and prostate operations. She was asked once again whether she might choose to have a lumpectomy performed before going forward with the more drastic procedure. "Look," she told him, "please don't wake me [during the operation] to have a conversation about it. Just do it. It shouldn't take you long, because there isn't much there to take off. Dolly Parton I'm not."[23]

She came through the surgery and postoperative period with amazing stoicism, concerned always for Ronnie and how this would affect him. When the nurse came out to tell him the results, he broke down and sobbed. Without thinking, the woman put her arms around him to comfort him. This was not the president of the United States. This was the husband of a woman who had just had a malignant tumor removed along with her left breast, and who only God could be sure was now clear of the disease forever. Nancy's first words to Ronnie were, "They took my breast. I feel so sorry for you."[24]

"That's all right, honey. I've always been a leg man, myself," he replied. Then he took her hand in his and professed his love for her.[25]

It was not until four days after the operation that Patti called her mother. They had not spoken in two years, and the conversation was awkward. Finally, Patti suggested that Nancy might want reconstructive surgery, and if she did, Patti knew of a good doctor. Nancy told her she couldn't think about another operation, having just survived this one. "I was glad she called," Nancy wrote later. "[Although] I longed to hear something more comforting about what I had just gone through." She came home to the White House on October 22, six days after the operation. That weekend they went to Camp David, and Nancy wrote in her diary: "I still haven't shown Ronnie—me. Even though he says it doesn't make any difference, and I believe him, I somehow can't bring myself to do it yet. I'll know when the time is right."[26]

On the twenty-sixth, having returned from Camp David feeling somewhat stronger, she had made a date for tea at the White House with television comedian Joan Rivers and was taking a short rest beforehand when Ronnie came into the room and sat down on the edge of the bed. His grim expression conveyed to her that something was wrong. "What is it? Tell me? What is it?"

"Honey," he said, "Edie is now with Loyal."[27]

She flew to Arizona with Ronnie for the funeral although she was not yet fully recovered. Everyone in the family was there except Patti, who had called Elaine Crispin and asked her to tell her mother that she had to be out of the country on business—a lie—but she later claimed that she simply could not face the entire family at this time. Edith's death was difficult for Nancy, even though she had been lingering for over a year and it was expected. There were so many ghosts in their past, so many things that perhaps neither of them had been able to dispel. "I think I made her proud of me," she told Elaine Crispin.

Emotion and exhaustion confined her to the White House for several weeks upon her return. She had pushed herself too hard, and the doctors were afraid she might have a relapse. Reagan was an adoring, attentive partner. They had dinner on silver trays, both of them in red robes (hers a present from Betsy Bloomingdale), and watched old movies. The proposed meeting in Washington with the Gorbachevs had finally become reality and would take place in December—less than a month away—and there were plans to discuss about "what to do with them," Raisa especially. The state dinner in their honor had to run smoothly despite the clamor for invitations and the difficult decisions about the final guest list.

The state dinner was to be entirely supervised by Nancy, and she went at it with great enthusiasm. There was also to be a tour with Raisa of the White House and the family quarters, followed by a tea on December 11. Nothing had changed. Although given two weeks to reply to the invitation, Mrs. Gorbachev waited until two days in advance before agreeing to come for a tour, but prescribing that it had to be at 11:30 in the morning and include coffee, not tea, as she had to leave for a luncheon by 12:30. This gave Raisa only one hour for the visit, and so she declined the offer to visit the family quarters. It was a terrible insult to Nancy that could have damaged the relationship between the two countries, but Nancy let it slide. When she arrived, Raisa was as graceless as she had been in Geneva. This was only six weeks since Nancy's mastectomy and the death of her mother. Raisa never asked after her hostess's health or extended condolences. As she sped through the official rooms of the White House, she continued her Soviet lectures to her hostess and guides and seldom glanced Nancy's way. When Nancy placed her hand on her arm at one moment, Raisa pulled away. It was remarkably bad behavior, made worse later when she told a reporter (having not seen the family quarters), "A human being would like to live in a regular house. . . . [the White House] is like a museum."[28]

As a general rule, state dinners are black tie. The Gorbachevs, however, sent word that tuxedos were not worn in the Soviet Union as they were the sign of bourgeois capitalism. An early evening ending at ten-thirty was requested, and so Nancy canceled the usual cocktail hour that gave guests a chance to get acquainted. Dinner was to be served at eight P.M. Raisa, in a dramatic black gown, and Gorbachev in a business suit, arrived a half hour late and then took their time going down the receiving line, which meant some shuffling had to be done. Coffee was now to be served at the tables instead of in the Blue Room and Van Cliburn (who in 1958 had won the Tchaikovsky Piano Competition in Moscow) was asked to play only one selection as his part of the entertainment. Despite this, the Gorbachevs enjoyed his performance so much that they asked if he would play "Moscow Nights" as an encore, which he did.

Raisa did not send the obligatory thank-you note to her host and hostess. A cold war still raged between the two women, but Reagan and Gorbachev had made history on December 8, 1987, by signing a treaty to cut their nations' nuclear arsenals. Fifteen hundred Soviet warheads would be removed and all ground-launched intermediate-range missiles in Europe destroyed, while the United States would destroy all Pershing II and ground-launched cruise missiles and four hundred deployed warheads. On-site inspections of each nation by the other were part of the agreement as well.

It is interesting to note that while Nancy strongly supported an accord with Russia over nuclear arms, Raisa, the militant Marxist, had done her best to deter its progress. Her stratagem appeared to be to get Reagan angry through slights to his wife so that he would leave the negotiating table in anger. But the old Hollywood pro knew better than to back his opponent into a corner or slam a door in his face.

CHAPTER NINETEEN

A GRACEFUL EXIT

They were inextricably bound together, yet each had carved out an individual image. "[My father] refines things that he is thinking about by saying them out loud and talking to [Nancy]," Maureen, the Reagan offspring closest to them at this time, and the only one who shared the president's political confidence, related. "She refines things she is thinking in the same way and they give each other advice in that way. They have always done that and they always will . . . I think it all became possible [Reagan's political ascendancy] because of the relationship they have. . . . They are absolutely a team. You do not get one without the other—ever."[1] By 1988, the Reagans had been married for thirty-six years, and basically neither one of them had changed. *Grown, yes*, aged, of course, but not changed.

Curiously, they did not share deep interests in many of the same things. Reagan loved the outdoors and was happiest when on the back of a horse, riding the range, thinking things out, talking to God. "[My father] had something special with God," Patti once told Peggy Noonan. "He talked to God all the time. It didn't mean that he was any more special in God's eyes or that . . . God's speaking to anybody more than anyone else . . . it's that some people choose to listen. And talk back. And my father talked to God all the time. He just had conversations with God.

"When we'd go horseback riding at the Malibu ranch [when she was a preteen], just the two of us, I knew the way to get him to talk and to have a conversation was to talk about God . . . 'What do you think God thinks of this?' . . . If I went to that place we would have these wonderful conversations. . . . And he would just tell me sometimes, 'Well, I asked God about this and this is what he said back to me. . . .' "[2]

Nancy was not a deeply religious person, nor did she feel comfortable with nature, with animals, or with the demands of the land. But she was so determined to make their marriage succeed that she took an interest in his favorite things and did so without complaint, although at times with a lack of enthusiasm that was noticeable to others, but never to Ronnie. She enjoyed an active social life, the good things that came with success. Even before she met Reagan, she had viewed marrying him as a way for her to move up the social ladder. Nancy was something of a snob. She preferred the moneyed classes, the so-called top people. Reagan, on the other hand, had always been at ease with the workers on his ranches and at General Electric factories, old friends from Dixon, and the multitude of average citizens he met on tours or who visited him at the White House. It is revealing that, when interviewed by this author, those who knew Reagan in this way described him as "warm," "a real person," "caring," while his political coworkers referred to him most often as "aloof," "difficult to really know."

Reagan never forgot his roots. He was fond of saying that Dixon was a home to come home to. He contacted old friends when they were ill or had a death in their family and congratulated them on any good fortune. He knew how it felt to be poor and how his belief in God had strengthened him throughout his life. He sincerely believed God had sent Nancy to him and that he had almost lost her because he had not listened well. He would never again take that chance. Nancy never gave him the opportunity, for the one thing they both believed in was that a wife stood squarely behind her husband and, supported, protected, and dignified him—as Nelle had with Jack, and, although not so sacrificially, as Edith had done with Loyal. The strength of their teaming was that Nancy was empowered by the success of her husband, and Reagan grew more successful through her staunch belief in his power, his worthiness. He once told Maureen that in some ways he felt as though God was reaching out to him through Nancy.

For Reagan, the most grievous crime of the Soviet government was its religious repression; to him "the evil empire" meant a "godless country." Although the Reykjavik summit was deemed a failure, Reagan had come bearing a list of 1,200 Jews who had been denied the right to leave Russia so that they could worship in their faith, and he appealed to Gorbachev to let them emigrate so that they could do so freely. In due course many of those on his list were given exit visas.

On May 12, 1988, the Reagans stepped on Soviet soil for the first time to attend the Moscow summit. Once again Reagan brought with him a list of Soviet dissidents and members of separated families who wanted to rejoin their relatives in the United States. The majority had been denied the right to worship in the religion of their choice. When asked if he would act upon the U.S. requests, Gorbachev was reported to have replied, "There are too many lists."

Prior to his arrival, Reagan had informed Gorbachev that he intended to make human rights issues a focus of his visit. To dramatize the plight of Soviet Jews, he had planned with Nancy to see the Ziemans, a family of refuseniks. Before leaving Washington he had received a poignant letter from their twelve-year old daughter, Vera, a piano virtuoso who was known as "Moscow's Orphan Annie" because of her red hair and freckled face. "Unlike Annie I have a family, and it is about its fate that I want to write you," she began, then she explained that her family was Jewish and could not practice its faith, and that because she was a rising pianist, state-trained, the government would not allow them to go elsewhere.[3] Colin Powell, in his new job as national security adviser, was warned by Eduard Shevardnadze, the Soviet foreign minister, that if Reagan visited the Ziemans, the family would never be given an exit visa. Reagan was furious that he should be so threatened, but gave in to pressure from his staff to forgo the meeting. However, the Ziemans were invited to a reception for a hundred dissidents and refuseniks at Spaso House, the residence of the American embassy. Since it is deemed sovereign American territory, the Ziemans could meet with Reagan without interference. The family was concerned that their attendance at this affair might hinder their ability to obtain an exit visa, but it did not. Two months later they were given visas to emigrate.

Nancy has said that as a younger woman she could never in her wildest dreams have imagined that she would be visiting Moscow as the wife of the American president. Most probably true. After all, there had been only thirty-nine American first ladies in over two centuries. She also has written that she was terrified that she might do or say the wrong thing and thus, inadvertently, be the cause of World War III. She boned up for weeks on Soviet protocol; she took with her no formal gown and no outfit in her favorite red, which she had been told was not appropriate in Soviet political circles. The tension between the wives of the two world leaders had not eased. While the men were holding their first meeting, Raisa took Nancy on a tour of the Kremlin that included a visit to the fifteenth-century Assumption Cathedral, now a museum, where the coronation of the czars had taken place before the revolution. Nancy felt a "spirituality" still pervaded the ancient cathedral and, perhaps unwisely, asked Raisa (through her interpreter) if services were ever held there. Raisa's face flushed, and she grimaced as she spat out the word "*Nyet!*" There was a definite chill from that moment on.

This was not the case with the two men. At the Soviet state dinner held in the Kremlin's Hall of Facets, Nancy sat on Gorbachev's right. He was pleasant, almost charming, and at one point in the evening confided to Nancy that he felt a rare chemistry with Reagan, and though he understood it was not permitted by the American Constitution, he wished "he could stay on for another four years."[4] Reagan and Gorbachev met one on one as they had done in their other meetings, and as always with Reagan, these were the most successful. With strategic help from Secretary of State Shultz, Gen. Colin Powell, and Secretary of Defense Frank C. Carlucci and their staffs, the arms treaty between the two countries—although not signed during the Moscow summit—moved closer to agreement. Reagan also believed he had been fairly successful in presenting his arguments for human rights, especially on the issue of freedom to practice one's religion. At the time there were over four hundred and fifty thousand Jews who wanted to leave the Soviet Union, a number that Reagan was aware could present a problem.

"These people are part of your society and many of them must have important jobs," Reagan recalled that he told Gorbachev. "But did it ever occur to you . . . that maybe if these Jews were permitted to worship as they want to and teach their children the Hebrew language, that maybe they wouldn't want to leave the Soviet Union?

"That's how our country was started, by people who were not allowed to worship as they wished in their homeland, so they came to our shores, a wilderness across the Atlantic, and founded our nation. . . . I know [these Jews] must love their country as much as other Russians do, so perhaps if they were allowed to reopen their synagogues and worship as they want to, they might decide that they wouldn't have to leave and there wouldn't be that problem of a brain drain." A logical argument, one that must have made some impression upon Gorbachev because, although limited, some churches and synagogues did reopen during the following year. Reagan found Gorbachev to be "different from the Communists who had preceded him to the top of the Kremlin hierarchy. Before him, every one had vowed to pursue the Marxist commitment to a one-world Communist state; he was . . . the first to agree to destroy nuclear weapons, the first to suggest a free market and to support open elections and freedom of expression."[5]

It is likely that Gorbachev recognized the failure of the Russian system. He would later write in his book *Perestroika* that "the central planning and bureaucratic control of the Soviet economy sapped the people's incentive to produce and excel." Religious repression did not seem in his view to have been the cause of that failure.

There was no doubt that Reagan's trip to Moscow was a success. His popularity with the people there was a surprise to both the Soviets and the folks back home. When he and Nancy decided to walk through the Arbat, a pedestrian street lined with shops and cafes, on a warm Sunday morning, a crowd of well-wishers who just wanted to see them was beaten back by the KGB, to Reagan's anger and a muttered remark that the Soviet Union "is still a police state."[6] It was the only ugly display of police violence he encountered. Crowds lined the streets and cheered his motorcade wherever he went. He gave speeches to students, to Soviet writers and intellectuals, "spectacular performances [that] touched the deepest chords of the Russian psyche," Gorbachev's biographers, Dusko Doder and Louise Branson, wrote in their book *Gorbachev, Heretic in the Kremlin,* adding that one Muscovite said, "I'm not religious, but I was delighted to hear him end his speeches by saying, 'God bless you,' " which had not been heard in a public arena or on television since pre-Soviet days, in the early years of the twentieth century.[7]

When the Reagans returned home, the Iran-Contra investigations were continuing, but there was no longer any talk of impeachment. Nancy could relax. The president was not found to have committed any crime or to have participated knowingly in the scandal. There were two strong opinions in Washington on this. Surveys showed that the public were more enraged that arms had been sold to Iran than that the money had been diverted to the Contras. "Americans," Lou Cannon wrote, "were divided on the question of whether Reagan had known about the diversion, but they could see plainly that he had traded arms for hostages. The more he lied about this, the deeper his credibility problem became."[8]

Larry Speakes disagrees. "I'm just convinced that the President would not have approved the diversion of funds to the Contras. I don't buy the theory that the President nodded and winked on it. He just wasn't that kind of guy. I've seen him answer the question too many times, and I've discussed it with him privately too many times. Frankly, I don't believe the man can tell a lie. The man can make a mistake and the man can hear something so many times that he believes something is true when it really isn't, but he simply isn't a liar." Further, Speakes believes that "Poindexter took it on himself to mislead both the President and North, failing to inform Reagan what North was up to, and failing to inform North that the President didn't know about it."[9]

Whatever was the case, as Reagan's term of office neared its end, his popularity was at a dazzling new peak. The Reagans and the Gorbachevs were to have one more meeting, this time in Washington shortly before Christmas 1988, when the Russian leader came to the United States to address the United Nations. To Nancy's amazement, Raisa greeted her almost with the warmth of an old friend. At a luncheon given by Marcela Pérez de Cuéllar, the wife of the U.N. secretary-general, Nancy reports that Raisa took her aside to tell her that she would miss both Nancy and Reagan. "As for the two of us, it was destiny that put us at the place that we were, next to our husbands, to help bring about the relationship that our two countries now have. My husband and I hope you will return to the Soviet Union to see us."[10] Raisa Gorbachev, in fact, had never promoted goodwill between the two countries. Gorbachev was obviously a man of strong will and independent character who overrode his wife's personal convictions to put forth his own—which in the end she had to bend to. But this time Raisa spoke not of Marxism, nor lectured on the great Communist system. She seemed to have done, if not an about-face, a half turn toward conciliation.

In a speech to the United Nations Gorbachev announced that Soviet military forces would be reduced by 500,000 troops upon his return to Russia. After his speech Gorbachev and Reagan met. Reagan suggested that one day he would like to show his Russian friend the rest of the United States, especially California, where perhaps they could ride the trails on his ranch together. Gorbachev admitted that he had never ridden a horse and would not know on which side he should mount. "The left, the left!" Reagan snapped. Gorbachev laughed raucously.[11]

In Washington, D.C., autumn 1988 was cool and crisp, the trees spectacular as their leaves turned fiery shades of red, orange, and yellow. There was little speculation as to the final outcome of the presidential race between George Bush and the Democratic nominee, Governor Michael Dukakis of Massachusetts. Even with the seeming albatross of J. Danforth [Dan] Quayle as his running mate, Bush had been the front-runner throughout the campaign, benefiting from Reagan's popularity, glasnost with the Soviets, and his own eight-year stint as vice president. Reagan campaigned hard for Bush, raising more for the Republican Party than any of his predecessors. Bush had served Reagan well even though the two men had never really hit it off personally. Bush, son of the wealthy, autocratic Prescott Bush, former senator from Connecticut, had lived a privileged life, attending elite schools, Phillips Academy and Yale, before moving to Texas and becoming a millionaire by founding an oil company. His manner was calm and reassuring, which pleased voters. But he had won the Distinguished Flying Cross for bravery during World War II and had been a congressman, ambassador to the United Nations, chief of the U.S. Liaison Office in China, and director of the CIA. And despite the persistent, demeaning comment that he was a *wimp*, people who met him were always surprised by his imposing size (he was over six feet tall) and his physical fitness. (This was a man who, ten years later, would parachute from a plane in celebration of his seventy-fifth birthday.) Bush would later say that Reagan never thanked him for his help and would add that the Reagans did not seem "to want us upstairs in [the family quarters] in the White House." Barbara Bush complained that this seemed even more noticeable from the time her husband was elected on November 4, 1988, until he took the oath of office on January 20, 1989.[12]

It was in these last months of his second term that Reagan's suddenly diminishing powers of recall shocked his staff and first began to alarm Nancy. He was seventy-six, when his occupancy of the Oval Office ended. During his presidency he had survived a near-fatal assassination attempt, skin and colon cancer, and a prostate operation, and still he looked as fit and—in some cases, fitter than—any of his much younger staff members. His posture was erect, his skin taut, his hair abundant and, amazingly, not yet tinged with gray. No one thought of him as an old man. Therefore, these lapses of memory were unexpected. White House counsel Peter Wallison composed an aide-mémoire when Reagan was appearing before the Tower Commission during the Iran-Contra investigations, as it was apparent to him and other close advisers that the president was having difficulties with his recollections. "There are some things he remembers very poorly," Stuart Spencer, who was an unofficial consultant, later recalled, "but I think he wants to remember them very poorly. He really has a good memory."[13]

Maureen, defending her father at the time, said that, "despite what his critics say, Ronald Reagan has the closest thing to a photographic memory as I've ever seen. . . . He can sort through masses of information and consolidate and process it all in such a way that he understands it and the people who he explains it to will understand it. He can look at a program and tell you where we are in the scheme of things, and where we're going, and in two months' time you can ask him again and he'll have total recall."[14]

This was true. Reagan appeared to have a prodigious memory for facts. But at times he had trouble remembering names and faces. Nancy refused to believe that this was a sign of anything more than being overtaxed. Nor would she bow to the suggestion that he was "showing his age." Yes, his hearing was impaired, and perhaps he had to rest a bit more frequently. But he was still an extremely vital man with high energy, more like a man in his fifties than his seventies. They spent the week after the Christmas holidays at the ranch where he rode, axed wood and mended fences. Nancy had always felt more feminine when he was close at hand, broad-shouldered and towering over her, and she still did. The glint in his eye when he smiled at her had not dimmed.

During an earlier trip to California, Nancy had looked for a house for them to move into when they departed Washington. She found a sprawling, comfortable one-story, red-brick, ranch-style home with a heated swimming pool and small pool house on one and one-quarter acres in Bel Air, an elegant section of Los Angeles that adjoins Beverly Hills. The house was walled and gated, which would insure complete privacy and lend itself to the security measures afforded former presidents and their families. The original address of the house had been 666 St. Cloud Road. The number was changed, at Reagan's request, to *668* before they occupied it: 666 in the Bible's Book of Revelations is "the number of the beast," and often associated with satanical rituals. The estate was purchased for $2.5 million by Wall Management Services, a group of eighteen of the Reagans' close friends and associates, including Holmes Tuttle and Earle Jorgensen (old members of Reagan's so-called Kitchen Cabinet) and leased to the Reagans for three years, after which they would acquire the property for themselves. Once again the Reagans' friends had saved them from spending their own money.

Their eight-year voyage on the sea of history would soon end. Reagan was enormously popular despite Iran-Contra, an increase in the national debt from $712 billion in 1981 to more than $2 trillion in 1988, and exceptionally high unemployment. He had stood tall with the Russians and had helped the country regain its pride in being American. There is little doubt that Reagan contributed greatly to the end of the cold war and the tearing down of the Berlin Wall, even though neither occurred during his term in office.

He could have done much more than he did, especially where AIDS was concerned. The epidemic grew on his watch, and all the signs were there that it could become a plague. But it was not until mid-1987 and the AIDS-related death of film star Rock Hudson, who was a personal friend, that he came forward, unfortunately with too little, too late. Although not homophobic (Reagan was comfortable with homosexual friends, but not in discussions about homosexuality), he had a problem with pressing for public funds for research and medical help for what he considered at the time a self-inflicted disease. By 1987 he realized this was not the case, that innocents—many of them children born of AIDS parents—were at risk and were being discriminated against. Reagan found himself caught between two strong forces—the religious-right conservatives, whom he had been responsible for bringing full center into American politics, and Nancy, who felt empathy for individuals with AIDS and had always had a few close homosexual friends but feared Reagan would lose his popularity if he championed the AIDS cause. The religious right had been organizing "ad hoc campaigns against everything from the teaching of evolution to a woman's right to an abortion" for many years before Reagan's presidency. But they marched into major political battle with his campaigns, becoming heavy contributors to the Republican Party and gaining such a powerful base that it was no longer possible for a Republican candidate for the presidency to be nominated without their backing. "In effect," political analyst Neal Gabler has written, what the religious right did, "in taking over the GOP, was to convert one of America's two major parties from a political organization dedicated to effecting policy, as parties traditionally did, to one that was also dedicated to eradicating sin [so labeled by its own standards and judgment], which is an entirely new function."[15]

Nancy's point of view regarding funds for AIDS research ultimately won Reagan over. But while funds were allocated for AIDS research, they were not enough to stop the plague, and Reagan's words to the nation about AIDS—although delivered with his usual power to move his listeners—stopped short of true enlightenment.

Nancy had been the most controversial first lady of the twentieth century. Too many people seemed to love to hate her. She was too out-front, too polished and perfectly put together, always pushing, always expecting her due, and more. She was made for the grist mills of gossipmongers and writers who knew that exploitive books and articles seething with innuendo could increase their earnings. But it is entirely possible, as Michael Deaver claims, that there might never have been a President Reagan without Nancy. Although she may have been shamefully remiss in her interference in Oval Office matters, she deserves considerable credit for her influence on Reagan's approach to the Soviets.

In his televised farewell address to the nation, Reagan spoke about his legacy as "the Great Communicator": "I never thought it was my style or the words I used that made a difference; it was the content. . . . I wasn't a great communicator, but I communicated great things, and they didn't spring full bloom from my brow, they came from the heart of a great nation—from our experience, our wisdom, and our belief in the principles that have guided us for two centuries. They call it the Reagan revolution. Well, I'll accept that, but for me it always seemed more like the great rediscovery, a rediscovery of our values and our common sense."[16]

Perhaps Reagan was not a great president either; that will be determined by history. But he was a great American who gained the trust of major global leaders and of his fellow countrymen and women. Gorbachev called him "a really big person . . . a very great political leader," and Margaret Thatcher never stopped singing his praises.[17]

The Reagans' last days at the White House were filled with honors, ceremonies, and tearful goodbyes. They spent one final weekend at Camp David, and then, almost abruptly it seemed, it was January 19, the day before they would leave the White House forever. Although infrequently, the Bushes had been in the family quarters before, but Barbara had come by in the afternoon for a walk-through to decide where she wanted to put some of her personal belongings. Nancy was gracious, despite the disorder created by the preparations for their move. She had grown to love these rooms and conveyed this in her attitude as she greeted their next occupant. That night the Reagans spent quietly with Maureen and Dennis and Ted Graber, who had helped Nancy decorate the family quarters and was now working with her on the plans for their new house in Bel Air. The five of them had dinner in Reagan's private study before a glowing fire. Outside, a gale wind was blowing, and the weather report promised gray skies and bone-chilling temperatures next day. Maureen said they talked about the future, not the past. Her dad had no intention of riding off into the sunset.

Plans were already set for a speaking tour that would take him to Japan, a deal for an autobiography was being negotiated with the publisher Simon & Schuster, and architectural renderings for a presidential library in Simi Valley, California, were being drawn. Nancy seemed more depressed than the president about leaving the White House. She would miss the extraordinary service, the luxury of living there, and the power, life at the center of things, that came with being first lady. For eight years, the White House had been her home, now it would be Barbara Bush's. "I understand now what Mrs. Carter was feeling when I came to see these rooms for the first time. But then she only lived here half as long as we have," she told Maureen.[18]

Friday, January 20, 1989 was, indeed, gray and blustery. Nancy rose early, along with Reagan. After breakfast he went into his study and "just puttered about for a time." Then he went down to the Oval Office and wrote a note to the new president and stuck it into the top drawer that would shortly be his. On a pad of notepaper inscribed on the top "Don't let the turkeys get you down," he had written in his inimitable scrawl:

Dear George:
There'll be moments when you'll want to use this particular stationery. Well, go for it. George, I treasure the memories we share and wish you all the very best. You'll be in my prayers. God bless you and Barbara. I'll miss our Thursday lunches.

RON.[19]

He did not think anyone would come in that morning, but when he looked up, Colin Powell was standing in the doorway. "Mr. President," he said, "the world is quiet today." Behind Powell, his uniform impeccable, his medals gleaming, was a camera crew come to shoot the president's last moments in the Oval Office. "Here were the cameramen, the sound guys, the light holders and the grips," Powell recalled. "And there, all alone against the backdrop of the Oval Office [his desktop cleared, the room looking spare] was Ronald Reagan shooting his last take."[20]

For the past week Nancy had been overseeing the packing and shipping of all their personal items, separating their personal property from what belonged to the government. Rooms looked bare as pictures and paintings were stripped from the walls. Boxes were piled high in corners and in corridors. Suitcases were stacked in their dressing rooms; these were to accompany them on their flight back to California along with any personal items still unpacked in their bedroom and bathrooms. Rex Stouten assured them that the final packing would be done and all their possessions moved for them by the time they were to leave Washington after the inaugural ceremony. Nancy had no reason to doubt this, recalling her amazement eight years earlier at finding the family quarters ready for them only a few hours after the Carters departed.

When Reagan left the Oval Office, he turned back for one last look. Then he joined Nancy in the State Dining Room where all the members of the domestic staff were lined up to extend their personal goodbyes. Nancy had been overwhelmed by their numbers on the first day of Reagan's term. Now they were mostly familiar faces, many associated with a special memory—the preparers of the state dinners and holiday parties, the butlers who brought them their trays at night, the maids who ironed a dress on a moment's notice, the dog walkers, the telephone operators— the list seemed endless. The domestic staff had extended so much kindness and uncomplaining service during the trying times of their illnesses. Such care could never again be had. The Reagans, as all past presidents, were saying goodbye to a way of life as well as to a group of people.

They met with the Bushes and the Quayles for coffee (although no one drank any), as they had done with the Carters, and at eleven o'clock they started the ride up Pennsylvania Avenue to the Capitol. The president and president-elect rode in one car, Nancy and Barbara Bush in another. The two women had not become close friends, but Barbara had been most sympathetic during the difficult times of the assassination attempt, the Reagans' illnesses, and the death of her parents, and Nancy would never forget that. They didn't talk much, caught up in the awe of the moment, and neither seemed to notice the drear and chill of the day.

As they drove out of the gates of the White House, Nancy managed to say, "I hope the magnolia trees I [had] planted will do well. Maybe my grandchildren will see them one day."[21]

Mrs. Bush nodded her head agreeably.

Nancy was solemn-faced as she watched George Bush being given the oath of office by Chief Justice Rehnquist. Without glancing down, her hand touched Reagan's. He seemed far more at ease. At the end, when Justice Rehnquist addressed Bush as "Mr. President," Reagan stood erect, shoulders squared. Only up close could the signs of aging be seen on his face. His hair was still untouched by gray, and at a quick glance he looked curiously younger than the new president. The same could be said of Nancy and silver-haired Barbara Bush.

The wind whipped at them as the Reagans, escorted by the Bushes, were helped into the helicopter that would take them to Andrews Air Force Base to board—not Air Force One, but AF27000—for California. As they lifted up into the cheerless, hoary sky the pilot circled the White House from above. "Look, dear," Reagan pointed to Nancy, "there's our bungalow."[22] Members of the press, including Sam Donaldson and Lou Cannon, flew back with them on AF27000. The chef presented a celebratory cake and champagne as a toast. On their arrival in Los Angeles, skies now of a golden hue, the thermometer at a warming seventy-seven degrees, they were greeted by the marching band of the University of Southern California. They went directly from the airport to their new house with, miraculously, all the suitcases they had left behind in the family quarters of the White House loaded into a car that followed them. Just as miraculously, the bed had been set up, the new furniture that Ted Graber had purchased was in place, flowers filled the main rooms, and the refrigerator was stocked with foods they both enjoyed.

When they were alone at last, Nancy admits that they clung together and cried. "It all seemed unreal and overwhelming," she explained later.[23] She also made note of the fact that if the Twenty-second Amendment to the Constitution had not limited the president's term of office, they would have been able to remain in the White House another four years. It seems that Nancy had done a complete about face from her position in 1984 and was now reluctant to forfeit power. But Reagan believed that such life changes were God's will and that He would also have plans for what His servant might do next. The important thing was to listen closely. He was fully prepared to do that.

CHAPTER TWENTY

LIFE CONTINUES, MEMORY FADES

T he Reagans had not had time to settle into their new home and what was essentially a different life when the media attacked them with extraordinary venom. Reagan was accused of cashing in on his presidency, accepting over $2 million for a speaking tour in Japan, signing up for six-figure engagements elsewhere, and agreeing to write his autobiography for $2.6 million. (Edmund Morris was reported as being paid $4 million dollars for his biography of the president, a contract signed in 1985.) As usual, Nancy did not get away without censure. She had also received seven figures for her memoir, *My Turn*, published by Random House shortly after they returned to California. (Kitty Kelley's advance for her scathing unauthorized biography *Nancy Reagan*, to be published by Simon & Schuster, Reagan's publisher, was also in the million-dollar orbit.)

Why the Reagans' high-paying contracts should have received such bad press is puzzling. Reagan was the most popular president, both at home and abroad, to leave office since Eisenhower (although the general had begun American involvement in Vietnam, sent paratroopers to enforce desegregation in Little Rock, Arkansas, allowed the Soviets to gain the lead in the space race, and done nothing when the Red Army rolled into Hungary in 1956). Reagan was also the most famous speaker, political or otherwise, since Roosevelt and Churchill and Kennedy. People wanted to hear and see him and were willing to pay top dollar to do so. There had not been a similar outcry over Nixon's financial windfall from his speeches and books after leaving the presidency in disgrace. Eisenhower, Ford, and Carter were all paid well for their autobiographies and speaking engagements, to which the press gave little attention.

Nancy was particularly upset about the criticism. In financial terms, the presidency had caused the Reagans to dip into their savings. The president's annual salary at that time was $200,000. That seems a tidy sum. However, when Reagan was inaugurated in 1981, he was certainly comfortable, but most of his assets were not income producing. The ranch, which he was determined to keep, was expensive to maintain. Presidents pay their own food bills, and as all items are ordered in and then passed by security, these costs are considerably higher than the average home outlay. Moreover, Reagan had continued to tithe ten percent of his salary to the church. Given Nancy's near obsession with their bank balance, it was not surprising that she should have encouraged Reagan to accept the offers when they came in.

A president's retirement pension is commensurate with his former salary and rises with the cost of living as the years progressed. Reagan would also receive $150,00 a year for five years for an office, staff, and office expenses. (The federal government would pay more for the Secret Service bodyguards, their equipment and vehicles, to protect the presidential couple, than Reagan would receive from his pension.) Both the Reagans would be covered with health insurance but not for some extras like private nurses at home, and Nancy would be entitled to the almost humiliating sum of $20,000 a year in the event of Reagan's death (which is what Jacqueline Kennedy received after her husband's assassination). This represented the height of sexism in government, especially if the amount of time and hard work a first lady contributes in what is essentially a nonpaying seven-day-a-week, fifty-two-weeks-a-year job, is taken into consideration. One cannot help but wonder, when a woman is elected president in the future, whether her husband would be expected to contribute the same effort without compensation.

Both of the Reagans had help on their books, but they were responsible for the tone and insight, inside information, and the telling stories of important and personal events. Nancy acknowledges Bill Novak as her collaborator, although his name does not appear on the cover. Neither does Robert Lindsey's whom Reagan credits inside with being "with me every step of the way."[1] Reagan met frequently with Lindsey, and they would talk; Lindsey would take notes, his wife Sandra would type them up. Lindsey put them in prose, and Reagan checked the pages. The book has an honest ring to it because Lindsey has beautifully caught Reagan's voice.

Michael Korda, editor in chief of Simon & Schuster, was in charge of the project. Korda, who also edited three of this author's early books, is an author in his own right (and seems to take a unique pleasure in skewering his more famous authors—Jacqueline Susann, Ronald Reagan—in profiles for the *New Yorker*, with a somewhat dubious but entirely readable end result). He had a horse farm in New York State, and his wife, Margaret, bred horses and was an accomplished horsewoman, having won a glittering array of silver cups for her prowess. Reagan quickly picked up on this mutual interest and his calls to Korda would often include a wish to speak to Margaret about her horses (and his). Korda vividly recalls his first meeting with Reagan in his new California office in June 1989.

"He was dressed in a light summer suit and smiled as naturally as if we had been friends all our lives. He had the kind of suntan and presence that only movie stars possess—a bigger-than-life quality that is purely physical, and that makes it hard to take your eyes off them even when they're not doing anything. His head was big, majestic, deeply seamed, his hands were gnarled, sinewy, and well cared for, but they were still a workingman's hands—they seemed Lincolnesque."[2]

Reagan's new offices were in one of the many towers in Century City, an area once the back lot of Twentieth Century–Fox, now boasting some of the most expensive real estate in Los Angeles. As behooved a former president, Reagan's office suite, which commanded a spectacular view of the city, was decorated in simple Americana. Korda recalls that the staff "all had perfect teeth, and many of the men wore red-white-and-blue patterned ties, while most of the women wore red-white-and-blue scarves. It wasn't exactly a uniform, but almost."[3]

One long wall in the reception room was a floor-to-ceiling glass-fronted museum case, where dozens of Reagan's saddles, presented to him as gifts, were on display. A Remington cowboy-on-a-horse statue sat on a wood plinth in a corner. Reminders of his beloved ranch life abounded and in his private office was a plethora of silver-framed pictures of Nancy alone, Nancy with him, and the two of them—mostly with famous people.

The Reagans were looking forward to spending the Fourth of July and Nancy's birthday on July sixth with their old friends Bill and Betty Wilson at their magnificent ranch in the Mexican state of Sonora (Bill Wilson had served under Reagan as the first U.S. ambassador to the Vatican and had also been responsible for finding Rancho del Cielo for the Reagans). The morning of July fourth was a spectacular day. The sun was glittering, the air so clear, the sky so blue, that it seemed as though you could see forever. The Wilsons' ranch included some of the most beautiful country in Sonora and riding paths that allowed fantastic views. Two Secret Service men came with them, but as Reagan and Wilson were the superior equestrians, they led the group. Reagan was on a spirited horse. That had never bothered him, but it did mean that horse and rider were not yet well acquainted.

They were proceeding down a rocky, downhill slope, when there was a rustle underfoot, most probably a snake, and Reagan's horse bucked wildly several times, his rider holding on tenaciously before being thrown off the animal onto the hard, graveled earth, his head hitting a rock. When his two Secret Service bodyguards and Bill Wilson reached him a split second later, he was stunned. He tried to sit up while the others restrained him.

One of the bodyguards used his cell phone to get assistance and within ten minutes the whir of a helicopter could be heard overhead. Reagan was flown, with Nancy, to Raymond W. Bliss Army Community Hospital at Ft. Huachuca, Arizona, where after X-raying and examining him, the doctors assured him that he had sustained bruises and a minor concussion but no serious injuries. "Well, honey," he grinned at Nancy, "I guess I had my own private rodeo." At his insistence they were flown back to the Wilsons' ranch by helicopter that same afternoon, accompanied by Capt. Juan Lopez, a U.S. Army doctor and the hospital's chief nurse, Lt. Col. Paul Farineau. The next day, against their advice and

Nancy's admonitions, he was back up in the saddle. "There is nothing better for the insides of a man than the outsides of a horse," he was fond of saying.[4]

In all the years of their marriage, Nancy had worried about many things but never Ronnie's handling of a horse. She had been badly frightened by the accident. She noticed small lapses of memory from that time on, and always blamed the fall from the horse as being the major cause of the disease that would eventually assail him as it had Nelle, and only recently, Neil, who no longer recognized his younger brother. A small blood clot had shown up when Reagan was reexamined in Los Angeles shortly after his return from Mexico, but it dissolved without surgery within a week.

The Reagans always had annual examinations at the Mayo Clinic in Rochester, Minnesota, and both were scheduled on September 7 for their 1989 checkup. Nancy was found to be in good health, but a CAT scan (not usually included in a general examination but done because of the earlier blood clot) located fluid on the right side of Reagan's brain (a condition that is known as a chronic subdural hematoma). A relatively simple procedure was ordered, which involved drilling a hole in the right side of the head and draining the fluid. Reagan entered St. Mary's Hospital in Rochester, where, on September 9, he underwent an hour-long surgery performed by a team of Mayo Clinic doctors. They removed the fluid on his brain.

He remained at St. Mary's, Nancy at his side, until September 16, his natural good humor seeming untouched as he joked about "the GI haircut" the doctors had given him. On Friday the fifteenth, he was visited by the maverick Soviet Communist Boris Yeltsin. Through interpreters the two men exchanged jokes. One example of Yeltsin's humor is a story he told about his first encounter with the Statue of Liberty: "I flew around it in a helicopter and I felt much freer, so I asked the pilot to fly around it again and then I felt completely free."

Yeltsin, who had been pushing Gorbachev to move faster with perestroika (restructuring) and glasnost reforms, had recently called for the "entire Soviet centralized bureaucracy to be dismantled in order to allow private cooperative groups to associate freely among themselves, sell their wares directly in the marketplace and deal directly with Western enterprises." He also called for "liberalization of foreign exchange controls for Soviet currency."[5] But he was silent about allowing the refuseniks to leave Russia, and Reagan could not let the opportunity pass without stressing the importance of doing so if the Soviet Union wished to have good relations with the West.

The Reagans flew home from Rochester in an army plane, Reagan appearing in fine form, although the doctors had insisted he cancel all speeches and travel for four weeks. There was much to fill their days. Nothing had prepared them for the amount of correspondence they would receive and be obliged to answer. They took an enormous interest in the construction of the Ronald Reagan Presidential Library in Simi Valley, a forty-minute drive from St. Cloud Road. There had been a groundbreaking ceremony the previous November. Now there was something new to see almost every week. The site was spectacular, one hundred acres, twenty-nine of them on the very top of a mountain that overlooked a 360-degree vista from snow-capped peaks to the ocean, and glancing down a valley gracefully curved around the foothills below. The property had been donated, but the library itself is one of eleven presidential libraries maintained by the National Archives and Records Administration.

Reagan had specific requests. The library was to be set so that the rear of the vast building would have huge glass expanses that placed the panoramic view directly before a visitor. He also wanted to replicate the Oval Office as it was during his occupancy, and he did not want the room to be scaled down. The architect Hugh Stubbins argued that the height of the ceilings in the library was considerably lower than that of those at the White House. "Then dig," Reagan replied.

"Dig, Mr. President?"

"Yes. Lower the floor and put in stairs leading down to it."

And they did.[6]

The measurements are exact. Doors, windows, and moldings were copied from the original. Exact replicas were made of the furniture, the rug, the paintings on the walls, and the view outside the Oval Office window. (One key feature is an authentic copy of "The Resolute," the desk that John F. Kennedy had used as well, which had been a gift from Queen Victoria to President Rutherford B. Hayes in 1880.) As a final touch, Reagan had all the items he once had on his desk arranged as they were when he occupied the Oval Office. The library museum and library facilities and archives are state of the art. On the second floor, behind locked doors and down a windowed corridor, are his and Nancy's private sitting-room offices, furnished with the pieces (desk, chairs, tables, sofas) that they had had in the family quarters of the White House, red-and-white flowered fabric on the upholstered pieces and the drapes.

In the lower bowels of the building is a massive, temperature-controlled, security-monitored storeroom for the more than hundred thousand gifts presented to the Reagans while he was in office. These belong to the federal government, as a president is not allowed to keep any gift over $180 (that figure had doubled by the year 2000), unless he cared to pay for the item at its assessed value. Tens of dozens of drawers are filled with gifts (including a solid gold evening bag, from a Saudi prince, the initials NR in well-cut diamonds); elephants of all description and size, many of them jeweled, others of finely tooled leather or carved wood; hundreds of saddles and boots and other riding equipment, silver of all types—salvers, candlesticks, boxes (most engraved or decorated with precious or semiprecious stones); and one personal item that the Reagans had bought at auction—the red leather booth from Chasen's where Ronnie had proposed to Nancy.

In November 1989 the Berlin Wall was torn down after a series of dramatic demonstrations. East Germany had resisted Gorbachev's reform policies and in attempting to establish itself in the tradition of old-style, rigid Communism found itself at the center of an uprising, with tens of thousands of East Germans fleeing to West Germany through Hungary and Czechoslovakia, many losing their lives in their run for freedom. Reagan's cry of "Tear down that wall, Mr. Gorbachev!" had been heard, although the action had taken place on Mr. Bush's watch. Reagan was jubilant and thrilled when a huge chunk of the wall was shipped to the Ronald Reagan Presidential Library and erected in the rear courtyard in time for its gala opening on November 4, 1991. The dedication of the library brought together all the other living presidents to honor Reagan—Richard Nixon, Gerald Ford, Jimmy Carter, and George Bush, along with their wives. The two presidential widows, Lady Bird Johnson and Jacqueline Kennedy Onassis, were also invited, but Jackie, under treatment for cancer, did not attend. President Ford told this author that it was a great afternoon and that "a spirit of high regard was held by all those present." He and Reagan seemed to have lost any trace of their past animosity. It was a happy occasion, and the five men lined up with broad smiles for a memorable photo shoot.

The fall of the Berlin Wall set in fast motion the total collapse of Communist governments in Eastern Europe and added to Gorbachev's problems. Party defections from right and left threw the Soviet Union into chaos. Gorbachev assumed the position of president with dire results. The economy of the country worsened. Food supplies dwindled. Bread became a luxury, housewives having to stand in lines for hours in order to buy a loaf, and even then the cost was so high that workers—unpaid for months—could not afford the price. Yeltsin challenged Gorbachev for the presidency and won, but was unable to remove him from power. Finally, in December, 1991, the two men and the ruling body of the Soviet Union agreed that the USSR would cease to exist on January 1, 1992. The Evil Empire had been toppled, and although George Bush was in the White House, people did not forget that it was Ronald Reagan who had been the instigator in its collapse.

The publication of two books—Patti's autobiography, *The Way I See It* (1992), and Kitty Kelley's *Nancy Reagan* (1990)—both skewering Nancy, and in Patti's case sometimes her father—were painful reminders to Nancy of how vulnerable she was. Patti's memoir, more searing than her novel had been, was by far the most difficult for her mother to accept. Nancy claims she did not read Kelley's book, but she did thumb through her daughter's with great sadness. At the time it seemed there never would be good relations between Patti and her mother. Her father tried to comfort Nancy, but admitted he found it difficult to understand why Patti had been so cruel to someone who loved her as much as Nancy did and who had tried (in his manner of thinking) to do her best.

Reagan believed that retirement was for other people, not for him. He dressed impeccably every morning, and was driven to his spacious office suite, spending several hours at his desk talking to a few select people and conducting the usual rituals of a former president. Hundreds of letters arrived every week requiring an answer, including endless requests for him to make a public appearance. He accepted very few. A former secretary claims that at least until the end of 1992, when she left his employ, Reagan closely followed domestic and foreign affairs and kept in touch with former presidents Ford and Carter and the incumbent president, George H. W. Bush. (She could not recall that he ever spoke directly with Bush's successor, Bill Clinton.)

Sometime toward the end of 1993 Nancy became alarmed after they had flown to Chicago, where Reagan was to give a speech. Once they had been driven to their hotel and led into their suite, he turned to her and said, "I'm afraid I don't know where I am."[7]

Marion Jorgensen, at whose home he had always spent election eves, recalled an evening about this same time when he came into her living room with Nancy and suddenly a puzzled look clouded his face as he glanced at his hostess and then out the window, "This place is familiar to me," he said. "I know I've been here before."[8] And then came a dinner for Mrs. Thatcher where he repeated a paragraph in his honoring speech to her without realizing he had done so.

The times he seemed confused, not sure of where he was became more frequent. He would enter a room purposefully and than pause, a look of some bewilderment in his puzzled eyes. Long moments could pass with him in this state, and often he needed assistance to return to his desk. "Who are you?" he asked a secretary who had been with him for years.[9]

Nancy's fear mounted. Ronnie had always had two distinct sides to his personality. On the one hand he was gregarious, enjoying the company of a few or of many; stories, theories, commentary with great enthusiasm, often shot with a touch of down-home humor. He could also be a loner, withdrawn. His daughter Patti recalls that shortly before he was elected president she looked over at him "standing in the middle of a crowd, alone. People were around him but no one was talking to him.... It was one of those cocktail party moments that usually goes [*sic*] unnoticed. Except I noticed, and I remembered it."[10]

Early in their relationship Nancy had accepted Ronnie's moments of separateness. She understood, when others did not, that he was an extraordinary man. But he was never hesitant in showing her how much he loved her or in telling her and anyone who would listen how indispensable she was to his life. And he never was shy about expressing his love for her in public by holding her hand, or placing his large, well-muscled arm around her narrow, delicate shoulders. "Powder down your lipstick," he once telegraphed when he was out barnstorming for GE. He was on his way home and could not wait to kiss her.[11] She had received from him well over a hundred letters, notes, telegrams, and cards, all declaring his great love for her. The presidency and the passing years had not stopped their flow, but his growing confusion had. No longer could Nancy attribute his lapses to ordinary forgetfulness. She now refused to leave his side except for those times when he was in his office and surrounded by loyal and protective staff.

Still, it was difficult for her to admit that anything deeply serious was taking place. He retained his social skills. He seemed to be willing himself to hang on to some semblance of the normal. They saw their old, trusted friends—Betsy Bloomingdale, the Deutsches, the Wicks, the Jorgensens, and the Annenbergs, among numerous others. They visited people's homes, or their friends came to theirs. Nancy became almost custodial, not wanting Ronnie to be placed in any situation that could lead to public embarrassment. By the summer of 1994 his lapses, his moments of confusion, worsened, and he submitted to medical tests and a brain scan at the Mayo Clinic. The dreaded diagnosis of Alzheimer's disease was made. At this time he was cognizant enough—his lapses interspersed with reasonably lucid intervals—to understand what he had and what it meant.

"His courage was outstanding," one close friend says, "but so was Nancy's."[12]

He and Nancy discussed what he should do. She pledged that she would, as always, remain by his side. Theirs was an unalterable love.

Determined to make something good of this tragic news, Reagan decided to tell the American people the truth, so that perhaps he could take some of the stigma off the disease. He sat down and began writing a draft the way he had always begun his speeches. He wrote it at his desk in the comfortable library of the Bel Air house, Nancy seated across from him as he moved his pen with a somewhat shaky hand. Most of his speeches had been written in this manner, marked with hen scratches as he edited his first thoughts. This letter took longer than usual, but the first draft of his last communication to the American people has only one correction—a line through the letter *I* in the middle of a sentence where he might have forgotten, for a moment, what he wanted to say. The draft is in his distinct hand.

On November 5, 1995, he bade the country his moving, brave good-bye, ending with: "I intend to live the remainder of the years God gives me on this earth doing the things I have always done. I will continue to share life's journey with my beloved Nancy and my family. . . . Unfortunately, as Alzheimer's Disease progresses, the family often bears a heavy burden. I only wish there was some way I could spare Nancy from this painful experience. When the time comes I am confident that with your help she will face it with faith and courage. . . ." (See appendix 8 for the complete text of his farewell letter.)[13]

Nancy was once quoted as saying about her relationship with the media, "If it rains, I get blamed for it." Now they rallied to her side. It helped—but only a little bit. Her concentration was on how to make Ronnie's life meaningful in view of his inevitable decline and on how to protect him and to preserve his dignity.

He continued with his daily trips to his office. There was a pretense that things were as they had always been, at least in the first years after the end of his administration. But he remained behind closed doors while "business as usual" was being conducted by his staff. Only a few trusted colleagues were allowed to visit him. Before they arrived, Nancy ordered the staff to make sure that framed photographs of that person with Reagan or of events in which the guest had participated be placed in strategic positions on tables and shelves so as to catch his eye as he ushered the guest into his private study. Before the visitor's arrival,

Nancy (or a secretary on her orders) would walk Ronnie around the room looking at the photographs to refresh whatever residual memories existed: "This is when he visited us at the ranch." "Here you both are on the plane during the second presidential campaign."[14] He would then repeat to his guest what he had just been told when he or she arrived moments later and he took them on a tour through his office. By 1998 his condition had so deteriorated that Nancy decided the office had to be closed and that Ronnie should be seen only by close family members. She called some of his oldest associates, like Michael Deaver, who for three decades had been his loyal aide and longtime family friend, to come and say goodbye.

When Deaver entered, Reagan "was sitting at his desk reading a large book. . . . he didn't look up," Deaver recalled. "He looked pretty good, I thought. Blue suit, French cuffs—for a man then in his late eighties, he was well turned-out." Deaver realized that he could stand there all day without Reagan taking notice of him and that he would "have to take charge if there was going to be any conversation."

"Hi," Deaver blurted, moving toward the desk.

After an awkward pause, Reagan looked up, his gaze "questioning and unrecognizing."

"Yes," he said, his voice polite. Then he returned his attention to the open book.

"Whatcha reading?" Deaver asked.

"A horse book," he replied.

Deaver glanced over at what Reagan was holding in his hands. "It was a picture book about Traveller, General Robert E. Lee's horse. I felt like crying," he recalled.[15] Reagan had no memory of who Deaver was or how close the two once had been, for a good part seeing each other daily, over a span of thirty years.

Nancy kept her fears mostly to herself, although she spoke of them to confidants Betsy Bloomingdale and Merv Griffin, "and if anyone knew her true feelings it was them."[16] She converted the house into a home where Ronnie could receive round-the-clock care and yet not be isolated from her. She was with him on a daily basis and supervised his mealtimes whenever possible. She talked to him about the family and all that was going on, despite the knowledge that little of what she said made sense to him. (This was in the late 1990s.) According to one staff member, "Mrs. Reagan was remarkable. She kissed the president's forehead, gently pushed his hair back from it, patted his hand and smiled—oh, my, how she smiled at him. It broke your heart. But at some point he would look at her and smile back. I don't believe she ever did, or ever could, let go of the idea that he knew who she was. Whether he did or not, he was aware that she was someone who cared for him, and he responded to that."[17]

During the last year of his cognition, Reagan's faith in God never appeared to waver. He was never known to have asked why God could have allowed this to happen to him, nor to display anger toward Him. Like Nelle, he accepted God's will. This disease, after all, was not man's doing. Nancy was no martyr. She was frustrated at times. Frightened at others. She grieved for what their life once had been. But Ronnie was in a safe place. He was not in pain, nor was he aware of what he had lost. For Nancy, the hardest thing to accept was that for Ronnie the past had slipped away. He no longer remembered that he had been the president of the United States, he no longer recognized his children, or even recalled their existence, nor knew that he had shared with Nancy a splendid love. These were the things that were almost unbearable. But for as long she lived, she would become his memory.

She took over the supervision of his correspondence (which still came in at a tremendous rate), as well as her own, along with all decisions that had to be made on their personal affairs and on the running of their household. She kept up with the newest medications for Alzheimer's and had frequent consultations with his doctors and their accountant. As always, the large expenditures for the house and care were of great concern to her. But in 1998 she sold Rancho del Cielo for a reported $6 million to the Young America's Foundation, a conservative group with its main offices in Santa Barbara, for use as a conference center. When not dealing with his care or spending time with Ronnie, Nancy threw herself into numerous charitable projects, into working with the staff at the Ronald Reagan Presidential Library, into the compilation of a book composed of Ronnie's love letters to her through the years (published as *I Love You, Ronnie*), and in 2002 she privately lobbied support for stem-cell research in hopes that the results of such work could eventually help early victims of Alzheimer's disease.

With the passage of the years, Nancy's greatest fear had been of a time when she would have to face life without Ronnie. Now she was fearful of how she would cope while he was alive. She wanted, above all, to maintain for him his dignity, to preserve in the minds of the people of the world an image of him conveying strength and purpose, the leader of the free world. Her job, as she saw it, was to protect his image as vigilantly as she would protect the man, especially now that he could not look after himself.

Her father's decline brought Patti close, for the first time in years, to her mother. Nancy managed to put aside her ill-feelings regarding Patti's literary excursions into their family history. "I need her now, more than ever," Nancy was known to have said.[18] With her father slipping away from her, Patti was, as she would say, shocked as to "how the years could have gone by so fast, how we [her father and herself] could have been so reckless with time, with words, with our hearts." One day, during a visit when he no longer recognized her, she took his hand in hers and remembered "how his hands had once chopped firewood and assembled Christmas toys for [Ron and herself]. When, I wondered, did his fingers lose their calluses, when did they become so delicate?"[19] Patti would never be able to have that reconciliatory confrontation with her father, the exchange that she always had hoped would lead to his understanding her. Now she wished that she had better understood him, but this re-alization came too late. She would not let this happen with her mother.

With Nancy so involved with his care, Maureen took on the task of being her father's spokesperson, appearing at various venues where he was to be honored in some way. One of her favorite journeys was to Dixon, where, she said, her "father's heart has always been . . . and it always will be." He had often told her stories of growing up in what he called "the greatest town in America."[20] Dixon, with the help of Con-gress, was setting up the house on Hennepin Street where he had lived from 1924 to 1928 as a national historic site. The streets he walked on his way to school and church were named the Ronald Reagan Trail. A statue of him was placed in Lowell Park. At the dedication of all these tributes to the humble hometown boy who had become president, Maureen would appear, flashing her winning Reagan smile, filled with exuberance and tales about the father whom she idolized, never a bad word said, never a mention of his years of inattention. Maureen and Dennis, who were childless, had adopted Rita, a young girl of color, toward the end of Reagan's presidency, and he had taken much pleasure in teaching her how to swim. By the late nineteen-nineties Rita was in her teens and accompanied her mother to Dixon. "My grandfather wasn't always a 'honcho,'" Rita commented to a group of teenagers at Ronald W. Reagan Middle School in Dixon. "He started out as a guy, just like us."[21] The Reagans had three grandchildren—Cameron and Ashley Reagan and Rita Revell—but none of them carried the genes of Nancy or Ronald Reagan.

Ronald Reagan celebrated his eighty-sixth birthday, February 6, 1997, with Nancy, blew out a candle on his favorite chocolate cake, and was still sharp enough to make a comment (possibly scripted for him) that this was "the forty-seventh anniversary of my thirty-ninth birthday." Until 1999 he managed to play a few supervised holes of golf once or twice a week. The time finally came when he had to be moved to the separate suite that adjoined the master bedroom that Nancy had prepared for him. After a fall in 2001, when he broke his hip, Nancy hired three shifts of nurses to care for him upon her return home from the hospital, his hip now pinned. She complained to friends about the financial burden and about the inequitable pension given presidents upon their retirement, but never about the physical and emotional difficulties of her life.

Perhaps the one kind thing his memory loss spared Reagan was the grief when Maureen died in August 2001 of a melanoma that had spread to the bone. Through the years Mermie had become the child to whom he was the closest.

Nancy's aura had done a complete about-face. Now she was viewed with grave respect by the media. After the death of Jackie Kennedy Onassis, Nancy was accorded the status of the brave widow, without actually being widowed. Her beloved other had lived on year after year after year, the once strapping physique that had made her feel so feminine now frail; the vibrant voice that had so stirred the patriotic instincts of his countrymen and women a faint whisper; his past, the most glorious a man born in the United States could experience—the humble boy rising to the presidency—lost to him. Nancy would sit by his bed and talk to him. Although he did not comprehend what she was saying, nor was Nancy certain he actually knew who she was, her voice did touch something that memory had once lighted, and he seemed calmed, reassured. He would smile, and the smile transformed his pale, almost skeletal face so that the man he once was became fleetingly apparent again.

Nancy published her book of his love letters in 2001 to show the world just how much she had meant to him. She christened an aircraft carrier, the USS *Ronald Reagan*, which was twenty stories high and could go twenty years without refueling its nuclear engines, a use of nuclear power that she knew Reagan would have heartily approved. She accepted the nation's highest honor, the Congressional Gold Medal, in both their names. Her past iniquities were not forgotten, but they paled under the bright, steady light of her devotion. She stood for loyalty in the extreme and symbolized a love that satisfied the weepiest sentimentalist.

The Reagan presidency was also being rethought by the public and political pundits. He had earned a reverence from the nation's citizens that was akin to worship. He had seen his country as being confronted by evil, "and the Communist states as simply the latest enemy that needed to be defeated rather than accommodated."[22] Whether he was largely responsible for the dismantling of the Berlin Wall and the collapse of the Soviet state remains for history to decide. But he had made his mark. He would be long remembered and held in obeisance by many (and perhaps in disfavor by many as well). And while you cannot compare the Reagans' marriage to those of John and Abigail Adams, James and Dolley Madison, or Franklin and Eleanor Roosevelt, because each couple has its own dynamics, throughout history they will always be thought of as a team. Could Nancy ever have wished for more?

ACKNOWLEDGMENTS

This book has been a long time in the making. It has been over twenty years now that I began work on *Early Reagan: The Rise to Power*, a biography of Ronald Reagan that was in its original concept to take him to the eve of his January 20, 1981 presidential inauguration. He was at the time two weeks short of his seventieth birthday, the oldest man to be elected president of the United States. Many of my extensive interviews were conducted with this in view and I sought out information about his early years along with his political career. Partway through I realized that it would have to be done in two volumes. *Early Reagan* thus ended on the eve of his election as governor of California.

Early Reagan: The Rise to Power was published in 1987. Ronald Reagan remained in the White House after a landslide reelection and was then enmeshed in the Iran-Contra affair. I decided that a second volume would have to wait. I am now grateful that I did. In the years that intervened before this book was begun, I came to the decision that once Nancy Davis married Ronald Reagan, they melded so into one another, their impact was so great on each other's life, that the only way to understand either one of them was to tell the story of their unique marriage. I am convinced that if Ronald Reagan had not married Nancy Davis, he would not have been president of the United States. That is how *The Reagans: Portrait of a Marriage* evolved.

For the first chapters in this book I have gone back to those early interviews, speaking to many of the people who previously had given so generously of their time and memories and who did so once again. I am especially grateful to the good folk of Dixon, Illinois where I conducted roundtable interviews of six to eight people, allowing one person's memories to spur another. I repeated this approach in Hollywood and Sacramento, as well as interviewing others on a one-to-one basis.

I owe a tremendous debt of gratitude to President Gerald R. Ford, who was so graciously forthcoming and to former first lady Nancy Reagan who, although I did not interview her for this book, never placed any obstacle in my path. She showed extreme kindness toward me and my husband and made my early days of research at the Ronald Reagan Presidential Library a very special experience. I have worked in many research libraries, but never have I encountered more helpful, good-natured, and knowledgeable archivists than at the RRPL. No query ever went unanswered, and no research request was overlooked. I was given access to material not yet catalogued. Thank you, thank you, Diane Barrie! And to you, Steve Branch and Josh Tannenbaum, photo archivists of the highest order, more thanks. Not to be overlooked were the helping hands of Greg Cumming, Megan Lee, David Bridge, John P. Langellier (curator), Mike Dugan, and the many others at the RRPL who also never turned aside a request.

My great appreciation to the late Maureen Reagan; to the delightful Armand Deutsch; to Susan Granger; to Dixonite William (Bill) Thompson, whose interviews clarified so much of Reagan's early years and who so generously shared all of his Reagan correspondence, clippings, and memorabilia with me; and to Stella Grobe (Loveland Community House, Dixon). The late Lew Wasserman, Benjamin Thau, Joy Hodges Scheiss, and John (Jack) Dales gave generously of their time and added much insight, as did Michael Dean Edwards, Earl B. Dunckel, Jean Kinney, Roddy McDowell, Colleen Moore, and Larry Kramer. Additional gratitude to Benjamin J. Guthrie (clerk, U.S. House of Representatives), James K. Hall (former chief, Freedom of Information-Privacy Acts Section, U.S. Dept. of Justice, Washington, D.C.), Reverend Benjamin A. Moore (Disciples of Christ Church), Thomas W. Shepherd, First Christian Church (Disciples of Christ, Los Angeles), Kristine Kreuger (Academy of Motion Picture Arts and Sciences), and Penny Circle (secretary to President Gerald R. Ford).

In the course of the many years I have been working on this project, the staffs of many libraries and archives have been helpful. I openly thank them all. Researchers all owe a debt to their perseverance and assistance. Many people contributed to this book but have asked to remain anonymous. Still, I owe them my gratitude and extend it here, as I do to the many others who I interviewed for *Early Reagan* and whose tapes, questionnaires, and notes contained pertinent material that I have incorporated here.

I have worked with many copy editors during my rather long writing career. None was more diligent or easier to agree with than Donald J. Davidson, who also managed a sense of humor that made the medicine go down easier. My excellent editor at St. Martin's Press, Hope Dellon, cheered me on with her enthusiasm. Ellis Levine was extremely helpful, as were Kris Kamikawa of St. Martin's Press and Marcelle Garfield Cady, an able research assistant.

To Mitch Douglas, my agent for the past twenty-five years, and Buddy Thomas, his patient and accommodating assistant, many, many thanks.

Yet, despite the marvelous cooperation I have had in the writing of this book, it could not have been achieved without the help of my husband, Stephen Citron, an acclaimed biographer in his own right who gave of his time and counsel, accompanying me to dusty archives and giving me the full benefit of his excellent insight and research capabilities.

I am indebted to you all.

EXCERPT FROM GUEST COLUMN FOR LABOR COLUMNIST VICTOR RIESEL'S SYNDICATED COLUMN FEBRUARY, 1950.

This column was the basis for a speech by Ronald Reagan given shortly thereafter to LAMBDA Fraternity.

... Day after day in this year's hearings by the House Committee on Un-American Activities, the same story has been unfolded—a story of Communist frustration and failure in the party's bold plot to seize control of the talent guilds and craft unions, through which the subversive brethren hoped eventually to control the content of films and thus influence the minds of 800,000,000 movie goers. ... the Red propagandists and conspirators in this country were trying to carry out orders for Joseph Stalin, who had said: "The cinema is not only a vital agitprop device for the education and political indoctrination of the workers, but is also a fluent channel through which to reach the minds and shape the desires of people everywhere. The Kinofikatsiya [turning propaganda into films] is inevitable. The task is to take this affair into your hands, and vigorously execute it in every field."

So the Red enemies of our country concentrated their big guns on Hollywood. And they failed completely. But not before they had succeeded in bringing about two years of disastrous strikes and bloody fighting in which American workmen battled other American workmen at the studio gates. And, unfortunately, not before the Communists had fooled some otherwise loyal Americans into believing that the Communist party sought to make a better world. Those dupes know today that the real aim of the Communist party is to try to prepare the way for Russian conquest of the world. ...

... I believe that all participants in the international Communist conspiracy against our nation should be exposed for what they are—enemies of our country and of our form of government. And any American who has been a member of the Communist party at any time but has now changed his mind and is loyal to our country should be willing to stand up and be counted, admit "I was wrong," and give all the information he has to the government agencies who are combatting the Red plotters. We've gotten rid of the Red conspirators in Hollywood. Let's do it now in other industries.

AMERICA THE BEAUTIFUL
COMMENCEMENT ADDRESS,

William Woods College, Fulton, Missouri, June 2, 1952

... I feel duty bound to inform you that I am going to try to give you some remarks from my mind and my heart, but they certainly will not be an address. If I had a text for anything I am going to say, you have heard it in the opening hymn, "American the Beautiful." I know that this is not particularly a fashionable subject. Too many tub-thumping politicians on too many Fourths of July have paid word tribute in platitudes to the 4th of July speech and waved the flag. All of us as we grow older have a tendency to grow a little cynical, to find fault, to see the things that should be done and as we're younger we're a little impatient with sentiment and emotion. We are a little reluctant to show it, we're impatient for change, and we want correction of those things that are wrong and should be done and so, perhaps, none of us pay enough attention to the very thought behind this land of ours....

America is less of a place than an idea, and if it is an idea, and I believe that to be true, it is an idea that has been deep in the souls of man ever since man started on his long trail from the swamps. It is nothing but the inherent love of freedom in each one of us, and the great ideological struggle that we find ourselves engaged in today is not a new struggle. It's the same old battle. We met it under the name of Hitlerism; we met it under the name of Kaiserism; and we have met it back through the ages in the name of every conqueror that has ever set upon a course of establishing rule over mankind. It is simply the idea, the basis of this country and of our religion, the idea of the dignity of man, the idea that deep within the heart of each one of us is something so God-like and precious that no individual or group has a right to impose its or his will upon the people, that no group can decide for the people what is good for the people so well as they can decide for themselves.

I, in my own mind, have thought America as a place in the divine scheme of things that was set aside as a promised land. It was set here and the price of admission was very simple: the means of selection was very simple as to how this land should be populated. Any place in the world and any person from those places; any person with the courage, with the desire to tear up the roots, to strive for freedom, to attempt and dare to live in a strange and foreign place, to travel half across the world was welcome here. And they brought with them to the bloodstream that has become America that precious courage, the courage that they, and they alone in their community, in their nation, in their family, had in the first place, to this land, the hometown, to strive for something better for themselves and for their children and their children's children. I believe that God in shedding his grace on this country has always in this divine scheme of things kept an eye on our land and guided it as a promised land for these people.

There is a legend about the group of fathers of this country meeting in a long debate in Independence Hall regarding the signing of a Declaration of Independence. As the hours wore on and the talk was filled with the sound of treason, traitors, heads rolling, we shall hang, at the very peak of this, there stood up a man and spoke out and with his voice all was stilled. He said, "Sign that document, sign it if tomorrow your heads roll from the headsman's axe. Sign that document because tomorrow and the days to come, your children and all the children of all the days to come will judge you for what you do today." As he went on speaking his oratory was so great, his words so sincere and so moving that there was a sudden movement to the front of the room, and the Declaration of Independence was signed. When the ceremony was completed and they turned to find the man that had swayed the issue, they could not find him. The doors were guarded, and they asked the guards and no one had seen anyone leave; and no one knows to this day although his words are recorded, who the man was nor could they find anyone who had spoken the words that caused the Declaration to be signed.

Since that day, and down through the years, we have seen grow an American personality. We who have within our nation and within ourselves all the bloodstreams of all the national origins in the world know that today there is an American personality, something that stamps us indefinable as what we are. . . .

[S]omeone once during [World War II] marveled that we seem to be the only people that could laugh and fight at the same time. I don't think this stems from any love of fighting, it just stems from the rich warm humor that comes from confidence in the belief all that is good, that is inherited in all of us.

I think it was best illustrated out in a lonely Pacific Island one day. A B-24 came in, buzzed the field, circled, and asked for landing instructions. Suddenly the control tower, as they buzzed the runway, saw a one-star flag painted on the side of this plane, and there was a hasty call for the Officer of the Day and the Commanding Officer with the announcement that a general was coming in. So they hastily mustered the guard and the Officer of the Day stood there as the plane landed and pulled to a stop. The crew came forth and the top ranking man was a youngster about 22 years old, a Major. They looked beyond him and asked, "Where's the General?" and he said, "General? There's no General, this is all of us." "But the one-star flag?" He said, "Oh that is a service flag. Our tailgunner's grandmother works at Lockheed."

It is said to you and to all of us that this is a man's world. You young ladies are getting ready to set foot into this man's world. I am not going to take issue with this particular belief or this claim. It's been said for as long as men have controlled the means of saying anything that a short time ago during World War II a new word was coined to this man's world, the term "momism." Many articles were written deploring the influence of the American female on the men of this man's world and blaming them for the fact that a large number of the young men have been unable or unwilling to face the test of war in behalf of their country. I am not going to take issue with this, but if blame is to be attached to the females of our country, if women are going to be blamed under the term of "momism" for this group of men who could not meet the test, then certainly credit must be due, and credit must be given where it is due. For if "momism" is responsible for those failures then "momism" must be responsible for the sixteen million young men who did meet those tests. "Momism" must have been responsible for the happenings in a B-17, the ball turret gunner was wounded, and the turret was jammed so they could not get him out. Finally, the pilot had to order, Bail out, and as the men started to leave the plane, the trapped wounded kid in the ball turret knew he was being left behind and he cried out in terror. Even the dry words of the situation in military language for heroism cannot hide the drama and the nobility of what took place then. The last man to leave the plane saw the co-pilot sit down and take the boy's hand and he said, "Never mind, son, we'll ride it down together." Congressional Medal of Honor posthumously awarded. . . .

You young ladies are going to embark on many graduation days on through your lives. There is a form of graduation day that marks each one of our passing from one phase of life to another, but none will be more important nor linger in your minds more than this. None will be more important from a standpoint of making a decision, of choosing your way. I know it is very easy for all of us to say; the events in the world are so large, the happenings of our nation are so great; what can I as an individual do; I have no place in this; this is for people who control the movements of mankind. . . .

Now you, in making a choice in embarking upon a course, can choose a form of "momism" as the boys I have talked about in the B-17, the boys your age, tonight or today are standing, I guess it is night there now, in Korea. . . . General Ridgway spoke of their courage, their heroism a few days ago. These are the boys that you are going to marry. You are going to teach and heal and mother their sons. You have an opportunity to decide now whether to this man's world you will contribute men who will believe in a love of humanity and love of their fellow men regardless of race or creed or national origin. If you embark on the right course and do this, you may bring closer the day when your sons and their sons will not have to prove their worth by bleeding all that they are and all they ever hope to be into the sands of some far-flung beach head. And now on this day of congratulations to you, I would like on behalf of all these people around you who have preceded you into the world, I would like to bid you welcome. We need you, we need your youthful honesty, we need your courage, we need your sweetness, and with your help I am sure we can come much closer to realizing that this land of ours is the last best hope of man on earth. God bless you!

RONALD REAGAN

NELLE REAGAN'S LETTER TO MARY AND JAY SIPE (DIXON, ILLINOIS)

Written July 15, 1957, Los Angeles, California

Darling Mary and Jay,

Was I ever happy when I wrote a letter to you wishing that the Dixon Friends would write me; that was when I developed a bad heart attact [sic] and they come very often so that I really expect to go in one of them some time, and what a wonderful response from my Dixon Friends.

I bet the post office here in California thought—My, this Mrs. Reagan must have a load of Friends back in Dixon, Illinois, it was just like a shower, the box was running over when the mail man dropped it in [through a slot in her front door], it was all over the floor, and I just cried for joy over every letter I read, how very grand of all of you dear ones to bring me such happiness. I just can't find words to express my great love to you all.

I am a shut in. I can't drive a car any more so it was sold this last week. I will be 74 years young this month of July, and am grateful to God, to have spared this long life. Yet when each attact [sic] comes I whisper—"Please God, let it be now, take me home," but He still isn't ready for me, or He would take me; there must be something I haven't done, and He don't [sic] want me until my tasks are done.

Neil picked me up in his car Monday on his way home from work and took me to his home for a nice dinner and later he and Bessie brought me home, they wanted me to stay overnight, but when the heart attacts [sic] come, I cry out with pain, its so awful and I just couldn't disturb their rest that way so Neil finally gave in and they took me home.

I wish you and Jay could come and visit me. Do try and see old Nellie Gray [her own nickname for herself] once more before I pass on, I hope this dream of mine will come true.

I must close now, the doctor says I must not write long letters, but one can't get enough on a post card. I am going to answer each letter [from Dixon] but must rest now.

I love you both so much, Nelle.

AMENDMENT XXV TO THE CONSTITUTION OF THE UNITED STATES

The proposed amendment was sent to the states July 6, 1965,

by the Eighty-ninth Congress. It was ratified February 10, 1967.

Section 1: [Succession of Vice President to Presidency] In case of the removal of the President from office or of his death or resignation, the Vice President shall become President.

Section 2: [Vacancy in office of Vice President] Whenever there is a vacancy in the office of the Vice President, the President shall nominate a Vice President who shall take office upon confirmation by a majority vote of both Houses of Congress. [This was invoked when Vice President Spiro Agnew resigned and Gerald Ford was voted in to replace him].

Section 3: [Vice President as Acting President] Whenever the President transmits to the President pro tempore of the Senate and the Speaker of the House of Representatives his written declaration that he is unable to discharge the powers and duties of his office, and until he transmit to them a written declaration to the contrary, such powers and duties shall be discharged by the Vice President as Acting President. [President Reagan did not at any time during his hospitalization after the assassination attempt invoke this section.]

Section 4: . . . within twenty-one days after Congress is required to assemble [and it is determined] by two-thirds vote of both Houses that the President is unable to discharge the powers and duties of his office, the Vice President shall continue to discharge the same as Acting President; otherwise, the President shall resume the powers and duties of his office.

JOHN HINCKLEY'S LETTER TO JODIE FOSTER

Dear Jodie:

There is a definite possibility that I will be killed in my attempt to get Reagan. It is for this very reason that I am writing you this letter now.

As you well know by now, I love you very much. The past seven months I have left you dozens of poems, letters and messages in the faint hope you would develop an interest in me. Although we talked on the phone a couple of times [these were calls put through to Foster at Yale and in which she spoke only briefly to him to ask him not to contact her again] I never had the nerve to simply approach you and introduce myself. Besides my shyness, I honestly did not wish to bother you. I know the many messages left at your door and in your mailbox were a nuisance, but I felt it was the most painless way for me to express my love to you.

I feel very good about the fact that you at least know my name and how I feel about you. And by hanging around your dormitory I've come to realize that I'm the topic of more than a little conversation, however full of ridicule it may be. At least you know that I'll always love you.

Jodie, I would abandon this idea of getting Reagan in a second if I could only win your heart and live out the rest of my life with you, whether it be in total obscurity or whatever.

I will admit to you that the reason I'm going ahead with this attempt now is because I just cannot wait any longer to impress you. I've got to do something now to make you understand in no uncertain terms that I am doing all of this for your sake. By sacrificing my freedom and possibly my life I hope to change your mind about me. This letter is being written an hour before I leave for the Hilton Hotel.

Jodie, I'm asking you to please look into your heart and at least give me the chance with this historical deed to gain your respect and love.

I love you forever.

[signed] John Hinckley

RONALD REAGAN'S
REMARKS AT A COMMEMORATIVE CEREMONY AT BERGEN-BELSEN CONCENTRATION CAMP IN THE FEDERAL REPUBLIC OF GERMANY

May 5, 1985

Chancellor Kohl and honored guest, this painful walk into the past has done much more than remind us of the war that consumed the European Continent. What we have seen makes unforgettably clear that no one of the rest of us can fully understand the enormity of the feelings carried by the victims of these camps. The survivors carry a memory beyond anything that we can comprehend. The awful evil started by one man, an evil that victimized all the world with its destruction, was uniquely destructive of the millions forced into the grim abyss of these camps.

Here lie people—Jews—whose death was inflicted for no reason other than their very existence. Their pain was borne only because of who they were and because of the God in their prayers. Alongside them lay many Christians—Catholics and Protestants.

For year after year, until that man and his evil were destroyed, hell yawned forth its awful contents. People were brought here for no other purpose but to suffer and die—to go unfed when hungry, uncared for when sick, tortured when the whim struck, and left to have misery consume them when all there was around them was misery.

I'm sure we all share similar first thoughts, and that is: What of the youngsters who died at this dark stalag? All was gone for them forever—not to feel again the warmth of life's sunshine and promise, not the laughter and the splendid ache of growing up, nor the consoling embrace of a family. Try to think of being young and never having a day without searing emotional and physical pain—desolate, unrelieved pain.

Today, we've been grimly reminded why the commandant of this camp was named "the Beast of Belsen." Above all, we're struck by the horror of it all—the monstrous, incomprehensible horror. And that's what we've seen but is what we can never understand as the victims did. Nor with all our compassion can we feel what the survivors feel to this day and what they will feel as long as they live. What we've felt and are expressing with words cannot convey the suffering that they endured. That is why history will forever brand what happened as the Holocaust.

Here, death ruled, but we've learned something as well. Because of what happened, we found that death cannot rule forever, and that's why we're here today. We're here because humanity refuses to accept that freedom of the spirit of man can ever be extinguished. We're here to commemorate that life triumphed over the tragedy and the death of the Holocaust—overcame the suffering, the sickness, the testing and, yes, the gassings. We're here today to confirm that the horror cannot outlast hope, and that even from the worst of all things, the best may come forth. Therefore, even out of this overwhelming sadness, there must be some purpose, and there is. It comes to us through the transforming love of God.

We learn from the Talmud that: "It was only through suffering that the children of Israel obtained three priceless and coveted gifts: The Torah, the Land of Israel, and the World to Come." Yes, out of this sickness—as crushing and cruel as it was—there was hope for the world as well as for the world to come. Out of the ashes—hope, and from all the pain—promise.

So much of this is symbolized today by the fact that most of the leadership of free Germany is represented here today. Chancellor Kohl, you and your countrymen have made real the renewal that had to happen. Your nation and the German people have been strong and resolute in your willingness to confront and condemn the acts of a hated regime of the past. This reflects the courage of your people and their devotion to freedom and justice since the war. Think how far we've come from that time when despair made these tragic victims wonder if anything could survive.

As we flew here from Hanover, low over the greening farms and the emerging springtime of the lovely German countryside, I reflected, and there must have been a time when the prisoners at Bergen-Belsen and those of every other camp must have felt the springtime was gone forever from their lives. Surely we can understand that when we see what is around us—all these children of God under bleak and lifeless mounds, the plainness of which does not even hint at the unspeakable acts that created them. Here they lie, never to hope, never to pray, never to love, never to heal, never to laugh, never to cry.

And too many of them knew that this was their fate, but that was not the end. Through it all was their faith and a spirit that moved their faith.

Nothing illustrates this better than the story of a young girl who died here at Bergen-Belsen. For more than two years Anne Frank and her family had hidden from the Nazis in a confined annex in Holland where she kept a remarkably profound diary. Betrayed by an informant, Anne and her family were sent by freight car first to Auschwitz and finally here to Bergen-Belsen.

Just three weeks before her capture, young Anne wrote these words: "It's really a wonder that I haven't dropped all my ideals because they seem so absurd and impossible to carry out. Yet I keep them because in spite of everything I still believe that people are good at heart. I simply can't build up my hopes on a foundation consisting of confusion, misery, and death. I see the world gradually being turned into a wilderness. I hear the ever approaching thunder which will destroy us too; I can feel the suffering of millions and yet, if I looked up into the heavens I think that it will all come right, that this cruelty too will end and that peace and tranquility will return again." Eight months later, this sparkling young life ended here at Bergen-Belsen. Somewhere here lies Anne Frank.

Everywhere here are memories—pulling us, touching us, making us understand that they can never be erased. Such memories take us where God intended His children to go—toward learning, toward healing, and, above all, toward redemption.

They beckon us through the endless stretches of our heart to the knowing commitment that the life of each individual can change the world and make it better.

We're all witnesses; we share the glistening hope that rests in every human soul. Hope leads us, if we're prepared to trust it, toward what our President Lincoln called the better angels of our nature. And then, rising above all this cruelty, out of this tragic and nightmarish time, beyond the anguish, the pain and the suffering for all time, we can and must pledge: Never again.

REMARKS AT A JOINT GERMAN-AMERICAN MILITARY CEREMONY AT BITBURG AIR BASE IN THE FEDERAL REPUBLIC OF GERMANY
May 5, 1985

Thank you very much. I have just come from the cemetery where German war dead lay at rest. No one could visit there without deep and conflicting emotions. I felt great sadness that history could be filled with such waste, destruction, and evil, but my heart was also lifted by the knowledge that from the ashes has come hope and that from the terrors of the past we have built forty years of peace, freedom, and reconciliation among our nations.

This visit has stirred many emotions in the American and German people, too. I've received many letters since first deciding to come to Bitburg cemetery; some supportive, others deeply concerned and questioning, and others opposed. Some old wounds have been reopened, and this I regret very much because this should be a time of healing.

To the veterans and families of American servicemen who still carry the scars and feel the painful losses of that war, our gesture of reconciliation with the German people today in no way minimizes our love and honor for those who fought and died for our country. They gave their lives to rescue freedom in its darkest hour. The alliance of democratic nations that guards the freedom of millions in Europe and America today stands as living testimony that their noble sacrifice was not in vain.

No, their sacrifice was not in vain. I have to tell you that nothing will ever fill me with greater hope than the sight of two former war heroes who met today at the Bitburg ceremony; each among the bravest of the brave; each an enemy of the other forty years ago; each a witness to the horrors of war. But today they came together, American and German, General Matthew B. Ridgway and General Johannes Steinhoff, reconciled and united for freedom. They reached over the graves to one another like brothers and grasped their hands in peace.

To the survivors of the Holocaust: Your terrible suffering has made you ever vigilant against evil. Many of your are worried that reconciliation means forgetting. Well, I promise you, we will never forget. I have just come this morning from Bergen-Belsen, where the horror of that terrible crime, the Holocaust, was forever burned upon my memory. No, we will never forget, and we say with the victims of that Holocaust: Never again.

The war against one man's totalitarian dictatorship was not like other wars. The evil war of nazism turned all values upside down. Nevertheless, we can mourn the German war dead today as human beings crushed by a vicious ideology.

There are over two thousand buried in Bitburg cemetery. Among them are forty-eight members of the SS—the crimes of the SS must rank among the most heinous in human history—but others buried there were simply soldiers in the German Army. How many were fanatical followers of a dictator and willfully carried out his cruel orders? And how many were conscripts, forced into service during the death throes of the Nazi war machine? We do not know. Many, however, we know from the dates on their tombstones, were only teenagers at the time. There is one boy buried there who died a week before his sixteenth birthday.

There were thousands of such soldiers to whom nazism meant no more than a brutal end to a short life. We do not believe in collective guilt. Only God can look into the human heart, and all these men have now met their supreme judge, and they have been judged by Him as we shall all be judged.

Our duty today is to mourn the human wreckage of totalitarianism, and today in Bitburg cemetery we commemorated the potential good in humanity that was consumed back then, forty years ago. Perhaps if that fifteen year-old soldier had lived, he would have joined his fellow countrymen in building this new democratic Federal Republic of Germany, devoted to human dignity and the defense of freedom that we celebrate today. Or perhaps his children or his grandchildren might be among you here today at the Bitburg Air Base, where new generations of Germans and Americans join together in friendship and common cause, dedicating their lives to preserving peace and guarding the security of the free world.

Too often in the past each war only planted the seeds of the next. We celebrate today the reconciliation between our two nations that has liberated us from that cycle of destruction. Look at what together we've accomplished. We who were enemies are now friends; we who were bitter adversaries are now the strongest of allies.

In the place of fear we've sown trust, and out of the ruins of war has blossomed an enduring peace. Tens of thousands of Americans have served in this town over the years. As the mayor of Bitburg has said, in that time there have been some six thousand marriages between Germans and Americans, and many thousands of children have come from these unions. This is the real symbol of our future together, a future to be filled with hope, friendship, and freedom.

The hope that we see now could sometimes even be glimpsed in the darkest days of the war. I'm thinking of one special story—that of a mother and her young son living alone in a modest cottage in the middle of the woods. And one night as the Battle of the Bulge exploded not far away, and around them, three young American soldiers arrived at their door—they were standing there in the snow, lost behind enemy lines. All were frostbitten; one was badly wounded. Even though sheltering the enemy was punishable by death, she took them in and made them a supper with some of her last food. Then, they heard another knock at the door. And this time four German soldiers stood there. The woman was afraid, but she quickly said with a firm voice, "There will be no shooting here." She made all the soldiers lay down their weapons, and they all joined in the makeshift meal. Heinz and Willi, it turned out, were only sixteen; the corporal was the oldest at twenty-three. Their natural suspicion dissolved in the warmth and the comfort of the cottage. One of the Germans, a former medical student, tended the wounded American.

But now, listen to the rest of the story through the eyes of one who was there, now a grown man, but that young lad that had been her son. He said: "The Mother said grace. I noticed that there were tears in her eyes as she said the old, familiar words, 'Komm, Herr Jesus. Be our guest.' And as I looked around the table, I saw tears, too, in the eyes of the battle-weary soldiers, boys again, some from America, some from Germany, all far from home."

That night—as the storm of war tossed the world—they had their own private armistice. And the next morning, the German corporal showed the Americans how to get back behind their own lines. And they all shook hands and went their separate ways. That happened to be Christmas Day, forty years ago.

Those boys reconciled briefly in the midst of war. Surely we allies in peacetime should honor the reconciliation of the last forty years.

To the people of Bitburg, our hosts and the hosts of our servicemen, like that generous woman forty years ago, you make us feel very welcome. Vielen dank. [Many thanks.]

And to the men and women of Bitburg Air Base, I just want to say that we know that even with such wonderful hosts, your job is not an easy one. You serve around the clock far from home, always ready to defend freedom. We're grateful, and we're very proud of you.

Four decades ago we waged a great war to lift the darkness of evil from the world, to let men and women in this country and in every country live in the sunshine of liberty. Our victory was great, and the Federal Republic, Italy, and Japan are now in the community of free nations. But the struggle for freedom is not complete, for today much of the world is still cast in totalitarian darkness.

Twenty-two years ago President John F. Kennedy went to the Berlin Wall and proclaimed that he, too, was a Berliner. Well, today freedom-loving people around the world must say: I am a Berliner. I am a Jew in a world still threatened by anti-Semitism. I am an Afghan, and I am a prisoner of the Gulag. I am a refugee in a crowded boat foundering off the coast of Vietnam. I am a Laotian, a Cambodian, a Cuban, and a Miskito Indian in Nicaragua. I, too, am a potential victim of totalitarianism.

The one lesson of World War II, the one lesson of nazism, is that freedom must always be stronger than totalitarianism and that good must always be stronger than evil. The moral measure of our two nations will be found in the resolve we show to preserve liberty, to protect life, and to honor and cherish all God's children.

That is why the free, democratic Federal Republic of Germany is such a profound and hopeful testament to the human spirit. We cannot undo the crimes and wars of yesterday nor call back the millions back to life, but we can give meaning to the past by learning its lessons and making a better future. We can let our pain drive us to greater efforts to heal humanity's suffering.

Today I've traveled 220 miles from Bergen-Belsen, and, I feel, forty years in time. With the lessons of the past firmly in our minds, we've turned a new, brighter page in history.

One of the many who wrote me about this visit was a young woman who had recently been bas mitzvahed. She urged me to lay the wreath at Bitburg cemetery in honor of the future of Germany. And that is what we've done.

On this fortieth anniversary of World War II, we mark the day when the hate, the evil, and the obscenities ended, and we commemorate the rekindling of the democratic spirit in Germany.

There's much to make us hopeful on this historic anniversary. One of the symbols of that hate—that could have been that hope, a little while ago, when we heard a German band playing the American National Anthem and an American band playing the German National Anthem. While much of the world still huddles in the darkness of oppression, we can see a new dawn of freedom sweeping the globe. And we can see in the new democracies of Latin America, in the new economic freedoms and prosperity in Asia, in the slow movement toward peace in the Middle East, and in the strengthening alliance of democratic nations in Europe and America that the light from that dawn is growing stronger.

Together, let us gather in that light and walk out of the shadow. Let us live in peace.

Thank you, and God bless you all.

RONALD REAGAN

ADDRESS TO THE NATION ON THE EXPLOSION OF THE SPACE SHUTTLE *CHALLENGER,* JANUARY 28, 1986

Ladies and gentlemen, I'd planned to speak to you tonight to report on the state of the Union but the events of earlier today have led me to change those plans. Today is a day for mourning and remembering. Nancy and I are pained to the core by the tragedy of the shuttle *Challenger.* We know we share this pain with all of the people of our country. This is truly a national loss.

Nineteen years ago, almost to the day, we lost three astronauts in a terrible accident on the ground. But we've never lost an astronaut in flight; we've never had a tragedy like this. And perhaps we've forgotten the courage it took for the crew of the shuttle. But they, the *Challenger* Seven, were aware of the dangers, but overcame them and did their jobs brilliantly. We mourn seven heroes: Michael Smith, Dick Scobee, Judith Resnik, Ronald McNair, Ellison Onizuka, Gregory Jarvis, and Christa McAuliffe. We mourn their loss as a nation together.

For the families of the seven, we cannot bear, as you do, the full impact of this tragedy. But we feel the loss, and we're thinking about you so very much. Your loved ones were daring and brave, and they had the special grace, that special spirit that says, "Give me a challenge, and I'll meet it with joy." They had a hunger to explore the universe and its truths. They wished to serve, and they did. They served all of us. We've grown used to wonders in this century. It's hard to dazzle us. But for 25 years the United States space program has been doing just that. We've grown used to the idea of space, and perhaps we forget that we've only just begun. We're still pioneers. They, the members of the *Challenger* crew, were pioneers.

And I want to say something to the schoolchildren of America who were watching the live coverage of the shuttle's takeoff. I know it is hard to understand, but sometimes painful things like this happen. It's all part of the process of exploration and discovery. It's all part of taking a chance and expanding man's horizons. The future doesn't belong to the fainthearted; it belongs to the brave. The *Challenger* crew was pulling us into the future, and we'll continue to follow them.

I've always had great faith in and respect for our space program, and what happened today does nothing to diminish it. We don't hide our space program. We don't keep secrets and cover things up. We do it all up front and in public. That's the way freedom is, and we wouldn't change it for a minute. We'll continue our quest in space. There will be more shuttle flights and more shuttle crews and, yes, more volunteers, more civilians, more teachers in space. Nothing ends here; our hopes and our journey continue. I want to add that I wish I could talk to every man and woman who works for NASA or who worked on this mission and tell them: "Your dedication and professionalism have moved and impressed us for decades. And we know of your anguish. We share it."

There's a coincidence today. On this day 390 years ago the great explorer Sir Francis Drake died aboard ship off the coast of Panama. In his lifetime the great frontiers were the oceans, and an historian later said, "He lived by the sea, died on it, and was buried in it." Well, today we can say of the *Challenger* crew: Their dedication was, like Drake's, complete.

The crew of the space shuttle *Challenger* honored us by the manner in which they lived their lives. We will never forget them, nor the last time we saw them, this morning, as they prepared for their journey and waved goodbye and "slipped the surly bonds of earth" to "touch the face of God."

RONALD REAGAN

FAREWELL TO THE NATION
November 5, 1994

My Fellow Americans,

I have recently been told that I am one of the millions of Americans who will be afflicted with Alzheimer's Disease.

Upon learning this news, Nancy and I had to decide whether as private citizens we would keep this a private matter or whether we would make this news known in a public way.

In the past Nancy suffered from breast cancer and I had my cancer surgeries. We found through our open disclosures we were able to raise public awareness. We were happy that as a result many more people underwent testing.

They were treated in early stages and able to return to normal, healthy lives.

So now, we feel it is important to share it with you. In opening our hearts, we hope this might promote greater awareness of this condition. Perhaps it will encourage a clearer understanding of the individuals and families who are affected by it.

At the moment I feel just fine. I intend to live the remainder of the years God gives me on this earth doing the things I have always done. I will continue to share life's journey with my beloved Nancy and my family. I plan to enjoy the great outdoors and stay in touch with my friends and supporters.

Unfortunately, as Alzheimer's Disease progresses, the family often bears a heavy burden. I only wish there was some way I could spare Nancy from this painful experience. When the time comes I am confident that with your help she will face it with faith and courage.

In closing, let me thank you, the American people, for giving me the great honor of allowing me to serve as your President. When the Lord calls me home, [the letter "I" is scratched out here] whenever that may be, I will leave with the greatest love for this country of ours and eternal optimism for its future.

I now begin this journey that will lead me into the sunset of my life. I know that for America there will always be a bright dawn ahead.

Thank you my friends. May God always bless you.

Sincerely,
Ronald Reagan

NOTES

ABBREVIATIONS USED IN THE NOTES

AE   *Anne Edwards*

AMPAS *Academy of Motion Picture Arts and Sciences*

ELD   *Edith Luckett Davis*

GRF   *Gerald R. Ford*

NR   *Nancy Reagan*

RR   *Ronald Reagan*

RRPL *Ronald Reagan Presidential Library*

SAG   *Screen Actors Guild*

UCLA *University of California, Los Angeles*

CHAPTER ONE: ENTER NANCY

Material for this chapter came from interviews by AE, archival material in the AM-PAS Library, Ronald Reagan Presidential Library, and the UCLA Library private collections. Books used were Nancy Reagan, *My Turn*, and Patti Davis, *The Way I See It*.

1. "He asked me" through "Sold": Edith Luckett Davis interview, Arizona, 1983. Anne Edwards Archive, University of California at Los Angeles, Private Collections. Taped with Neil Reagan and Jean Kinney.

2. Edith Luckett remained a supporting player throughout her career (ending with her marriage to Dr. Loyal Davis), which never translated from theater to movies as did the careers of so many of her contemporaries. The Russian actress Nazimova (Alla Yakovlevna Leventon) toured the United States to much acclaim before World War I. She capitalized on her sensuous exoticism. When her stage popularity waned in 1916, she turned to the silent screen. Her acting was highly stylized, bizarre, and yet haunting. The public did not take to her, and she returned to the stage at about

the time talking pictures made their debut. In the 1940s she played character roles in several successful films: *Blood and Sand* (1941), *The Bridge of San Luis Rey* (1944), and *Since You Went Away* (1944). She died in 1945 at the age of sixty-six. Although Edith Luckett Davis and Nazimova remained lifelong friends, Nancy seldom saw her godmother.

3. "a one-legged man": ELD interview.

4. "treated her with great love": NR, *My Turn*, p. 70.

5. "Mother was not only outgoing": Ibid., p. 70.

6. "quickly came to love": Ibid., p. 71.

7. "I always dreaded": Ibid., p. 71.

8. "was thousands of miles": Ibid., p. 70.

9. "I've fallen in love": ELD interview.

10. "I was happy for Mother": NR, *My Turn*, p. 73.

11. "in the third or fourth grades": Chris Wallace, "*First Lady*," p. 4.

12. "no question about that": Ibid., p. 7.

13. "They were too close": Margaret McLean interview, 1985.

14. "She called [Loyal] 'Daddy' ": Ibid.

15. "She was a flirt": ELD interview.

16. Petition filed in Cook County Circuit Court of Illinois, April 19, 1938.

17. "You can call me": Kitty Kelley, *Nancy Reagan*, p. 43.

18. "Nancy's social": Girl's Latin School Annual, 1939.

19. "Some of the girls": NR classmate confidential interview.

20. "Screen tests": Armand Deutsch interview, Beverly Hills, 2001. In the six years between her graduation from Smith and her contract with Metro-Goldwyn-Mayer, Nancy Davis appeared in four plays, but only one on Broadway. The other three were road companies starring her mother's good friend, Zazu Pitts, who made a name for herself on screen portraying addled ladies. Off-screen Pitts was a reactionary and a virulent red-baiter. She took Davis under her wing and shared her strong political beliefs with her.

21. "I had never": Ibid.

22. "I think Nancy's relationship": MGM player confidential interview.

23. "My greatest ambition": AMPAS Archives, Nancy Reagan Papers.

24. Nancy Davis's original test arrangements were changed at the last moment. Multiple Academy Award nominated director and cinematographer George Cukor and George Folsey, respectively, replaced the staff technicians who had been assigned the job of filming the test. Nancy has claimed that she cannot recall how the test was set up, or who was responsible for bringing her to Hollywood. It has been variously reported that Spencer Tracy, an old friend of Edith Luckett Davis's, had arranged her daughter's screen test; that the screen test was payback to Nancy for kindness extended to Tracy's hearing-impaired son (previous to her signing with MGM). When the boy was a visitor to New York City, Nancy put him up in her apartment. It has also been said that after having visited the Davises in Chicago, Benny Thau (also previous to Nancy's studio contract) had agreed to help Nancy get started on a movie career. Perhaps all of the above are true—or none of them. However, the former MGM executives interviewed on behalf of this book, and for an earlier volume by this author, *Early Reagan*, are in accord that Thau brought

Nancy, whom he had yet to meet, out to Hollywood at the request of both Clark Gable and Spencer Tracy and that Thau had been personally taken with Nancy from their first meeting at MGM.

By 1949, the year of Nancy Davis's screen test, Cukor had been nominated by the Academy of Motion Picture Arts and Sciences as Best Director for *Little Women* (1934); *The Philadelphia Story* (1940); and *A Double Life* (1947). He had made many critically acclaimed and successful films before that date, including *Dinner at Eight, David Copperfield, Camille,* and *Gas Light.* He also directed several key scenes in *Gone With the Wind,* and would win the Oscar at last in 1964 for *My Fair Lady.* George Folsey was nominated for an Academy Award in Cinematography nine times in the years between 1934 and 1963, but he never won.

Some of MGM's leading actresses during 1949–1953, Nancy Davis's major years at the studio, were Lana Turner, Hedy Lamar, Ava Gardner, Elizabeth Taylor, Greer Garson, Jennifer Jones, Alexis Smith, Leslie Caron, June Allyson, Kathryn Grayson, Vera Ellen, Cyd Charisse, Jane Powell, Katharine Hepburn, Deborah Kerr, Arlene Dahl, Esther Williams, Judy Garland, and a very young Marilyn Monroe.

25. "Sinatra knew": Peter Lawford interview, Los Angeles, 1985.

26. "Nancy was desperate": MGM player confidential interview (previously cited, n. 22).

27. "Her eyes were glued": Roddy MacDowall interview, New York, 1997.

28. Reagan and the FBI: Papers secured through the Freedom of Information Act, although heavily censored, confirmed Reagan's connection at SAG as an informer for the FBI. AE also conducted dozens of interviews with SAG members (for the years 1948–1954 regarding Reagan's undercover activities. Most of this material is in the Anne Edwards Archive, UCLA Special Collections.

29. "two men": Jack Dales interview, 1987.

30. "There was a lot of political talk": Jill Schary Robinson interview, New Milford, Conn., 1986.

31. "Reagan and Nancy met": Miriam Schary interview, New Milford, Conn., 1983.

32. "In the end, we stopped the Communists": RR, *An American Life*, p. 114.

33. "None of us": Dalton Trumbo interview, London, 1985. Of the many hundreds of men and women whose lives were destroyed by HUAC, no one was ever found guilty of any traitorous act. These hearings, and the blacklisting that followed, constitute one of the most shameful periods in the history of the United States in the twentieth century. John Howard Lawson and Dalton Trumbo were two of the nineteen Hollywood writers, directors, actors, and producers first called before the committee. The other men (no women among them) were Alvah Bessie, Herbert Biberman, Lester Cole, Edward Dmytryk, Ring Lardner Jr., Albert Maltz, Samuel Ornitz, Adrian Scott, Robert Rossen, Bertolt Brecht, Larry Parks, Lewis Milestone, Irving Pichel, Gordon Kahn, Richard Collins. One thing all these men had in common was that none of them had served in the army, having been too old, not a citizen (Bertolt Brecht), or deferred for health reasons. For that common reason, no veterans' committee would stir up problems.

Both Lawson and Trumbo, as well as a number of the others named above, served terms of one year in federal prisons for refusing to state their political affiliation to the committee, a demand they firmly believed was unconstitutional. Lawson's career was ruined, but Trumbo made a brilliant comeback, winning an Academy Award for his screenplay for *The Brave One* (under the pseudonym Richard Rich), and going on to write celebrated screenplays for *Spartacus*, *Exodus*, *Hawaii*, and *Papillion*, among others.

34. Ronald Reagan, *An American Life*, p. 121. The two other Nancy Davises mentioned by Reagan were Nancy Davis Hunt, a professional ice skater who had no links to any Communist front groups, and in fact was not a member of SAG but of the Screen Extras Guild; and Nancy (Lee Strauss) Davis, an actress and the wife of producer Jerome Davis, who later said, "Nancy and I both signed the amicus brief to the Supreme Court in 1949, but we weren't Communists. We simply believed that Lawson and Trumbo should not be persecuted for their beliefs." SAG bylaws prohibit duplication of actors' names, but at the time that Nancy Davis (Reagan) signed her contract with MGM, Jerome Davis's wife was on the inactive list. When she resumed work, she used the name Nancy Lee Davis.

Nancy Lee Davis reappeared in Nancy's life in 1953 when she was being considered for a role in a Columbia Pictures film. She was rejected because the investigation firm that checked such things for the studio found that a Nancy Davis had signed the previously noted amicus curiae brief that had precipitated the first meeting between Nancy and Reagan. Reagan and Jack Dales wrote angry letters stating she was not the Nancy Davis so accused and demanded and received a written apology. But she was not cast in the film.

35. "the name confusion": Ibid.
36. "a starlit sky": *Movieland*, July 1952.
37. "the Guild is in need": Screen Actors Guild archives.
38. "one morning": RR, *An American Life*, p. 123.
39. " 'Let's get married' ": Ibid.

CHAPTER TWO: ALL SHE EVER WANTED
Extensive interviews were conducted for the information regarding Reagan and SAG including Jack Dales and many of SAG's board members and executives. SAG also gave me access to its archives. Edith Luckett Davis was interviewed and taped in 1983, as was Neil Reagan (Anne Edwards Archives, UCLA Special Collections). Nelle and Jack Reagan's family history was researched through Illinois records and interviews held in Tampico and Dixon, Ill. The author also spent several weeks interviewing Dixon residents and church parishioners and held several roundtable discussions among his former associates in that city. Interviews were also carried out in Eureka, Ill., and Los Angeles, Calif.

1. "I can see": NR, *I Love You, Ronnie*, p. 13.
2. "Jane was too involved": Confidential interview.
3. "Well, it looks . . . our first meeting": Neil Reagan interview.
4. "Nothing better": Dixon Round Table Interviews, Dixon, Ill., April 17–21, 1986.
5. "not in the drab": Charles Lamb interview. Lamb was the Dixon historian.
6. "which was fine": RR, *Where's the Rest of Me?*, p. 9.
7. "bouts with the dark demon": Ibid.

8. "He just would drink": Louis Sindlinger interview, Dixon, Ill.

9. "The President still": Letter from Benjamin H. Moore to AE, Sept. 27, 1986.

10. "when he invited Christ": In *Bread of Life*, May 1981. Monthly publication of Ridgewood Pentecostal Church, May 1981.

11. "make the Bible": Roundtable conducted by AE in Dixon, Ill.

12. "If Nelle had": Dixon Round Table Interviews, Dixon, Ill., April 17–21, 1986.

13. "She had a way": LS interview, Dixon, Ill.

14. "a pretend world": Roundtable (n. 11)

15. "Dixon was always": *Dixon Evening Telegram*, Feb. 4, 1984.

16. " 'Dutch'. . . . And took his knocks": Ralph McKinzie interview, Eureka, Ill., 1985.

17. Eureka College Student strike: Eureka College Archives.

18. "Ronnie would express": Lawrence Williams interview, Los Angeles, 1986. UCLA Library Private Collections, AE Archive.

19. "Committing what he": Ibid.

20. "It was obvious . . . to board at school": Maureen Reagan, *First Father, First Daughter*, p. 94.

21. "Dad could give": Michael Reagan, *On the Outside Looking In*, p. 243.

22. "talked about Dad": Ibid., p. 243.

23. "Nancy and I got along": Ibid., p. 92.

24. "Ronnie wanted to keep": NR, *My Turn*, p. 101.

25. "O.K. It's official": Maureen Reagan, *First Father, First Daughter*, p. 94.

26. "I would have preferred.": Ibid., n. 24.

27. "the gift of life": RRPL, Telegram Archive.

28. "a damned hard man": Barry Goldwater interview, Phoenix, Ariz., 1985.

29. "After just a few days": NR, *I Love You, Ronnie*, p. 29.

CHAPTER THREE: A HOME OF THEIR OWN

For the Lew Wasserman/MCA material, Dennis McDougal's 1998 biography, *The Last Mogul*, was a prime reference, along with Dan E. Moldea's *Dark Victory: Ronald Reagan, MCA and the Mob* (1986). For information on Chautauqua, *Dixon Evening Tribune*, Aug. 12, 1923. Dixon, Illinois.

1. "Lew": Lew Wasserman interview, 1985.

2. "cool and well turned out": ELD interview.

3. "Dave Chasen . . . was such a dear man": NR, *I Love You, Ronnie*, p. 21.

4. "a bit precipitously": NR, *My Turn*, p. 103.

5. "[What I was told] . . . wanted a boy": Patti Davis, *The Way I See It*, pp. 20–21.

6. "I didn't know much": NR, *My Turn*, p. 146.

7. "The few times I felt good . . . against her": Michael Reagan, *On the Outside Looking In*, p. 65.

8. "Well at last . . .": NR, *My Turn*, p. 125.

9. "some up to four hours": *Hollywood Citizen*, Feb. 15, 1954.

10. "alone": Ibid.

11. "Is Las Vegas": *Variety*, Mar. 24, 1954.

12. "Never again": AE, *Early Reagan*, p. 446.

CHAPTER FOUR: CORPORATE LIFE

1. "So you won't have to be": RRPL, Correspondence—Nancy Davis Reagan.
2. "How MCA baited": Earl B. Dunckel interview, 1986.
3. "We had been very definite": Ibid.
4. "The wife of our man": Benjamin H. Moore interview, 1986.
5. GE's building a new home, including "Where?": Ibid.
6. "There was nothing of the posturing": Dunckel interview.
7. "With all the 'missing you,' ": RR, *I Love You, Ronnie*, pp. xii–xiii.
8. "For My Mommie Poo . . ." RRPL, Correspondence—Nancy Davis Reagan.
9. "He couldn't see": Dunckel interview.
10. "generally having . . . take it or leave it amounts to": Ibid.
11. "I got to see": RRPL, Radio Speech, March 27, 1968.
12. "I went over to her": ELD interview.
13. "Edith taught me": Loyal Davis, *A Surgeon's Odyssey*, p. 228.
14. "It will have everything": Los Angeles Times, Sept. 9, 1957.
15. "Nancy and Ronnie are just alike": ELD interview.
16. "I was never told why": Patti Davis, *The Way I See It*, p. 28.
17. "What happened between arrival": Patti Davis, *The Way I See It*, pp. 28–29.
18. "It seemed Mom and I": Michael Reagan, *From the Outside Looking In*, p. 68.
19. "So help me God": Kitty Kelley, *Nancy Reagan*, p. 108.
20. "I thought that at last": Michael Reagan, *From the Outside Looking In*, p. 76.
21. "The 'half' part": Patti Davis, *The Way I See It*, p. 30.
22. "She's too busy": Michael Reagan, *From the Outside Looking In*, p. 75-77.
23. "Michael is my older brother . . . move in with them": Maureen Reagan, *First Father, First Daughter*, p. 97.
24. "Dearest Mommie Poo": RRPL, Correspondence RR/NDR.
25. "I am a shut in": Nelle Reagan to Mary and Jay Sipe, Jul. 15, 1957. Courtesy Loveland Museum, Dixon, Ill.
26. "His mother's decline": Confidential interview, Los Angeles, 2001.

CHAPTER FIVE: I LOVE YOU, NANCY

1. "How come you moved in on me": RRPL, Correspondence RR/NDR undated.
2. "We knew there was going to be": Jack Dales interview, Los Angeles, Calif., 1986.
3. "Nancy is not being asked": Lew Wasserman interview, Los Angeles, Calif., 1986.
4. "if she came by": Patti Davis, *The Way I See It*, p. 75.
5. "Why do you always say": Ibid., p. 58.
6. "You are not living up": Michael Reagan, *From the Outside Looking In*, p. 89.
7. "You are the offspring": Ibid., pp. 89–90.
8. "he is more complex": Susan Granger interview, Feb. 17, 2000.
9. "What you see": Ibid.
10. "Pray as I am praying": RR to Sam Harrod Jr., December 19, 1952. Private archive.

11. "Can you believe": RR campaign speech (repeated several times in different venues) for Richard Nixon, 1962, RRPL.

12. "Dutch had just finished": AE, *Early Reagan*, p. 479.

13. "If it wasn't": Ibid.

14. "Ron can't be pushed": Ibid., p. 480.

15. "Remember when Churchill": *Los Angeles Times*, Nov. 19, 1964.

16. "It was the Communists": Maureen Reagan interview, Dixon, Ill. Aug. 21, 2000.

17. "Couldn't she have changed her suit?" Patti Davis, *The Way I See It*, p. 82.

18. "the proliferation": RRPL, Speeches, 1964.

19. "You and I": Ibid.

20. "the most successful": *Washington Post*, Oct. 29, 1964.

21. "At about midnight": RR, *An American Life*, p. 142.

22. "After the Goldwater": RR, *An American Life*, p. 143.

23. "Nancy had no more interest": Ibid., p. 145.

24. "It soon got": RR, *An American Life*, p. 148.

25. "In the beginning Nancy": Confidential interview.

26. "How do you say no": RR, *An American Life*, p. 147–48.

27. "Why do you lie like this": *Patti Davis, The Way I See It*, p. 69.

28. "so splurged with color": *Los Angeles Times*, Jan. 5, 1966.

CHAPTER SIX: ON THE CAMPAIGN TRAIL

1. "What I wanted": NR made this exact statement in *My Turn*, and in television interviews with Barbara Walters and Diane Sawyer.

2. Ronnie and Sills, including "small-town Illinois roots": Armand Deutsch interview

3. "Something happened in the sixties" and "Jane Wyman": Morella and Epstein, *Jane Wyman: A Biography*, p. 211.

4. "dig a hole": Maureen Reagan, *First Father, First Daughter*, p. 146.

5. "If you pay someone": Ibid., p. 147.

6. "For me to read aloud": Ibid., p. 149.

7. "Taking someone with celebrity status,": *Los Angeles Times*, June, 19, 2001.

8. "I'm running against an an actor": TV political commercial, June 20, 1966.

9. "Brown's campaign . . . from Hollywood": TV news interview, July 9, 1966.

10. "Ronnie always voiced . . . we weathered it": Armand Deutsch interview.

11. "now working for the other fellows": Jack Dales interview.

12. "It was an explosive situation": Ibid.

13. "Nancy was indispensible": Staff member, Roberts-Spencer confidential interview.

14. "As I am sure you know": Richard Nixon to RR, June 9, 1966. RRPL, Box 29.

15. "I just talked": George Murphy to RR, Aug. 10, 1966, ibid.

16. "They can cut off": *Sacramento Bee*, Oct. 17, 1966.

17. "He was a real guy": Interviews with attendees of Reagan's 1966 fund-raisers and campaign stops.

18. "She was a patient listener": Nancy Reagan staff member confidential interview.

19. "get out of that [organization]" AE, *Early Reagan*, p. 303.

20. "dirty campaign. . . . I have ever been in": Television interview, Oct. 1966.

21. "on the slightest provocation": Ibid., note 16.

22. "I'm going to do a little Harry Truman": *Sacramento Bee*, Oct. 1966.

23. "trying to appear": Confidential interview.

24. "This is the first time": RR to George Murphy, Nov. 1966. RRPL, Correspondence.

25. "Congratulations": Richard Nixon to RR, Nov. 1966, RRPL, Telegrams.

26. "not make too much": RRPL radio campaign broadcast, Oct. 22, 1966.

27. "both my parents . . . fat butt . . . anything": Patti Davis, *The Way I See It*, pp. 117, 116.

28. "If you had to list it": Maureen Reagan, *First Father, First Daughter*, p. 154.

29. "At that hour": Maureen Reagan, *First Father, First Daughter*, p. 155.

30. "A splash of red": Ibid.

31. "These were the Republicans": Bill Boyarsky, *Sacramento Bee*, Feb. 1967.

32. "Every once in a while": RR to Elonwy Neer, Jan. 7, 1967. Courtesy of Elonwy Neer (private papers), interviewed in Dixon.

33. "I LUV U": NR, *I Love You, Ronnie*, p. 86.

34. "My Darling First Lady": Ibid., p. 96.

35. "Somewhere between Betty Davis": Confidential interview.

CHAPTER SEVEN: THE GOVERNOR'S LADY

1. "That horse": Kae Spector interview, Paso Robles, 2001.

2. "Feels kind of": Bill Boyarsky, *The Rise of Ronald Reagan*, pp. 140–41.

3. "I can see him sitting": Skinner, Anderson, and Anderson, *Reagan in His Own Hand*, p. xv.

4. "He was constantly writing": Ibid., p. xvii.

5. "I was always amazed": Ibid.

6. "When we had people": NR, *My Turn*, p. 135.

7. "the queen bee": *New York Times Magazine*, Nov. 5, 2000.

8. "Billy Haines": Ibid.

9. "took up a collection": NR, *My Turn*, p. 138.

10. "Why Red": Bill Boyarsky, *The Rise of Ronald Reagan*, p. 221.

11. "reminiscent of a luxurious": Bill Boyarsky, *The Rise of Ronald Reagan*, p. 177.

12. "Dismissing an incompetent": Michael Deaver, *A Different Drummer*, p. 63.

13. "Nancy had her own": Confidential interview.

14. "Reagan always got to don": Deaver, *A Different Drummer*, 64.

15. "I almost felt": AE, *Early Reagan*, p. 167.

16. "simply on the supposition": Bill Boyarsky, *The Rise of Ronald Reagan*, pp. 189–90.

17. "He would boldly announce": Ibid.

18. "What I recall most clearly": Patti Davis, *The Way I See It*, p. 127.

19. "He thought we could save": Maureen Reagan, *First Father, First Daughter*, p. 162.

20. "It was easier": Maureen Reagan, *First Father, First Daughter*, p. 162.

21. "The next day": Michael Reagan, *From the Outside Looking In*, p. 116.

22. "thought that the war": Charles E. Goodell, *Political Prisoners in America*, p. 127.

23. "which cast considerable doubt": Ibid.

24. "As governor, I": RRPL, Broadcast.

25. "He was the amazing": Michael D. Edwards interview, Los Angeles, Calif., Jan. 2002.

26. "far from the fray . . . at Berkeley, protesting . . .": Patti Davis, *The Way I See It*, p. 94.

27. "radical black girl . . . everyone": Ibid., p. 107.

28. "full technological resources": Campaign literature, 1965.

29. "Over dinner": Ibid., p. 116.

30. In correspondence with Sinatra during the writing of *Judy Garland*, I inadvertently brought to his attention that one year after her death Judy Garland remained in a file drawer at Hyde Park Cemetery, New York. The cost of her interment had not been paid. The cemetery director informed me of Sinatra's gracious act (made within a few hours of receipt of my letter) and that he had said no expense should be spared.

31. "several leaders of the state. . . . A favorite son . . . convention.": RR, *An American Life*, p. 176–77.

CHAPTER EIGHT: THE YEARS BETWEEN

I owe a great debt of gratitude to President Gerald R. Ford, who gave so graciously of his time in a lengthy interview with me; quotes from this interview appear here and in chapter 9.

1. "Sometimes it must": NR, *I Love You, Ronnie*, p. 106.

2. "the tax-and-spend": RR, *An American Life*, p. 185, 186.

3. "Is this true?": Transcript of radio news conference, RRPL. Radio Broadcasts, 1970.

4. "She's been subjected": RR, *An American Life*, p. 184.

5. "conspiracy of the press": Quoted in Henry Kissinger, *Years of Upheaval*, p. 94.

6. "In September, 1973": Ibid.

7. "Stuck with Nixon": Lou Cannon, *President Reagan: The Role of a Lifetime*, p. 55.

8. "Nixon should have": Patti Davis, *The Way I See It*, p. 191.

9. "deceived the country": RR, Press conference, Aug. 27, 1974.

10. "Suddenly, I found": NR, *My Turn*, p. 145.

11. "The previous eight": RR, *An American Life*, p. 191.

12. "The road was so steep": Ibid., p. 193.

13. "Then we turned": Ibid.

14. "We'd get a fire going": "First Lady," p. 158–59.

15. "on a cloud": RR, *An American Life*, p. 194.

16. "I think people": Ibid., p. 195.

17. "When we were building": Peggy Noonan, *When Character Was King*, p. 114.

18. "You don't understand": Edmund Morris, *Dutch*, p. 390.

19. "That campaign was so exciting": NR, *My Turn*, p. 178.

20. "The liberals had had": RR, *An American Life*, p. 199.

21. "the lost vision": Ibid.

22. "Ron has wanted to . . . but I failed": Gerald R. Ford, *A Time to Heal*, p. 294.

23. "Actually, I expected to win": Ibid.

24. "I can do": Confidential interview, March 8, 2001.

25. "John doesn't look you in the eye": NR, *My Turn*, p. 180.

26. "He was like": Confidential interview, March 8, 2001.

27. "knit dresses": NR, *My Turn*, p. 185.

28. "The Reagan strategy . . . voted it down": Gerald R. Ford, *A Time to Heal*, p. 397.

29. "The biggest blow": NR, *My Turn*, p. 189.

30. "I think we both knew": RR, *An American Life*, p. 203.

31. "I will lay me down": Old English ballad, anon.

32. "You know what I regret": RR, *An American Life*, p. 204.

CHAPTER NINE: ON THE STEPS OF THE WHITE HOUSE

1. "had to get up": Nancy Reagan, *I Love You, Ronnie*, p. 103.

2. "the most desirable woman in the world": Ibid., p. 132.

3. "I can still see": Morris, *Dutch*, p. 390.

4. "Mankind has survived. . . . I'll be right back": RRPL, Pre-Presidential Papers, Radio.

5. "who were awkward and tentative": Patti Davis, *The Way I See It*, p. 237.

6. "What I remember most. . . . There's no gag order": Ibid.

7. "Honey . . . it looks as though": NR, *My Turn*, p. 205.

8. "Every night": Ibid, p. 206.

9. "You got Deaver!": Scene re-created from NR, *My Turn*, p. 206, Michael Deaver, "Behind The Scenes," p. 167, and RR, *An American Life*, p. 209.

10. "I recall the sequence of events . . . clear terms": GRF interview.

11. "We were cautious . . . adult and child": Patti Davis, *The Way I See It*, p. 240.

12. "I'm very clear . . . operate with two presidents": GRF interview.

13. "Stop . . . I'll make the decision . . . on the phone": Michael Reagan, p. 176.

14. "to make a difference": Personal conversation with Lillian Gordy Carter, 1983.

15. "had serious weaknesses": RRPL/Presidential Debates/1980.

16. "a second White House": Reagan staff member confidential interview.

17. "There was a terrible crush": Reagan neighbors on St. Onofre Drive.

18. "grabbed a towel. . . . Not bad at all": NR, *My Turn*, p. 221.

CHAPTER TEN: MARCHING INTO HISTORY

1. "a hero embodies": Norman Mailer, *The Presidential Papers of Norman Mailer*, p. 159.

2. "a crusader, the first missionary . . . economic despair": Editorial, *New York Times*, Jan. 18, 1981.

3. "a vision for the future": Felton, *A Shining City*, p. 26.

4. "to shape policy or exert power": Mary Finch Hoyt, *New York Times*, Jan. 18, 1981.

5. "What do you think . . . wood left over": Michael Reagan, *On the Outside Looking In*, p. 183.

6. "I couldn't even jog": John Gay, *Los Angeles Times*, Jan. 15, 1981.

7. "Hello, there": Mrs. Donald Hubbs, quoted in ibid.

8. "the chill in Mrs. Carter's . . . low rent.": This scene has been recreated from NR, *My Turn*, p. 225.

9. "Putting an end . . . sexual preferences": Michael Reagan, *On the Outside Looking In*, p. 182.

10. The scene on Air Force One and the letters that Nancy wrote en route to Washington, D.C., are from NR's own recollections and those of two of the recipients of her letters written on Air Force One stationary.

11. "Blair House": NR, *My Turn*, p. 227.

12. "they're made for": Armand Deutsch interview, Beverly Hills, 2001.

13. "parties within parties": NBC television interview with Barry Goldwater, Jan. 19, 1981.

14. "laser beams": *New York Times*, Jan. 21, 1981.

15. "Almost every day . . . Thank you": Museum of Broadcasting (Tape) Capital Center, Largo, Md., Jan. 19, 1981.

16. "You know": RR, White House Press Conference, Feb. 6, 1981.

17. "Governor": Deaver, *A Different Drummer*, p. 85.

18. "face was pale": NR, *My Turn*, p. 231.

19. Ibid.

20. "As we drove . . . that day": RR, *An American Life*, pp. 225–26.

21. "If we can just": Walter Cronkite, NBC Inauguration Day coverage, Jan. 20, 1981.

22. "They did it": Frank Reynolds, ABC Inauguration Day coverage, Jan. 20, 1981.

23. "He's not even": Phil Jones, CBS Inauguration Day coverage, Jan. 20, 1981.

24. "This is just": George Will, ABC Inauguration Day coverage, Jan. 20, 1981.

25. The writing of Reagan's first inaugural address: RRPL/Notes/papers/01/81.

26. "With thanks": Michael Deaver.

27. "bouffant hairdos": Washington Post, Jan. 21, 1981.

27. "awed . . . humbling": Susan Granger interview, Independent News Alliance, Dec. 21, 1981.

CHAPTER ELEVEN: MEET THE PRESS

1. "It's hell": Helen Thomas, *Front Row at the White House*, p. 240.

2. "vulgar . . . a traitor": William O. Stoddard, *Inside the White House in War Times*, p. 95.

3. "Harry, the President . . . of the people" Joseph Lash, *Eleanor and Franklin*, p. 94.

4. "Jackie is superb": Paul F. Boller Jr., *Presidential Wives*, p. 357.

5. "They're the second . . . the first ladies": Helen Thomas, *Front Row at the White House*, p. 239.

6. "I never made . . . to my husband": Edith Bolling Wilson, *My Memoir*, p. 56.

7. "Sometimes I feel": Paul F. Boller, *Presidential Wives*, p. 285.

8. "Of all the first ladies": Thomas, *Front Row at the White House*, p. 272.

9. "I believe": Ibid.

10. "We did the best": *Washington Post*, Jan. 25, 1981.

11. "A thanksgiving service": Ibid.

12. "I'd find myself . . . you made it": RR, *An American Life*, p. 245.

13. "brain-noting": Bill Thompson interview, Dixon, II., 1986.

14. "The first time . . . lifeguard": Ibid.

15. "We have a new . . . discussed": Larry Speakes, *Speaking Out*, p. 62.

16. "It was one thing": Ibid.

17. "Y and H . . . wisest": Ibid., p. 63.

18. "Well, guys, it looks": Ibid.

19. "find a black . . . turned out": Bob Colacello, *Vanity Fair*, "The Reagans," August 1998.

20. "On the day . . . game is played": Speakes, *Speaking Out*, p. 64.

21. "He was obsessed . . . slighted": NR, *My Turn*, p. 241–242.

22. "I've seen presidents": RRPL, Private Papers.

23. "an irresistible": Armand Deutsch interview, 2001.

24. "should have crossed . . . California": RR, *An American Life*, p. 389.

25. "enjoyed looking": Confidential interview.

26. "[My Nancy has] made one man": RRPL, Correspondence—Nancy Davis Reagan.

27. "where Lyndon . . . country": NR, *My Turn*, p. 250.

28. "a gag poster": Ibid., p. 247.

CHAPTER TWELVE: "OH, GOD, IT'S HAPPENING AGAIN!"

The events in this chapter have been recreated by extensive research. The Ronald Reagan Presidential Library contains substantial material on March 30, 1981, and its immediate aftermath. The Department of the Treasury, Office of the General Counsel, contains an important paper: "Management Review on the Performance of the U.S. Department of the Treasury in Connection with the March 30, 1981, Assassination Attempt on President Ronald Reagan," Department of the Treasury, Aug. 1981.

Books used were: Herbert L. Abrams, *The President Has Been Shot*, Norton, N.Y., 1992; Ronald Reagan, *An American Life*, Simon & Schuster, N.Y., 1990; Nancy Reagan, *My Turn*, Random House, N.Y., 1989; Larry Speakes, *Speaking Out*, Scribner's, N.Y. 1988; Peggy Noonan, *When Character Was King*, Viking, N.Y. 2002; Michael K. Deaver w/ Mickey Herskowitz, *Behind the Scenes*, Morrow, N.Y. 1987; Michael Reagan, *On the Outside Looking In*, Zebra, N.Y. 1988; Maureen Reagan, *First Father, First Daughter*, Little Brown, Boston, 1989; Lou Cannon, *President Reagan: The Role of a Lifetime*, Touchstone/Simon & Schuster, N.Y., 1991; Lawrence I. Barrett, *Gambling With History*, Doubleday, N.Y. 1983; Patti Davis, *As I See It*, Putnam, N.Y., 1992; Lyn Nofziger, *Nofziger*, Regnery Gateway, Washington, D.C., 1992; Helen von Damm, *At Reagan's Side*.

Articles used were: *The New York Times*, March 31, 1981–April 14, 1981; *Los Angeles Times, The Washington Post*, March 31, 1981–April 14, 1981; *Time, Newsweek*, as above.

Washingtonian, August, 1981; *American Medical News*, April 10, 1981; *Rolling Stone*, Aug. 5, 1982 (Specifically the article "The Dark Side of the American Dream," by Aaron Latham.

Additional research: Academy of Motion Picture Arts & Sciences; Office of the Federal Registers Weekly Compilation of Presidential Documents, April 6, 1981, pp. 67–72.

1. "Good morning": RRPL, RR Diary.
2. "leaned over the bed": Ibid.
3. "Any of the regulars?": Michael Deaver, *Behind the Scenes*, p. 14.
4. "an isolated terrorist . . . decisions": *Newsweek*, Apr. 6, 1981.
5. "an encroachment": Ibid.
6. "In the perfect . . . mechanic.": Ibid.
7. "frightened the shit": Ibid.
8. "Haig may have . . . alternatives": *Time*, Apr. 6, 1981.
9. "a scene so peaceful . . . Jackson": NR, *My Turn*, p. 246.
10. "like living . . . in an eight-star": RR, *An American Life*, p. 250.
11. "If it is Mr. Lincoln's": Maureen Reagan interview.
12. "The joke was": *Newsweek*, Apr. 14, 1981.
13. "for reasons I'll never know": RR, *An American Life*, p. 259.
14. "extol the virtues": Reagan's speach: Office of the Federal Register's *Weekly Compilation of Presidential Documents*, Apr. 6, 1981, pp. 367–72.
15. Comments of bystanders compiled from *Washington Post*, *Time*, and *Newsweek*.
16. "I was almost to the car": RR, *An American Life*, p. 260.
17. "When he landed": Ibid., 259.
18. "cover and evacuate": Peggy Noonan, *When Character Was King*, p. 169.
19. "paralyzed with pain": RR, *An American Life*, p. 259.
20. "There was something": Peggy Noonan, *When Character Was King*, p. 170.
21. "bleeding into": *Newsweek*, Apr. 1, 1981.
22. "his eyes rolled": Aaron Latham, *Rolling Stone*, Aug. 5, 1982.
23. "and found the President. . . . Touch and go": Larry Speakes, *Speaking Out*, p. 6.
24. "his head split open": Michael Deaver, *Behind the Scenes*, p. 18.
25. "I thought to myself": Larry Speakes, *Speaking Out*, p. 6.
26. "Who's holding my hand?": RR, *An American Life*, p. 260.
27. "Honey" and "As long as I live . . . deserve": Ibid. pp. 260, 261.
28. "Who's minding" and "There's a little chapel": Michael Deaver, *Behind the Scenes*, p. 18–19.
29. "didn't want . . . deal with": *American Medical News*, Apr. 10, 1981.
30. "I hope you're a Republican": RR, *An American Life*, p. 261.
31. "All in all": Ibid.
32. "They're strong men . . .": NR, *My Turn*, p. 8.
33. "I am in charge here!" *Newsweek*, Apr. 13, 1981.

The complete order of presidential succession is: 1. Vice President, 2. Speaker of the House, 3. President pro tempore of the Senate, 4. Secretary of State, 5. Secretary of Treasury, 6. Secretary of Defense, 7. Attorney General, 8. Secretary of

Interior, 9. Secretary of Agriculture, 10. Secretary of Commerce, 11. Secretary of Labor, 12. Secretary of Health and Human Services, 13. Secretary of Housing and Urban Development, 14. Secretary of Transportation, 15. Secretary of Energy, 16. Secretary of Education, 17. Secretary of Veterans Affairs.

34. "To see the man": Confidential interview.

35. "[Bush] took his seat": Larry Speakes, *Speaking Out*, p. 9.

36. "It's okay, Dad": NR, *My Turn*, p. 10.

37. "With all the": RR, *An American Life*, p. 255.

38. "Nothing can happen": Ibid.

39. Reagan's notes while he was in hospital were reported in *Newsweek*, *Time*, and in several of the books used in the preparation of this chapter. They were originally reported by Larry Speakes and Lyn Nofziger in press conferences; and RR and NR recorded various of them in their diaries.

CHAPTER THIRTEEN: AFTERMATH

1. "I should have": Michael Deaver, *Behind the Scenes*, p. 20.

2. "If I had seen": Ibid., p. 24.

3. "What made you think": Ibid.

4. "I quickly said . . . to shoot us": RR, *An American Life*, p. 261.

5. "I would have": RRPL, Telegrams, 1981.

6. Notes in hospital written by RR: Various sources compiled including NR, Peggy Noonan, Michael Deaver, Larry Speakes, *Newsweek*, *Time*.

7. "People reach out . . . distance": Patti Davis, *The Way I See It*, p. 271.

8. "His skin was pale": Ibid., p. 272.

9. "Patti and Ron were already . . . Thanksgiving": Michael Reagan, *On the Outside Looking In*, p. 196.

10. "Obviously in pain": Ibid.

11. "I had weeks": Peggy Noonan, *When Character Was King*, p. 190.

12. "talking nonsense": Ibid.

13. "We pushed to get him out": Abrams, *"The President Has Been Shot,"* p. 71.

14. "I thanked God": RR, *An American Life*, p. 262.

15. "For the first two days": Abrams, *"The President Has Been Shot,"* p. 71.

16. "I had the thought . . . lower lobe": Ibid.

17. "swept the department": Ibid.

18. "a Woodrow Wilson": Abrams, *"The President Has Been Shot,"* p. 72.

19. "walking with": Ibid.

20. "The first full day . . . paid me a call": RR, *An American Life*, p. 264.

21. "proud and patriotic": Ibid.

22. "Now, Dick": Chris Wallace, *First Lady*, p. 23.

23. "the future": RR, *An American Life*, p. 257.

24. "two spiders": Ibid.

25. "how do we go about": RR, *An American Life*, p. 264.

26. "if he ever feared . . . God's forgiveness": Patti Davis, *The Way I See It*, p. 272, 273.

27. "good natural looks": *Newsweek*, Apr. 13, 1981.

28. "a glum, seedy": Ibid.

29. "Outside of being a Nazi": Ibid.

30. "There's a plot": Lincoln Caplan, *The Insanity Defense and the Trial of John W. Hinckley Jr.*, p. 54.

31. "scowled in disbelief": *Newsweek*, Apr. 13, 1981.

32. "The United States was born": *Times* (London), Apr. 1, 1981.

CHAPTER FOURTEEN: JUST SAY NO

1. "may be all right" and decoration of White House: *New York Times*, Nov. 2, 2000, and Abbott and Rice, *Designing Camelot*.

2. "The most dramatic": Edmund Morris, *Dutch*, p. 438.

3. "a program that will balance": RR State of the Union speech, Feb. 18, 1981.

4. "In the 3d part": RRPL, Private Papers.

5. "I could never get over": Helene von Damm, *At Reagan's Side*, pp. 71–72.

6. "He would put up . . . to the right": Peggy Noonan, *When Character Was King*, pp. 149–150.

7. "didn't get to see the tender side": Ibid., p. 150.

8. "was nowhere near": Helene von Damm, *At Reagan's Side*, p. 72.

9. "Nancy wanted to": Peggy Noonan, *When Character Was King*, p. 152.

10. "This is a man without ideas": Jacques Attali, *Verbatim*.

11. The royal wedding and Mrs. Reagan: *London Times, Observer, Sunday Express* July 1981. Also Anne Edwards, *Diana and the Life She Led*.

12. "Princess Margaret tied a balloon": Charles Earl Spencer interviews, 1997.

13. Naming of Just Say No: NR, *I Love You, Ronnie*, p. 144.

14. Visitors to the White House: Jerry Herman interview, 2002.

15. "Nothing up ahead": Confidential interview.

16. "sounded pleased . . . Is Maureen going to run?": Maureen Reagan, *First Father, First Daughter*, p. 282, 283.

17. "I hope not . . . I'm sorry": Ibid., p. 283.

18. "Coming into the living": Chris Wallace, *First Lady*, p. 102.

19. "Money doesn't buy": Often used by Nancy Reagan in appearances promoting Just Say No.

20. "those big eyes focus . . . cared about": Chris Wallace, *First Lady*, p. 108.

CHAPTER FIFTEEN: A DEATH IN THE FAMILY

1. For material and quotes on Camp David: John L. Gerik, *A History of Camp David, 1942–72*.

2. "loved nature . . . drifts of magnolia . . . the queen": Robert Caro, *Means of Ascent*, p. 55.

3. "despite his outbursts": RR, *An American Life*, p. 396.

4. "Haig sought": Lou Cannon, *President Reagan: The Role of a Lifetime*, p. 167.

5. "it was his personality": Ibid.

6. "repeated displays": Ibid., p. 166.

7. "whispered to him": Ibid.

8. "fired up by demagogues": RR, *An American Life*, p. 554.

9. "Our military strength": RRPL, Speech to British Parliament, June 8, 1982.

10. "It's as ugly": RR's response to correspondents covering the event, *Time and*

Newsweek, June 14 and June 15, 1982.

11. "One day in March": Helen Thomas, *Front Row at the White House*, p. 273.
12. Parody lyrics: Ibid., p. 274.
13. Description of NR at Gridiron event: Ibid., p. 275.
14. Parody of lyrics: Ibid.
15. "I came": *Washington Post*, March 25, 1982.
16. "It was a curious . . . authority": Confidential interview.
17. "Just remember": Confidential Interview.
18. "Nancy in tears": RR diary, Aug. 9, 1982. RRPL.
19. "Talked to Nancy": RR diary, Aug. 15, 1982. character. RRPL.
20. "I was afraid that my mother": Chris Wallace, *First Lady*, p. 147.
21. "It was when": Ibid.
22. "Dr. Loyal . . . sweetheart": RR diary, Aug. 15, 1982. RRPL.
23. "that threatened to rupture": Larry Speakes, *Speaking Out*, p. 193.
24. "We played some outrageous games": Chris Wallace, *First Lady*, p. 23.

CHAPTER SIXTEEN: THE POWER AND THE GLITTER

Interviews were conducted with Bill Thompson August 2002. Thompson was also kind enough to send me copies of his correspondence with RR, which were extremely insightful. Numerous books (by Attali, Fitzgerald, Kornbluh, Martin, Secord, Walsh, and Weinberger), articles (*U.S. News, Time*), and newspaper coverage (*Washington Post, New York Times*) provided background on the Iran-Contra situation. The Ronald Reagan Presidential Library also has voluminous material under the heading of Iran-Contra. Several members of the Reagans' staff were interviewed with the agreement that I would not use their names, and I have quoted from those interviews. Larry Kramer was helpful in regard to AIDS.

1. "I'd go so far . . . Nancy had to approve": Helene von Damm, *At Reagan's Side*, p. 237.
2. "There was more than pillow talk . . . with her": Confidential interview.
3. "She was *much* more . . . history": Helene von Damm, *At Reagan's Side*, p. 239.
4. "During Reagan's . . . a big stick": *New York Times*, Feb. 12, 2002 editorial page.
5. "he was possessed": Peggy Noonan, *When Character Was King*, p. 259.
6. "I haven't heard from you": Ibid.
7. "As far as he was concerned": NR, *I Love You, Ronnie*, p. 164.
8. "Dear Glamour Puss": Ibid., p. 166.
9. "but never a raised voice . . . shined *always*": Confidential interview.
10. "She seemed . . . afternoon": *Newsweek*, March 7, 1983.
11. "talking about our children": NR, *My Turn*, p. 262.
12. "I know I promised": Ibid.
13. The underground chambers of the Ronald Reagan Presidential Library in Simi Valley, California, are crammed full of presents given to the Reagans while he was in office. They belong to the government. They range from magnificent jewels and silver and gold artifacts from Saudi Arabian royals to charming offerings from well-wishers—quilts, drawings, good-luck charms, hundreds of elephant objects, an imposing number of saddles, and countless oddities and lovely antiques. On occasion, pieces are brought up to the main floor for public display.

14. RR to Bill Thompson, Jul. 13, 1983.

15. "I KNOW him": Rev. Adrian Rogers interview, 1982.

16. The Reagans' visit to Dixon was recreated through interviews with numerous participants, including Bill Thompson and an anonymous friend of NR's from her Metro days.

17. "all white males . . . discriminated against": Maureen Reagan, *First Father, First Daughter,* p. 296, 297.

18. "began shuttling": Ibid., p. 299.

19. "I felt we had": RR, *An American Life,* p. 484.

20. "As president, I was at the helm": RR, *An American Life,* p. 484.

21. "For the chief . . . stupidity": Barbara Tuchman, *The March of Folly,* p. 386.

22. "Nancy has very good political": Spencer quoted in Chris Wallace, *First Lady,* p. 118.

23. "I think it's going to be tough": Ibid.

24. "She was very concerned": Rollins quoted in Chris Wallace, *First Lady,* p. 109.

25. "The man I was seeing": Patti Davis, *The Way I See It,* p. 300.

26. "combine aggressiveness": Lou Cannon, *President Reagan: The Role of a Lifetime,* p. 447.

27. "Right from the start": NR, *My Turn,* p. 266.

CHAPTER SEVENTEEN: FACING THE DEMONS

Books used for this chapter include *What Does Joan Say?* by Joan Quigley, *Reagan's America: Innocents at Home,* by Garry Wills, as well as books listed in chapter 16 notes.

1. "so superlative": Joan Quigley, *What Does Joan Say?* p. 43.

2. "Nancy always seemed pinched": Ibid.

3. "I needed to get . . . White House": Ibid., p. 69.

4. "the hour and minute . . . Evil Empire": Ibid., p. 135.

5. "What a shock": Donald T. Regan, *For the Record,* p. 172.

6. "Surely he could": Confidential interview.

7. "thinly disguised": NR, *My Turn,* p. 166.

8. "What did you expect?": Patti Davis, *The Way I See It,* p. 221.

9. Full text of Reagan's 1985 Inaugural Address: RRPL, Speeches, 1985.

10. "Dutch called us": Bill Thompson interview, Dixon, Ill., May 2, 2002.

11. RR to the Thompsons, Feb. 12, 1985.

12. "Comrades, this man": Edmund Morris, *Dutch,* p. 517.

13. "the beginning of": RR, *An American Life,* p. 376.

14. "was in political": Lou Cannon, *President Reagan: The Role of a Lifetime,* p. 431.

15. "I said [the picnic . . .]": Joan Quigley, *What Does Joan Say?,* p. 121.

16. "All of a sudden": Cannon, *President Reagan: The Role of a Lifetime.* p. 516.

17. "walked past the mounds": RR, *An American Life,* p. 382.

18. "Everywhere here": RRPL, Speeches, 1985.

19. "She was the greatest": RRPL, Radio speeches, 1984–85.

20. "Let's get it done": NR, *My Turn,* p. 273.

21. "delayed . . . July 13": Joan Quigley, *What Does Joan Say?,* p. 12.

22. "It was a result": RR, *An American Life*, p. 502.

23. Re: Deaver's departure. In October 1987 Michael Deaver was found guilty of perjury and violating lobbying restrictions imposed on former senior White House aides. Stories that Nancy Reagan cut off relations with him at that time are false. Although she avoided face-to-face contact with him as both Deaver himself and White House advisers wished, the first lady sent encouraging notes to Deaver through emissaries. When Reagan completed his second term, she saw Deaver once again. In 2002 she wrote the foreword to his book *A Different Drummer.*

24. "a force to be avoided": Confidential interview.

25. "in defiance of congressional": *New York Times*, Aug. 17, 2002.

26. "with satellite photography": Ibid.

CHAPTER EIGHTEEN: THE BEST OF TIMES AND THE WORST OF TIMES

1. "I felt it was ridiculous": NR, *My Turn*, pp. 336–37.

2. "For all you know": Colin Powell, *My American Journey*, p. 360.

3. "talked and talked . . . political system": NR, *My Turn*, p. 338.

4. "It made her look . . . the Great": Ibid., p. 339–340.

5. "When I was told": RR, *An American Life*, p. 635.

6. Ibid., p. 636.

7. "I'd learned a few lessons . . . inappropriate": Ibid., p. 637.

8. "The [space shuttle] . . . extremely old": Larry Speakes, *Speaking Out*, p. 93.

9. "Tell them": Ibid.

10. "that Reagan was the worst": Tip O'Neill, *Man of the House*, pp. 360–363.

11. "Perhaps she has something": *New York Times*, Oct. 12, 1986.

12. "Scared the daylights": Larry Speakes, *Speaking Out*, p. 303.

13. "The door is open": Dusko Doder and Louise Branson, *Gorbachev: Heretic in the Kremlin*, p. 194.

14. "more politically astute [Donald Reagan]": Lou Cannon, *"President Reagan: The Role of a Lifetime,"* p. 640.

15. "I'll be goddammed": Quoted in ibid., p. 643. However, it is unlikely that Deaver is quoting Reagan correctly. He was never known to take the Lord's name in vain. It was against the principles of his religion. Nancy claims that she never heard him profane the Lord's name, nor during her bid to get Donald Regan fired, did Reagan tell her "to get off my goddamned back." At least five of his close associates and members of his family (including Neil Reagan) claim Reagan had to have been misquoted.

16. "their arms interlocked . . . the President": Larry Speakes, *Speaking Out*, p. 209.

17. "I met with my West German hosts . . . like animals": RR, *An American Life*, p. 681.

18. "Behind me stands . . . tear down this wall!": RRPL, Speeches, Germany.

19. "Something that he got": Larry Speakes, *Speaking Out*, p. 285.

20. Oliver North's testimony: For current accounts see: *New York Times, Newsweek, Time, Washington Post* during July 1987.

21. "had an expression": NR, *My Turn*, p. 286.

22. "It would mean a lot": Patti Davis, *The Way I See It*, p. 317.

23. "Look, please don't wake me up": NR, *My Turn*, p. 293.

24. "They took my breast . . . leg man myself": Ibid., p. 294.

25. "That's all right": RRPL, Private Papers, Oct. 1987.

26. "I was glad . . . when it's right": NR, *My Turn*, p. 297.

27. "What is it": NR, *My Turn*, p. 300.

28. "[The White House] is like": *New York Times*, Dec. 12, 1987.

CHAPTER NINETEEN: A GRACEFUL EXIT

This chapter was helped greatly by a personal interview with Maureen Reagan in Dixon, Ill. August 25, 2000.

1. "[My father] refines things": Chris Wallace, *First Ladies*, p. 32.

2. "[My father] had something special . . . back to me": Peggy Noonan, *When Character Was King*, p. 156.

3. "Unlike Annie I have": Lou Cannon, *President Reagan: The Role of a Lifetime* p. 704.

4. "he could stay on": NR, *My Turn*, p. 355.

5. "These people are part . . . expression": RR, *An American Life*, p. 706.

6. "is still a police": Lou Cannon, *President Reagan: The Role of a Lifetime*, p. 704.

7. "It was the only ugly display . . . God bless you": Doder and Branson, *Gorbachev*, pp. 111–12.

8. "Americans were divided": Lou Cannon, *President Reagan: The Role of a Lifetime*, p. 628.

9. "I'm just convinced . . . about it": Larry Speakes, *Speaking Out*, p. 297.

10. "As for the two of us": NR, *My Turn*, p. 364.

11. "The left! The left!": Lou Cannon, *President Reagan: The Role of a Lifetime*, p. 710.

12. "to want us upstairs": Edmund Morris, *Dutch*, p. 657. Re the Bushes visiting the Reagans in the family quarters of the White House: Nancy Reagan says that the Bushes had been guests of theirs once during Reagan's first term, but had only attended state dinners during his second term. George Bush had met with Reagan in the family quarters while he was recuperating from surgery after the assassination attempt, and the Bushes had watched the 1984 election results with the Reagans. Barbara Bush also visited the family quarters twice during the last weeks of Reagan's presidency.

13. "There are some things": Lou Cannon, *President Reagan: The Role of a Lifetime*, p. 633.

14. "despite what his critics say": Maureen Reagan, *First Father, First Daughter*, p. 318.

15. "ad hoc campaigns" and "in effect": *Los Angeles Times*, Nov. 2, 2000.

16. "I never thought it was my style": RRPL, Speeches Archive (1986–1988).

17. "a really big": *New York Times*, Feb. 6, 2001.

18. "I understand now": Maureen Reagan interview, Dixon, Ill. Aug. 25, 2000.

19. "Dear George": RR, *An American Life*, p. 722. The reference to the turkeys in this letter is to the wild turkeys that would walk across the White House lawns and foul them.

20. "Here were the cameramen": Colin Powell, *My American Journey*, p. 395.

21. "I hope the magnolia trees": NR, *My Turn*, p. 368.

22. "Look, dear": Ibid.

23. "It all seemed unreal": Ibid.

CHAPTER TWENTY: LIFE CONTINUES, MEMORY FADES

1. "with me every step": Acknowledgments to RR, *An American Life*.

2. "He was dressed": *New Yorker*, Oct. 6, 1997.

3. "all had perfect teeth": Ibid.

4. Description of Reagan's fall from horse, medical statements, and Nancy's reactions are from *Washington Post*, Sept. 9–20, 1989.

5. "I flew around" and "entire Soviet": *Washington Post*, Sept. 15, 1989.

6. "Then dig": Fred Hummel, project manager, RRPL, interview.

7. "I'm afraid I don't know where I am": Peggy Noonan, *When Character Was King*, p. 321.

8. "This place is familiar": Ibid.

9. "Who are you?": Reagan staff member confidential interview.

10. "standing in the middle": Patti Davis, *The Way I See It*, p. 334.

11. "Powder down your lipstick": RRPL, Telegrams, Nancy Reagan Archive.

12. "His courage": Confidential interview.

13. "I intend to live my life": RRPL, Speeches Archive, 1989–.

14. "This is when": Confidential interview.

15. "was sitting at his desk ... crying": Michael Deaver, *A Different Drummer*, p. 220–221.

16. "and if anyone knew": Confidential interview.

17. "Mrs. Reagan ... to that": Ibid.

18. "I need her": Confidential interview.

19. "how his hands had once chopped": *Los Angeles Times*, August, 2001.

20. "father's heart had always been": *Telegraph*, Dixon, Ill., Aug. 25, 2000.

21. "My grandfather": Ibid.

22. "and the Communist states": *New York Times*, Feb. 11, 2002.

*The eleven presidential libraries as of 2002 are Ronald W. Reagan, Gerald R. Ford, Jimmy Carter, Lyndon B. Johnson, Harry S. Truman, The Nixon Project (not associated with The Nixon Library in Yorba Linda, Calif.), John F. Kennedy, Herbert Hoover, Franklin D. Roosevelt, Dwight D. Eisenhower, and George H. W. Bush.

†Some 59,850 pages of documents were transferred in 2001 from the Herbert Hoover Library, where they had originally been kept sealed, to the Ronald Reagan Presidential Library, where archivists began the giant task of cataloging it so that it could be available to the public. Only 150 pages of Reagan papers (considered security sensitive) remained sealed in 2002, a low number for presidential libraries, many of which have tens of thousand of documents still sealed and not scheduled for release for decades to come.

BOOKS

Abbott, James A., and Elaine M. Rice. *Designing Camelot*. Washington, D.C.: Van Nostrand Reinhold, 1998.

Abrams, Herbert L. *"The President Has Been Shot."* New York: Norton, 1992.

Anderson, Martin. *Revolution: The Reagan Legacy*. Palo Alto, Calif.: Hoover Institution Press, 1990.

Attali, Jacques. *Verbatim*, vol. 1 (1981–1986). Paris: Fayard, 1993.

Barrett, Lawrence I. *Gambling with History*. New York: Doubleday, 1983.

Boller, Paul F., Jr. *Presidential Wives*. New York: Oxford University Press, 1988.

Boyarsky, Bill. *The Rise of Ronald Reagan*. New York: Random House, 1968.

Brown, Edmund. *Reagan and Reality*. New York: Praeger, 1970.

Brownstein, Ronald. *The Power and the Glitter*. New York: Pantheon, 1990.

Cannon, Lou, *Reagan*. New York: Putnam, 1982.

———. *President Reagan: The Role of a Lifetime*. New York: Simon & Schuster, 1991.

Caplan, Lincoln. *The Insanity Defense*. Boston: David Godine, 1984.

Cole, Lester. *Hollywood Red*. Palo Alto, Calif.: Ramparts Press, 1981.

Davis, Loyal. *A Surgeon's Odyssey*. Garden City, N.Y.: Doubleday, 1973.

Davis, Patti. *The Way I See It*. New York: Putnam, 1992.

Deaver, Michael K., with Mickey Hershkowitz. *Behind the Scenes*. New York: William Morrow, 1987.

———. *A Different Drummer*. New York: HarperCollins, 2001.

Donaldson, Sam. *Hold On, Mr. President*. New York: Random House, 1987.

Douglas, Helen Gahagan. *A Full Life*. Garden City, N.Y.: Doubleday, 1982.

Doder, Dusko, and Louise Branson. *Gorbachev: Heretic in the Kremlin*. New York: Viking, 1990.

Edwards, Anne. *Early Reagan*. New York: Morrow, 1988.

———. *Ever After: Diana and the Life She Led*. New York: St. Martin's Press, 2000.

———. *Throne of Gold: The Lives of the Aga Khans*. New York: Morrow, 1995.

Edwards, Lee. *Ronald Reagan: A Political Biography*. San Diego, Calif.: Viewpoint Books, 1967.

Federal Writers' Project of the Works Progress Administration of Northern California, *California, A Guide to the Golden State*. New York: Hastings House, 1967.

Felton, D. Erik. *A Shining City: The Legacy of Ronald Reagan*. New York: Simon & Schuster, 1998.

Fitzgerald, Frances. *Way Out There in the Blue*. New York: Touchstone Books, 2000.

Ford, Betty, with Chris Chase. *The Times of My Life*. New York: Harper & Row, 1978.

Ford, Gerald R. *A Time to Heal*. New York: Harper & Row, 1979.

Gerik, John L. "A History of Camp David, 1942–72," updated 1999 by Master Chief McGlendon, Ronford, and Travis Martin, Washington Government office, 1999.

Goodell, Charles E. *Political Prisoners in America*. New York: Random House, 1973.

Haig, Alexander M., Jr., *Caveat*. New York: Macmillan, 1984.

Johnson, Paul. *Modern Times: The World from the Twenties to the Eighties*. New York: Harper & Row, 1983.

Kelley, Kitty. *Nancy Reagan: The Unauthorized Biography*. New York: Simon & Schuster, 1991.

Kissinger, Henry A. *White House Years*. Boston: Little, Brown, 1979.

———. *Years of Upheaval*. Boston: Little, Brown, 1982.

Kornbluh, Peter, and Malcolm Byrne, eds. *The Iran-Contra Scandal: The Declassified History*. New York: New Press, 1993.

Kramer, Larry. *Just Say No*. New York: St. Martin's Press, 1991.

Lash, Joseph P. *Eleanor and Franklin*. New York: Norton, 1971.

Leamer, Lawrence. *Make-Believe*. New York: Harper & Row, 1983.

Leighton, Frances Spatz. *The Search for the Real Nancy Reagan*. New York: Macmillan, 1987.

Mailer, Norman. *The Presidential Papers*. New York: Bantam, 1964.

Martin, Al. *The Conspirators: Secrets of an Iran-Contra Insider*. Pray, Mont: National Liberty Press 2002.

Mayer, Jane, and Doyle McManus. *Landslide*. Boston: Houghton Mifflin, 1988.

McDougal, Dennis. *The Last Mogul*. New York: Crown, 1998.

Moldea, Dan E. *Dark Victory: Ronald Reagan, MCA and the Mob*. New York: Viking, 1986.

Morella, Joe and Edward Z. Epstein, *Jane Wyman: A Biography*, Delacourte Press, NY, 1988.

Morris, Edmund. *Dutch*, New York: Random House, 1999.

Noonan, Peggy. *What I Saw at the Revolution*. New York: Random House, 1990.

———. *When Character Was King*. New York: Viking, 2001.

Nofziger, Lyn. *Nofziger*. Washington, D.C.: Regnery Gateway, 1992.

Navasky, Victor. *Naming Names*. New York: Viking Press, 1980.

O'Neill, Tip, with William Novak. *Man of the House*. New York: Random House, 1987.

Patterson, Bradley H. *The Ring of Power*. New York: Basic Books, 1988.

Perret, Geoffrey. *A Dream of Greatness, the American People, 1945–1963*. New York: Coward, McCann & Geoghegan, 1979.

Powell, Colin, with Joseph E. Persico. *My American Journey*. New York: Random House, 1995.

Quigley, Joan. *What Does Joan Say?* New York: Birch Lane Press, 1990.

Reagan, Maureen. *First Father, First Daughter*. Boston: Little, Brown, 1989.

Reagan, Michael, and Joe Hyams. *On the Outside Looking In*. New York: Zebra Books, 1988.

Reagan, Nancy, with Bill Libby. *Nancy.* New York: Morrow, 1980.

————. *My Turn.* New York: Random House, 1989.

————. *I Love You, Ronnie,* New York: Random House, 2001.

Reagan, Ronald W., with Richard G. Hubler. *Where's the Rest of Me?* New York: Duell, Sloan & Pearce, 1965.

————. *An American Life.* New York: Simon & Schuster, 1990.

————. *A Time for Choosing: The Speeches of Ronald Reagan, 1961–1982,* ed. by Alfred A. Balitzer and Gerald M. Bonetto. Chicago: Regnery Gateway, 1983.

————. *Ronald Reagan Talks to America.* Old Greenwich, Conn.: Devon Adair, 1983.

Regan, Donald T. *For the Record.* New York: Harcourt, Brace, Jovanovich, 1988.

Reston, James. *Deadline.* New York: Random House, 1991.

Ryan, Frederick J., ed. *Ronald Reagan, the Great Communicator.* New York: Perennial, 1995.

Secord, Richard, with Jay Wurts. *Honored and Betrayed.* New York: Wiley, 1992.

Shilts, Randy. *And the Band Played On.* New York: St. Martin's Press, 1987.

Shultz, George P. *Turmoil and Triumph.* New York: Scribner's, 1993.

Skinner, Kiron K., Annelise Anderson, and Martin Anderson, eds. *Reagan in His Own Hand.* New York: Free Press, 2001.

Speakes, Larry, with Robert Pack. *Speaking Out.* New York: Scribner's, 1988.

Stockman, David A. *The Triumph of Politics.* New York: Harper & Row, 1986.

Stoddard, William O. *Inside the White House in War Times.* New York: Webster, 1890.

Thomas, Helen. *Front Row at the White House.* New York: Scribner's, 1999.

Tuchman, Barbara. *The March of Folly: From Troy to Vietnam.* New York: Knopf, 1984.

Van Damm, Helene. *At Reagan's Side.* New York: Doubleday, 1989.

————. *Sincerely, Ronald Reagan.* Ottawa, Ill.: Green Hill Publishers, 1976.

Wallace, Chris. *First Lady: A Portrait of Nancy Reagan.* New York: St. Martin's Press, 1986.

Walsh, Lawrence E. *"Firewall: The Iran-Contra Conspiracy and Cover-Up.* New York: Norton, 1997.

Weinberger, Caspar W. *Fighting for Peace.* New York: Warner Books, 1990.

Wills, Garry. *Reagan's America: Innocents at Home.* New York: Doubleday, 1987.

Woodward, Bob. *Veil: The Soviet Wars of the CIA, 1981–1987.* New York: Simon & Schuster, 1987.

MAGAZINES

Architectural Digest

Time, 04/06/81, 04/13/81, 04/20,81. (Almost every issue from this last date through 01/20/89 carries pertininent material about the Reagans.)

Rolling Stone, 08/05/82.

Newsweek 04/06/81, 04/13/81 and 04/20/81 through 01-20-89.

New Yorker 07/02/84.

New Republic, 11/15/80, 07/12/82, etc.

Redbook ("The Secret Life of John Hinckley Jr.") May 1985.

Saturday Evening Post

Congressional Quarterly (1982)

Vanity Fair

NEWSPAPERS
Boston Globe
Dixon Evening Telegraph
Los Angeles Times
London Times
Manchester Guardian
New York Times
Observer (London)
Sacramento Bee
Sunday Express (London)
Wall Street Journal
Washingtonian
Washington Post
U.S. News and World Report

ARCHIVES
Ronald Reagan Home, Dixon, Ill.
Ronald Ragan Society, Dixon Public Library, Dixon, Ill.
Ronald Reagan Presidential Library, Simi Valley, Calif.
Private Collection, Wm. C. Thompson, Dixon, Ill.
Loveland Museum, Dixon, Ill.
Eureka College, Eureka, Ill.
Gerald R. Ford Presidential Library, Ann Arbor, Mich.
National Archives and Records Service, Washington, D.C.
Academy of Motion Pictures Arts and Sciences, Beverly Hills, Calif.
Screen Actors Guild, Los Angeles, Calif.
Hoover Institution of War, Revolution and Peace, Palo Alto, Calif.
Museum of Television and Broadcasting (New York, N.Y., and Beverly Hills, Calif.)
Broadcast Pioneers Library, Washington, D.C.
Television Information Office, New York, N.Y.
Beverly Hills Library, Beverly Hills, Calif.
University of Wisconsin, Madison, Wisc. (Film archive)
University of Southern California (Warner Bros. Film Archives), Los Angeles, Calif.
University of California, Los Angeles, Calif. Special Collections
University of California, Berkeley, Calif. (Regional Oral History Office)